The History of Bankruptcy

Always a natural companion to capitalism, bankruptcy has become much more prevalent in the public consciousness since the global financial crisis. Not only have there been the spectacular failures of multinational banks and corporations, but also the rate of personal bankruptcy in North America and Europe has reached levels not seen since the 1930s.

This volume takes up bankruptcy in early modern Europe, when its frequency made it not only an economic problem but a personal tragedy and a social evil. Using legal, business and personal records, the chapters in this volume examine the impact of failure on business organizations and practices, capital formation and circulation, economic institutions and ethics, and human networks and relations in the so-called "transition" to modern society, from the early sixteenth to the early nineteenth century. One group of chapters concentrates on the German-speaking world and shows a common concern for the microeconomics of bankruptcy, that is, for such issues as the structure of the firm, the nature of its capital and the practices of its partners, especially their assessment of risk. Another group of chapters shifts the focus from Central to Western and Northern Europe and away from the microeconomics of the early modern firm to an institutional consideration of bankruptcy. The final group of chapters turns to Southern Europe, especially the Mediterranean basin, to assess bankruptcy not as an unfortunate result of crisis, but as an intentional response to crisis. All of the contributions are the result of original research; many of the scholars publish in English for the first time.

All of the chapters are founded on close archival research, offering insights not only into business organization and practice but also into social and cultural aspects of economic life from the late sixteenth to the early nineteenth century.

Thomas Max Safley is Professor of History at University of Pennsylvania, USA.

Routledge explorations in economic history

Edited by Lars Magnusson
Uppsala University, Sweden

1 **Economic Ideas and Government Policy**
Contributions to contemporary economic history
Sir Alec Cairncross

2 **The Organization of Labour Markets**
Modernity, culture and governance in Germany, Sweden, Britain and Japan
Bo Stråth

3 **Currency Convertibility**
The gold standard and beyond
Edited by Jorge Braga de Macedo, Barry Eichengreen and Jaime Reis

4 **Britain's Place in the World**
A historical enquiry into import controls 1945–1960
Alan S. Milward and George Brennan

5 **France and the International Economy**
From Vichy to the Treaty of Rome
Frances M.B. Lynch

6 **Monetary Standards and Exchange Rates**
M.C. Marcuzzo, L. Officer and A. Rosselli

7 **Production Efficiency in Domesday England, 1086**
John McDonald

8 **Free Trade and its Reception 1815–1960**
Freedom and trade: volume I
Edited by Andrew Marrison

9 **Conceiving Companies**
Joint-stock politics in Victorian England
Timothy L. Alborn

10 **The British Industrial Decline Reconsidered**
Edited by Jean-Pierre Dormois and Michael Dintenfass

11 **The Conservatives and Industrial Efficiency, 1951–1964**
Thirteen wasted years?
Nick Tiratsoo and Jim Tomlinson

12 **Pacific Centuries**
Pacific and Pacific Rim economic history since the 16th century
Edited by Dennis O. Flynn, Lionel Frost and A.J.H. Latham

13 **The Premodern Chinese Economy**
Structural equilibrium and capitalist sterility
Gang Deng

14 **The Role of Banks in Monitoring Firms**
The case of the crédit mobilier
Elisabeth Paulet

15 **Management of the National Debt in the United Kingdom, 1900–1932**
Jeremy Wormell

16 **An Economic History of Sweden**
Lars Magnusson

17 **Freedom and Growth**
The rise of states and markets in Europe, 1300–1750
S.R. Epstein

18 **The Mediterranean Response to Globalization before 1950**
Sevket Pamuk and Jeffrey G. Williamson

19 **Production and Consumption in English Households 1600–1750**
Mark Overton, Jane Whittle, Darron Dean and Andrew Hann

20 **Governance, the State, Regulation and Industrial Relations**
Ian Clark

21 **Early Modern Capitalism**
Economic and social change in Europe 1400–1800
Edited by Maarten Prak

22 **An Economic History of London, 1800–1914**
Michael Ball and David Sunderland

23 **The Origins of National Financial Systems**
Alexander Gerschenkron reconsidered
Edited by Douglas J. Forsyth and Daniel Verdier

24 **The Russian Revolutionary Economy, 1890–1940**
Ideas, debates and alternatives
Vincent Barnett

25 **Land Rights, Ethno Nationality and Sovereignty in History**
Edited by Stanley L. Engerman and Jacob Metzer

26 **An Economic History of Film**
Edited by John Sedgwick and Mike Pokorny

27 **The Foreign Exchange Market of London**
Development since 1900
John Atkin

28 **Rethinking Economic Change in India**
Labour and livelihood
Tirthankar Roy

29 **The Mechanics of Modernity in Europe and East Asia**
The institutional origins of social change and stagnation
Erik Ringmar

30 **International Economic Integration in Historical Perspective**
Dennis M.P. McCarthy

31 **Theories of International Trade**
Adam Klug
Edited by Warren Young and Michael Bordo

32 **Classical Trade Protectionism 1815–1914**
Edited by Jean Pierre Dormois and Pedro Lains

33 **Economy and Economics of Ancient Greece**
Takeshi Amemiya

34 **Social Capital, Trust and the Industrial Revolution**
1780–1880
David Sunderland

35 **Pricing Theory, Financing of International Organisations and Monetary History**
Lawrence H. Officer

36 **Political Competition and Economic Regulation**
Edited by Peter Bernholz and Roland Vaubel

37 **Industrial Development in Postwar Japan**
Hirohisa Kohama

38 **Reflections on the Cliometrics Revolution**
Conversations with economic historians
Edited by John S. Lyons, Louis P. Cain and Samuel H. Williamson

39 **Agriculture and Economic Development in Europe since 1870**
Edited by Pedro Lains and Vicente Pinilla

40 **Quantitative Economic History**
The good of counting
Edited by Joshua Rosenbloom

41 **A History of Macroeconomic Policy in the United States**
John H. Wood

42 **An Economic History of the American Steel Industry**
Robert P. Rogers

43 **Ireland and the Industrial Revolution**
The impact of the Industrial Revolution on Irish industry and society, 1801–1922
Andy Bielenberg

44 **Intra-Asian Trade and Industrialization**
Essays in memory of Yasukichi Yasuba
Edited by A.J.H. Latham and Heita Kawakatsu

45 **Nation, State and the Industrial Revolution**
The visible hand
Lars Magnusson

46 **A Cultural History of Finance**
Irene Finel-Honigman

47 **Managing Crises and De-globalisation**
Nordic foreign trade and exchange 1919–1939
Edited by Sven-Olof Olsson

48 **The International Tin Cartel**
John Hillman

49 **The South Sea Bubble**
Helen J. Paul

50 **Ideas and Economic Crises in Britain from Attlee to Blair (1945–2005)**
Matthias Matthijs

51 **Bengal Industries and the British Industrial Revolution (1757–1857)**
Indrajit Ray

52 **The Evolving Structure of the East Asian Economic System since 1700**
Edited by A.J.H. Latham and Heita Kawakatsu

53 **German Immigration and Servitude in America, 1709–1920**
Farley Grubb

54 **The Rise of Planning in Industrial America, 1865–1914**
Richard Adelstein

55 **An Economic History of Modern Sweden**
Lennart Schön

56 **The Standard of Living and Revolutions in Russia, 1700–1917**
Boris Mironov

57 **Europe's Green Revolution and Others Since**
The rise and fall of peasant-friendly plant breeding
Jonathan Harwood

58 **Economic Analysis of Institutional Change in Ancient Greece**
Carl Hampus-Lyttkens

59 **Labour-Intensive Industrialization in Global History**
Edited by Gareth Austin and Kaoru Sugihara

60 **The History of Bankruptcy**
Economic, social and cultural implications in early modern Europe
Edited by Thomas Max Safley

The History of Bankruptcy

Economic, social and cultural implications in early modern Europe

Edited by Thomas Max Safley

Routledge
Taylor & Francis Group
LONDON AND NEW YORK

First published 2013
by Routledge
2 Park Square, Milton Park, Abingdon, Oxon OX14 4RN

Simultaneously published in the USA and Canada
by Routledge
711 Third Avenue, New York, NY 10017

Routledge is an imprint of the Taylor & Francis Group, an informa business

British Library Cataloguing in Publication Data
A catalogue record for this book is available from the British Library

Library of Congress Cataloging in Publication Data
The history of bankruptcy : economic, social and cultural implications in early modern Europe / edited by Thomas Max Safley.
p. cm.
1. Bankruptcy–Europe–History. 2. Europe–Economic conditions.
I. Safley, Thomas Max.
HG3769.E85H57 2012
332.7'50940903–dc23 2012031999

ISBN: 978-0-415-68730-0 (hbk)
ISBN: 978-0-203-06683-6 (ebk)

Typeset in Times New Roman
by Wearset Ltd, Boldon, Tyne and Wear

Printed and bound in the United States of America by Publishers Graphics, LLC on sustainably sourced paper.

Contents

Contributors

Paola Avallone, Institute for the Study of Mediterranean Society, Italy.

Thomas Brennan, United States Naval Academy, USA.

Mauro Carboni, University of Bologna, Italy.

Natacha Coquery, University of Nantes, France.

Dave De ruysscher, Free University of Brussels, Belgium.

Paul Fischer, University of Augsburg, Germany.

Massimo Fornasari, University of Bologna, Italy.

Mark Häberlein, University of Bamberg, Germany.

Mina Ishizu, London School of Economics, UK.

Håkan Jakobsson, Umeå University, Sweden.

John MacLeod, University of Glasgow, UK.

Klas Nyberg, University of Stockholm, Sweden.

Thomas Max Safley, University of Pennsylvania, USA.

Jérôme Sgard, Centre for International Studies and Research, Paris, France.

Dana Štefanová, University of Vienna, Austria.

Andre Wakefield, Pitzer College, USA.

1 Introduction

A history of bankruptcy and bankruptcy in history

Thomas Max Safley

Insolvency and bankruptcy are persistent realities of economic life that have long provoked comment and criticism. As early as the sixteenth century, an Augsburg chronicler remarked about one of the most notorious bankrupts of his day that:

> he often oppressed the common good and the poor man with his commercial activity, not only with large, reputable wares, but also with smaller, poorer goods. He bought up ash wood in good times, and brought it to market at better times, the same with wine, and lute strings, and often bought the entire supply of a good at a higher price than it was worth in order to put pressure on his competitors, who could not afford to buy it, after which he would raise the price of the good in all lands and sell as he pleased. No merchant worth 50,000 or 100,000 gulden could trade in comparison with him, because he profited wherever he wished.[1]

Here was profit-seeking in every saleable good, speculation in commodity futures, competition on price-point, manipulation of foreign markets and an utter disregard for every non-advantageous consideration. The account detailed how complex credit transactions combined with opportunistic business partners led to a bankruptcy that resulted in extended litigation and ended with the ruin of his family and hundreds of his creditors. That he died in chains—the last detail of the account—was little more than justice. This chronicler and others after him[2] immortalize the greed, and question why the bankrupt lost sight of the early modern merchant-financier's maxim, *servare modum finemque tenere*, Lucan's attribution to Cato, urging moderation in pursuit of reasonable goals, which serves today as the motto of the House of Rothschild. Apart from Villani's report of the fourteenth-century collapse of the great trading companies of the Bardi and Peruzzi,[3] it is one of the earliest existing accounts of an actual bankruptcy.

Some 200 years later, an anonymous moralist of the eighteenth century decried bankruptcy and bankrupts in general:

> They steal under the appearance of an honorable man. They cut a figure with other people's money. They win friends with unrighteous Mammon.

> They are the best of men, because they give everything to their wives. When they are unable to carry on, they give up their good names as well as their businesses. They pay no one. It is said, they were unfortunate. They lose everything and live afterward from the wealth of their wives as comfortably as before.[4]

His text points at many of the same issues: profit and greed, credit and debt, nonpayment and deception, reputation and punishment. Yet, there is no assumption of a good man gone astray. There is no just ending.

His tone suggests that something has changed. What had emerged in the sixteenth century as an economic and social problem had become a sign of economic decline and moral decay, an index of social and personal failure. Bankruptcy had moved from being something extraordinary, like the sighting of a comet or the birth of a two-headed calf, to being something systemic. Capitalistic practices no longer needed to be described; they could be assumed. Bankrupts all deserved the rope, a prescription not necessarily original in itself,[5] because the damage they caused was not limited to a group of reckless highflyers. Merchants and bankers relied on other people's capital. When they misrepresented the investment risks or mismanaged financial affairs, they robbed others of their fortunes, their homes, their jobs and their futures. They were often the least affected by the consequences of their deeds. Recent events echo these sentiments, even as the prescriptive measures against bankruptcy have lost most of their draconian bite.

This volume attempts to address the transition framed by the two commentators. Its contributors take up bankruptcy in early modern Europe from a wide variety of perspectives. At the heart of their inquiries lie questions about the identity and fate of bankrupts, the generation and redistribution of wealth, the organization and reorganization of enterprise and the emergence and transformation of institutions over time. Together they make clear that what has become generally known as "commercial capitalism," by no means new in the sixteenth century, was practiced in new forms, underwritten by new institutions and associated with new meanings in the eighteenth.

Bankruptcy belongs to the essence of capitalism. Though failure, conceived in its broadest terms, can occur under any kind of economic system, the particularities of bankruptcy suggest a close identification with one particular kind. While no precise definition of capitalism finds universal approval, scholars agree generally that it involves private ownership of the means of production, creation of goods and services for profit in a market and, to a varying degree, governmental support for private property in the form of appropriate legal institutions. These characteristics—private property, market activity, legal institutions—appear readily in the reports and reflections of chronicler and moralist.

They inform the very definition of the term. The root, bankrupt, appears in English in the sixteenth century, as a term borrowed from the French (*banqueroute*) and Italian (*banca rotta*) to identify "the wreck or break-up of a trader's business in consequence of his failure to pay his creditors; or the shutting up or desertion of his place of business without paying his liabilities."[6] The Italian *banca rotta* referred transparently to the destruction of a merchant's trading table, or bank, usually located in the marketplace among those of other merchants, when he failed to pay his debts. Bankrupt was commonly taken to mean:

> a merchant, trader or other person, whose property and effects, on his becoming insolvent, are administered and distributed for the benefit of all his creditors, under that system of statutory regulations called the Bankrupt or Bankruptcy Laws. As these laws (which began in England with Acts 34 and 35 Henry VIII, c. 4) were originally directed against fraudulent traders, who absconded with the property of their creditors, or eluded the attempts of creditors to get at them.

The earlier senses were: in law, "a trader who secretes himself, or does certain other acts tending to defraud his creditors" (Blackstone); popularly, "one who has brought himself into debt by reckless expenditure or riotous living; a fugitive from his creditors, a broken man in sanctuary or outlawry."[7]

Bankruptcy carried an enduring implication of dishonesty and profligacy, because the malversation of private property made it offensive. In legal parlance and in common usage today, bankruptcy has been largely stripped of moral censure and has come to refer strictly to the legal process that begins with a declaration—either by bankrupt or creditors—of a person's inability to pay his or her debts. It is "The state of a person who has been adjudged by a court to be insolvent. The court orders the compulsory administration of the bankrupt's affairs so that his assets can be fairly distributed among his creditors."[8] It distinguishes itself thus from insolvency, that is, the unofficial financial situation from which bankruptcy results, and default on any single debt or obligation. The involvement of a court of law provides a forum and—significantly, for the historian—produces a record, in which the related questions of the financial state of the bankrupt, his actions and intentions and the causes and consequences of his bankruptcy are examined, disputed and, occasionally, resolved. These definitions confirm again and again the systematic existence of private property invested for productive purposes in the market and protected by an array of legal institutions. Their change over time indicates that the social and legal responses to bankruptcy became more sophisticated.

That the term came into much more frequent, colorful and varied usage in the sixteenth century is not mere happenstance. It seems likely that bankruptcy became more frequent from the late fifteenth century. Whether this was indeed the case and why it might have been so remain matters of conjecture. It is hard to ignore the numbers of bankruptcies that begin to mount in the sixteenth century.

Take as a single example the German imperial city of Augsburg. As early as 1560, the local chronicler Paul Hektor Mair counted no fewer than 26 merchants who "became bankrupt and, because of debts, sought sanctuary, fled the city, or suffered arrest until they settled and were released."[9] Had he been able to extend his count to 1580, as Jakob Strieder did in 1938, the total would have risen to 70 "great and famous commercial houses."[10] More recent surveys have set at 63 the number of bankruptcies in Augsburg between 1529 and 1580.[11] If one extends the period of study to 1800, the number may rise as high as 250, and this reflects only those cases that came to the attention of the authorities. Similar numbers may be developed for other, early modern, commercial centers.

The causes were manifold. The inconsistencies of state finance certainly played a part in many bankruptcies. The ambitions of princes and the costs of their policies rose rapidly from the fifteenth century, and merchants with disposable capital were willing to provide credit, accepting the real risk of non-payment for a high rate of interest. The results were both spectacular returns and equally spectacular ruptures.[12] The Spanish suspension of payments, followed by the Dutch, French and Portuguese, all of which occurred in the sixteenth century, swept away those merchant bankers not so far-sighted as to have diversified their engagements.[13] Commercial developments finished the rest. European silver mining, the great source of capital for overseas exploration and Renaissance culture, suffered a steady decline in productivity and profitability after the mid-sixteenth century. A rising tide of minerals, particularly silver, and other commodities from the Americas and Asia speeded the fall. The consequences of a so-called "rise of the Atlantic economies"[14] have been debated among scholars,[15] but they generally agree that the European economy as a whole experienced inflationary expansion, with different localities or regions profiting at different points in time. A growing, global economy, based ever more intensely on imported and exported commodities, created competitive challenges and disadvantages to which many merchants were not equal.

The resulting bankruptcies have created the impression of a turning-point in economic history. Until very recently, those of the sixteenth century marked the end of "The Age of the Fugger," "The Catastrophe of the Early Capitalist Age," or "The Collapse of Southern- and Middle-European Early Capitalism."[16] Though close studies of the economies of Europe at that time reveal few unequivocal indicators of crisis,[17] they continue to associate this wave of failures with capitalistic practices in a society and economy that seem deserving of the term. Joseph Schumpeter, whose work in many ways defines the modern discussion of failure and capitalism argued that there was no separating the two, that the one was intrinsic to the other. He wrote:

> A society is called capitalist if it entrusts its economic process to the guidance of the private businessman. This may be said to imply, first, private ownership of nonpersonal means of production … second, production for private account, i.e., production by private initiative for private profit.[18]

He thus calls attention to the individual entrepreneur as the agent, to private enterprise as the modality and to personal profit as the motive of change under capitalism. As he explains in *Business Cycles*, entrepreneurs are "New Men," whose enterprises are "New Firms" that pursue "innovation" by creating new commodities, forming new organizations or opening new markets.[19] Even as it drives capitalism forward, innovation provokes resistance, because it threatens the status quo.[20] This is the essence of "creative destruction," as he defines it in *Capitalism, Socialism and Democracy*, which "incessantly revolutionizes the economic structure from within, incessantly destroying the old one, incessantly creating a new one."[21] For Schumpeter, well aware that capitalism wreaks havoc on social relations and undermines moral values, the benefits of increased prosperity outweigh the costs in human suffering.

A close study of failure suggests a more ambivalent view. The chapters that follow take up bankruptcy, insolvency and default to explore various aspects of economic life in the early modern period. They examine the identities of and relationships among debtors and creditors. They reconstruct the organizations and workings of their businesses. They trace the consequences of failure. And they set it in the larger context of economic and social change. They reveal an economy profoundly capitalistic before the coining of the neologism.

Several of the chapters in this volume address the bankrupts and their creditors. Bankruptcy litigation and negotiation includes direct and indirect testimonies by these agents, not only those who failed, but also those who succeeded, who demanded payment and, in many instances, continued in business. Their documented statements permit examination of their heritages and educations, identities and self-representations, to say nothing of their social relationships and communities.

Mark Häberlein analyzes the 1590 bankruptcy of Leonhard Sulzer Heirs, luxury traders in Augsburg. Theirs was a family firm in the narrow sense that capital came from and direction was in the hands of members of the immediate family. Moreover, they borrowed, lent and cooperated most intensely and intimately with a fairly narrow range of merchant families, bound to them by ties of kinship and marriage. Most importantly, these patterns of organization and association persisted over generations with the result that merchant-entrepreneurs in Augsburg, a leading economic center of the day, were by no means "new men," but rather scions of established mercantile families, educated in the traditional manner and related by marriage and association along customary lines. Yet, newcomers appear as well, if less often in the early modern period.

Klas Nyberg and *Håkan Jakobsson* use the bankruptcies of 80 wholesalers in late eighteenth-century Stockholm to analyze the character of their financial relations. Credit, security and property were not, they argue, merely quantifiable economic concepts but also expressions of social and business relationships. The ability of migrants to form enterprises and enter markets in the community of Stockholm wholesalers involved, among other things, gaining access to capital, overcoming barriers to mobility and achieving membership in social or corporative groups. Logically and historically, failure transforms social barriers to entry into a trade or market and, thus, transforms the community of economic agents over time. Accordingly, these studies of bankruptcy suggest that identity could be a fluid social construct and that economic success and failure may have depended not so much on a merchant's given identity at any one time, but rather more on the capacity of that identity to change.

That social relations and structures might play a role in economic life is not a new concept, the recent arguments of economic sociologists notwithstanding. In the nineteenth century, Emile Durkheim, Karl Marx and Max Weber all argued that economic exchanges are social relationships.[22] These studies offer evidence of the degree to which social connections of various sorts might have influenced access to capital, avenues of cooperation and attempts at settlement. Häberlein and Nyberg and Jakobsson argue explicitly that, among large-scale, early modern merchants, credit flowed to a very considerable extent along the ties of kinship networks.

Thomas Brennan analyzes some 750 cases of default among rural peasants and traders in eighteenth-century Champagne and finds that their credit networks were based no less on repeated association or cooperation than on ties of marriage or relationship. His argument seems to accord with Craig Muldrew's that rising default and insolvency were functions of growing population size and economic activity.[23] These worked to dilute, disrupt and disintegrate networks of commercial or financial relationships. *Natacha Coquery* pursues a similar train of thought in her study of the bankruptcies of 120 shopkeepers, most in the luxury trades of jeweler and tapestry-maker, in eighteenth-century Paris. She emphasizes the absolute necessity of credit for the economic life of the place and period as well as the "embeddedness"[24] of credit–debt transactions in social relationships, which is to say, the tendency of shopkeepers to borrow from and lend to members of their own trade associations, often engaging in repeated exchanges over time. In eighteenth-century Paris, as in Champagne and sixteenth-century Augsburg, capital seems to have flowed over networks of relationship, based on various kinds of association, the stronger the relationship the readier the flow.

The question of social connections among debtors and creditors, "embedding" their economic transactions in non-economic relationships and meanings, raises what Diego Gambetta refers to as that "elusive notion of trust."[25] Brennan, Coquery, Häberlein and Nyberg and Jakobssen all insist that the capacity to engage in business required more than the capital. It also required trust, a personal reputation for consistently meeting one's obligations, as an essential element of the social basis of economic life. Where Muldrew claims perhaps too sweepingly that credit was the motor of early modern commerce,[26] they and a host of other, contemporary economic historians suggest that trust was the motor of credit. Repeated, satisfactory exchanges created intimate relationships. Embeddedness worked to the same end. The trust that supposedly emerged as a result of such intense, multiplex relationships functioned as a barrier against opportunistic behavior. It helped to assure the fulfillment of honorable or contractual obligations where more formal mechanisms, be they legal or extra-legal sanctions, again supposedly, were inadequate. Bankruptcy could destroy trust, but it also provided a forum for its reification. The parties discussed how it came into being, how it was understood and how it ceased to be. Successful resolutions that satisfied the creditors and discharged the bankrupts, referred to as "accords" could reestablish it.

These chapters not only examine the economic function of social categories, relationships and values, but also invite their reexamination. What exactly do these contemporary terms—family, network, trust—mean in the context of economic life? Their definitions may be relatively familiar, but their applications often fail to capture the shadings of degree and the varieties of experience. Families may be understood in terms of kinship and marital ties, but these ties do not necessarily determine or predict intimacy of communication or cooperation. A father or brother is not necessarily a more intimate relation than an uncle or brother-in-law. Networks may be understood in terms of varieties of social connections and interactions that vary in degrees of intensity, but these relationships do not determine or predict solidarity or opportunism in economic behavior. Embedded relationships, so-called, neither absolutely preclude opportunism nor consistently guarantee cooperation. Trust may be understood in terms of a confidence in or reliance upon some person, thing or statement without investigation, evidence or guarantee,[27] but such a willingness to believe can have varying degrees, take varying forms and yield varying outcomes. All trust is not alike, as Oliver Williamson has argued.[28] In other words, these terms often lack empirical rigor. They undoubtedly play a role in economic life, as much today as 500 years ago; but they cannot easily be abstracted from specific relationships and specific circumstances; and they do not reliably predict economic or social behaviors. For these reasons, perhaps, the social reinforcement of economic transactions has gradually given way to less personal standards and structures, even as it has not entirely been displaced by them. The study of bankruptcy suggests that the results of failure could be creative as well as destructive.

A second group of chapters takes up the business forms and behaviors of bankrupts and, by extension, their pursuers. The documentation of bankruptcies includes charters that reveal exactly how companies were organized. It often extends to correspondence, contracts and accounts that reveal the bankrupt's strategy and conduct—the evaluation of engagements, the assessment of the competition and the determination of goals for his company—and how they changed in the face of evolving market conditions and risk assessments.

Many of the contributions to this volume treat family firms. Rather than a single type, family firms could range in scale from small, such as Coquery's urban shopkeepers or Brennan's rural peasant holding, such as Brennan's rural wine producers, to large, such as Häberlein's international luxury traders or Nyberg and Jakobsson's wholesalers. What family firms have in common and what makes them unique is their dependence on internal arrangements, often maintained over generations, rather than on external laws. As Ron Harris put it:

> Management was based on the generational hierarchy within the family. All family members contributed the whole of their labor capability to the firm

> and enjoyed the use of family capital. Profits were distributed according to need and tradition, or plowed back in to the firm. Interest in the firm was transferred from one generation to the next by way of succession, according to family and inheritance laws, and regional and class customs.[29]

In practice, the family firm did not require the resources of all family members, but it drew the majority of its business leadership and a large portion of its start-up capital from the family. All members might benefit, but only the investors received a share of the profits. Low start-up costs and elastic forms might explain both the family firm's survival and its ubiquity to this day.

Paola Avallone examines the family firms of merchant bankers of early modern Naples, and shows how, as a result of their failures in a crisis period, 1580–1623, the state began to penetrate them, imposing auditors and overseers and eventually replacing them with a state-sponsored bank, the *Banco delle Due Sicilie*, in 1815. It was organized along strikingly different lines, with more clearly articulated, formal operating rules and regulations and more specialized, bureaucratic structures and functions. As she makes clear, governance and capitalization proved essential weaknesses of early modern merchant banks that contributed directly to their instability and failure. *Mauro Carboni* and *Massimo Fornasari* tell a strikingly similar story in Bologna. The failures of private banking houses during the late sixteenth century resulted in their replacement, not in an act of state-sponsored reorganization and not by state-sponsored financial institution in the strict sense, but rather by a gradual process of consumer preference for a state-sponsored charity, the *Monte di pietà*, that rose from the function of public pawnshop to that of a public bank in the early seventeenth century. And, again, informal structures and insufficient capitalization led to financial instability and failure that prompted, in turn, both state penetration and organization and institutional development. *Dana Štefanová* exposes some of the same problems and development, albeit from a very different perspective. Her chapter on the Schwarzenberg Bank in late eighteenth- and early nineteenth-century Vienna and its approach to insolvent and bankrupt clients looks more directly at questions of organization and governance, both of the bank itself and of two insolvent merchants, Johann Georg Paziazi and Johann Tost. The response to insolvency involved constant attention to specific circumstances, rather than a rigid application of *a priori* procedures or rules. As in the Italian cases, the development of business forms in the broadest sense—that is, the adaptation and adoption of specific structures, procedures, means and ends—was the result of empirical knowledge, gathered from past experiences and tailored to specific circumstances.

These cases of bankruptcy show the firm in action—usually, in crisis—and offer thus evidence of structure and function, governance and strategy, that builds upon the prescriptive statements of charters and regulations. Bankruptcies exposed structural deficiencies of early modern commercial or financial enterprises: inadequate capitalization, deficient administration, insufficient information. They also revealed the steps taken to amend these deficiencies: development of larger, specialized bureaucracies; mobilizing new, secure sources of capital base; articulating new rules for or forms of control.

The survival of a variety of business records makes bankruptcy a unique and uniquely ironic laboratory for the study of premodern business practice, a kind of anti-Chandler approach that seeks evidence of "the visible hand" not so much in cases of success as those of failure.[30] *Mina Ishizu* relies upon correspondence and accounts in her analysis of the 1811 bankruptcy of the Liverpool mercantile firm, John Leigh & Company. She examines the interplay of credit instruments, financial markets and business failure, taking the reader into questions of trust and exposing them to the development of financial practice. The closing of a single bank, due either to discounting the bills of untrustworthy merchants or to refusing to discount merchants they deemed untrustworthy, could create a ripple effect that cast other banks and merchants into bankruptcy in its wake. Her study confirms broadly the arguments of Avallone, Carboni and Fornasari and Štefanová that bankruptcy could be a potent empirical mechanism, prompting innovation and development in economic practices and institutions and forcing merchants to refine their techniques. Accordingly, entrepreneurs may well have spent more time adapting and reacting than innovating; the capacity to adapt to changing circumstances might be no less important in a constantly changing market environment.

These chapters, too, not only explore issues of business practice but pose questions about it. What was the relationship between business practice and business failure? Bankrupts consistently portrayed themselves as the victims of fortune, a malign turn of events, be they accidental—shipwreck, fire or theft—or personal—disease, disability or death—that could not be forecast or measured. How can they be held strictly accountable for what is completely unpredictable? Creditors sought to discover not only what the bankrupt had, so they could recover their loans and minimize their losses, but also what the bankrupt knew. Was he aware of the risks and provided adequate surety? Bookkeeping, for example, was a tool for answering such questions. It is generally thought to have developed as a result of growing complexity. Extensive business required accurate controls. An accurate record of a company's receipts and expenditures, profits and losses, could be used as a check on information gleaned, commodities exchanged and prices paid. They permitted the assessment of uncertainty and risk, constant themes in the discussion and resolution of bankruptcy. Creditors and magistrates sought to compel each bankrupt to surrender these books, to reveal his capital, that is, the disposition of his resources, the extent of his liabilities and the accuracy of his knowledge. Coquery notes the familiar relationship between inadequate or inaccurate bookkeeping and suspicious or fraudulent bankruptcy. Its close analysis has yet to be attempted.

The final group of chapters addresses the institutional context of early modern business. Indeed, many recent studies argue that institutions determine capitalism, that is, that capitalism can only exist in the presence of certain institutional arrangements.[31] As important as the institutional context of economic life doubtless is, too great an emphasis on it may reduce economic agents and their behaviors—as well as businesses and businessmen themselves—capitalism, if one will—to the level of dependent variables. The studies presented here suggest that economic behaviors and economic institutions affect one another discursively.

The collapse of commercial enterprises worked like a centrifugal force, spreading financial crisis outward from one firm to the next, one city to the next, one state to the next.[32] Coming in waves, it provoked changes in the institutions that organize and regulate economic life, even as economic institutions shaped the occurrence and course of failure. As the chapters by Avallone and Carboni and Fornasari indicate, the failure of private banks encouraged this intervention in the form of state-sponsored, public banks from the late sixteenth century. Such institutions as the *Casa di San Giorgio* in Genoa (1586), the *Wisselbank* in Amsterdam (1609) and the *Banco publico* of Nuremberg (1621), to say nothing of the *Banco* in Naples or the *Monte* in Bologna, worked to stabilize financial markets and restrict private bankruptcies by securing capital deposits, regularizing credit–debt relations, imposing legal regulations and dispersing risk. Even among private banks, as Štefanová's work on the Schwarzenberg suggests, bankruptcy could compel change, as it forced the bank to develop its procedures and improve its administration. They all make the implicit case that practices influenced policies and statutes, even as they were influenced by them.[33]

Andre Wakefield examines the *Zucht- und Tollhaus* at Celle in the eighteenth century to consider the bankruptcy of a public institution, the result of the misguided housekeeping of one of its chief administrators. Clearly, in an age when state officials might bear personal responsibility for the organizations or offices in their charge, bankruptcy was not limited to private enterprises. In a public enterprise as in private banks, however, it could lend itself to schemes for fiscal reform. Cameralists understood bankruptcy as a means to force payment of debts but, more interestingly, also made it a metaphor for mismanagement and waste. Nor did the process cease with literary imagery. Concern for bankruptcy influenced their thinking about proper public administration and political economy.

The discursive relationship of economic failure and institutional change applies no less to the development of the law. Bankruptcies are highly complex matters, involving litigation and negotiation that can extend over many decades and leave voluminous documentation. They are also fluid affairs, given to extraordinary variation based on the personalities and circumstances involved. The actions and tactics of debtors and creditors alike are predicated in large part upon the bankruptcy laws and legal practices of the time and place. All of the contributions to this volume pay attention to the subject in varying degrees, an absolute necessity given that bankruptcy resolution is a legal process at heart. And, they all make more or less explicit that bankruptcy statutes addressed and, in many cases, formalized those procedures and principles that had long been practiced informally by bankrupts and their creditors. Practice precedes policy.

Paul Fischer examines the late-medieval and early modern statutory codes of the imperial city of Augsburg, as well as other cities and territories of the Holy Roman Empire, to show the gradual emergence of basic bankruptcy principles that have traction in law to this day. Limiting independent execution by individual creditors, guaranteeing the equal treatment of all creditors and distinguishing degrees of culpability on the part of the bankrupt all emerge in the course of the early modern period. Interestingly, they exist in informal practice long before they are embodied in statutory law. *Dave De ruysscher* takes up similar sources and issues, but in the great commercial and financial center of Antwerp, and finds a similar development. Relying upon early statute texts and settlement contracts, as well as fragments of early bankruptcy proceedings, he traces the development of what he calls "equitable practices," essentially the equal treatment of all creditors, the legal prohibition of individual settlements or executions and the consideration of bankruptcy as non-fraudulent. These crystallized in the legal reform of 1516 but, as in Augsburg, were evident in quotidian practice far earlier. *John MacLeod* takes a careful look at one aspect of this development, the reception of the *actio Pauliana*, that is, the challenge to fraudulent conveyance—the transfer of property made to swindle, hinder or delay a creditor or to put such property beyond his or her reach—in Scots Law with the passage of the 1621 Bankruptcy Act. His analysis of case law and legal opinion demonstrates the complex process of change that took credit–debt relations as well as multiple legal traditions into account and that sought to protect creditor interests in the face of conflicted circumstances. In general and across Europe, therefore, patterns begin to emerge over the course of the early modern period. Bankrupts were forbidden to remove or withhold property from their creditors; creditors were forbidden to seize the bankrupt's property in individual acts of private execution. Rather, bankrupts were to submit to their creditors, and creditors were to act in common. They were required to register their debts with the authorities and pursue settlement through the offices of a commission of representatives, selected from among their ranks and empowered by the authorities.

Yet, attention to general patterns of development may obscure noteworthy differences, as *Jérôme Sgard* makes clear. His comparison of early modern bankruptcy law in Britain and France exposes what he calls its two poles: *ex ante* sanctions, that is the development of state-imposed, punitive measures to prevent bankruptcy; and *ex post* negotiations, the preservation of private settlements between debtor and creditors. He characterizes the British approach in terms of the former and the French in terms of the latter. Though both states pursued programs of trade legislation intended to promote economic growth in mercantilist terms, they adopted quite different legal and institutional approaches to the problem of bankruptcy.

Institutional approaches to economic history enjoy considerable favor among contemporary scholars, as noted, and scholars generally accept that economic development cannot be understood apart from the specific circumstances of the period and place in which it occurs. Questions remain, however. If, as these chapters suggest, economic practices and institutions exist in discursive, reciprocal relationships, each affecting and being affected by the other, how are institutions and institutional effects best to be studied? Institutions are too often treated as though they form a corpus, of which all economic agents are aware and upon which they all draw, not unlike traditional *Ideengeschichte*. It is not necessary, strictly speaking, to show their specific origins, context or function. These things are simply there. Because they are "there" in the sense that reference is made to them, their economic effects are often assumed rather than demonstrated. The complex ways economic institutions and practices, whether political, legal, social or cultural, were actually influenced by and sought to influence bankruptcies deserve further, empirical consideration.

These studies of bankruptcy indicate that, by the close of the early modern period, failure had worked a "institutional change" in the Northian sense, that is, a change in the "rules of the game," in the larger social, political and economic structures that direct human interaction and exchange. The slow development of bankruptcy law reveals how authorities gradually learned to manage business failure in a more orderly, uniform manner. These laws were pragmatic as well as systematic: they were applied according to the circumstances and necessities of each case; and they treated the debtor's assets as subject to the creditors' claims, as their property de facto.[34] The state's role remained essentially passive; it did not stipulate specific solutions. Rather, it provided a framework intended to minimize the disruptions that might result from bankruptcy and it confirmed the solutions reached by the involved parties. By enforcing the distinction between honest and dishonest insolvency, it encouraged debtors to negotiate with their creditors. By compelling creditors to act in common, it promoted settlements that were orderly, rational and occasionally compassionate. Over the course of the early modern period, private executions and draconian methods yielded slowly to the fundamental elements of modern due process, including public settlements, creditor equality and monitored negotiations.

The contributions to this volume underscore the empirical nature of early modern capitalism; it can be understood as a praxis of counting houses and marketplaces, where persons made decisions and faced consequences.[35] Even the contemporary institutions of economic life were rooted in and responsive to quotidian realities. Debtors and creditors adapted established commercial structures and functions, applied them to current markets and available marketplaces, appropriated the legal processes of settlement in individual ways and reshaped their economic practices accordingly.

They make clear the transformative process at work in the early modern period. The altered consciousness of commentators from the sixteenth to the eighteenth century, the refined definitions of bankruptcy in the same period and the increasing numbers of events all testify to the fact. The reliance on social networks, never entirely absent, if not perfectly understood, shifts from an emphasis on kinship to an emphasis on cooperation, that is, from a reliance on the solidarities of blood and marriage to the experience of repeated satisfactory transactions. Business organizations begin to evolve—often as a consequence of failure and crisis—from the family firm, with its informal arrangements and domestic structures, to various forms of chartered companies with formal, contractual rules and hierarchies. Bankruptcies encourage—indeed, compel—changes in institutional structures and procedures that rely unexpectedly upon preexisting, traditional arrangements. This is especially clear in the evolution of bankruptcy law across the continent.

Finally, as a group, the contributions to this volume offer evidence of the ubiquity of capitalistic practices in early modern Europe. From the counting houses of great trading and banking companies to the shops of urban artisans and the holdings of rural peasants, credit and debt relations—financial markets—determined the pace of economic life. Not an economic elite, but an astonishingly broad swath of society made frequent, sophisticated use of private property—their own and others'—for the purposes of profitable exchange. They used that property, in the form of capital accumulated and borrowed, to gain entry or access to markets and marketplaces that were local, regional and international, often at great distances from the point of production. States provided institutions in the form of laws—principles and procedures—to regulate and secure these activities, often confirming established practice long after the fact. Not only were capitalistic practices ubiquitous, but broad sections of early modern society deserve the predicate capitalist. These studies of bankruptcy can serve as a reminder how failure and its consequences—economic, social and moral—contribute to the "great transformation" to our time.[36]

Notes

1 Aber mit seiner kauffmannschatz hat er offt den gemeinen nutz und armen mann truckt, nit allein mit groser namhaffter gut und war sunder auch mit schlechter, klainer war. Er hat die eschenholz bei guttem weg auffkaufft, und wenn beser weg ist gewessen, zu markt gefiert, des gleichen wein und foren und die seitten auff die lauthen, und hat offt ain gantze war mit ainander auffkaufft, theurer, dan es wert ist gewessen, damit er die andern kauffleut nach gefallen truck, die solichs nit vermigt haben, darnach hat er in die war ain auffschlag in allen landen darein gemacht und sie verkaufft nach seinem willen. kain kauffmann hat mit 50000 fl oder 100000 fl nichtz, gegen im geschetzt, künden handlen, dann er hat gewunnen, was er gewelt hat.

"Die Chronik von Clemens Sender von den ältesten Zeiten der Stadt bis zum Jahre 1536; Fortsetzungen der Chronik des Hector Mülich von Demer, Walther und Rem", in *Die Chroniken der deutschen Städte vom 14. bis ins 16. Jahrhundert*, Vol. XXIII (Leipzig 1894), 220

2 E. Kern, Studien zur Geschichte des Augsburger Kaufmannshauses der Höchstetter (Berlin 1935), 32.

3 Giovanni Villani claimed the Peruzzi carried debts in excess of 600,000 florins, most of it loaned to the English King Edward III, when they declared bankruptcy in 1343. See P.H. Wicksteed, *Villani's Chronicle: Being Selections from the First Nine Books of the Croniche Fiorentine of Giovanni Villani* (London 1906). For a modern treatment of the "super company" and its eventual demise, see E.S. Hunt, *The Medieval Super-Companies: A Study of the Peruzzi Company of Florence* (Cambridge, UK 1994).

4 Sie stehlen unter dem Schein eines ehrlichen Mannes. Sie machen Figur mit anderer Leute Geld. Sie erwerben sich Freunde mit dem ungerechten Mammon. Sie sind die besten Männer; denn die schenken alles ihren Weibern. Wenn sie

hernach nicht weiter können, so geben sie ihren ehrlichen Namen mit samt der Handlung auf. Sie zahlen niemand. Es heisst, sie wären unglüklich gewesen. Sie wären um allen kommen und leben hernach von dem Vermögen ihrer Frauen ebenso gemächlich als zuvor.

("Von dem bürgerlichen Stande," *Augsburger Intelligenzzettel* 37 (1752))

5 One need only consider the array of criminal codes up to and including the *Reichspolizeiordnung* of 1548 to see the association of bankruptcy with theft, each of which could end on the gallows. See also T.M. Safley, "Die Frage einer frühneuzeitlichen Standardisierung des Rechtsprozesses in Bankrottsfällen am Beispiel des Höchstetter Konkurs 1529," in: T.M.J. Möllers (ed.), *Vielfalt und Einheit: Wirtschaftliche und rechtiche Rahmenbedingungen von Standardisierung* (Baden Baden 2008), 107–26.

6 *OED* online, "bankruptcy, n."; "insolvency, n." (Oxford 2012). http://proxy.library.upenn.edu:2266/view/Entry/96926?redirectedFrom=insolvency (accessed 16 July 2012).

7 The *OED* makes reference to Blackstone and Thomas More. See especially, More's Apologia (*1533 T. More* Apol. *xxi, in Wks. 881/2* Suche bancke rouptes ... which whan they haue wasted and missespent their own, woulde than be very faine ... robbe spirituall and temporall to).

8 J. Law and E.A. Martin, "bankruptcy *n.*" *A Dictionary of Law* (Oxford 2009). www.oxfordreference.com/views/ENTRY.html?subview=Main&entry=t49e334 (accessed 16 July 2012).

9 *Die Chroniken der deutschen Städten vom 14. bis ins 16. Jahrhundert*, Vol. 33, 2nd ed. (Göttingen, 1965–67), 78–81.

10 J. Strieder, "Der Zusammenbruch des süd- und mitteleuropäischen Frühkapitalismus," in: H.-F. Deininger (ed.), *Das Reiche Augsburg: Ausgewählte Aufsätze Jakob Streiders zur Augsburger und süddeutschen Wirtschaftsgeschichte des 15. Und 16. Jahrhunderts* (Munich 1938), 46. Cf. W. Zorn, *Augsburg: Geschichte einer europäischen Stadt*, 3rd ed. (Augsburg 1994), 236.

11 M. Häberlein, *Brüder, Freunde und Betrüger: Soziale Beziehungen, Normen und Konflikte in der Augsburger Kaufmannschaft um die Mitte des 16. Jahrhunderts* (Berlin 1998), 397–9. See also his contribution to this volume.

12 Early modern financiers have been described as "the creatures of the great monarchs, who needed them but always could, and did, break them when reason of state demanded it." H.G. Koenigsberger and G.L. Mosse, *Europe in the 16th Century* (New York 1968), 53.

13 Häberlein, *Brüder, Freunde und Betrüger*, 38–9. See also R. Carande, *Carlos V. y sus banqueros*, 3 vols. (Madrid 1942/47); R. Hildebrandt, "The Effects of Empire: Changes in the European Economy after Charles V," in: I. Blanchard, A. Goodman and J. Newman (eds.), *Industry and Finance in Early Modern History: Essays Presented to Geroge Hannersley on the Occasion of his 74th Birthday* (Stuttgart 1972), 58–76; H. Kellenbenz, "Die frühen Bankgeschaäfte der Fuggerschen Faktorei in Sevilla," *Revue internationale d'Histoire de la Banque* 8 (1974): 200–15; H. Kellenbenz, *Die Fugger in Spanien und Portugal bis 1560*, 2 vols. (Munich 1990).

14 R. Davis, *The Rise of the Atlantic Economies* (Ithaca, NY 1973).

15 Davis's book appeared to laudatory reviews, but these included gentle warnings; Martin Wolfe and Jacob Price both noted the relative lack of attention paid to Mediterranean economies. See their reviews respectively in: *American Historical Review* 79 (1974): 1142; *Hispanic American Historical Review* 55 (1975): 332–3. Scholars have taken up and amplified these concerns. See especially the works of Domenico Sella, e.g., *Crisis and Continuity: The Economy of Spanish Lombardy in the Seventeenth Century* (Cambridge, MA 1979).

16 R. Ehrenberg, *Das Zeitalter der Fugger: Geldkapital und Creditverkehr im 16. Jahrhundert*, 2 vols. (Jena 1896), Vol. II, 174–8; J. Kulischer, *Allgemeine Wirtschafts-*

geschichte des Mittelalters un der Neuzeit (Munich 1958); J. Strieder, "Der Zusammenbruch des süd- und mitteleuropäischer Frühkapitalismus."

17 I. Bog, "Wachstumsprobleme der oberdeutschen Wirtschaft, 1540–1618," *Jahrbücher für Nationalökonomie und Statistik* 179 (1966): 493–537; H. Kellenbenz, "Gewerbe und Handel, 1500–1648," in: H. Aubin and W. Zorn (eds.), *Handbuch der deutschen Wirtschafts- und Sozialgeschichte*, Vol. I (Stuttgart 1971), 414–64; H. Kellenbenz, "Augsburger Wirtschaft, 1530 bis 1620," in: *Welt im Umbruch: Augsburg zwischen Renaissance und Barock*, Vol. I (Augsburg 1980), 51–71; F. Lütge, "Die wirtschaftliche Lage Deutschlands vor Ausbruch des Dreißigjährigen Krieges," in: F. Lütge (ed.), *Studien zur Sozial- und Wirtschaftsgeschichte* (Stuttgart 1963), 336–95; B. Roeck, *Eine Stadt in Krieg und Frieden: Studien zur Geschichte der Reichsstadt Augsburg zwischen Kalenderstreit und Parität*, 2 vols (Göttingen 1989); E. Schremmer, "Die Wirtschaftsmetropole Augsburg," in: M. Spindler (ed.), *Handbuch der bayrischen Geschichte*, Vol. III (Munich 1971), 1080–96.

18 J.A. Schumpeter, "Capitalism," *Encyclopedia Britannica*, Vol. VI (New York 1946), 801.

19 On "new men" and "new firms," Schumpeter wrote,

> In accordance with our conception of New Men setting up New Firms, we also assume that would-be entrepreneurs do not already happen to own part or the whole of the assemblage of producers' goods which they need in order to carry out their plans, or any assets which they could exchange for what they need.

Hence, by implication, they were individuals without access to the goods required to begin new enterprises, outsiders in the market. Their firms had no foundation in previous enterprises but came into being *de novo*. See J.A. Schumpeter, *Business Cycles* (New York 1939), 108.

20 Schumpeter understood "innovation" not in the sense of the discovery or invention of something new, be it a technique, product or market, but rather as the achievement or realization of that new thing in the sense of it being placed in the market and, for a time, achieving a monopoly status by virtue of its newness or uniqueness. See J.A. Schumpeter, "The Creative Response in Economic History," *Journal of Economic History* 7 (1947): 149–59.

21 For the entire discussion, see J.A. Schumpeter, *Capitalism, Socialism and Democracy* (New York 1942), Ch. 7.

22 R. Swedberg, "Max Weber's Central Text in Economic Sociology," in: M. Granovetter and R. Swedberg (eds.), *The Sociology of Economic Life* (Boulder, CO 2001).

23 C. Muldrew, *The Economy of Obligation: The Culture of Credit and Social Relations in Early Modern England* (Basingstoke/New York 1998), 95; C. Muldrew, "'Hard Food for Midas': Cash and its Social Value in Early Modern England," *Past and Present* 170 (2001): 78–120.

24 M. Granovetter, "Economic Action and Social Structure: The Problem of Embeddedness," in: M. Granovetter and R. Swedberg (eds.), *The Sociology of Economic Life* (Boulder, CO 2001).

25 D. Gambetta, *Trust: Making and Breaking Cooperative Relations* (Oxford 1990).

26 Muldrew, *The Economy of Obligation*.

27 *OED* online, "trust, n." (Oxford 2012). http://proxy.library.upenn.edu:2266/view/Entry/207004?rskey=BnlVJr&result=1&isAdvanced=false (accessed 21 July 2012).

28 O.E. Williamson, "Calculativeness, Trust, and Economic Organization" *Journal of Law and Economics* 36 (1993): 453–86.

29 R. Harris, *Industrializing English Law* (Cambridge, UK 2000), 28.

30 A.D. Chandler, *The Visible Hand: The Managerial Revolution in American Business* (Cambridge, MA 1993).

31 The acknowledged founder of this school is Douglass C. North. For an introduction, see his *Institutions, Institutional Change and Economic Performance* (Cambridge,

UK 1990). Among many other studies, by way of example see: R.H. Coase, "The New Institutional Economics," *Journal of Institutional and Theoretical Economics* 140 (1984); A. Greif, *Institutions and the Path to the Modern Economy: Lessons of Medieval Trade* (Cambridge, UK 2006); G.M. Hodgson, *Economics and Institutions: A Manifesto for a Modern Institutional Economics* (Cambridge, UK 1988); W. Lazonick, *Business Organisation and the Myth of the Market Economy* (Cambridge, UK 1991); D.N. McCloskey, "The Enclosure of Open Fields. Preface to a Study of Its Impact on the Efficiency of English Agriculture in the Eighteenth Century," *Journal of Economic History* 32 (1972); D.C. North, "Structure and Performance: The Task of Economic History," *Journal of Economic Literature* 16 (1978); D.C. North, *Structure and Change in Economic History* (New York 1981); D.C. North, *Understanding the Process of Economic Change* (Princeton, NJ 2005); D.C. North and R.P. Thomas, "An Economic Theory of the Growth of the Western World," *Economic History Review* 22 (1970); D.C. North and R.P. Thomas, *The Rise of the Western World: A New Economic History* (Cambridge, UK 1973); N. Rosenberg and L.E. Bridzell, *How the West Grew Rich: The Economic Transformation of the Industrial World* (New York 1986); C. Tilly, "The Demographic Origins of the European Proletariat," in: D. Levine (ed.), *Proletarianisation and Family History* (London 1984); O.E. Williamson, *Markets and Hierarchies: Analysis and Anti-trust Implications* (New York 1975); O.E. Williamson, "Transaction Cost Economics: The Governance of Contractual Relations," *Journal of Law and Economics* 22 (1979); O.E. Williamson, *The Economic Institutions of Capitalism* (New York 1985); O.E. Williamson and S. Winter (eds.), *The Nature of the Firm: Origins, Evolution and Development* (Oxford 1985).

32 Economic collapse—the suspension of payments and the cessation of operations—struck the "great and famous commercial houses," but most bankrupts were middling men-on-the-make, not the great financiers but modest merchants or improving masters, not bankers who served the mighty but rather men who lived beyond their means. R. Hildebrandt, "The Effects of Empire," 62–4.

33 T.M. Safley, "Die Frage einer frühneuzeitlichen Standardisierung."

34 A. Flessner, "Philosophies of Business Bankruptcy Law: An International Overview," in: J. Ziegel (ed.), *Current Developments in International and Corporate Insolvency Law* (Oxford 1994), 19–28.

35 Cf. T. Safley, *Charity and Economy in the Orphanages of Early Modern Augsburg* (Leiden 1996), 12 and *passim.*

36 K. Polanyi, *The Great Transformation: The Political and Economic Origins of Our Time* (Boston 1944).

Part I

Social contexts

2 Merchants' bankruptcies, economic development and social relations in German cities during the long 16th century

Mark Häberlein

The Sulzer firm of Augsburg: a case study

In 1589 the brothers Anton, Wilhelm and Georg Sulzer, who came from a well-established merchant family in the imperial city of Augsburg and jointly ran the trading company "Leonhard Sulzer's heirs" (*Leonhard Sulzer sel. Erben*), were unable to repay their debts. In this situation, Anton and Wilhelm Sulzer opted for a *cessio bonorum*, a cession of property, and handed over their assets, including two spacious houses in the center of town, to a committee of their creditors. The creditors in turn sold these houses to the rich merchant Hans Steininger for almost 14,000 florins. This sale, however, met with fierce opposition from the third Sulzer brother, Georg, and his son, Matthias. Georg and Matthias Sulzer repeatedly petitioned the city court to prevent the alienation of family property, which in their view was contrary to the last will of Georg's grandfather Leonhard Sulzer. This will, drawn up in 1532, had explicitly stipulated that the houses were to remain in the family, and Matthias, as the bankrupts' closest kinsman, attempted to regain possession of them. Moreover, Matthias Sulzer and his sister, Maria, claimed that their deceased mother's inheritance, which amounted to 10,600 florins, was tied up in these houses.[1]

In January 1591, the committee of the Sulzers' creditors submitted their response to the Augsburg city court. They denied Matthias and Maria Sulzer's claims, stating that their father had actually sold off a farm in the village of Hiltenfingen that had been part of their maternal inheritance. In the committee's view, the major portion of this inheritance was still tied up in the trading company. During the following summer, rumors spread that Matthias Sulzer was secretly paying off individual creditors, including the Kraffter firm and Hans Bodecker, in order to satisfy his father's debts. To prevent further mischief, the city council imprisoned him in August 1591 and interrogated him repeatedly. These interrogations, along with the investigations of the city council's commissioners, Christoph Böcklin and Lukas Ulstett, revealed that the Sulzer bankruptcy was "a rather confused and intricate matter" (*ain zimblich verwirdte, intrigierte sach*).[2]

According to the documents compiled by the city court, the Sulzer brothers had carried on an extensive long-distance commerce in luxury goods, mostly precious stones and pearls as well as spices, Indian textiles, mirrors, arms, writing desks and small altars made of ebony wood.[3] Commission agents represented their interests in the major commercial centers of southern and western Europe: in Lyons, Matthäus Spon's heirs[4] held rubies in store for the Sulzer company; in Venice, Christoph Ott[5] handled sales of gems for them; and in Hamburg, Gilles de Greve[6] received shipments of pepper and garnets. The firm's trade network also extended to Antwerp, Middelburg, England and Seville. In the years before the firm's bankruptcy, however, the Sulzers' commercial activities appear to have focused on Lisbon, then Europe's center for the import of precious stones and other luxury goods from Asia.[7] Merchant firms from Augsburg and Nuremberg had rushed to the Portuguese capital after the Portuguese discovery of the sea route to India and had established several trading posts there in the early years of the sixteenth century.[8] While most of them had withdrawn by mid-century, some, like the Sulzers, continued to pursue opportunities there in the gem and spice trades. In 1579 they founded a separate company for the Portugal trade (*Portugiesische Handlung*), which was administered by Georg Sulzer and his son Matthias.[9]

The relationship between the firm "Leonhard Sulzer's heirs" and the Portugal Company was controversial, however. While Matthias Sulzer claimed that the Portugal Company was a completely independent undertaking of Georg Sulzer, in which he executed his father's will, the creditors saw the Portugal Company as an integral part of the Sulzer family firm and suspected that Georg and Matthias Sulzer used the Lisbon branch to alienate trade goods, pay off their own creditors and transfer the bankrupt Georg Sulzer's assets to his son. Commissioners Christoph Böcklin and Lukas Ulstett found it difficult to disentangle the matter, since both firms had operated under Georg Sulzer's name until he transferred the entire Portugal Company to his son.[10] In 1592, Matthias Sulzer fled the imperial city and filed suit before the imperial chamber court both against his creditors for seizing his property and against Augsburg's city government for imprisoning him. These cases dragged on for years.[11]

The Sulzer case reveals several central features of merchants' bankruptcies in the long sixteenth century. One important aspect is the frequency of business failure: while the sixteenth century witnessed the rise of a large number of south German merchant families to fame and fortune—most notably the Fuggers and Welsers of Augsburg—failure was common as well, and bankruptcies throw light on structural problems of the early modern economy. A second aspect is the importance of family and kinship for early modern trade: the Sulzer company was a family enterprise in which family members and relatives had invested their dowries, inheritances and surplus capital. Under these circumstances, the failure of a merchant company inevitably affected kinship networks and amounted to a crisis in social relations.[12] Finally, the Sulzer case indicates that city councils and courts—at least in important commercial centers like Augsburg—had developed formal procedures for handling merchants' bankruptcies by the late sixteenth century. In the following chapter, I will address these points in more detail. While the economic impact of individual firms' bankruptcies on the south

German merchant community should not be exaggerated, I argue that business failure severely affected kinship ties, gender relations and notions of honor, trust and reputation. In addition, they forced city governments to confront the complex issues involved in settling bankruptcy cases.

Business failure and economic development

During the sixteenth century, merchant companies from south German cities and towns—above all from Augsburg and Nuremberg, but also from Ulm, Memmingen, Constance and Strasbourg—forged commercial links across the European continent and established trading posts in major European commercial centers like Antwerp, Venice, Lyons, Seville and Lisbon. The largest firms invested in mining and smelting operations in Tyrol, Slovakia, Bohemia, Saxony and Thuringia and became bankers to the Holy Roman Emperor, western European monarchs and German territorial princes.[13] But many of those firms exceeded their means. The city of Augsburg in particular experienced a long series of business failures that brought down dozens of major trading houses between the 1520s and the outbreak of the Thirty Years War.

In 1529, the Höchstetter firm, a major supplier of Alpine copper to markets in Italy, the Netherlands, France and Portugal, collapsed after a failed attempt to gain control of the European mercury market.[14] The international credit crisis caused by the Spanish and French state bankruptcies in 1557 was followed by a number of insolvencies of Augsburg firms, and the economic recession of the early 1570s resulted in yet another series of failures. Thus the year 1574 witnessed the collapse of the important Haug-Langnauer-Linck company and of Melchior Manlich's firm.[15] Konrad Rot went bankrupt in 1580 after the breakdown of his effort to monopolize the distribution of Indian pepper in Europe.[16] Altogether, I have counted 62 merchant bankruptcies in Augsburg between 1529 and 1580 and another 57 business failures from 1580 to 1620.[17] These failures culminated in the bankruptcy of the prestigious Welser company in 1614.[18]

At least until the 1570s, the merchants of Nuremberg, who may have taken a more cautious attitude toward financing business ventures, were apparently spared a comparable history of failure, although the series of court protocols in the Nuremberg city archives, the *libri litterarum* and *libri conservatorii*, still await systematic study. A number of prominent Nuremberg firms did break down during the last decades before the outbreak of the Thirty Years War, however. These included the Gößwein and Rottenburger companies in 1588, the Dutch merchant Johann de Meere in 1594, the Italian merchant-banker Carlo Albertinelli, who left behind heavy debts when he fled the Franconian city in 1609, and Albertinelli's countryman, Bartolomeo Corolanza, in 1615.[19]

Economic historians have long concentrated on the largest of these firms and have ascribed their failure to over-investment in risky fields of business, such as state finance, the opening of new trade routes (like the Levant trade from the port of Marseille) and the exploration of new mining areas (such as the English copper mining venture of the Haug-Langnauer company in the 1560s).[20] But the

Sulzer bankruptcy of 1589 hardly fits this pattern: the sources do mention a loan of some 3,500 florins to the Portuguese crown, but this constituted merely a small portion of their overall investments. In comparison with major firms like the Fuggers or Welsers, the Sulzers traded on a substantially smaller scale: in 1590 the Portugal Company had assets of 31,500 florins, while outside creditors claimed some 27,000 florins.[21] Indeed, bankruptcies affected a large number of middling and small merchants as well as major companies, and they hit traders in secondary commercial centers as well as the well-known international merchant bankers of Augsburg and Nuremberg. This is particularly true for the last decades before the Thirty Years War, when most south German merchants shied away from high-risk investments in new trading areas or in state finance.[22]

This observation calls for a reconsideration of the causes of business failure in the context of general economic trends. Several merchants who went bankrupt in the late sixteenth century pointed to the disruption of trade routes in France and the Netherlands, countries torn by religious wars since the 1560s. The Jenisch company of Augsburg, which had to suspend payments to its creditors in 1592, claimed that it had incurred heavy losses due to warfare in the Netherlands,[23] and Johann de Meere, a Flemish immigrant merchant who went bankrupt in Nuremberg in 1594, specified the "damages" which he had suffered on account of insecure trade routes as well as unreliable business partners. According to de Meere, business partners in Antwerp and Hamburg, who owed him large sums, had gone bankrupt, and a grain shipment from Hamburg to Lisbon had been captured by English corsairs.[24] The early 1570s and the 1590s in particular were times of economic crisis, when depressed prices for commercial goods, insecure trade routes and a general scarcity of credit forced numerous firms out of business.[25]

Moreover, central European commerce went through a period of structural change and readjustment between 1570 and 1620. The establishment of new commercial communities—especially Flemish and Walloon merchants who had fled the war-torn Netherlands and Italian firms who set up branches north of the Alps—in cities like Nuremberg and Frankfurt increased competition there and may have crowded out some older firms. Many members of these new merchant groups specialized in the trade of luxury goods and thus entered the very field in which the Sulzer company operated.[26] Nor should we discount internal developments, like the inability of some merchants to find able and competent successors for their businesses and the attractiveness of alternative career options for the urban elites, like prestigious posts in city governments or territorial administrations, military commissions or the acquisition of real estate in the countryside.[27] By the late sixteenth century, the fortunes of the Sulzer firm apparently depended on one member of the younger generation—Georg Sulzer's son, Matthias—and he may not have been a particularly able or trustworthy businessman.

In any case, even the failure of more than 100 merchant firms in Augsburg between 1529 and 1620 does not signify that southern German long-distance commerce collapsed before the Thirty Years War, as Jakob Strieder, a leading German economic historian of the early twentieth century, once argued.[28] Only eight of the 55 large and middling Augsburg firms mentioned in an agreement on fixed currency exchange rates in 1585 actually went bankrupt during the following quarter-century.[29] Moreover, the number of large taxpayers in the city of Augsburg, who were taxed for a fortune of at least 20,000 florins, rose by 46.3 percent from 80 to 117 between 1558 and 1604, whereas the overall number of taxpayers rose by merely 14.8 percent from 8,770 to 10,069 during the same time period. While these figures cannot be taken as unequivocal signs of economic health, as some individuals may have moved their wealth from business to personal holdings, it still appears that the number of wealthy merchants in the Swabian imperial city continued to expand right up to the Thirty Years War, even though some very large fortunes had been annihilated by business failure.[30] In a study of commercial relations between the southern German cities and Venice, Reinhard Hildebrandt showed that transalpine trade actually doubled in volume over the course of the sixteenth century and was essentially sound around 1600.[31]

Other scholars have also rejected the hypothesis of a general economic decline—or even collapse—of southern German long-distance trade before the Thirty Years War. To be sure, there were clear signs of crisis, such as inflation, overproduction in the all-important textile sector and growing competition from immigrant traders, and southern German merchants had to adjust to structural changes in the European economy, such as the shift from the Mediterranean to the Atlantic world. Yet, there is ample evidence for a continuing dynamism and growth of central European commerce in the late sixteenth and early seventeenth centuries.[32] Merchants' bankruptcies in German cities during this period should not, therefore, be interpreted as indicators of a failing economy but rather as signs that these merchants operated in an environment characterized by a high degree of uncertainty and growing competition from new merchant groups.

Kinship, gender and credit

Early modern merchant firms were tied up in intricate networks of kinship and credit. In Thomas Max Safley's words, "the positive emotions of family life and the transcendent morals of Christian religion ... were essential prerequisites for conducting business in an age notably lacking in reliable techniques for risk-assessment and management."[33] Therefore business failures sent ripples—or in some cases shock waves—through entire merchant communities. Like the Sulzer firm, sixteenth-century merchant companies typically consisted of groups of two to eight partners who signed a company contract (*Gesellschaftsvertrag*) and invested a fixed amount of capital "at gain or loss" (*zu Gewinn und Verlust*) in the joint enterprise. Most companies were either owned by single individuals or by small groups of persons with close kinship connections to one another—brothers, fathers and sons, in-laws, cousins or combinations of these. This applies to large international companies like the Fugger, Welser and Höchstetter firms of Augsburg or the Tucher and Imhoff companies of Nuremberg as well as to numerous middling and smaller firms.[34]

The significance of kinship ties was not limited to the formation of trading partnerships, but also extended to other aspects of these companies' business operations. Of particular importance was the role of family members and kinfolk in supplying capital. The bankruptcy of the brothers Anton, Wilhelm and Georg Sulzer in 1590 provides a telling example. As a long-established merchant family, the Sulzers were tightly integrated into the far-flung kinship networks of Augsburg's economic and social elite. Their mother Regina came from the respected patrician Imhof clan. Anton Sulzer's marriage to Maria Konradina Heel in 1562 connected him to the Lauginger, Hörmann and Bimmel families, while his brother Georg's marriage to Regina Manlich in 1557 established further links with the Hörmann, Rem, Linck and Walther families. Wilhelm Sulzer's wife Richardis Eiselin was closely related to the Jenisch family, and his sister Regina had married a member of the Haug family in 1567. Finally, Wilhelm Sulzer's daughter Anna became the wife of Anton Bernhard Rehlinger, a scion of one of Augsburg's most prominent patrician clans, in 1580. This impressive lineup of the imperial city's elite is also reflected in a list of the Sulzer's creditors at the time of their bankruptcy, which included no fewer than seven Rehlingers, four Welsers, three Imhofs, three Herwarts, as well as members of the Haug, Hörmann and Lauginger families. Although the available sources do not tell us how their kinship connections influenced these investors' decisions to provide the Sulzer brothers with capital, the empirical evidence suggests that these ties constituted important bonds of trusts between firms and their investors.[35]

Other south German merchant families were just as dependent on the capital investments of relatives. In fact, the extensive mining activities of Augsburg's large merchant firms, which controlled a significant part of the European copper market and were engaged in the mining of gold, silver, tin, lead and mercury,[36] would have been inconceivable without their reliance on large sums of deposit capital. Depositors did not share in a firm's profits but received a fixed interest rate that typically ranged from 5 to 8 percent. Analysis of the sources of capital deposited in sixteenth-century Augsburg merchant firms reveals that a high proportion—often more than one-half—of these firms' outside capital came from the owners' relatives. When the Haug-Langnauer-Linck company was founded in 1531, it accepted a total of 211,000 florins in outside capital from 73 different creditors. Only 82,000 florins were deposited by persons who neither worked for the Haug-Langnauer-Linck nor were related to the firm's associates, with relatives supplying most of the capital. Fourteen years later, 61 percent of the company's deposit capital of slightly over 200,000 florins belonged to relatives and a further 17.5 percent to employees. In 1553, relatives and employees once again accounted for two-thirds of the Haug-Langnauer-Linck firm's deposit capital, which now amounted to over 250,000 florins, and in 1557 the share of depositors neither related to nor employed by the Haug-Langnauer-Linck dropped to merely one-sixth. When the firm of Christoph Manlich and his brothers went bankrupt in 1564, about 60 percent of the 102,850 florins which the brothers owed to 44 creditors came from members of their kinship network.[37] Family members and close relatives also provided important brokerage services, and merchants who were engaged in conflicts frequently relied on the support of kinfolk.[38]

Given the importance of family members and relatives as trading partners, sources of capital, brokers and supporters in conflict situations, their behavior in bankruptcy cases was crucial. Since significant portions of deposit capital usually came from the owners' circle of relatives, a firm's failure threatened the loss of these relatives' investments and therefore strained kinship ties. On the other hand, the support of kinfolk could be an important asset in settling insolvency cases. Bankrupt merchants often tried to accommodate their relatives by paying them off first, thereby dividing the ranks of the creditors along kinship lines. Such a division is evident in the case of Hans Paul Herwart's bankruptcy in 1576. Herwart, a prominent patrician merchant who had over-extended his own resources when he lent Melchior Manlich the huge sum of 120,000 francs to support Manlich's Levant trade via Marseille, initially mortgaged his entire property to a group of six persons that included his brothers Hans Heinrich and Hans Jakob along with his brothers-in-law Stefan Endorfer and Heinrich Rehlinger. Herwart's settlement with his close relatives enraged his other creditors, however, who demanded to be treated on equal terms with this kinship group. Both parties settled their differences in a contract which specified Hans Paul Herwart's obligations to his creditors, his wife's privileged claims to her husband's property and the mode in which Herwart's relatives as well as the other creditors were to be repaid from the bankrupt's estate.[39] Matthias Sulzer was likewise accused of having paid off relatives to the detriment of other creditors.[40]

In other instances, relatives were suspected of helping bankrupts to hide some of their assets from their creditors' and the authorities' eyes. The creditors of the insolvent Zangmeister brothers of Memmingen, for example, became suspicious when the bankrupts' brother-in-law, Hans David Ott, was reported to have left the town with a Latin warrant for Venice, where he might try to sell the Zangmeisters' stored goods for the benefit of his relatives.[41] In general, business failures reveal the extent as well as the limits of kinship obligations in early modern German towns. Whereas the bankruptcy of a merchant firm and the accompanying loss of capital could be seen as a breach of trust and might shatter the confidence of the bankrupts' own relatives, notions of familial honor and kinship solidarity as well as the close ties between the merchant community and the city council could work to promote mutual agreements and the restoration of strained relationships.[42]

As the Sulzer case indicates, merchants' bankruptcies could also affect gender relations. When Anton and Wilhelm Sulzer handed over their property to their creditors in 1590, their wives not only swore that they had not hidden any assets but helped to bring about the settlement by relinquishing their "female freedoms" (*weibliche Freiheiten*) and settling with 20,000 out of the 32,000 florins that they had invested in their husbands' firm. Matthias Sulzer, on the other hand, claimed his mother's inheritance against his creditors, and his wife Constantia Adelgaiss later sued the Sulzer creditors for restitution of her dowry of 4,000 florins.[43]

In early modern south German towns, a woman's marriage portion (*Heiratsgut*) as well as her inherited property legally remained her own but were administered by her husband, who frequently invested them in his business. After the husband's death, city law required the widow to be put under the care of two male guardians, if the deceased had not explicitly exempted her from guardianship in his will.[44] With the advice of their guardians, wealthy widows frequently deposited capital in merchant companies, often in those headed by their sons or sons-in-law. A firm's failure thus threatened not only its owners' fortunes, but their wives' and female relatives' means of sustenance as well. Women who had invested substantial sums in bankrupt firms might face poverty and the loss of social status. On the other hand, wives' property rights might be of crucial importance in the settlement of bankruptcy cases. The marriage portion, being legally her own property, was exempt from the bankrupt's estate, and the city authorities regarded dowries, along with the capital of foster children or public institutions, as "privileged debts" whose payment had priority over other claims to the bankrupt's estate. Therefore, if a wife claimed her whole property, she might be able to support her family from it; but if she relinquished part of it or yielded her claim to priority, she might aid the settlement of the case. The handling of the marriage portion consequently became a central issue in bankruptcy proceedings and illustrates the flexible character of debt settlements in imperial cities.[45]

Bankruptcy and the law

In the course of the sixteenth century, legal procedures for handling bankruptcy cases were introduced both at the local and imperial levels. Faced with a string of business failures, Augsburg's city council issued three bankruptcy ordinances between 1564 and 1580. Codifying legal practices which had already been applied in earlier bankruptcy cases, these ordinances provided for the seizure and safekeeping of insolvent firms' assets, the establishment of committees representing the interests of creditors, and the imprisonment of debtors until they had come to a settlement with their creditors. In addition, the 1580 ordinance associated business failure with the loss of male honor when it decreed that bankrupts were to be excluded not only from the prestigious patrician and merchant drinking halls, but from all "gatherings of honest people" (*ehrlicher leuth Zusamenkünfften*), and had to take their seats among the women during weddings and funerals. Their children were not allowed to wear gold chains unless they had inherited this right from their mothers.[46] At the imperial level, the police ordinances (*Reichspoliceyordnungen*) of 1548 and 1577 drew a distinction between honest merchants, who had failed because of unfortunate circumstances like the loss of trade goods at sea, and fraudulent bankrupts who sought to cheat their creditors.[47] This distinction remained crucial in the bankruptcy legislation of German territorial states throughout the early modern period.[48]

The Augsburg ordinances provided the general framework for bankruptcy proceedings in the imperial city in the late sixteenth and early seventeenth centuries, including the settlement of the Sulzer case. Accordingly, a committee represented the creditors in negotiations with the Sulzer brothers and the city council; a cession of property was executed; and the contract drawn up between Anton and Wilhelm Sulzer and their creditors in 1590 explicitly stipulated that "divine fate" had caused their financial difficulties. At the same time, the city council retained considerable flexibility in bankruptcy proceedings. There is no evidence, for example, that Anton and Wilhelm Sulzer, who cooperated with their creditors and whose wives relinquished part of their dowry, were ever put in jail. Their nephew, Matthias, on the other hand, was imprisoned for 16 months to prevent him from hiding assets and evading his creditors. In part, the different treatment of Matthias Sulzer and his uncles may reflect the difficulties of sorting out this "confused and intricate matter." But, more importantly, this flexibility was characteristic of a city government that had already accumulated considerable experience in the handling of bankruptcy proceedings and that took the bankrupts' reputation and trustworthiness into account.[49] While business failures could shatter mercantile careers and frequently resulted in prolonged conflicts, there is ample evidence that insolvent merchants, their kinfolk and city governments sought to maintain the honor of bankrupts' families and restore harmony within strained social networks.

Conclusion: remembering and forgetting bankruptcy

In 1618 the brothers Wolf Leonhard and Hieronymus Sulzer compiled a *Stammenbeschreibung der Sulzer*, a genealogical work on their family that featured copious biographical notes on the male family members. This work—actually the continuation of an older genealogy written by Christoph Sulzer in 1540—includes several pages on the brothers Georg, Anton and Wilhelm Sulzer. We learn from them that Georg Sulzer, born in 1535, was trained as a merchant from his youth and was "much experienced and practiced" (*wol erfahren vnndt geyebt*) in commerce. Moreover, Georg had obtained a seat on the imperial city's Small Council in 1571 and became an overseer of public building projects (*Bauherr*) in 1572; he held both posts until 1589, when he temporarily left the city. He eventually returned to Augsburg and died there in January 1603.[50] The family chronicle further describes Anton Sulzer as "the friendliest and most charitable" of the brothers (*ist vnder sein Bruedern der freindtlichst vnndt guetthätigst gewest*) and informs readers that Georg Sulzer's son Matthias received a commercial education in his youth, was sent to Italy (*Welschlandt*) to learn the language, had married Constantia Adelgaiss from Antwerp in 1587 and eventually became a postmaster in Rheinhausen.[51] The authors of the family chronicle remained conspicuously silent on the bankruptcy of the Sulzer company in 1589. Business failure was not allowed to stain the memory of an ancient and respected family that traced its roots in Augsburg back to the fourteenth century, whose members had made their mark in commerce, urban government, the legal profession, the military and chivalric tournaments, and some of whom had been accepted into the ranks of the urban patriciate in 1538.[52]

Georg Kölderer, a commercial employee of the Weiß family and a diligent chronicler of urban life in the late sixteenth century, was less obliging. In late November 1589, Kölderer wrote, a rumor (*ain geschray*) spread that the Sulzers had become insolvent. The chronicler learned that Anton Sulzer had fled the city and that his brother Georg denied his involvement in the firm's affairs. Kölderer even gave an exact estimate of the Sulzers' debts—99,803 florins—and offered two explanations for the brothers' failure. First, he noted that the Sulzers had supported the "new calendar," the Gregorian calendar that the Augsburg city council had introduced in 1583 and that Protestants like Kölderer bitterly opposed.[53] This rather curious explanation indicates that the chronicler may have seen the bankruptcy of the Protestant Sulzer brothers as a form of divine punishment for their alleged betrayal of their co-religionists. Second, Kölderer hinted at the symptoms of a general economic crisis: the world was becoming poorer and poorer, and there was so little employment and money available that people might well use the services of an alchemist.[54]

The silence of the Sulzer family chronicle on a bankruptcy, about which the chronicler Georg Kölderer had a number of observations and surmises to offer, underscores that bankruptcies in early modern German towns were contested affairs. They were contested not only in city council chambers and law courts, where insolvent merchants, their relatives and their creditors presented their claims, negotiated settlements and argued over matters of trust and honor, but also in historical memory. Bankruptcy cases thus offer a wealth of insights into kinship ties, social norms and economic behavior in the pre-industrial period which historians have not yet fully explored.

Notes

1 Stadtarchiv Augsburg, Stadtgerichtsakten, no. 176 (no pagination); see also Stadtarchiv Augsburg, Kaufmannschaft und Handel, no. 24; Schuld-, Klag- und Appellationssachen, part 2, box XXVI.
2 Stadtarchiv Augsburg, Stadtgerichtsakten, no. 176.
3 See the inventory of goods which the Sulzer company had entrusted to the firm's partner Georg Sulzer ("Verzaichnung der durch die Leonhard Sultzerischen gesellschaffter Georgen Sultzer vertrauten Wahren"): Stadtarchiv Augsburg, Stadtgerichtsakten, no. 176. Cf. also Stadtarchiv Augsburg, Kaufmannschaft und Handel, no. 24, ff. 90–108, 156–8, 164–5.
4 In the final third of the sixteenth century, the heirs of Matthäus Spon, a merchant who hailed from the city of Ulm, acted as commissioned agents for a number of south German firms in the French city. See G. Seibold, *Die Manlich: Geschichte einer Augsburger Kaufmannsfamilie* (Sigmaringen 1995), 149; W. Reinhard (ed.), *Augsburger Eliten des 16. Jahrhunderts: Prosopographie wirtschaftlicher und politischer Führungsgruppen 1500–1620* (Berlin 1996), 1140; M. Häberlein, "Commerce, formation et réseaux de compatriotes: la ville de Lyon vue par des marchands de l'Allemagne du Sud au XVIème et au début tu XVIIème siècle," in: J.-L. Gaulin and S. Rau (eds.), *Lyon vue d'ailleurs (1245–1800): Échanges, compétitions et perceptions* (Lyon 2009), 141–59, esp. 149–50.
5 Christoph Ott and his brother Hieronymus were the sons of David Ott, a merchant from Ulm who had moved to Venice. In the final third of the sixteenth century, the

Ott firm handled the Venetian affairs of the Fuggers and other south German firms. An important part of their business was the purchase of artwork and luxury items for central European customers. See S. Backmann, "Kunstagenten oder Kaufleute? Die Firma Ott im Kunsthandel zwischen Oberdeutschland und Venedig (1550–1650)," in: K. Bergdolt and J. Brüning (eds.), *Kunst und ihre Auftraggeber im 16. Jahrhundert: Venedig und Augsburg im Vergleich* (Berlin 1997), 175–97; M. Häberlein, *The Fuggers of Augsburg: Pursuing Wealth and Honor in Renaissance Germany* (Charlottesville and London 2012), 107, 111, 127; R. Dauser, *Informationskultur und Beziehungswissen: Das Korrespondenznetz Hans Fuggers (1531–1598)* (Tübingen 2008), 82, 84; S. Wölfle, *Die Kunstpatronage der Fugger 1560–1618* (Augsburg 2009), 274–9 and *passim*.

6 This Hamburg merchant had business dealings with several Augsburg firms between 1570 and his death in 1604, including copper exports to England for the Paler-Weiß company and the reception of pepper shipments from Lisbon for the wealthy patrician merchant Marx Rehlinger. In the early 1590s, he also handled business transactions for Georg Fugger's heirs and the Welser company of Augsburg, who held the monopoly contract for marketing Portuguese imports of Indian pepper in Europe. See H. Kellenbenz, *Unternehmerkräfte im Hamburger Portugal- und Spanienhandel 1590–1625* (Hamburg 1954), 201–3, 224; Reinhard, *Augsburger Eliten*, 72 (no. 127) 311 (no. 447), 382 (no. 549), 595, 597 (no. 910), 609 (no. 923), 680 (no. 1042), 714 (no. 1088); R. Hildebrandt (ed.), *Quellen und Regesten zu den Augsburger Handelshäusern Paler und Rehlinger 1539–1642: Wirtschaft und Politik im 16./17. Jahrhundert. Part 1: 1539–1623* (Stuttgart 1996), 116 (no. 74), 151 (no. 111), 202–3 (no. 170); M. Kalus, *Pfeffer–Kupfer–Nachrichten: Kaufmannsnetzwerke und Handelsstrukturen im europäisch-asiatischen Handel am Ende des 16. Jahrhunderts* (Augsburg 2010), 85, 88, 95–7, 99, 102, 122, 195, 197.

7 On Lisbon's position in the early modern world economy, see J. Munro, "Patterns of Trade, Money, and Credit," in: T.A. Brady, Jr., H.A. Oberman and J.D. Tracy (eds.), *Handbook of European History 1400–1600: Late Middle Ages, Renaissance and Reformation. Vol. 1: Structures and Assertions* (Leiden 1994), 147–95, esp. 168–70; T.D. Walker, "Lisbon as a Strategic Haven in the Atlantic World," in: W. Klooster and A. Padula (eds.), *The Atlantic World: Essays on Slavery, Migration and Imagination* (Upper Saddle River, NJ 2004), 60–75, 194–5; T.D. Walker, "Lisbon," in: J.J. McCusker (ed.), *History of World Trade since 1450*, 2 vols. (Detroit 2006), II: 463–5.

8 See W. Großhaupt, "Commercial Relations between Portugal and the Merchants of Augsburg and Nuremberg," in: J. Aubin (ed.), *La Découverte, le Portugal et l'Europe: Actes du Colloque Paris, les 26, 27 et 28 mai 1988* (Paris 1990), 359–97; J. Pohle, *Deutschland und die überseeische Expansion Portugals im 15. und 16. Jahrhundert* (Münster 2000).

9 Stadtarchiv Augsburg, Stadtgerichtsakten, no. 176; Kaufmannschaft und Handel, no. 24, ff. 64–71; C. Warnemünde, "Augsburger Handel in den letzten Jahrzehnten des 16. Jahrhunderts und dem beginnenden 17. Jahrhundert" (unpub. Ph.D. diss., University of Freiburg, 1956), 155–9; Reinhard, *Augsburger Eliten*, 829–30 (no. 1292), 832–3 (no. 1296).

10 Stadtarchiv Augsburg, Stadtgerichtsakten, no. 176.

11 Bayerisches Hauptstaatsarchiv München, Reichskammergericht, no. 12643, 12644.

12 M. Häberlein, *Brüder, Freunde und Betrüger: Soziale Beziehungen, Normen und Konflikte in der Augsburger Kaufmannschaft um die Mitte des 16. Jahrhunderts* (Berlin 1998); T.M. Safley, "Bankruptcy: Family and Misfortune in Early Modern Augsburg," *Journal of European Economic History* 29 (2000): 53–72.

13 Surveys include H. Kellenbenz, "Wirtschaftsleben der Blütezeit," in: W Baer, J. Becker and G. Gottlieb (eds.), *Geschichte der Stadt Augsburg von der Römerzeit bis zur Gegenwart*, 2nd edn. (Stuttgart 1985), 258–301; M. Diefenbacher, "Handel im Wandel: Die Handels- und Wirtschaftsmetropole Nürnberg in der frühen Neuzeit

(1550–1630)," in: B. Kirchgässner and H.-P. Becht (eds.), *Stadt und Handel. 32. Arbeitstagung in Schwäbisch Hall 1993* (Sigmaringen 1995), 63–81; and E. Landsteiner, "Kein Zeitalter der Fugger: Zentraleuropa 1450–1620," in: F. Edelmayer, P. Feldbauer and M. Wakounig (eds.), *Globalgeschichte 1450–1620: Anfänge und Perspektiven* (Vienna 2002), 95–123.

14 See E. Kern, "Studien zur Geschichte des Augsburger Kaufmannshauses der Höchstetter," *Archiv für Kulturgeschichte* 26 (1936): 162–98; T.M. Safley, "Staatsmacht und geschäftliches Scheitern: Der Bankrott der Handelsgesellschaft Ambrosius und Hans, Gebrüder Höchstetter, und Mitverwandte im Jahr 1529," *Österreichische Zeitschrift für Geschichtswissenschaften* 19 (2008): 36–55; T.M. Safley, "The Question of Early Modern Business Culture: Methodological Reflections on the Firm 'Ambrosius and Hans, the Brothers Höchstetter and Associates', 1524–1529," *Wiener Zeitschrift für Geschichte der Neuzeit* 9 (2009): 7–23.

15 F. Hassler, *Der Ausgang der Augsburger Handelsgesellschaft David Haug, Hans Langnauer und Mitverwandte (1574–1606)* (Augsburg 1928); H. Kellenbenz, "Le banqueroute de Melchior Manlich en 1574 et ses répercussions en France," in: *Villes, bonnes villes, cités et capitals: Études d'histoire urbaine (12e–18e siècle) offertes à Bernard Chevalier* (Tours 1989), 153–9; Seibold, *Die Manlich*, 146–53.

16 R. Hildebrandt, "Wirtschaftsentwicklung und Konzentration im 16. Jahrhundert: Konrad Rot und die Finanzierungsprobleme seines interkontinentalen Handels," *Scripta Mercaturae* 4 (1970): 25–50.

17 Häberlein, *Brüder, Freunde und Betrüger*, 397–9 and *passim*; M. Häberlein, "Firmenbankrotte, Sozialbeziehungen und Konfliktlösungsmechanismen in süddeutschen Städten um 1600," *Österreichische Zeitschrift für Geschichtswissenschaften* 19 (2008): 10–35.

18 See J. Müller, "Der Zusammenbruch des Welserschen Handelshauses im Jahr 1614," *Vierteljahrschrift für Social- und Wirtschaftsgeschichte* 1 (1903): 196–234; J. Müller, "Der Verlauf des Welserschen Gantprozesses im Jahre 1614," *Zeitschrift des Historischen Vereins für Schwaben und Neuburg* 30 (1903): 42–74; and R. Hildebrandt, "Der Niedergang der Augsburger Welser-Firma (1560–1614)," in: M. Häberlein and J. Burkhardt (eds.), *Die Welser: Neue Forschungen zur Geschichte und Kultur des oberdeutschen Handelshauses* (Berlin 2002), 265–81.

19 L.F. Peters, *Der Handel Nürnbergs am Anfang des Dreißigjährigen Krieges: Strukturkomponenten, Unternehmen und Unternehmer. Eine quantitative Analyse* (Stuttgart 1994), 133, 135–8, 194–9, 306–9, 363, 473, 488, 501, 535–41; Häberlein, "Firmenbankrotte," 15–17.

20 The classic study of merchant capitalism and financial crises in the sixteenth century is R. Ehrenberg, *Das Zeitalter der Fugger: Geldkapital und Creditverkehr im 16. Jahrhundert*, 2 vols. (Jena 1896). On the Levant trade of the Melchior Manlich company, see A.-E. Sayous, "Le commerce de Melchior Manlich et Cie d'Augsbourg à Marseille et dans toute la Méditerrannée entre 1571 et 1574," *Revue Historique* 176 (1935): 389–411; Kellenbenz, "Le banqueroute"; Seibold, *Die Manlich*, 140–5. On the Haug-Langnauer firm in English copper mining, see G. Hammersley, "Technique or Economy? The Rise and Decline of the English Copper Industry, ca. 1550–1650," in: H. Kellenbenz (ed.), *Schwerpunkte der Kupferproduktion und des Kupferhandels in Europa, 1500–1650* (Cologne 1977), 1–40; A. Hoechstetter-Müller, "Die 'Company of Mines Royal' und die Kupferbergwerke in Keswick, Cumberland, zur Zeit Joachim und Daniel Hoechstetters (1526–1580)," in: P. Fassl, W. Liebhart and W. Wüst (eds.), *Aus Schwaben und Altbayern: Festschrift für Pankraz Fried zum 60. Geburtstag* (Sigmaringen 1991), 75–91.

21 Stadtarchiv Augsburg, Stadtgerichtsakten, no. 176.

22 Cf. Häberlein, "Firmenbankrotte," 14–22.

23 Stadtarchiv Augsburg, Kaufmannschaft und Handel, ad 28.

24 Bayerisches Hauptstaatsarchiv München, Reichskammergericht, no. 8611, quad. 12.

25 See R. Hildebrandt, "Die Krise auf dem europäischen Kupfermarkt 1570–1580," in: W. Kroker and E. Westermann (eds.), *Montanwirtschaft Mitteleuropas vom 12. bis 17. Jahrhundert* (Bochum 1984), 170–8; H. Schilling, "The European Crisis of the 1590s: The Situation in German Towns," in: P. Clark (ed.), *The European Crisis of the 1590s: Essays in Comparative History* (London 1984), 135–56.

26 On the Italian and Flemish immigrant merchants in Nuremberg, see L. Bauer, "Die italienischen Kaufleute und ihre Stellung im protestantischen Nürnberg am Ende des 16. Jahrhunderts (Zu einem Bericht an die Kurie vom Jahre 1593)," *Jahrbuch für fränkische Landesforschung* 22 (1962): 1–18; Peters, *Der Handel Nürnbergs*, 99–104 and *passim*; Diefenbacher, "Handel im Wandel," 73–6. On the Flemish and Walloon immigrant communities in Frankfurt, see H. Schilling, *Niederländische Exulanten im 16. Jahrhundert: Ihre Stellung im Sozialgefüge und im religiösen Leben deutscher und englischer Städte* (Gütersloh 1972); F. Berger (ed.), *Glaube Macht Kunst: Antwerpen–Frankfurt um 1600* (Frankfurt am Main 2005).

27 A classic example is the Fugger family of Augsburg. While the family firm continued to operate until the mid-seventeenth century, family members gradually withdrew from active involvement in the firm's management and focussed on other fields such as court service, urban politics, military office, the management of rural estates and art patronage. This largely left the day-to-day management of the Fugger company in the hands of salaried employees. See S. Haberer, "Handelsdiener und Handelsherren – Andreas Hyrus und die Fugger," *Zeitschrift des Historischen Vereins für Schwaben* 88 (1995): 137–55; S. Haberer, *Ott Heinrich Fugger (1592–1644): Biographische Analyse typologischer Handlungsfelder in der Epoche des Dreißigjährigen Krieges* (Augsburg 2004), 99–152; Häberlein, *The Fuggers of Augsburg*, 99–124, 146–8, 199–219. In Nuremberg, all but two patrician families had withdrawn from active commerce by the early seventeenth century. See Peters, *Der Handel Nürnbergs, passim*. On these developments, see also M. Häberlein, "Sozialer Wandel in den Augsburger Führungsschichten des 16. und frühen 17. Jahrhunderts," in: G. Schulz (ed.), *Sozialer Aufstieg: Funktionseliten in Spätmittelalter und Früher Neuzeit. Büdinger Gespräche 2000–2001* (Munich 2002), 73–96.

28 J. Strieder, "Der Zusammenbruch des süd- und mitteleuropäischen Frühkapitalismus," in: H.F. Deininger (ed.), *Das Reiche Augsburg: Ausgewählte Aufsätze Jakob Strieders zur Augsburger und süddeutschen Wirtschaftsgeschichte des 15. und 16. Jahrhunderts* (Munich 1938), 45–9. Strieder's assessment has been frequently repeated in later works. See, e.g., W. von Stromer, "Die oberdeutschen Geld- und Wechselmärkte: Ihre Entwicklung vom Spätmittelalter bis zum Dreißigjährigen Krieg," *Scripta Mercaturae* 10 (1976): 23–49, esp. p. 40; and H. Schilling, *Aufbruch und Krise: Deutschland 1517–1648* (Berlin 1988), 52–3.

29 Hildebrandt, *Quellen und Regesten*, 194–6 (no. 163); Häberlein, "Firmenbankrotte," 21–2.

30 R. Hildebrandt, "The Effects of Empire: Changes in the European Economy after Charles V," in: I. Blanchard, A. Goodman and J. Newman (eds.), *Industry and Finance in Early Modern History: Essays Presented to George Hammersley to the Occasion of his 74th Birthday* (Stuttgart 1992), 58–76.

31 R. Hildebrandt, "Die wirtschaftlichen Beziehungen zwischen Oberdeutschland und Venedig um 1600: Konturen eines Gesamtbildes," in: B. Roeck, K. Bergdolt and A.J. Martin (eds.), *Venedig und Oberdeutschland: Beziehungen zwischen Kunst und Wirtschaft* (Sigmaringen 1993), 277–88.

32 F. Lütge, "Die wirtschaftliche Lage Deutschlands vor Ausbruch des Dreißigjährigen Krieges," in: F. Lütge, *Studien zur Sozial- und Wirtschaftsgeschichte: Gesammelte Abhandlungen* (Stuttgart 1970), 336–95, esp. 358–9; I. Bog, "Wachstumsprobleme der oberdeutschen Wirtschaft 1540–1618," *Jahrbücher für Nationalökonomie und Statistik* 179 (1966): 493–537, esp. 515–16; Kellenbenz, "Wirtschaftsleben der Blütezeit," 291–3; B. Roeck, *Eine Stadt in Krieg und Frieden: Sudien zur Geschichte*

der Reichsstadt Augsburg zwischen Kalenderstreit und Parität, 2 vols. (Göttingen 1989) I: 511–14; Peters, *Der Handel Nürnbergs*, 55.

33 Safley, "Methodological Reflections," 10.

34 E. Lutz, *Die rechtliche Struktur süddeutscher Handelsgesellschaften in der Zeit der Fugger*, 2 vols. (Tübingen 1976); Häberlein, *Brüder, Freunde und Betrüger*, 341–2, 377–9; M.A. Denzel and Ulrich Pfister, "Handelsgesellschaft," in: F. Jaeger (ed.), *Enzyklopädie der Neuzeit*, Vol. 5 (Stuttgart 2007), 97–101, esp. 99–100.

35 For the list of the Sulzers' creditors, see Stadtarchiv Augsburg, Augsburger Geschlechter, ad 34 (Sulzer). For their kinship connections, see Reinhard, *Augsburger Eliten*, 827 (no. 1289), 829–30 (no. 1292), 832–3 (no. 1296), 834 (no. 1298). Cf. also Häberlein, "Firmenbankrotte," 22–3.

36 Cf. R. Hildebrandt, "Augsburger und Nürnberger Kupferhandel 1500–1619: Produktion, Marktanteile und Finanzierung im Vergleich zweier Städte und ihrer wirtschaftlichen Führungsschicht," in: H. Kellenbenz (ed.), *Schwerpunkte der Kupferproduktion und des Kupferhandels in Europa 1500–1650* (Cologne 1977), 190–224; E. Westermann, "Zur Silber- und Kupferproduktion Mitteleuropas vom 15. bis zum frühen 17. Jahrhundert: Über Bedeutung und Rangfolge der Reviere von Schwaz, Mansfeld und Neusohl," *Der Anschnitt* 38 (1986): 187–211; H. Kellenbenz, "Kapitalverflechtung im mittleren Alpenraum: Das Beispiel des Bunt- und Edelmetallbergbaus vom fünfzehnten bis zur Mitte des siebzehnten Jahrhunderts," *Zeitschrift für Bayerische Landesgeschichte* 51 (1988): 13–50.

37 F.-W. Ringling, "Sixteenth-Century Merchant Capitalism: The Haug-Langnauer-Linck & Relatives of Augsburg as a Case Study" (unpub. Ph.D. diss., University of Rochester, 1979), 73, 94–5, 102, 116, 119, 129, 131; Häberlein, *Brüder, Freunde und Betrüger*, 243–54.

38 Häberlein, *Brüder, Freunde und Betrüger*, 374–92.

39 H. Herwarth von Bittenfeld, "Fünf Herwarthische Urkunden," *Zeitschrift des Historischen Vereins für Schwaben und Neuburg* 9 (1882): 117–57, esp. 147–55; Häberlein, *Brüder, Freunde und Betrüger*, 308–9.

40 Stadtarchiv Augsburg, Stadtgerichtsakten, no. 176.

41 A. Westermann, "Die Zahlungseinstellung der Handelsgesellschaft der Gebrüder Zangmeister zu Memmingen 1560," *Vierteljahrschrift für Social- und Wirtschaftsgeschichte* 6 (1908): 460–516, esp. 485–6.

42 On the importance of the concepts of trust and honor in early modern economic relations, see T.M. Luckett, "Credit and Commercial Society in France, 1740–1789," (unpub. Ph.D. diss., Princeton University, 1992), 45–90; Häberlein, *Brüder, Freunde und Betrüger*, 274–87; C.S. Muldrew, *The Economy of Obligation: The Culture of Credit and Social Relations in Early Modern England* (Houndmills and Basingstoke 1998), *passim*; S. Gorißen, "Der Preis des Vertrauens: Unsicherheit, Institutionen und Rationalität im vorindustriellen Fernhandel," in: U. Frevert (ed.), *Vertrauen: Historische Annäherungen* (Göttingen 2003), 90–118.

43 Stadtarchiv Augsburg, Personenselekt "Sulzer"; Stadtgerichtsakten, no. 23; Häberlein, "Firmenbankrotte," 26–7.

44 L. Roper, *The Holy Household: Women and Morals in Reformation Augsburg* (Oxford 1989), 148–50, 172–6.

45 Häberlein, *Brüder, Freunde und Betrüger*, 360–73.

46 R. Hildebrandt, "Zum Verhältnis von Wirtschaftsrecht und Wirtschaftspraxis im 16. Jahrhundert: Die Fallitenordnungen des Augsburger Rates 1564–1580," in: A. Mächler, E. Grünert, H. Kraemer and K.-R. Seidel (eds.), *Historische Studien zu Politik, Verfassung und Gesellschaft: Festschrift für Richard Dietrich zum 65. Geburtstag* (Bern 1976), 153–60; Häberlein, *Brüder, Freunde und Betrüger*, 323–6, 331–6.

47 M. Weber, *Die Reichspolizeiordnungen von 1530, 1548 und 1577: Historische Einführung und Edition* (Frankfurt am Main 2002), 198–9, 252–4.

48 See the example of the Saxon bankruptcy ordinance of 1724 analyzed in R. Beachy, "Bankruptcy and Social Death: The Influence of Credit-Based Commerce on Cultural and Political Values," *Zeitsprünge. Forschungen zur Frühen Neuzeit* 4 (2000): 329–43. Beachy's argument that the 1724 Saxon ordinance marks a shift from an older discourse on usury to a modern discourse on business failure (ibid., 331–5) is untenable, however, as it completely ignores the sixteenth-century discourse on bankruptcy.

49 Stadtarchiv Augsburg, Personenselekt "Sulzer"; Stadtgerichtsakten, no. 176; Häberlein, "Firmenbankrotte," 24–30.

50 "[D]as Er sich von hier hinweg begeben, nachgehendß wider hiehero kommen, und den 14 Jan. 1603 gestorben." Staats- und Stadtbibliothek Augsburg, 2o Cod. Aug. 132, f. 55r.

51 Staats- und Stadtbibliothek Augsburg, 2o Cod. Aug. 132, ff. 56r, 69r. On Matthias Sulzer's tenure as postmaster in Rheinhausen, see W. Behringer, *Im Zeichen des Merkur: Reichspost und Kommunikationsrevolution in der Frühen Neuzeit* (Göttingen 2003), 180–1, 193–4, 197, 356.

52 See C. Emmendörffer and H. Zäh (eds.), *Bürgermacht & Bücherpracht: Augsburger Ehren- und Familienbücher der Renaissance* (exhibition catalogue) (Lucerne 2011), 224–5.

53 Cf. Roeck, *Eine Stadt in Krieg und Frieden*, I: 125–88, P. Warmbrunn, *Zwei Konfessionen in einer Stadt: Das Zusammenleben von Katholiken und Protestanten in den paritätischen Reichsstädten Augsburg, Biberach, Ravensburg und Dinkelsbühl von 1548–1648* (Wiesbaden 1983), 360–75.

54 "Inn summa alle welltt will verarmen, und ist kain gelltt unter denn Leuthen so wol auch gar schmale und kleine Narung, das man wol ains goldt- und Silbermachers bedörffte." Staats- und Stadtbibliothek Augsburg, 2o Cod. S 43 (Kölderer chronicle, vol. 5), f. 18v. On Kölderer, see B. Mauer, *"Gemain Geschrey" und "teglich Reden": Georg Kölderer—ein Augsburger Chronist des konfessionellen Zeitalters* (Augsburg 2001).

3 Debt and default in 18th-century Champagne

Thomas Brennan

Introduction

Debt is stalking the land, once again. Obsession with debt has seized the domestic, national and world stage. It is worth remembering that public debt, and the failure to deal with it, brought down an Old Regime little more than 200 years ago. It is equally interesting to remember that the proliferation of debt instruments facilitated a commercial revolution in the centuries preceding that collapse. Credit quickened the sclerotic flows of supply and demand, ameliorated the inadequacies of the money supply, and allowed the countryside to escape from autarky. This dual nature of debt, as blood flow and blood loss, shapes my approach to the study of debt in a little corner of France a few decades before the Revolution. The failure to meet one's debts, litigated in various seigneurial and royal courts in Champagne, opens a window on to the flow of goods and services in an early modern economy. This kind of default was all too common in a world of low liquidity and widespread poverty. It was litigated in a process that let creditors get their delinquent debtors' attention and sometimes even their goods. More importantly, the process left records that allow us today to learn about the flow of debt and, behind it, of the commercial economy.

It is no longer a surprise to historians of the pre-modern countryside to find the use of credit at a very local level. An older tradition that painted a picture of rural autarchy, of an agricultural economy "turned in on itself," where "autoconsumption of all primary goods, and especially grains, remained the rule," has given way to a vision of the countryside "in motion" and connected to regional and national markets.[1] To help animate these rural markets, peasants sought credit from towns and from other peasants. Historians have been finding the records of their debts and of well-developed systems of credit already in the Middle Ages.[2] And where an older tradition emphasized the oppressive, even predatory, burden of debt on peasants, recent work has presented more balance between the practical advantages of credit and its weight on the poor.[3]

To uncover this debt, I have studied not bankruptcy but its less dramatic cousin, default. Bankruptcy or, more correctly in old regime France, insolvency (*faillite*) involved a debtor seeking court protection and entailed an elaborate process of verifying creditors' claims and arranging for an orderly distribution of assets or, perhaps, more time to repay the debts.[4] Long before this process, however, most debtors had been involved in litigation by individual creditors for individual loans on which they had defaulted. Such mundane debt litigation was more likely to involve a wider range of debtors from more walks of life and, thus, tell us more about the everyday incidence of debt throughout the society.

The choice of the region around the city of Reims in the province of Champagne is inspired by its embrace of several distinct economic regions, all connected to a major provincial city. It is most famous for its wines, which were transformed in the eighteenth century from a traditional supply of common red wines to a national market into an international and, for its time, highly industrialized sparkling white wine. It was also the center of a textile industry that was slowly falling on hard times. And it produced a range of agricultural and forest products for local consumption. Studying the patterns of default in villages from each of these economic regions allows us to look for contrasts in the patterns of exchange and the role of commercial debt in a rural economy.

The basis for this study is a sample of default cases in 16 seigneurial courts which produced over 750 cases in a span of four years—from 1769 through 1772.[5] These are practically the only courts in the region whose registers have survived. Court registers kept track of all the cases brought before the court, though not always in much detail. Yet, they routinely identified the parties by name, profession and residence, the amount being contested and, often, the nature of the debt. They would record the decision, which included assigning court costs to the losers.[6] Creditors brought debtors to these courts as a step in an elaborate ritual that could result in the seizure of goods and even imprisonment. For the price of minor court costs that were mostly borne by the debtor, the creditor gave formal notice of his impatience and initiated a legal record of debt that could become useful in the future. Debtors rarely contested the case and creditors rarely went through with seizures or imprisonment.[7] Elsewhere in France, a study of seigneurial courts has found that suits for default were the single most common case and made up a third of all the civil cases in the late eighteenth century.[8] The distribution of the cases in Champagne suggests that suits for default in this province could be a good deal more or less common, depending on the region. The geography of how many suits were handled by each of the courts, points to a clear distinction between the courts to the south and west, and those to the east of the city. The courts to the east saw fewer than five cases in a year, whereas the rest had one or two dozen, with the exception of two villages in the south, along the Marne River that saw four or six dozen. This, in turn, is a reflection of economic differences between an upland region to the south where vines held sway, and the arable plain to the east where poor farming was supplemented by cottage weaving.

In fact, several of the busier courts, particularly five of them in the south, served dozens of local villages and sometimes overlapped. This contrasts with most of the smaller seigneurial courts, which heard exclusively cases against inhabitants of their own village. The courts of the eastern villages were more typical of seigneurial justice in the rest of France, which have been found to have covered a parish or less in most cases.[9] Thus these 16 courts covered defaulters in 43 different villages in the area, particularly those in the Mountain of Reims, to the south of the city. At least half of the villages seem to have been barely active, with only one or two suits per year, but without having the records of their own seigneurial courts it is difficult to say how many defaulters there were. Those with their own seigneurial courts, however, averaged ten cases a year, and a few had two or three dozen. The villages with seigneurial courts and two others that clearly also relied on them averaged one default for every 15 households per year, though there is considerable variation.

Credit and debt in early modern society

The activity in this region looks rather pale compared to the more commercial society across the Channel. Craig Muldrew has charted the number of suits for default as a function of population in the town of King's Lynn and has provided figures for other English courts. He has found a high point of nearly three suits per household per year in the early seventeenth century but a rapid decline to less than one suit for every three households in the early eighteenth century and less than one for 12 households by the late eighteenth century.[10] Muldrew argues that this decline represents a growing maturity of credit relations, but it is hard to make a similar case for Champagne without a longer survey. Elsewhere, in France, the recourse to rural courts for default seems to have been increasing over the eighteenth century, despite a fairly general decline in the rate of total litigation.[11] More importantly, Muldrew and others argue for a connection between rates of litigation and economic activity; a study of seigneurial courts in northern Burgundy notes that such litigation is "indicative of the economic interdependence of the countryside."[12] Thus, the fact that a half dozen of the Champagne villages, especially a cluster of them in the south, were seeing more than one default for every ten households underscores the commercial sophistication of the villages along the Marne River.

The debts brought to court mirror the range of debt instruments available to the old regime, from least to most formal, and suggest their commercial origins in the exchange of goods and services. All but a few of the cases identified something about the type of debt under dispute; nearly half of them were for promissory notes. These were written promises of payment, a kind of check that could be negotiable. They were fairly informal, written out by the debtor and rarely notarized, though they gained formal legal status when registered at a bureau of the *contrôle des actes*.[13] As we shall see, this process of registration allows us to get a more global perspective on these debts. Unfortunately, the court records rarely identified what the promissory note had been used to pay for, but the average was only 72 livres and the median sum was only 36 livres. This was the cost of a horse, on the one hand, or a barrel of wine, on the other. One suit claimed 66 livres for "100 bales of vine props." These non-notarized debts were worth somewhat more, on average, than a large number of even more informal debts for goods, services and loans that were being litigated for default.

Most of these suits referred to no written records of the debt, except for a quarter of them that invoked the seller's account book. The other three quarters simply identified the "sale and delivery" of goods that were specified in considerable detail or the loan of money to someone "in their need" or the performance of some job. With an average of 50 livres and a median of only 18, most of these debts clearly transcended the petty exchanges of daily living yet frequently refer to the sale of food or goods. Neither these oral debts nor the account books would be registered in the *contrôle des actes*. Only a few other suits could point to written contracts, which averaged somewhat more than either the promissory notes or the informal debts, and these did find their way into the register of acts. They were closer in scale to the more formal, notarized debts called obligations, although these too made up only a few percent of the total default suits. A somewhat larger number of cases resulted from the most formal and long term of all the debt instruments available to the old regime, the annuity (*rente*). Borrowers "sold" annuities for large sums that were used to purchase houses, offices or other long-term investments or, sometimes, to consolidate a long list of smaller debts.[14] They did not represent commercial exchanges in the way that non-notarized contracts did. Debtors were not obliged to "buy back" or repay these annuities, but they owed 5 percent annual payments on their loan. More than 10 percent of these cases sued debtors for falling behind on their annual interest payments, so they tended to be for lower sums. In some cases, these suits indicate serious financial hardships, like a modern foreclosure, but others resulted from disputes over inheriting such debts. Such suits were actually fairly rare and limited to a few villages.

Most of the documented debts, and even some of the oral ones, gave a date for the transaction, which shows that creditors waited an average of 56 months to sue for default, though the median was only 20 months. This kind of impatience suggests that creditors did not expect long waits, but it depended on the kind of debt. The average annuity in arrears had been created almost 16 years before the litigation; the average obligation was six-and-a-half years overdue. The rest averaged only 35 months, with a median of 18 months. Indeed, some of the delay may have been due to the time needed to get on the docket. The average written, un-notarized debt was registered only 34 months after it was signed but then added a month or two before the court case. Some of this delay

Table 3.1 Types of debt

Type of debt	*N*	*%*	*Average amount in livres*
Promissory notes	334	43	72
Goods, services, loans	176	23	50
Contracts	31	4	148
Obligations	25	3	196
Annuities	94	12	93
?	118	15	39
Total	778	–	77

may also have been due to the choreography of litigation. The registration of a debt clearly indicated an intent to sue the defaulter, but creditors might have waited to see if the threat was enough.

Default in rural Champagne

In 750 suits, there were only 440 different individual defaulters, meaning that nearly a third of them were involved more than once. Yet, all but a dozen of these appeared five times or fewer, and only three appeared more than ten times. All this suggests that suits for defaulting represented a more transitory problem of liquidity, such as plagued many businesses on occasion and were, therefore, less serious than a genuine failure. Other information about these defaulters supports this conclusion, though their professions are fairly ambiguous. A little over half of them were identified as vine growers, which tells us nothing about their wealth but does tell us that they made their living producing a highly commercial product. Another 9 percent claimed to be "laboureurs" and so substantial farmers. Barely 5 percent claimed to be merchants, and the rest were mostly identified as various artisans.

This could be a fairly motley population, but, fortunately, it is possible to learn a great deal more about them from the unusually detailed tax records of this region. Most of the villages around Reims drew up a *taille tarifée* around 1770, in which assessors identified the amount of land—in several categories, including vines and arable—owned by each household and the amount of income it produced.[15] By translating these revenues into the local arable land values, it is possible to distinguish between social categories: the landless, those with less than five hectares who were basically wage earners; those with five to ten hectares who might enjoy a precarious independence under favorable circumstances; those with more than ten hectares who could probably support themselves from their land; and those with more than 30 hectares who formed a tiny elite of *laboureurs*.

Of 440 individual defaulters identified in the suits, nearly two-thirds can be identified in the tax records of the period. Of these, there are enough people from a dozen villages to offer some meaningful figures on their relative social and economic position in their local society.[16] Taken together, these 250 defaulters were little more than 10 percent of the households in their villages, yet they appear surprisingly representative of their village populations. They worked an average of more than ten hectares of arable land, or its equivalent in vineyards, which was only a little over the average of all the households in these villages.[17] They owned 84 percent of what they worked, which was essentially the same for their neighbors. The average covered a range of conditions, of course, and here we see some differences with the general population. Only 12 percent were landless, which is only two-thirds of the village profile. Evidently this group was too poor to be creditworthy and, so, less likely to default. Nearly a third of both groups owned or rented less than five hectares of land, an amount that did no more than supplement their wages. This was the largest social group in these villages but not the largest group in the population of defaulters. Instead, it was the households with five to ten hectares that led among defaulters and over-represented their village role by nearly 50 percent. This is a particularly interesting group, since there is some debate about whether a household required five or ten hectares to achieve self-sufficiency in this world. Thus, this group owned and worked enough land to give it a precarious independence, depending on the natural and business climate and a host of personal factors. It is not surprising, then, to find them over-extended proportionately more often than their neighbors. The defaulters in the two highest categories, those farming more than ten and those with more than 30 hectares, were somewhat under-represented but their strength is surprising. The fact that these groups, which tended to be securely independent and even prosperous, made up one-quarter of defaulters reminds us that default was not simply a measure of failure.

The general profile of these dozen villages obscures important differences, however, in the local ecologies and economies of the region. The area is now known for its wines, but barely a third of the villages in the region were truly viticultural economies. Instead, the region was divided fairly evenly between the production of wine, woolens and wood, with a few villages producing only grain. We can see from the map (Note 18) that these villages were not all equally likely to produce defaulters. The social profile of defaulters in the four kinds of villages shows even more clearly what differentiated their relation to debt.

The arable villages to the east of Reims had relatively few defaulters, but they came from the wealthy categories of their communities. The defaulters in the arable villages worked a third more land than the average and owned 50 percent more; they came disproportionately from those groups whose ten and even 30 hectares of land produced a surplus and involved them in the local grain trade. Their defaults attest not to poverty but to commercial vitality.

The defaulters from viticultural villages were noticeably less wealthy than those in arable villages, but little different from the average in their own villages. Yet, the 71 percent of defaulters owning the equivalent of five to 30 hectares of arable were somewhat more common than the 62 percent of the general viticultural villagers. It should be noted that vineyards were so much more profitable than arable land, by some ten to 15 times in the best villages, that members of this group might own less than one hectare of vines but still have the precarious independence of a farmer with almost ten hectares of arable. Nearly all in this group were vine growers and so commercially quite active, relying on the wine market to make a living and buying, rather than growing, their own grain. It is not surprising to find them frequently in debt to wood merchants for their vine props and barrels. Vine growers of every size participated actively in the market and defaulted on a regular basis. Although some of this may be attributed to a couple of bad harvests, it appears to be tied more to the level of commercial activity.

The defaulters in the mixed economy worked less land than those in the viticultural villages, but some 20 percent more than others in their own villages. However, they owned little more than half of the land they were working and less than their village average. Whether we consider land worked or owned, the defaulters holding between five and ten hectares figured most prominently and were vastly over-represented compared to their relative place in these villages' social makeup. This was unlikely to be enough land to give them either full employment or independence, though they were not destitute. In this economy they eked a living from rented land, relatively mediocre vines and exploiting the forests that surrounded them. A number of them supplemented their income with artisanal and small retail functions; several were tavern owners. Defaulters from all other groups were under-represented, though there were a surprising number from those without land.

This is distinctly more prosperous, however, than the profile of defaulters in the textile villages, to the northeast of Reims. The large majority of defaulters lived as dependent peasants, most of whom were identified as weavers, with less than five hectares. This was the largest group of peasants in these villages, but they also produced a disproportionate number of defaulters. This group, too, was forced to buy its food on the market and earn a living from wages, but their default attests more to their poverty than to their commercial engagement. Another measure of the textile workers' economic situation can be found in the percentage that had been forced to go into long-term debt with a perpetual annuity. Whereas less than half of the defaulters in viticultural or mixed villages owed *rentes*, and only one-fifth of those in arable villages did, nearly two-thirds of the defaulting weavers also owed long-term debts, and most were being sued for falling behind in their payments.

So, default could be a kind of failure, as the poor weavers of Champagne sinking under the weight of their debts must have felt. And, more generally, the third of defaulters who worked less than five hectares were undoubtedly facing serious financial problems. The rest, however, were doing as well as or better than their peers, and their defaults were more often a kind of over-extension. They probably tell us as much about the commercial vitality of parts of the Champagne countryside as they do about the trouble people had paying their bills. These debts reveal, instead, the variable engagement of the economies around Reims in the commercial life of the region.

The identity of the creditors and their relation to these debtors lends weight to this argument. The social profile of creditors in these courts reinforces the point that they were suing for payment of goods and services. In more than 700 suits where the profession of the creditor was identified, the largest group (43 percent) were merchants. Of these, more than a third (39 percent) were identified as wood merchants. The court records reveal a flourishing trade in wood products circulating between the forests of the wooded plateau south of Reims and peasants, particularly vine growers, along the slopes around the plateau. Peasants made up more than a fifth of the creditors, fairly evenly divided between large farmers (*laboureurs*) and vine growers. The *laboureur* could be found extending credit for his grain and hay, for his plowing or for money lent, since these were the wealthy members of their villages and were owed by nearly everyone. A variety of rural artisans made up another 16 percent, of which nearly a third were millers. Only 14 percent belonged to the elites, legal, professional or otherwise. These creditors were also rustics in the large majority, even in the shadow of the city of Reims. Only 12 percent lived in the city; the rest lived in the countryside and lent to relatively close neighbors. About a quarter had lent money within the same village. The rest were only separated from their money by an average of seven kilometers.

The geography of these transactions also suggests their commercial nature and, more generally, offers a rich window into the flow of credit, debt and commercial transactions throughout this region. A map of these transactions shows several distinct patterns (see Figure 3.1).[18] Most of the courts, in the middle and top half of the map, show a hub with local spokes, attached both to Reims and to smaller communities nearby. The one to the northwest was a small town with a weekly market and annual fair that offered artisanal and financial services to its neighbors. But the villages east of Reims, which were most involved in arable and textiles, interacted only weakly and with a limited range of other villages. In contrast, the handful of courts in the south of the map were nearly lost in a dense tangle of connections to each other as well as farther away that suggests a more intense but less focused local economy. Viticultural villages on the southern slopes of the plateau exchanged with each other and with villages in the forests on top of the plateau. They also exchanged with several of the small towns along

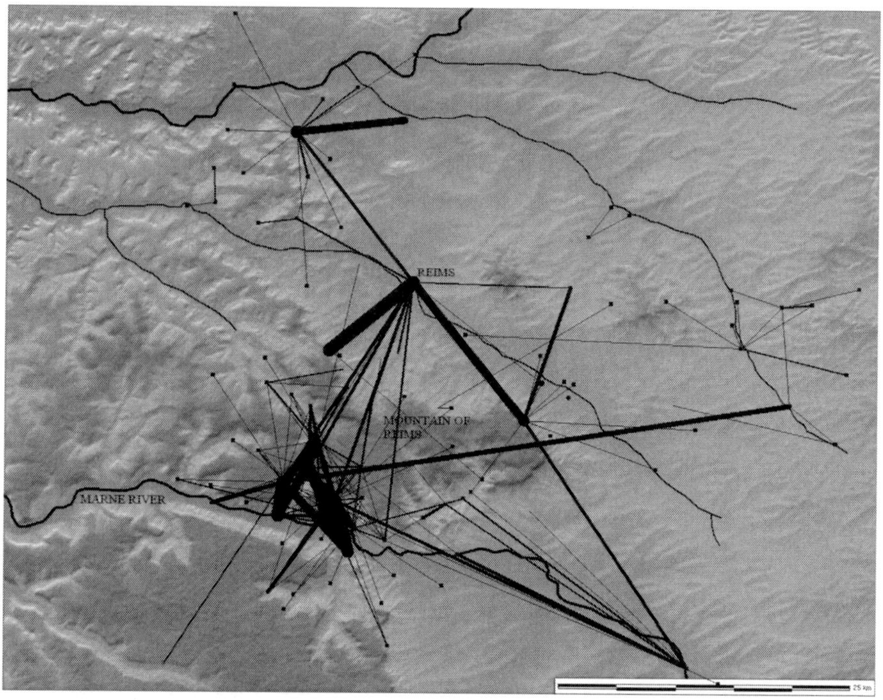

Figure 3.1 Rural default in seigneurial courts.

the river that also had weekly markets and semi-annual or seasonal fairs. This activity attests, in part, to the lively trade in wood produced by the plateau villages to serve the needs of the vine growers. Indeed, much of the trade between this cluster and Reims was actually with wood merchants based in the city who clearly worked on the plateau. It also shows the commercial sophistication of the Marne River system, which had long enjoyed a close connection to the Parisian market and had pioneered the development of sparkling champagne.[19] Commerce with ports and markets along the river knit much of the plateau into an economic unit, and default in this zone, I would argue, was a sign of its sophistication rather than its poverty.

Network analysis

To better understand the dynamics of these debts it is helpful to study them with the tools of social network analysis. Although network analysis is generally applied to individuals, there are too few recurring individuals in this sample; rather, there are individuals in villages that show up regularly. If we consider the villages involved in these documents as nodes in a network of goods and services being paid with debt, it is possible to see which ones played the most important role in the flow of commerce and thus to distinguish between the kinds of economic systems in the region and see how they might have shaped debt and commercial patterns. Network analysis offers measurements of a network's density, centrality and cohesion.[20] Where nodes are all connected to each other, the network is dense, cohesive, but uncentralized or egalitarian; where all are connected to one but not each other, the network is the reverse.[21] In between these extremes, a network will have nodes that form more or less cohesive groups, depending on how many other nodes they are connected to, and these groups can display a hierarchy of more integrated cores and less integrated peripheries. Although network analysis is used more often to study the internet or biology, it has recently been used to study markets in the early modern French economy. Guillaume Daudin has argued that "the more important the transactions are in a region the more one expects the commercialization network to be egalitarian: that is, everyone exchanges his goods with everyone else." This he contrasts with a weak system of exchanges and a more centralized network where "each exchanges only with a given center."[22] This insight can be applied to the region around Reims. In the context of Champagne, it will be no surprise to learn that a major city like Reims dominated much of the commercial and financial activity of the region, but it is also interesting to learn if other communities engaged in lateral transactions and where markets had most integrated groups of villages.

Measurements of cohesion highlight the very different connections among these villages and bring to light the much greater financial integration of certain parts of the region. Two-thirds of the 115 villages that appear in these records, for example, were only loosely connected to the rest, through only one intermediary. In most cases this was a single inhabitant who had lent money to someone in one of the main villages. This system formed a network of very low density (0.0152), suggesting little integration of the commercial and financial activity of the region.[23] A half-dozen sites with very high (betweenness) centrality measures acted as the hubs of distinct sub-groups, most only loosely connected to the rest.[24] These nodes included the city of Reims, the arable villages, two of the viticultural villages and one of the mixed *bourgs* mentioned above, but did not include the textile villages. This describes a largely fragmented and still very localized rural economy. The textile villages, in particular, participated very little in this exchange economy or at least in the exchange of financial instruments that allowed it to function.

In contrast, there were a dozen villages that were so closely integrated that each one had financial connections with at least half of the group and some with all of them. They lay along the Marne River, on the slopes to its north and in the forests on the plateau of the Mountain. Most were viticultural villages, but three of them were part of the mixed economy of forest products, herds and arable that complemented the viticultural economies around them. Not surprisingly, three of the dozen villages were actually small towns, two of them with weekly markets, and one was Reims. Clearly these three facilitated the connection of this system to a larger, national market, but none of them dominated the system. With a much higher network density (0.4487) and very low centrality measures for each node, this system describes an intense and essentially egalitarian interaction among these villages. They were surrounded by another half dozen villages that lay nearby and had somewhat looser connections to this system, connecting to at least four others. The geography of this system matches almost exactly the dense cluster of interacting villages in the south of the map on Figure 3.1; the network analysis confirms the sense that they formed a far more economically integrated group than the rest of the villages in the region. The shape of exchanges revealed by defaults appears to distinguish between very different parts of the region's commercial system.

The landscape of rural credit and debt relations

What makes this argument hard to sustain is the unrepresentative selection of the seigneurial courts that survived the World Wars. Many of these courts happened to come from the Marne River and the Mountain of Reims, in fairly close proximity to each other. To get a better sense of debt defaults that had been litigated throughout the region in and around Reims, however, there is a way to approximate the civil cases generated by all of the courts in this area. The written debts made informally between individuals but without the help of a notary were legally required to pay a small stamp tax and have the debt written down in the registers of the *contrôle des actes*. Only this registration gave these debts a legal status as judicial evidence, and the records of seigneurial courts routinely mention that the written debts presented to them had been duly registered, usually within weeks of the trial date. Holders of un-notarized debts appear rarely to have bothered with such registration unless they intended to take the debtor to court, so it is likely that the non-notarized debts that were registered signal the beginning of a court case. Thus these registers can identify more globally the incidence of default that led to the kinds of civil cases considered earlier, as well as all of the notarized debts in this region.

There are some real problems with using the *contrôle* as a proxy, however. Little more than half of the cases before the civil courts, according to our sample, were based on the written un-notarized debts that would be registered prior to a court case. Almost all of these were promissory notes, along with a few contracts and accounts due. The notarized debts, like obligations, were rarely contested in these courts, although more than 10 percent sued people for failing to pay their yearly annuity. But since all notarized debts were registered, it is difficult to know which ones resulted in a civil suit. The rest of the debt litigation, amounting to a third of the cases, was based either on documents, like account books, that were not registered or on verbal claims of goods sold, work done or money loaned. Thus, if we ignore the debts that were registered anyway, because they had been drawn up by a conscientious notary, the register of acts only tells us about half of the debts that were litigated before civil courts. Nevertheless, this allows us to see more general patterns of debt and default in the region.

The bureau of the *contrôle des actes* of Reims and the ten *bureaux* around it recorded nearly 4,000 informal, un-notarized debts during a 24 month period that coincides with the four years covered by the seigneurial courts.[25] These rural *bureaux* were ten of the 12 bureaux within 25 kilometers of the city. They certainly registered most of the debt contracts in a radius of 30 kilometers around Reims. The frequency of cases, in which someone was involved either as creditor or debtor, in the 200 principal communities in this region was one per 24 households, with the median being one in 15, but the actual geography of default suggests a more complex reality. The city of Reims had more frequent cases, at one in 12, as did many other villages, almost all of them to the south of the city. A map of the villages more frequently involved in debt locates them all along the Marne River and around the Mountain of Reims. These are the principal viticultural villages, though they include many of the mixed villages along the top of the Mountain. They averaged one litigation for every seven households and include most of the villages covered by the seigneurial courts discussed above.

The register of acts makes it is possible, first of all, to compare the period of this study with earlier moments in the century. From years sampled in earlier decades for several of these *bureaux*, we can see that the registration of promissory notes and other informal debts had risen gradually through the century, but not noticeably during the difficult economic times at the beginning of the 1770s. The average in three of these *bureaux* for three different years from the 1740s was only 57 percent of the level for the same *bureaux* in the early 1770s, and the average for three different years from the 1750s in seven of these *bureaux* was 74 percent of their level in 1770. But the average of three different years from the 1760s in five of these *bureaux* was 22 percent greater than the period at the beginning of the 1770s. The 1760s were chiefly a time of low grain prices and relative prosperity. They were, however, also a time of financial disruption.[26]

At several points during the decade and again in 1770, the Parisian discount rate climbed and credit became scarce. The greater number of debt registrations and, presumably, litigations may signal financial tightening rather than underlying economic hardship.

The larger sample of debts matched the smaller sample from the courts in some ways, though there are interesting differences. Creditors in the larger sample waited 33 months, on average, between the signing of the debt and their registration, but this average is distorted by a few very long delays; the median was only 11 months. There appears to have been no clustering around a particular delay, as if, for example, the promissory note was usually accorded a year before being called in. Nor was there any obvious relationship between the time delay and the amount of money owed (R=–0.0463), as if large sums were registered more urgently. Of 2,434 creditors identified by name, a sixth of them appeared multiple times. In the large majority of these cases, this was less than half a dozen times, yet 60 creditors appeared more often than that. A score of them presented themselves more than ten times, two-thirds of them merchants of various kinds, but also a widow and a single woman. It is not hard to understand that ironmongers, horse merchants or wood merchants might have dealings with enough people that they had to pursue multiple defaulters. The widow was probably settling the affairs of a merchant husband, though that is not explicit. Only one of the merchants raises troubling questions. A single wood merchant from the village of Chaumuzy registered 149 debts in several of the *contrôle des actes* during these two years. His average debt was 13 months old, as opposed to the 33 months that the whole region averaged, and half of his debts were three months old or less. The most troubling aspect of his behavior is that two-thirds of these debts were registered on a single day's visit to one of the *bureaux*, and almost half of these were less than a month old. It is hard to see all of these debts indicating imminent litigation, even if this merchant was having trouble with some of them and was particularly litigious. This one individual, at least, does not support the assumption that registration indicates default, and the cases from that day that were less than a month old have not been included.

Out of 3,700 defaulters, there were actually very few recidivists. More than three-quarters of them appeared only once in the registration and, of the 480 who appeared more frequently, more than half only appeared twice. Only four appeared as many as a dozen times. This makes the larger sample of default look like a rather more random collection of borrowers, but the sample also covers half as much time as that drawn from the seigneurial courts. Only half of these individuals were identified by profession, but the profile is also rather different from that of the seigneurial court defaulters. The largest group was vine growers, at more than a quarter of the defaulters, with nearly a fifth more from those identified as laboureurs. Thus farmers of various kinds made up barely half of the defaulters. There were more merchants of various kinds, though they still amounted to little more than 10 percent. The rest were a range of artisans and small retailers. The social makeup of these defaulters was also closer to the average of their villages than the defaulters before the seigneurial courts. When considering the defaulters from the same dozen villages consulted earlier, plus those from another half-dozen villages, the defaulters from the arable and viticultural villages continued to be richer than the average, but those from the textile and mixed economies were essentially identical to the rest of their villages and came less heavily from the more marginal levels of these societies. The kind of misery that emerged in a few of the seigneurial courts was much less pronounced in the larger sample, although many of the "typical" peasants were obviously quite poor.

The *contrôle des actes* allows us to see the flow of financial transactions across the whole of the region, undistorted by the selection of seigneurial courts (see Figure 3.2). It confirms some elements of that smaller sample but reveals new features. Not surprisingly, the city of Reims played a much larger role in this map than in the previous one. Over a quarter of the region's loans were made by residents of the city, and the average loan was nearly twice as large as for the whole sample. They lent money to people in more than 100 villages and towns, so they dealt with more than a third of the villages within 30 kilometers, but not equally. More than twice as many of their loans went to the city's south than to its north, particularly to the viticultural villages along the north slope of the Mountain of Reims, indicating its intense involvement in their economies. The city clearly also reached out to its north and northeast, but these interactions were less concentrated and less intense. Rather, the real activity, once again, was

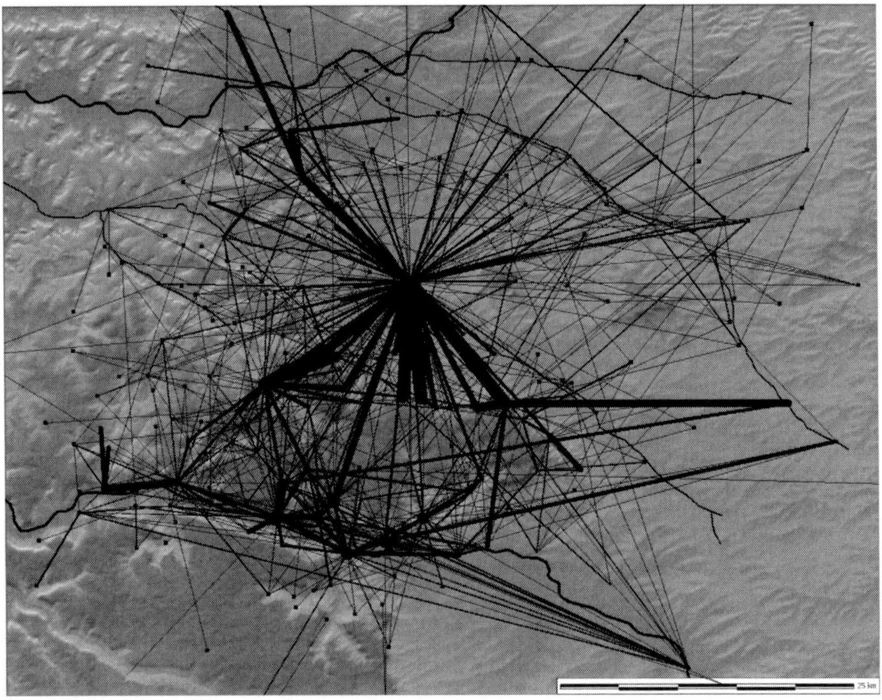

Figure 3.2 Financial transactions recorded in the *contrôles des actes*.

around the Mountain and the Marne. The connections between small towns along the river shows up even more clearly than in Figure 3.1, although there is a similar concentration of activity around the same villages that had such active seigneurial courts. The more comprehensive map (see Figure 3.2) confirms the vitality of this section, though the rest of the map now appears more active as well.

A network analysis of this global map, however, offers a clearer picture of its internal dynamics. Once again it identifies a core of the most integrated locations and the surrounding layers of cohesion. A core of 15 locations were most tightly cohesive, each connected to at least half of the others and some with nearly all. These locations include eight of the 13 that formed an inner core in the sample from the seigneurial courts. Thus there is considerable similarity between the network dynamics of the smaller sample and of the larger snapshot. The larger network adds to the inner core important towns to the east and west of the inner core along the Marne River, as well as a node in Paris. This inner core clearly represented the commercial hub of the Marne River system, extending from Chalons sur Marne all the way down to Paris, but also including the city of Reims. It also included some of the most productive and expensive of the vineyards and one of the most active of the mixed-economy villages on the Mountain itself. The core network was quite egalitarian (with a density of 0.4619) which means, among other things, that no node dominated the network, as shown by their very low (betweenness) centrality measures. Again, this suggests the vitality of this river system. Credit circulated among these core towns at a high volume and in multiple directions; everyone exchanged with everyone else.

Further layers made the region's system progressively less egalitarian and more centralized. A second layer of 15 villages further populated the river valley but also extended on to the Mountain of Reims, adding more of the viticultural and the mixed-economy villages. Most of the additions had relatively few lateral ties and were, rather, connected to many of the original core. This system was less dense and less egalitarian, with Reims already emerging with a slightly more central role than any of the towns on the River. Yet, it is at the next level, with the addition of a third layer of 16, less cohesive, villages, that the network became distinctly more complicated. The network's density dropped dramatically (0.1541), as Reims gained greater dominance, with a centrality measure now four times greater than any other town. Most of the new villages lay along the north slope of the Mountain and interacted principally with Reims rather than with the villages to their south, although many of the neighbors along the north slope interacted with each other. They interacted also with the village of Chaumuzy, which emerged at this stage as the second most (betweenness) central location, though well behind Reims. In fact, the village of Chaumuzy had commercial ties with more different villages than all the communities in the region except the city of Reims. Not only the busy wood merchant, but another two dozen inhabitants were selling on credit to villages across the Mountain and along the River. Many of the lenders in Chaumuzy, who can be identified in the village's tax rolls, were wood, fruit and livestock merchants. The wood merchant, in particular, registered scores of small loans made to vine-growers in all the viticultural villages within a dozen kilometers, who had a constant need for wood to make vine props and barrels. He also exchanged with charcoal burners, woodsmen and barrel makers, not only selling on credit but also buying on credit. A village with a mixed economy like this, though only of a modest size, could provide a symbiotic partnership with the viticultural villages around it and, even though the records rarely specify the goods bought with credit, they indicate the intensity of the commerce that tied different ecological zones together.

Successive layers were, by definition, more diffuse but they did not always reflect greater dominance by Reims. Two villages in the next layer of 15 were located north of Reims, for the first time, though close to the city. Half of the rest lay along the Marne River, which raised the (betweenness) centrality of two of the towns on the river. Although Reims was still the dominant hub, its centrality measure was only three times greater than theirs. Other additions were scattered around the Mountain, so the system of the 61 villages in these first four layers still looked like a map of the Mountain and the River. The next layer, however, more than doubled the number of villages and came much closer to looking like a map of the whole region. The vast majority lay north of the Mountain, and more than half lay north of Reims, evenly divided to the northwest and northeast. Not surprisingly, Reims now dominated the whole network, with a (betweenness) centrality measure nine times higher than any other town. Two-thirds of these new additions were connected directly to this city, and many of the rest were only one step away. The new layer was hardly uniform in its relationship to the market. Whereas most of the villages to the northeast of Reims, both textile and arable villages, were connected to only three or four other villages besides Reims, several of the viticultural and mixed villages to the northwest were the (high-degree) hub of a dozen or so villages. This includes one of the small towns with a seigneurial court. A multidimensional scaling diagram of this system (see Figure 3.3) captures the contrast between the most

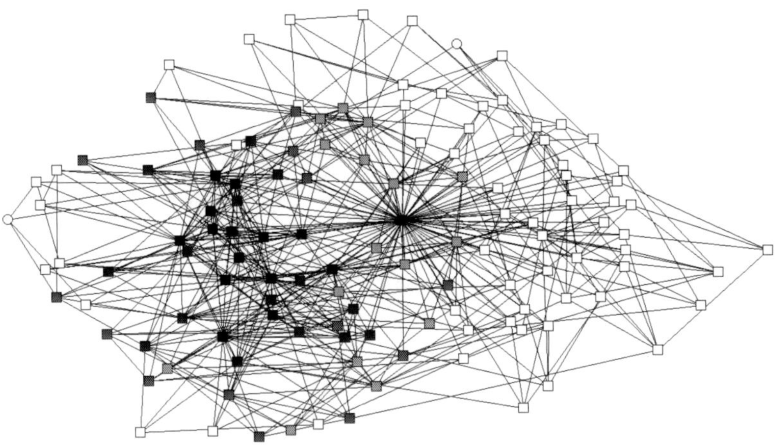

Figure 3.3 Network analysis of credit relations in Champagne.

cohesive core, on the left in dark shading, and the least, mostly on the right in white. The city of Reims is a clear hub for much of the low-density network on the right, in contrast with a higher density, more egalitarian network on the left. This suggests two very different commercial and financial systems, one dominated by the city but having little other activity, the other having the greater density of a more active market. The addition of another 160 villages to this system, in three more layers, does not alter the fundamental structure of the network. The last three layers are attached only loosely, sometimes to Reims but their increasing distance from Reims meant attachments to more peripheral locations. Reims remained highly central and the whole system very low density.

Conclusion

What this analysis gives us, first of all, is confirmation of the picture sketched by the seigneurial courts. The rates of default and of the financial activities underlying it were indeed greater in the south along the River than in the rest of the region. The River and the Mountain of Reims did indeed have a commercial and financial network that manifested itself as more cohesive and interconnected than elsewhere in the region. Multiple communities interacted vigorously with each other and with a wider world; none of them dominated the system but participated in a lively exchange with those around them. In contrast with a basically egalitarian system along the Marne River, there was another system centered on Reims. The system around Reims is not surprising; the city was the center of a textile industry and a wine trade of long standing. We can see how Reims had dominated the exchanges in its hinterland: this system had a very low density and a very high centrality. The city had imposed a commercial dependence on many of the villages in the region, particularly the textile villages to the east. In fact the city exchanged more often with viticultural villages, yet it had a different relationship with most of them. Rather than dominating the viticultural market, Reims was merely one of a number of poles in a complex system. Viticultural villages were generally more commercial and more connected to a range of trading partners, particularly those on and around the Mountain of Reims. This zone formed a dense commercial system that connected different economies and markets into a surprisingly egalitarian network. And, if we accept the argument that such a pattern indicates the relative intensity of commercial exchanges, then this was a strikingly dynamic and sophisticated market. The density of commercial ties around and across this mountain is all the more dramatic in light of the transportation challenges it faced. At the same time, we should note that viticultural villages profited from the competition between two commercial outlets, that of Reims and that of the Marne, with its ties to Paris. This gave them some independence from either and allowed them to develop their own commercial expertise. The central cluster in this system also revealed the close symbiosis between viticultural villages and the mixed zone in the interior. Whether exchanging wood or other products, the trade between these two zones bound them into a dense and egalitarian network. We see, finally, how the economy of vines encouraged a commercial culture among the vine growers and their economic partners. This would appear to be the real cradle of a commercial revolution in the province of Champagne.

Notes

1 See P. Goubert, *Cent mille provinciaux au XVIIe siècle: Beauvais et les Beauvaisis de 1600 à 1730* (Paris 1968), 116; A. Poitrineau, *La vie rurale en basse-auvergne au XVIIIe siècle* (1726–1789) (Paris 1965), 507, for classic examples of an older school. More recently, the work of J.-M. Moriceau, for example, *Terres mouvantes: les campagnes françaises du féodalisme à la mondialisation, 1150–1850: essai historique* (Paris 2002) and of G. Béaur, *Histoire agraire de la France au XVIIIe siècle* (Paris 2000).

2 C. Briggs, *Credit and Village Society in Fourteenth-Century England* (Oxford 2009) surveys the recent literature.

3 I have surveyed some of this literature in T. Brennan, "Peasants and Debt in Eighteenth-Century Champagne," *Journal of Interdisciplinary History* 37 (2006): 175–200. More recently, see L. Fontaine, *L'économie morale: pauvreté, crédit et confiance dans l'Europe préindustrielle* (Paris 2008).

4 See P.C. Reynard, "The Language of Failure: Bankruptcy in Eighteenth-Century France," *Journal of European Economic History* 30 (Fall 2001): 355–90, for a careful review of the legal literature defining bankruptcy. See also T. Luckett, "Credit and Commercial Society in France, 1740–1789" (unpub. Ph.D. diss., Princeton University, 1992); A.D. Kessler, *A Revolution in Commerce: The Parisian Merchant Court and the Rise of Commercial Society in Eighteenth-Century France* (New Haven, CT 2007).

5 AD Marne, B 1565 Jonchery sur Suippe, B 2482 Fleury la Riviere, B 2499 Nanteuille, B 2515 St Imoge, B 7448 St Souplet, B 9668 Fontaine, 24B 2 Auberive, 24B 20 Beine, 24B 253 Chigny, 24B 372 Cormicy, 24B 526 Epoye, 24B 664, 665, 666 Hautvillers, 24 B 853 Montigny, 24B 1026 Trigny, 24B 1054 Verzy, 24B 1074 Villedomange.

6 F. Mauclair, *La justice au village: Justice seigneuriale et société rurale dans le duché-pairie de la Vallière (1667–1790)* (Rennes 2008), offers a detailed discussion of the *registres de l'audience* on which this is based and of civil litigation of debts.

7 H. Piant, *Une justice ordinaire: justice civile et criminelle dans la prévoté royale de Vaucouleurs sous l'ancien régime* (Rennes 2006), 143–51. Luckett, "Credit," 100, argues for a "remarkably small" number of seizures and imprisonments. I have consulted the records of seizures in the baillage court, AD Marne 17B 1135, for the relevant period and have found none of the defaulters mentioned.

8 A. Crubaugh, *Balancing the Scales of Justice: Local Courts and Rural Society in Southwest France, 1750–1800* (University Park, PA 2001), 34.

9 Crubaugh, *Balancing the Scales*, 7, surveys his own and several other regions.

10 C. Muldrew, *The Economy of Obligation: The Culture of Credit and Social Relations in Early Modern England* (New York 2001), 232–8. This may not be too different from the figure of one in 14 given by G. Postel-Vinay, *La terre et l'argent: L'agriculture et le crédit en France du XVIIIe au début du Xxe siècle* (Paris 1998), 41, but it is rather difficult to know since he does not specify the kinds of loans that he is counting in that table.

11 Piant, *Une justice ordinaire*, 144, sees a rise in default litigation, but Mauclair, *La justice au village*, and others have found that total litigation generally declined.

12 Muldrew, *Economy of Obligation*, 226. J. Hayhoe, *Enlightened Feudalism: Seigneurial Justice and Village Society in Eighteenth-Century Northern Burgundy* (Rochester,

NY 2008), 107. Hayhoe has also calculated total litigation rates in his villages of one per 15 households. See Hayhoe, *Enlightened Feudalism*, 103–4.

13 P. Bossis, "L'endettement de la paysannerie au XVIIIe siècle dans les registres du contrôle des actes (étude de sources)," *Bulletin d'histoire économique et sociale de la Révolution française* (1977): 53–62.

14 See P. Hoffman, G. Postel-Vinay and J.-L. Rosenthal, *Priceless Markets: The Political Economy of Credit in Paris, 1660–1870* (Chicago 2000), for a discussion of this credit instrument and its use in Paris; see Brennan, "Peasants and Debt," for its use in Champagne.

15 See R. Lentz, *La taille tarifée en Champagne* (Paris 1928) and M. Touzeray, *L'invention de l'impot sur le revenu, la taille tarifée, 1715–1789* (Paris 1994), for the background to this decision and some of the details of its imposition.

16 AD Marne, C2202, C2210, C2211, C2232, C2233, C2240, C2246, C2261, C2292, C2341, C2347, 18E depôt 670.

17 Since vineyards were almost nine times more productive, on average, in this region, according to the assessments of the tax officials, it is only possible to compare landholdings by using the revenue estimates made by the assessors. I have simplified these estimates by turning them into the amount of arable land this would be worth in each village. See Brennan, "Debt," for a longer discussion.

18 I wish to thank Peter Guth, not only for the use of his mapping software, MICRODEM, but also for the many hours he has spent helping me use it.

19 T. Brennan, *Burgundy to Champagne: The Wine Trade in Early Modern France* (Baltimore, MD 1997), 240–71; B. Musset, *Vignobles de Champagne et vins mousseux: histoire d'un mariage de raison 1650–1830* (Paris 2008), 441.

20 A standard treatment of this subject can be found in S. Wasserman and K. Faust, *Social Network Analysis: Methods and Applications* (Cambridge 1994). The analysis in this article was done using UCINET and NETDRAW software.

21 Centrality in this article refers to betweenness, though L.C. Freeman, "Centrality in Social Networks: Conceptual Clarity," *Social Networks* 1 (1979): 227–38, discusses that and other measures of graph centrality. Cohesion is measured by k-cores, as outlined by S.B. Seidman, "Network Structure and Minimum Degree," *Social Networks* 5 (1983): 269–87, and I. Alvarez-Hamelin, L. Dall'Asta, A. Barrat and A. Vespignani, "k-core Decomposition: A Tool for the Visualization of Large Scale Networks," at http://xavier.informatics.indiana.edu/lanet-vi/k-cores_AHDBV3.pdf (accessed 16 October 2011).

22 G. Daudin, *Commerce et prospérité: La France au XVIIIe siècle* (Paris 2005), 137–9, argues that, because the variable costs of working through an intermediary are greater in a centralized network and the fixed costs of establishing a direct link are greater in an egalitarian network, an egalitarian network is more advantageous in a system with a high volume of transactions.

23 Network density is simply the percentage of possible links between nodes (villages) that actually exist; in this case, less than 2 percent.

24 The most useful measures here are degree centrality, which simply counts the number of nodes connected to a particular node, and betweenness centrality, which counts the number of shortest paths between other nodes that run through a particular node.

25 AD Marne, C 4126, C 4145, C 4272, 4295, C 4313, C 4328, C 4594, C 4644–46, C 5065, C 5094.

26 Musset, *Vignobles de Champagne*, 441, charts the rise of grain prices in the market of Reims from 1768 through the 1770s after much lower prices earlier. For financial problems, see T. Luckett, "Crises financières dans la France du XVIIIe siècle," *Revue d'histoire moderne et contemporaine* 43 (1996): 266–92.

4 Credit, trust and risk

Shopkeepers' bankruptcies in 18th-century Paris[1]

Natacha Coquery

Introduction

"Everybody buys bread on credit," wrote abbé Galiani in 1770 in his *Dialogue sur le commerce des blés*.[2] The general recourse to credit during the early modern age was an answer to the problem of money mobilization and mobility due to the lack of reliable credit institutions and specialized financial markets.[3] In the eighteenth century, commercial needs were satisfied with the traditional monetary and credit system. This system relied on private bankers and on old exchange techniques, supported by increases in price, stock, money and exchanges. South America provided additional support to the increasing circulation of payment means, money flows and commercial papers.[4] In this context of abundance, the gathering of capital remained nonetheless difficult for small entrepreneurs. The lack of liquid assets was general and payment in cash, rare.[5] So, the chain of credit was the basis of trade, as Daniel Defoe observed.[6] Craig Muldrew studied this credit economy of sixteenth and seventeenth-century England, in which everything was measured by monetary prices but where money was not the main means of exchange.[7]

Shops were one of the transfer hubs of credit and this was one of their chief attractions. Because of their profession, shopkeepers stood on the frontline, at the same time lending and borrowing credit. They were at the center of a widespread network of partners, wholesalers, brokers, customers and capitalists. Included in money matters, they participated actively in the networks of local credit, as did the notaries.[8] The lending of money was an articulation of power. The key issue was the control of credit. On it depended the success or the failure of any company, however small. Retailers were tangled up in credit. They lived between those who owed them money and those to whom they owed it. It was a double-edged weapon, as Fernand Braudel underlined: "A precarious balance always on the edge of the tumble."[9] Credit meant easy terms, speedy exchange and ready earnings. As Craig Muldrew wrote, it was the oil in the wheels. But it entailed vulnerability and uncertainty. A weak link in the chain could check it and lead to a break. Interdependence was formidable and led to a spate of bankruptcies. Credit made the exchange easy, but it linked it to risk. It was dangerous but inescapable. How did the shopkeepers manage time, inevitable and unpredictable, and synchronization, which were in the heart of the economic problem? How did they master money flows and capital investments in their various forms? In short, how did they manage uncertainty?[10]

Account books and statements kept within bankruptcy files give part of the answer.[11] The practice of accounting cannot be examined outside its own social and institutional context: it was a practice constructed within and formative of socio-economic relations; it was a trial-and-error adaptation to the evolution of the operating conditions and to the environment of businesses, a specific way to try to manage one's contemporaries and contemporary events.[12] In this way, accounting was both a kind of power and a kind of knowledge.[13] Indeed, credit systems reveal a strong social intricacy. Credit relations expose professional relations as well as hierarchies and tensions internal to the trading world. They were manifold links: of dependence and interdependence, of subordination and domination, of trust and mistrust. Looked for and dreaded links, credit–debt relations signaled power or success and failure or even ruin. In spite of the disputes due to debts and insolvency, the "invisible institution"[14] of trust, played a major part in exchanges. This is why such notions as reputation, honor or honesty weighed so heavily in the shopkeeper world.[15] Integration into the small business community was paramount in a career: winning and keeping the trust of lenders, suppliers and customers was mandatory.[16] Trust was necessary to create social links since common interests made an unstable and precarious basis. Trust united individuals, it made possible exchange.[17]

Bankruptcy analysis provides a good means of thinking over the relations among credit, trust and risk or, in other words, over cooperation and disagreement between shopkeepers. Bankruptcies highlighted the difficulties of time management and, more precisely, the absence of synchronization, the badly managed time shifts. Bankruptcy did not, however, necessarily signal closure, incapacity, mediocrity, tragedy or forfeiture. Some shopkeepers underwent several bankruptcies, which demonstrates its usually temporary nature. Bankruptcy also captured the efforts to recover from a wrongly assessed risk and the difficulty in escaping the pitfalls of credit, the control of which was a key to success. It especially highlighted the crucial role of credit in the interdependent relations that linked the actors in any exchange. Only a detailed study can show how important credit was, both in quality and quantity, in early modern society. Jewelers and tapestry-makers' shops provide a good ground for study since they represented two emblematic sectors of the expanding luxury and semi-luxury markets in the eighteenth-century Paris.[18] By virtue of their speciality—jewelers adorned the body; tapestry-makers adorned the household—they held cash and gave credit. They sold rare and costly goods that required substantial funds. They stood at the heart of a system of exchanges, because they gave credit both upward (to producers and wholesalers) and downward (to consumers).

What is to be understood, beyond the necessary credit relations that shopkeepers formed, is their seemingly inexhaustible business vitality. Most of the success and fame of the capital of fashion and luxury rested on this vitality. It can only be understood against its background: the "embeddedness" of individuals in social systems; the function of institutions setting the rules and regulating behaviours. These systems and institutions were themselves produced by individual strategies and behaviors.[19] At the end of the day, more than a sanction, more than an economic indicator, bankruptcy revealed the tensions and struggles within commercial society.[20] I shall first explain the causes of bankruptcy, i.e., the relations between credit, trust and embeddedness. Then I shall show the different ways in which these bankruptcies were resolved—by the commercial code, a pragmatic law framing the discussion between peers.

Credit, trust and embeddedness

The selected documents concern about 120 shopkeepers, mostly Parisian jewelers or tapestry-makers; 96 are clearly identifiable as to trade.[21] They bring to light two major points: the involvement of shopkeepers in the Parisian luxury market; and the embeddedness of shopkeepers in a network of commercial and credit relationships.

The market of the capital, boosted by the presence of the king and the court, aroused keen interests.[22] The amounts at stake, in terms of assets and liabilities, prove the integration of shops in the Parisian commercial exchange center: capital outlays and investments, working capital, fixed assets … all were expensive. Credit is visible in the statements, where it is identified as "dettes actives" for the assets due the shopkeeper and "dettes passives" for the liabilities owed by him. The omnipresence of credit was mandatory given the absence of liquid assets. Jean Meuvret observed the relative lack of substantial amounts of cash in the inventories: this shows that sixteenth-century shopkeepers did almost totally without cash in their working capital. In Niort, in the west of France, three centuries later, two bankrupts out of three had no cash at home at the time of their failure.[23] Accounts confirm this condition generally: the proportion of cash reached 1.5 to 2 percent of all assets among the most prosperous shopkeepers. Jeweler Augard's capital amounted to 26,000 livres *tournois* in 1750; his widow held 352 livres "which represent all the cash […] in the estate," i.e., 1.5 percent. Jeweler Buteux's assets amounted to 10,000 livres in 1779, out of which 186 livres, 2 percent, took the form of cash. The lack of liquid assets lead to a drastic increase in promissory notes issued by individuals—gentlemen, bourgeois, officers, clergymen, moneymen, shopkeepers—to merchants, bankers, shopkeepers and craftsmen.[24] These notes were credit instruments. All the accounting documents of the time—account books, post-mortem inventories, commercial statements—prove the large and varied usage of "credit paper" as Morellet called it in his *Prospectus d'un nouveau Dictionnaire de Commerce* (1769): fixed-term notes, bill of exchange, money orders, acknowledgments, drafts, etc. The most usual form of payment was a private acknowledgment of debt: these bills (*effets*) or notes (*billets*) amounted to short-term loans, sometimes renewable, at a high interest rate. As a consequence, the main difficulty in determining a shopkeeper's balance of payments was to check the notes: it was necessary to balance between assets and liabilities but also between assets, that is between "good debts," those likely to be paid (*bonne dette*) and "bad debt," those unlikely to be lost (*dette douteuse* or *mauvaise dette*).

For about 50 shopkeepers, their assets totalled to an average 54,000 livres, while their liabilities were slightly higher, on average 59,000 livres (see Table 4.1). The high figures emphasize the part played by shopkeepers and the credit they offered in the rapidly expanding Parisian luxury market during the last part of the eighteenth century. As a measure of that expansion, consider first that 87.5 percent of bankruptcies, 77 of 88 cases, took place after 1765.[25] Such global figures should not, however, be allowed to hide the intrinsic diversity of the shopkeepers' world (see table): total value of all assets varied from 500 to 400,000 livres; total liabilities varied from 3,000 to 375,000 livres; total accounts receivable varied from 400 to 191,000 livres; total good debts ranged from 0 to 168,000 livres; goods in store valued as much as 171,000 livres, total losses were valued from 1,300 to 116,000 livres; fortunes from 215,000 livres in debts to 97,000 livres in assets.

The high figures for accounts receivable, a good index of business vitality, indicate the wealth and reputation, leading to confidence and hence to credit. The average assets of 54 jewelers or goldsmiths reached 53,500 livres, that of 14 tapestry-makers 25,400 livres. Taking into account secure assets, i.e., assets without losses and bad debt,[26] the averages reached 54,400 livres for the 27 jewelers and 22,000 livres for the eight tapestry-makers considered. The accounts receivable average reached 3,080 livres for 40 jewelers, 15,300 for 11 tapestry-makers. Liabilities were even more impressive, and with good reason (they caused bankruptcy): the averages amounted to 59,000 livres for the 58 jewelers and to more than 32,200 for the 17 tapestry-makers. In 42, instances of losses reached 33,500 livres. Tension was constant between accounts receivable and accounts payable; the default of a single receivable account could lead to bankruptcy. That just shows how much shopkeepers were subordinated to their creditors and even more if in a tricky situation. Comparing accounts receivable, "dettes actives," of which the debts most likely to be paid, "bonnes dettes," are most important, and accounts payable, "dettes passives," of which the debts least likely to be paid, "mauvaises dettes," are most important, is sufficient to make the situation clear. The tapestry-maker Law held 3,455 livres in account receivable but 19,000 livres in bad debt; the jeweler Aubourg, 11,000 livres in account receivable but 10,000 livres in doubtful debt and 39,000 livres in bad debt; the jeweler Dezarot, 300 livres in account receivable but 31,500 livres in doubtful debt and bad debt and so on. Bankrupts failed to keep balance between account receivable and liability, between good or bad debts. They were overcome by credit.

There is no business without capital. Rising capital is critical for vitality and growth. Shopkeepers needed money to start their business, to increase it, to buy or renew stocks and to cope with cash-flow problems. In order to acquire capital, they appealed to credit, which formed the burden of liabilities in the statements. As such, the statements testify to the integration of the shopkeepers in the economic fabric.

Table 4.1 List of 88 failed Parisian shopkeepers, classified in increasing order of the liabilities (1750–80)

Name	*Trade*	*Year*	*Asset*	*Liabilities*
Dehanne	Jeweler	1784	4,380	3,080
Chartier (3)	Tapestry-maker, mirror dealer	1784	5,450	4,298
Schmit (1)	Goldsmith, jeweler	1783	–	4,352
Lecuyer (d[lle])	Jeweler (woman)	1791	3,058	4,370
Duchene	Tapestry-maker	1774	5,997	5,608
Degoest	Jeweler	1784	7,058	5,980
Dumont	Mounter	1750	3,498	6,009
Clément	Jeweler	1753	12,782	6,704
Poiret (2)	Watchmaker	1774	2,169	7,454
Ricard	Gilder	1772	21,786	7,872
Henchoz	Watchmaker	1780	–	8,950
Diodet	Jeweler	1779	2,770	9,294
Hubert	Haberdasher	1768	8,600	9,708
Delaunay	Goldsmith	1785	17,033	9,746
Lehaberdasher (widow)	Jeweler	1789	8,482	10,129
Schmit (2)	Goldsmith, jeweler	1787	7,190	10,483
Possieu (1)	Goldsmith, jeweler	1766	12,771	10,539
Charpentier	Tapestry-maker	1781	25,317	10,999
Fagard	Watchmaker	1780	–	12,731
Lecuyer	Jeweler	1780	5,021	13,091
Nollet (1)	Jeweler	1781	8,755	13,988
Labatte	Tapestry-maker	1776	11,713	14,174
Girard (1)	Jeweler	June 1780	16,750	16,142
Calame	Watchmaker	1785	7,466	16,790
Godefroy	Jeweler	1789	8,813	17,232
Terrasse	Jeweler	1774	1,380	17,779
Devaux	Tapestry-maker, mirror dealer	1726	11,398	18,496
Girard (2)	Jeweler	December 1780	14,209	19,837
Baudouin	Jeweler	1784	12,182	20,691
Delespine	Jeweler	1782	500	21,794
Morin	Tapestry-maker	1751	–	21,861
Blezimar	Jeweler	1779	14,997	23,184
Chartier (1)	Tapestry-maker, mirror dealer	1783	28,300	24,890
Poiret (1)	Watchmaker	1768	6,544	26,837
Chapuy (1)	Tapestry-maker	1781	30,207	27,277
Chapuy (2)	Tapestry-maker	1781	–	27,277
Dezarot	Jeweler	1779	41,607	27,689
Excoffon	Jeweler	1780	35,473	30,356
Combes (2)	Jeweler	1779	36,491	30,487
Pontet	Jeweler	1771	64,113	31,064
Wielland	Jeweler	1770	70,135	33,225
Hallot	Jeweler	1777	12,450	33,477
Charpentier	Haberdasher	1770	23,482	33,549
Chartier (2)	Tapestry-maker, mirror dealer	1783	22,100	34,890
Deshayes (2)	Tapestry-maker, mirror dealer	1742	16,893	35,652
Dubois	Trader	1779	–	36,202
Dupret	Jeweler	1766	53,740	38,148

Table 4.1 Continued

Name	*Trade*	*Year*	*Asset*	*Liabilities*
Brianchon	Tapestry-maker	1790	23,638	39,481
Sevenet	Jeweler	1779	11,200	39,905
Dufrainne	Jeweler	1777	–	40,033
Deshayes (1)	Tapestry-maker, mirror dealer	1738	65,763	41,351
Law	Tapestry-maker, mirror dealer	1788	44,112	43,254
Langlois (Claude)	Jeweler	1779	53,651	44,038
Lebœufve	Haberdasher, jeweler	1768	40,607	44,114
Pinson	Jeweler	1772	97,087	44,385
Guillermet	Jeweler	1781	10,481	44,423
Possieu (2)	Goldsmith, jeweler	1781	31,182	44,805
Leubat	Watchmaker	1789	36,290	45,159
Jobart	Jeweler	1778	32,615	46,244
Lonchamps	Jeweler	1788	12,629	46,419
Jourdain	Tapestry-maker, mirror dealer	1782	14,600	50,248
Grandin	Tapestry-maker, mirror dealer	1783	–	50,843
Martinet (1)	Jeweler	1777	47,940	53,316
Boquet	Jeweler	1770	33,011	56,495
Combes (1)	Jeweler	1781	33,870	56,806
Leconte (2)	Jeweler	1784	68,494	57,019
Aubourg	Jeweler	1783	63,027	57,792
Martinet (2)	Jeweler	1777	13,930	57,974
Bonein (2)	Haberdasher	1783	53,970	64,254
Virlouret	Hardware dealer	1784	57,825	66,204
Carelu	Jeweler	1742	–	69,947
Guy (3)	Jeweler	1780	51,870	71,802
Caumont	Mounter	1751	97,934	74,844
La Garenne (de)	Jeweler	1751	35,274	75,353
Langlois (Auguste) (1)	Jeweler	1789	–	76,722
Seriny	Jeweler	1715	81,100	81,013
Guy (2)	Jeweler	1779	53,060	84,143
Caplain	Tapestry-maker	1792	50,222	96,497
Langlois (Auguste) (2)	Jeweler	1789	185,085	105,868
Bonein (1)	Haberdasher	1782	126,601	111,521
Guy (1)	Jeweler	1777	85,856	115,197
Georges	Goldsmith	1790	118,171	127,084
Fortier	Jeweler	1789	61,810	149,015
Cerf Levy	Trader	1777	691,028	154,560
Clémencée	Jeweler	1783	227,587	207,075
Nollet (2)	Jeweler	1788	35,329	250,088
Leconte (1)	Jeweler	1778	389,479	292,732
Granchez	Jeweler	1787	398,890	376,817

Sources: bankruptcy statements (Paris archives), creditors' union contracts (National archives).

Note
Some shopkeepers filed several bankruptcies, they thus established several bankruptcy statements; the figure in parentheses specifies it.

The jewelers Baudouin, Blézimar and Charpentier and the tapestry-maker Deshayes owed 20,000 to 30,000 livres to about 30 persons; the tapestry- and mirror-makers Grandin and Jourdain owed 50,000 livres to about 20 persons; the jewelers Carelu and Combes 60,000 to 70,000 livres respectively to about 40 persons. To understand the relations linking the shopkeepers to their creditors, the list of creditors established as part of the legal process, begun by filing for bankruptcy, is invaluable.[27] The list included very specific information about the creditors and their credit: the persons owed, the amounts owed, the means of payment, the deadlines, etc. They make clear that the vast majority of creditors were actually shopkeepers and craftsmen, small and big. Credit relation criss-crossed among shopkeepers, which is precisely the basis of their embeddedness.

Let's study the jewelers. The 48 shopkeepers called upon 1,098 creditors of known profession (see Table 4.2).[28] Of these, 90 percent (985) belonged to various trades, including 170 merchants, 179 jewelers, 54 haberdashers and 45 goldsmiths. The bankers or "money sellers" represented hardly 1 percent. Few came from outside of the world of commerce: *bourgeois of Paris* (less than 3 percent), official circles (2 percent), nobility (1.5 percent). Observing the amounts paid, (from 3 to 50,600 livres) reveals the balance of power that gave form to commercial society. Merchants proved the single largest source of credit (25 percent of the amount loaned), followed by the very active goldsmiths (17 percent). The jewelers provided less credit than these two groups (9.8 percent) but still more than the *bourgeois de Paris* (4.6 percent). So, the Parisian retail jewelery was financially dependent upon merchants and goldsmiths, great capital holders, rather than members of their own craft. These substantial lenders mastered information because they—especially the merchants—participated in the international market and controlled the flow of commodities and capital.[29] Through credit as much as through goods, merchants and goldsmiths subordinated the shopkeepers. The vast majority of bankrupts were debtors toward merchants and (or) goldsmiths, even the smallest. The amounts at stake could be quite significant, ranging from 20,000 to more than 80,000 livres. In 1778 and again in 1784, the jeweler Leconte owed 82,000 livres to 24 goldsmiths, 77,000 livres to six merchants, 58,000 livres to 13 jewelers and 17,000 livres to a single *bourgeois de Paris*. In 1781 and 1788, the jeweler Nollet owed 62,000 livres to two merchants (more than 50,000 livres to Delaunay), 29,000 to 18 manufacturers in Beauvais and Rouen, 27,000 to two *bourgeois de Paris*, 26,000 to a wood dealer, 17,000 to a jeweler and 17,000 to a tapestry-maker.[30] The haberdasher-jeweler Granchez spent fortunes to supply his shop. According to one account, he owed various sums to more than 100 shopkeepers.[31] He owed 80,000 livres in goods to 14 merchants, including 18,000 to a merchant in the city (Grenier frères), 30,000 to three Londoners (Gray, Holy and Josué Ogier),[32] 7,000 to a merchant in Birmingham (Glover son and Frey) and 5,000 to two Swiss merchants (Dubois, of Neuchâtel, and Mallet, of Geneva).[33] These great merchants specialized in importation and redistribution on the Parisian market, revealing, once again, the strong hierarchy within the commercial world. The recurrence of a few names emphasizes the power of a dozen merchants as well as the diamond supremacy of the

Table 4.2 Distribution of the creditors (the position of whom is known) of 48 jewelers and goldsmiths, according to the amount of the claims

Trade or quality	*Amount of credit*	*%*	*Number*	*%*	*Number of claims*
Mounter	2,000	–	12	–	12
Count	2,250	–	2	–	2
Furbisher, gunsmith	3,200	–	10	–	10
Gilder	3,400	–	25	2	30
Grocer	3,700	–	9	–	8
Duke	5,000	–	1	–	1
Hardware dealer	5,500	–	3	–	5
Button maker	5,500	–	9	–	12
Wine dealer	6,600	–	14	–	13
Material dealer	6,800	–	4	–	4
Caster	7,300	–	16	–	18
Seller of roast meat	10,100	–	1	–	1
Joiner	10,500	–	14	–	14
Engraver	10,600	–	13	–	15
Tailor	11,200	–	17	–	17
Major girl	11,200	–	4	–	4
Manufacturer	17,100	–	9	–	7
Judge advisor (former main)	18,400	–	1	–	1
Lapidary	19,300	–	26	2	26
Adviser	20,500	–	2	–	2
Tapestry-maker	24,200	–	12	–	12
Painter	26,600	–	21	–	21
Servant	32,600	–	4	–	4
Banker	34,200	–	12	–	8
Captain	35,600	–	1	–	1
Cabinet-maker	37,300	–	11	–	11
Toy dealer	39,000	–	34	3	47
Watchmaker	39,500	–	32	3	32
Maker	40,600	1,5	24	2	24
Wood dealer	47,300	–	7	–	8
Shopkeeper	57,900	2,4	47	4	51
Bourgeois of Paris	113,500	4,6	29	2,5	25
Jeweler	344,400	13,8	170	15	199
Haberdasher	123,400	5	54	5	57
Goldsmith (jeweler)	412,600	17	45	4	222
Trader	615,800	25	170	15,5	193
Total	2,439,749	–	1,098	–	1,777

Source: Arch. de Paris (lists of creditors established by the consular jurisdiction and statements).

Netherlands: Léon Zacharie, a Rotterdam native (named nine times), and Israel Simon from Amsterdam (six); the hardware dealers Orcel (six), the jeweler Abraham Bernard Wolf (five), the goldsmith Tirard (five). On a smaller scale, lists of creditors show the dominant part played by some jewelers and the intertwining of relations.[34] Merchants and goldsmiths were hence the great suppliers of credit in Parisian jewelery and, consequently, masters of the market.

Small businesses also operated in accordance with intense horizontal relations, as shown by the multiplicity of creditors and the informal links between peers. Credit set trust as a key issue of commercial relations at the heart of shopkeepers' activity. Trust influenced many, widely held practices: associations among shopkeepers, common purchasing of goods and selling, gifts "in trust" or "on condition," i.e., goods deposited at each other's shops. Deposits among shopkeepers as well as associations formed a substantial part of the circulation of goods, inside the Parisian market and between Paris and provincial (Lyon, Montpellier...) and foreign (London, Naples, Genoa or even Constantinople) markets.[35] Deposits allowed shopkeepers to bypass rigid regulations. They rendered null and void, for example, the prohibition to hold several shops. "[D]elivered in trust [to Bélalie brothers] an enamelled china box with Flemish figures, to be sold for 30 livres."[36] "[To James Staphens, London shopkeeper] for entrusted goods ... 3,880 livres."[37]

But risk increased in trust-based relationships, because no protection was possible within trust relations: so-called gifts in trust were made over-the-counter. Association did not suppress risk either, although it sought to contain it: "In false losses in the association [with Master Roger] [...] and common loss for my of share ... 6,000 livres."[38] Distance increased uncertainty. The lender in trouble had little recourse in the face of betrayal. He had to write matters of trust on the debit side of the ledger. Deferred liabilities made up the lion's share of bad debts and losses. They were "debts lost with trust in the breakdown" (*dettes perdues au détail par confiance*) as the jeweler Lecuyer wrote, "money lent by trust" (*argent prêté sur parole*), "honor notes" (*billets d'honneur*),[39] bankrupt or dead shopkeepers' debts. Shopkeepers maintained among themselves lines of credit over years, paying by paper transfers and registration of account. Credit relied on acquaintance with a person and faith in the value of their signatures or promises, hence the importance of words such as "reputation," "credit" and "trust." "Lost with the named Frigelly, Italian residing in Genoa through goods I delivered to him in trust in 1777 ... 4,005 livres."[40] "several goods I entrusted to various individuals and consequent losses ... 2,500 livres."[41]

Profits and risk remained inseparable. "Profits appear very fortuitous, implying risks and chance: this which is this word is often used by players and shopkeepers."[42] Risk figured in bankruptcy. "It is the state of a shopkeeper [...] whose affairs are so disrupted that he cannot meet the commitments he made and pay the amounts he owes."[43] Bankruptcy was a crisis of both credit and confidence; "If trust eases so many matters, it also causes so many troubles in business when those who put trust in some people, suddenly withdraw it and deny credit to them to whom they used to give it."[44] What happened in cases of "breach of trust" (*abus de confiance*), of "faithless or indiscrete partners" (*sans foy et sans delicatesse*)?[45] Bankruptcy signaled a breach of trust, at least momentarily, and moved the basis of exchange on to the ground of mistrust and suspicion. Yet, the fundamental pragmatism of the commercial community remained. Relations wavered between sanction and compromise, because failure posed a new set of problems and risks: How could they avoid the expenses and get a chance to recover the debts?

Trust, crisis and discussion: how to settle and overcome the crisis

The embeddedness of the shopkeepers' community was the main factor triggering the crisis. Bankruptcy compromised both the shopkeeper's fortune and his reputation, i.e., the laboriously built image of his own value shown to the others. An individual was always imbedded in his social networks: he was always located, always locatable by those persons with whom he stood in relationships.[46] His success depended on reputation: without it, no credit, no respect.

Bankruptcy brought creditors and debtors face to face in a collective, contentious procedure: the courts were limited to giving binding effect to the collective decisions of the creditors, without detailing "the resolutions taken by the creditors' assembly."[47] The proceedings hinged then on discussion: dispute and arbitration were not necessarily antagonistic.[48] The confrontation between the bankrupt and his creditors generated texts of great interest for the historian, because shopkeepers are seldom heard. The choice of convention usually required several assemblies and hearings: the bankrupt had to submit a precise statement of his situation. Judged by his peers with neither compassion nor aggression, he sought to restore his trust. He had to find the arguments to avoid the worse—civil imprisonment and seizure of assets—or to be released if he was imprisoned. He had to suggest solutions that his creditors might accept or reject. They were both judge and jury since they assessed his situation, imposed sanctions and sought restitution, all while belonging to the same world as the bankrupt. Their actions depended on the bankrupt's statements and accounts. It depended also on his reputation, a measure of his integration and his station in the commercial community.

Bankruptcy offers a glimpse not only of the bankrupt's affairs, but also of the function of the shopkeepers' world, the commercial community. It exposes the degree of embeddedness of their inter-relationship and the role that trust played among them. It sets the commercial law, which governed conventions among bankrupts and their creditors, in contrast to the special procedure (*procédure extraordinaire*) of royal justice before the *Châtelet* and *Parlement*. Finally, bankruptcy resolution reveals how shopkeepers managed to overcome failure, or not.

The suspension of payment troubled the economic relations and harmed creditors. Creditors wavered between the punishment of fraud with its cumbersome procedures, on the one hand, and the protection of honest misfortune with its goal of settlement, on the other.[49] Fairness was a balance hard to find, because bankruptcy endangered different, often conflicting interests that had somehow to be safeguarded. The reading of documents makes clear the flexibility of the creditors, at least the acknowledged claimants who seemed open to trade-offs in order to preserve whatever they could. Deals were often struck outside the courts through the agency of notaries. Bankruptcy law was empirical, resulting from common ideas and collective practices,[50] but the procedures still involved strong guaranties. The first step toward a common solution was the formation of the "creditors' union" (*union des créanciers*). To establish themselves as a legal unity, creditors had to choose among them the director or trustee, whom, with the assistance of a notary, was in charge of operational procedures, of administrating and reallocating the bankrupt's assets, of filing the claims, etc. The procedure met in assembly to decide a specific course of settlement, usually after a thorough examination of the bankrupt's statement and, often, after a close interrogation of the bankrupt. Assemblies were meetings of strong discussion, where the solution to the crisis was debated and agreed as a group. The recurrence of such words as "having commonly deliberated" (*ayant délibéré ensemble*), "after examining the aforesaid statement and considering among themselves the most suitable terms for their real interests" (*après avoir examiné ledit état et réfléchi entre eux sur le party le plus convenable à leurs vrais intérêts*), "after conferring among themselves" (*après avoir conféré entre eux*), "considering the necessity to agree among themselves" (*considérant la nécéssité de s'entendre entre eux*), etc., all bear witness of it. "Necessity to agree" (*nécessité de s'entendre*): the words expressed the purpose of the creditor's union, i.e., to manage to settle accounts among peers despite tensions. The course of action was to avoid the inconveniences of the legal proceedings: "avoid expenses" (*éviter les frais*), shorten the "lengths of the legal discussion" (*longueurs dans la discussion en justice*). The creditors' union contract for the goldsmith Paul de Seriny made this perfectly explicit:

> these being informed of the bad state of affairs of master Seriny that none of his creditors seized and executed his furniture and have seized really his real property fearing that the various procedures and the setting up of several prosecutors generated significant expenses and lengths in the legal discussion of master Seriny's assets, what would be to the detriment of the creditors and would much decrease the bills' profit to be used for their payment, have gathered to prevent these inconveniences and decide on a common position favorable to their interests and after common deliberation they decided and agreed as follows.[51]

Pragmatism dominated: the mutually agreed arrangement between parties was the surest means to get paid, at least in part. If the collective procedure completed the bankrupt's ruin, the creditors might recover only a portion of their capital. This is why the direct agreement with the debtor was essential. Conciliatory words were plenty: "arrangement" (*arrangement*), "assent" (*acquiescement*), "have compromised" (*ont transigé*), "have agreed to the proposal" (*ont accepté la proposition*), "have subscribed" (*ont adhere*), "have extended" (*ont sursi*), etc. Arrangement often meant bargaining. Postponement dominated in the world of goods in attempts to settle conflicts over deadlines and cancellations, avoid dispossession, stop business activities or forced liquidation.[52] This is the "commercialist"[53] concept of bankruptcy.[54] Creditors were sceptical about the efficiency of the rigorist attitude, which implied long, costly and uncertain procedures. They preferred to speculate on the return to prosperity and on the bankrupt's wish for settlement. Generous deadlines were often granted, when no cancellation was requested.[55] If they were convinced of his honesty, creditors trusted the bankrupt and accepted his proposal "on the strength of the execution of the contracted obligation" (*sur la foi de l'exécution des obligations contractées*) or "on the strength of security" (*sur la foi du cautionnement*):

> the aforesaid masters and ladies creditors [...] convinced that, from the aforesaid master Bonein, there is no misconduct, nor dissipation, and full of confidence in his probity, his activity and intelligence, agreed on what follows. [...] They did him justice to recognize him as an exact and sincere shopkeeper.[56]

The creditors' union contract was chosen to settle a bankruptcy only in desperation, when the bankrupt was dead, presumed guilty of fraud or his business in such disarry as to render reorganization impossible. The deed constituted an *a priori* irredeemable forfeiture; the signatories pursued their individual interests, which explains *a posteriori* shifts in positions. The jeweler Langlois le Jeune was helped by his elder brother, to whom he owed almost 13,000 livres. After approving a debt waiver at the end of October 1789, the creditors opted for cancellation two months later. Waiving all the goods and accounts receivable had proven an unsound economic calculation. It was better to accept the elder brother's offer: a 40 percent payment of capital, 30,000 livres, at the rate of 6,000 livres every six months in return for the cancellation of the infamous abandoned deed. Fair is fair. The full weight of family solidarity was brought into the deal, as the following clearly shows:

> [Art. 6: Langlois l'Aîné's aim is] to ensure the aforesaid Langlois Jeune keeps his trade and avoids his complete ruin [...]. [The commitment he makes] will be effective only if [his brother] recovers his business and if debt waiver and resolution are stopped. [...]. [Art. 8] and it is in the interest of all the creditors to accept the aforesaid Langlois l'Aîné's resolutions since, they grant them 40 percent of their capital claims, while a debt waiver [...] presents difficulties, lengths and losses in its enforcement that do not allow to keep the same hope [the creditors guarantee Langlois le Jeune to have the present act carried out].[57]

Even imprisonment or flight seldom signaled the end of the negotiation or entailed greater severity: the greatest difficulties resulted not from the bankrupt but rather from his creditors, who often resisted acting in common through the creditors' union or pursued individual initiatives because they suspected the bankrupt of fraud. Negotiations started during the bankrupt's imprisonment or upon his return from flight. Conciliation proceedings did not distort the balance of power. Creditors could always threaten, and their trust remained limited:

"The aforesaid creditors shall retain their claims until they be completely paid" (*Lesdits sieurs créanciers garderont entre leurs mains les titres de leurs créances jusqu'à ce qu'ils en soyent entièrement payé*).[58] Negotiations sometimes included pressures and several shopkeepers spent a few months in prison until their situation was clarified.

Settling the bankruptcy was a touchy process. The room for maneuver remained narrow because the bankrupt relied on the creditors' willingness to delay payment or risk loss, even as he risked forfeiture and business death. If the creditors pushed rigor too far, even though justified, they lost any chance to recover their capital. Assemblies and deliberations were a close game.

The bankrupts' own words appear in that part of the legal proceeding known as the "Observations," sometimes in commenting statements but mainly in the contract signed with the creditors before a notary. The contract started with all the parties involved: the bankrupt, then the creditors. The bankrupt then produced his statement; he commented on it, and he suggested a plan of repayment. The creditors deliberated and delivered their verdict; they presented their justification for it. The act ended with the signature of all the people present. According to the bankrupts, bankruptcy resulted first from non-commercial factors such as unforeseen personal misfortunes.[59] Credit problems and business losses came second. The rigors of the market were often used as an excuse, because they enabled the bankrupts to dismiss any personal responsibility by blaming failure on either the lack of cash, the over-use of credit, compulsory or hasty sales (*ventes forcées* or *précipitées*). Yet, domestic expenses and unforeseeable accidents, such as fires, thefts, seizures, illnesses, etc., prevailed in their arguments. Nothing was mentioned about market conditions or economic transformations. Failure was not perceived as the consequence of an improper choice or a competitive climate. It was an individual accident, out of context. Bankrupts portrayed themselves as having no control over the world around them. An ideal of honesty and moderation that seems disconnected from economic realities haunted their self-narratives. P.-C. Reynard or W. Reddy showed how shopkeepers' confusion between private and public spheres demonstrated the lack of an autonomous commercial field.[60] Shopkeepers wished to demonstrate to creditors the burden of ordinary and modest family expenses (housing, nurse, illnesses, etc.). They tried to avoid any evidence of dissipation and fraud. Most of the bankrupts posed as victims. They cited "evil times" (*le malheur des temps*), "trade difficulties" (*la difficulté du commerce*), "unfortunate circumstances" (*des circonstances malheureuses*), and they begged for the "indulgence" (*indulgence*), "leniency" (*clémence*), "condescension" (*condescendance*) and "help" (*secours*). All insisted on the advantage of an agreement. The forces of credit and time were recurrent elements of their narrative. Bankrupts were aware of the damage but pleaded helplessness; they presented their resort to credit as mandatory and uncontrollable, because they could not master time frames. Several shopkeepers pointed to the key issues: duration and chronology of business. The watchmaker Fagard clearly related credits, losses and time:

> the credits he was bound to give and the losses he suffered because of these credits over several years, having significantly reduced his business and his fortune, forced him to fail in his commitments to them, all the more as the claims due to him for which he had some hope are of hard and difficult recovery [...]. And the above-named creditors, after acquainting themselves with the situation of the aforesaid master Fagard, having perfect knowledge of the losses he suffered because of the credit he had to give [...] made the decision was unanimously made and deliberated to rescue the aforesaid master Fagard.[61]

Admittedly, a capable shopkeeper did not get caught in a credit crunch but at the same time the omnipresence of credit explained the leniency of the creditors and the ease with which they granted cancellations or deadlines.

In the settlement process the reputation of the shopkeeper was vital. All the bankrupts asked their assembled creditors to choose terms "enabling them to continue their business" (*en état de continuer [leur] commerce*). The objective was to avoid the risk of legal and liquidation proceedings, to put an end to the "rigorous pursuits" (*poursuites rigoureuses*) and personal imprisonment, to get schedule of payments and, whenever possible, a cancellation of debts. "Avoid his complete ruin" (*éviter sa ruine totale*) was a near constant leitmotiv. To achieve this, bankrupts had to convince creditors of their "good faith" (*bonne foi*), their "honor" (*honneur*), their "integrity" (*probité*). They needed at all costs to distinguish themselves from fraudulent bankrupts. The ultimate goal was to recover the trust of their peers, to regain a position among them and to regain access to credit. The haberdasher Bonein insisted:

> He dares pride himself that the ease, which the cancellations just granted will give him, will enable him to extend his business by facilitating suppliers credit and turnover; he may then settle all his debts and, hence, fulfil his conscience and accurate integrity.[62]

Conclusion

Credit relations held an ambiguous intensity: they raised questions of economy and society, of finance and law. The shop represented an essential locus of the credit market on which flourishing commercial activity was based. It was in truth a market because credit had a cost, a perimeter of action and followed specific rules. It was nonetheless also informal, hence the questions about contractual relations, disputes, negotiation. Disputes between shopkeepers did not necessarily imply economic crisis or social dysfunction; they rather expressed the cheapest way to get legal guarantees to continue credit relations under difficult circumstances.[63] The common occurrence of postponement—a voluntary deed signed before a notary—meant that the bankruptcy settlement aimed in no way at breaking the links between the shopkeeper and his creditors but rather at strengthening them by law. The aim was to redefine the rules of the game between the actors who knew each other and were obliged to cooperate in the same field: The "postponement law,"[64] as Guyot defined it, provided the framework for stabilized relations. For many creditors, the objective was not to end the relation by demanding the complete refund of debts but rather to be able to continue it.

Notes

1 Many thanks to Marie-Agnès Dequidt for the translation.

2 S.L. Kaplan, *Le meilleur pain du monde: Les boulangers de Paris au XVIIIe siècle* (Paris 1996), p. 159.

3 J. Bouvier, "Vers le capitalisme bancaire: l'expansion du credit après Law," in F. Braudel and E. Labrousse (eds.), *Histoire économique et sociale de la France, 1660–1789*, Vol. II (Paris 1970), 301–21; H. Lüthy, *La Banque protestante en France: De la révocation de l'Édit de Nantes à la Révolution*, Vol. III (Paris 1959–61), 9–46.

4 E. Labrousse, "Inflation d'argent, inflation d'or: Le stock monétaire français: doublement, triplement?" in F. Braudel and E. Labrousse (eds.), op. cit., Vol. II, 394–5; M. Morineau, *Incroyables gazettes et fabuleux métaux: Les retours des trésors américains d'après les gazettes hollandaises, XVIe-XVIIIe siècle* (Paris 1985), 351–549; J. Meuvret, "Circulation monétaire et utilisation économique de la monnaie dans la France du XVIe et du XVIIe siècle," *Études d'histoire économique: Recueil d'articles. Cahier des Annales*, 32 (Paris 1971), 127–38.

5 L. Bergeron, "Les réseaux de la finance internationale," in P. Léon (ed.), *Histoire économique et sociale du monde*, Vol. III (Paris 1978), 119–35; F. Braudel, *Civilisation matérielle, économie et capitalisme, XVe-XVIIIe siècle* (Paris 1979), I: 411; Meuvret, "Circulation monétaire," pp. 127–38.

6 D. Defoe, *The Complete English Tradesman* (London 1726), 198.

7 B.L. Anderson, "Money and the Structure of Credit in the Eighteenth Century," *Business History* 12 (1970): 85–101; C. Muldrew, *The Economy of Obligation: The Culture of Credit and Social Relations in Early Modern England*, (Basingstoke 1998), 95; C. Muldrew, "'Hard Food for Midas': Cash and its Social Value in Early Modern England," *Past and Present* 170 (2001): 78–120.

8 P. Hoffman, G. Postel-Vinay and J.-L. Rosenthal, "Économie et politique: Les marchés du credit à Paris, 1750–1840," *Annales. Histoire, sciences sociales* 1 (1994): 65–98; P. Hoffman, G. Postel-Vinay and J.-L. Rosenthal, *Des marchés sans prix: Une économie politique du credit à Paris, 1660–1870* (Paris 2001); P. Léon, "Les nouvelles élites," in F. Braudel and E. Labrousse (eds.), *Histoire économique et sociale de la France, 1660–1789*, op. cit., Vol. II, 610 *et seq*.

9 "[É]quilibre précaire, au bord, sans fin, de la culbute," F. Braudel, *Civilisation matérielle*, op. cit., Vol. II, 57; J. Hoppit, "The Use and Abuse of Credit in Eighteenth-Century England," in N. McKendrick and R.B. Outhwaite (eds.), *Business Life and Public Policy: Essays in Honour of D.C. Coleman* (Cambridge 2002), 66–7.

10 J.-Y. Grenier, *L'Économie d'Ancien Régime: Un monde de l'échange et de l'incertitude* (Paris 1996), 425; B. Lepetit, "Le présent de l'histoire," in B. Lepetit (ed.), *Carnet de croquis: Sur la connaissance historique* (Paris 1999), 252 *et seq*.

11 I studied 140 accounting documents in the Paris Archives (*Archives de Paris*) and in the notary files from the National Archives (*Minutier central des Archives nationales*), including 61 bankruptcy files, 36 post-mortem inventories of estate, 24 contracts of postponement or of creditors' union which included assessments or debts statements.

12 B. Colasse, *Comptabilité générale: Questions et applications* (Paris 2003), 42.

13 A.G. Hopwood and P. Miller (eds.), *Accounting as Social and Institutional Practice* (Cambridge 1994), 1–2.

14 K.J. Arrow, *The Limits of Organization* (New York 1974).
15 Muldrew, "Hard Food for Midas," 83; Hoppit, "The Use and Abuse of Credit," 65.
16 J.-C. Martin, "Le commerçant, la faillite et l'historien," *Annales. Économies, sociétés, civilisations* 6 (1980): 1251–68.
17 A. Orléan, "Sur le rôle respectif de la confiance et de l'intérêt dans la constitution de l'ordre marchand," *Revue du mouvement anti-utilitariste dans les sciences sociales, À qui se fier? Confiance, interaction et théorie des jeux* 4 (1994): 17–36, esp. 19.
18 This work derives from a *habilitation à diriger des recherches* (professorial thesis) entitled "La boutique à Paris au XVIIIe siècle," University of Paris I, 2006. See also N. Coquery, *Tenir boutique à Paris au XVIIIe siècle: Luxe et demi-luxe* (Paris 2011), 273–300.
19 M. Granovetter, "Economic Action and Social Structure: The Problem of Embeddedness," *American Journal of Sociology* 91 (1985): 481–93; D.C. North, *Institutions, Institutional Change and Economic Performance* (Cambridge 1991). See also B. Pecqueur and J.-B. Zimmermann (eds.), *Économie de proximités* (Paris 2004), 21.
20 J.-C. Martin, *Commerce et commerçants à Niort au XIXe siècle: Les faillites, summary of Commerce et commerçants de Niort et des Deux-Sèvres aux XVIIIe et XIXe siècles* (Paris 1978), 500; J.-C. Martin, "Le commerçant, la faillite et l'historien," *Annales. Économies, sociétés, civilisations* 6 (1980): 1251–68, esp. 1251.
21 The corpus gathers 47 jewelers, nine goldsmiths, 17 tapestry-makers and tapestry-and-mirror makers, 11 watchmakers and two merchants for comparative purposes. The way shopkeepers called themselves was preserved as far as translation permitted. A total of 63 files are bankruptcy statements from the series D4B6 of Paris archives (*archives de Paris, Arch. de Paris*) or from the notary archives in the National archives (*minutier central des Archives nationales, A.N.*); 33 come from post-mortem assets inventories. Some files were too incomplete to be taken into account. The 88 statements used are spread as follows: one in 1715, one in 1726, one in 1738, two in 1742, one in 1750, three in 1751, three in 1753, one in 1762, two in 1766, three in 1768, three in 1770, one in 1771, two in 1772, three in 1774, one in 1776, six in 1777, two in 1778, eight in 1779, seven in 1780, six in 1781, three in 1782, seven in 1783, six in 1784, two in 1785, two in 1787, three in 1788, six in 1789, two in 1790, one in 1791, one in 1792 (see Table 4.1). The commercial crisis of 1777 appears, as do the years 1779–1784 or the year 1789, but a small sample makes a formal reasoning difficult.
22 N. Coquery, *L'hôtel aristocratique: Le marché du luxe à Paris au XVIIIe siècle* (Paris 1998); N. Coquery, "The Language of Success: Marketing and Distributing Semi-Luxury Goods in Eigtheenth-Century Paris," *Journal of Design History, Special Issue: Disseminating Design: The French Connection* 17 (2004): 71–89.
23 For Serge Chassagne, the absence of working capital due to the inelasticity of the financial market was one of the recurring defects of the Ancien Regime. "Cela tient parfois à la rareté du numéraire, toujours à l'inexistence d'un système de credit efficace, et aussi probablement à l'absence d'une comptabilité minutieuse et régulière," S. Chassagne, "Faillis en Anjou au XVIIIe siècle: Contribution à l'histoire économique d'une province," *Annales ESC* 2 (1970): 477–97, esp. 492–3, see also, 416; Meuvret, "Circulation monétaire," 132.
24 Bergeron, "Les réseaux de la finance internationale," 369; C. Carrière, *Négociants marseillais au XVIIIe siècle: contribution à l'étude des économies maritimes*, Vol. II (Marseille 1973), 793–874; D.A. Kent, "Small Businessmen and their Credit Transactions in Early Nineteenth-Century Britain," *Business History* 36 (1994): 47–64; Martin, *Commerce et commerçants*, 476–81.
25 Coquery, *Tenir boutique*, 286–300.
26 The statement uses the words account receivable (*dettes actives*) and liabilities (*dettes passives*).

Les dettes actives, c'est ce qui nous est dû; les dettes passives, c'est ce que nous devons. [...] on compte de trois sortes de dettes actives; celles qui sont bonnes et exigibles, celles qui sont douteuses, et celles que l'on croit absolument perdues. On compte aussi de trois sortes de dettes passives; l'argent de dépôt; ce qu'on doit aux particuliers, qui ne sont point négocians, ni marchands; et ce que l'on doit aux marchands et négocians avec lesquels on est en commerce.

See "Dettes," in J. Savary des Bruslons, *Dictionnaire universel de commerce...*, 3 vols (Paris 1741).

27 Bankruptcy law relied on two texts: the royal decree of 1673 and the statement of 1739. In Paris, three jurisdictions were in charge of commerce: the Châtelet, the commercial court (*la juridiction consulaire*), the Bureau of the City (*Bureau de la ville*). The royal decree of 1673 handed the bankruptcy jurisdiction over to the royal judge, but gave the power to check the claims, debt states and account books to the commercial court. Because of the increasing number of bankruptcies, a statement of 1715, renewed, handed absolute jurisdiction to the consular magistrates. After the reaction of the Châtelet, the statement of 1739, applicable in Paris, stated that in all bankruptcies and fraudulent bankruptcies the royal magistrates would not receive claim assertions and would not ratify any deadline contract without the titles being examined by the judges and consuls. See, among others: P. Dupieux, "Les attributions de la juridiction consulaire de Paris (1563–1792): L'arbitrage entre associés, commerçants, patrons et ouvriers au XVIIIe siècle," *Bibliothèque de l'École des chartes* 95 (1935): 116–48, esp. 134; J.-L. Lafon, "L'arbitre près la juridiction consulaire de Paris au XVIIIe siècle," *Revue historique de droit français et étranger* 51 (1973): 217–70; J.-L. Lafon, *Les Députés du commerce et l'Ordonnance de Mars 1673: Les juridictions consulaires: principe et compétence* (Paris 1979), 113–34; A.D. Kessler, *A Revolution in Commerce: The Parisian Merchant Court* (New Haven, CT 2007).

28 The number of creditors per shopkeeper ranged from five (the jeweler Sévenet) to 107 (the jeweler Granchez).

29 Grenier, *L'Économie d'Ancien Régime*, 417–18.

30 Arch. de Paris, D4B6 69–4518, Leconte; D4B6 82–5521, Nollet; D4B6 90–6197, Virlouret.

31 They were goldsmiths, jewelers, merchants, toy dealer, watchmakers, mirror-makers, caster, gilder, varnisher, enamel maker, cutler, fan-maker, the Queen's china factory, the royal crystal factory in Besançon, etc. Most of the claims were notes that were "ready made value in goods [...] and current account" ("tous faits valeur en marchandises [...] et en compte courant") (*Arch. de Paris*, D4B6 91–6280, creditors list, 1787, Granchez, deposition of Léon Zacharie, Jewish merchant, checked claims list).

32 Thomas Grey, 90e creditor on the list, merchant in London, represented by Dominique Daguerre then settled in the English capital but holding a shop *rue Saint-Honoré* in Paris. Daniel Holy's deposition (103e) mentioned London as place of residence although the business was in Sheffield. See C. Sargentson, *Merchants and Luxury Markets: The Marchands Haberdashers of Eighteenth-Century Paris* (London 1996), 126. Granchez also owed 25,000 livres to his son for "pension revenue and various refunds" ("produits de rentes et divers remboursemens").

33 The jeweler still owed 100,000 livres to 35 goldsmiths, out of which 19,000 to Blerzy and 17,000 to Marcillac, 18,000 to seven watchmakers, 12,000 to eight toy dealers, 8,800 to the Queen's china factory, 4,000 to two mirror-makers, etc.

34 Blezimar, bankrupt in 1779 with assets of 15,000 livres, was Granchez's (asset of 400,000 livres) and Clément's creditor (12,800 livres); Granchez, bankrupt in 1787, was Dezarot's (41,000 livres) and Diodet's creditor (2,800 livres)...

35 Company set between Diddet, Armenian shopkeeper in Constantinople, usually in Constantinople, residing *rue de l'Arbre-Sec* (Paris), and Casadur dit Chamas, Chaldean shopkeeper from Mesopotamia, same street, 6 August 1738, A.N., minutier central, et/X/445.

36 "[L]ivré par confiance [à Bélalie frères] une boëte de porcelaine en email figures flamande, pour être vendu la somme de 30)," Jobart's statement, jeweler haberdasher, 9 April 1778, Arch. de Paris, D4B6 67–4373.

37 "[À] James Staphens, marchand londonien pour marchandises confiées ... 3,880," Étienne Dubois's statement, agent merchant, *bourgeois de Paris*, 1779, Arch. de Paris, D4B6 42–2364.

38 "[E]n fausses pertes dans l'association [avec le sieur Roger] [...] et perte commune pour ma part de portion ... 6,000," Claude Guillermet's statement, privileged jeweler, 28 March 1781, Arch. de Paris, D4B6 80–5369.

39 Arch. de Paris, D4B6 77–5135, 26 May 1780, Jean Nicolas Lecuyer's statement, jeweler. The jeweler Claude-Luc Langlois was creditor of an "honor note" (*billet d'honneur*) (1,792 livres) owed by the marquis de Fénelon, of three "honor notes" (572 livres) owed by the baron de Fénelon and about ten others (*Arch. de Paris*, D4B6 70–4603, 19 January 1779, statement). Jouy, ribbon dealer, stated that, at the time of the first bankruptcy of the jeweler Guy, "about six or seven years ago" ("il y a six à sept ans environ"), he was creditor for 4,000 livres, none refunded, and that he has "again had the great weakness to give [...] another two thousand livres in cash about two to three months ago without asking for note nor acknowledgment" ("il a 'encore eu la plus grande faiblesse de donner [...] deux autres mille livres en espèces il y a environ deux ou trois mois sans prendre aucun billet ni reconnaissance") (*arch. de Paris*, D4B6 64–4154, June 1780, creditors list).

40 "Perdu avec le nommé Frigelly Italien demeurant a Gennes par marchandises de confiance que je lui ai livré en 1777 ... 4,005," Claude Guillermet's statement, privileged jeweler, 28 March 1781, Arch. de Paris, D4B6 80–5369.

41 "[P]lusieurs marchandises confiées à différens particuliers et pertes sur icelles ... 2,500," *Etat des dettes* ... (Statement of debts) of Jacques Lebœufve, haberdasher-jeweler, 22 August 1768, Arch. de Paris, D4B6 32–1723.

42 "Le gain semble être quelque chose de très casuel, qui suppose des risques et du hasard: voilà pourquoi ce mot est d'un grand usage pour les joueurs et pour les commerçants." Article "Gain" in the *Encyclopédie*. See J.-Y. Grenier, *L'Économie d'Ancien Régime*, 103.

43 "C'est l'état dans lequel se trouve un marchand [...] dont les affaires sont tellement dérangées, qu'il est dans l'impossibilité de remplir les engagemens qu'il a contractés, et d'acquitter les sommes dont il s'est rendu débiteur." See J.-N. Guyot, *Répertoire universel et raisonné de jurisprudence*... 17 vols (Paris 1784–85), 273.

44

> [S]i la confiance facilite une infinité d'affaires, elle cause aussi une infinité de maux dans le commerce lorsque ceux qui ont eu de la confiance pour quelques-uns la retirent tout d'un coup et refusent le credit à ceux auxquels ils avaient accoutumé d'en donner.

See S. Ricard, *L'Art de bien tenir les livres de comptes en parties doubles* ... (Amsterdam 1724).

45 *Arch. de Paris*, D4B6 70–4603, 19 January 1779, statement, preliminary observations, Claude-Luc Langlois, jeweler.

46 C. Dupuy and A. Torre, "Confiance et proximité," in B. Pecqueur and J.-B. Zimmermann (eds.), *Économie de proximités* (Paris 2004), 65–87.

47 "[*R*]*ésolutions prises dans l'assemblée des créanciers*," Royal decree of 1673. See G. Antonetti, "La faillite dans la pratique notariale à Paris aux XVIIe et XVIIIe siècles," *Revue internationale d'histoire du notariat, le Gnomon* 63 (1988): 4–11, esp. 5. Current practice deeds (stemming from collective creditors resolution) were worked out empirically to be used as regulation for bankruptcies before becoming the common law.

48 J.E. Shaw, "Liquidation or Certification? Small Claims Disputes and Retail Credit in Seventeenth-Century Venice," in B. Blondé, P. Stabel. J. Stobart and I. Van Damme

(eds.), *Le Parfait Négociant: Buyers, Sellers and Salesmanship in Medieval and Early Modern Europe (Italy, the Low Countries and England)* (Brepols 2006), 277–95.

49 N. Coquery and N. Praquin, "Règlement des faillites et pratiques judiciaires: De l'entre-soi à l'expertise du syndic (1673–1889)," *Histoire et Mesure* 23 (2008): 43–83.

50 J. Hilaire, *Introduction historique au droit commercial* (Paris 1986), 324.

51 [L]esquels estans informés du mauvais état des affaires dudit sieur Seriny qu'aucuns de ses créanciers ont saisy et exécuté ses meubles et fait saisir réellement ses immeubles craignans que les différentes procédures et l'établissement de plusieurs procureurs ne causent des frais considérables et des longeurs dans la discution en justice des biens dudit sieur Seriny, ce qui causeroit préjudice auxdits sieurs créanciers et diminuroit de beaucoup le produit des effets qui doivent servir à leur payement, se sont assemblés pour prévenir à ces inconvéniens et aviser à prendre de concert un party favorable à leurs interests et après avoir délibéré entre eux ils sont convenus et demeuréz d'accord de ce qui suit.

A.N., et/CXV/363, 29 October 1715, creditors' union contract, Paul de Seriny, goldsmith jeweler

52 J.-N. Guyot, *Répertoire universel*, Vol. I, 696–7.

53 Translator's note: bankruptcy, in this case, is seen from the shopkeepers' point of interest and not with a legal view.

54 Antonetti, "La faillite," 10.

55 [A]nd the aforesaid creditors [...] agreed to grant the aforesaid Calame the aforesaid cancellation complete of the interests and expenses [...] and to grant him a ten years deadline, six of which with no payment at all to then pay the principal claims in the four other years by quarter, with a first settlement date at the end of the seventh year.

A.N., et/LXV/476, 18 August 1785, Postponement, Christian Calame, watchmaker

("Et lesdits sieurs créanciers [...] sont convenus de faire audit Calame ladite remise pure et simple des intérêts et frais [...] et de luy accorder le délai de dix années dont six sans rien payer pour ensuite faire le payement des créances principales dans le cours des quatre autres années par quart d'année en année dont la première échéance à la fin de la septieme année.")

56 [L]esdits sieurs et dames créanciers [...] convaincus qu'il n'y a de la part dudit sieur Bonein ni inconduite, ni dissipation, et pleins de confiance dans sa probité, son activité et son intelligence, sont demeurés d'accord de ce qui suit. [...] ils lui rendirent la justice de le reconnoître pour un marchand exact et de bonne foy.

A.N., et/XXIX/566, 27 January 1782, convention, Joseph Bonein, haberdasher

57 [Art. 6: Le but de Langlois l'Aîné est] d'assurer audit sieur Langlois Jeune la conservation de son commerce et de prévenir sa ruine totale [...]. [L'engagement qu'il prend] n'aura d'effet qu'autant que [son frère] sera remis en possession de son commerce, qu'il ne sera donné aucune suite audit acte d'abandon ainsy qu'aux délibérations [...]. [Art. 8] et attendu l'intérêt dont il est pour tous les créanciers d'accepter les obligations dudit sieur Langlois L'Aîné puisqu'elles leur assurent la rentrée de 40 pour cent des capitaux de leurs créances tandis que l'abandon [...] présente dans son exécution des embarras, des longueurs et des pertes qui ne permettent pas de conserver le même espoir [les créanciers assurent à Langlois le Jeune de faire exécuter le présent acte.

A.N., et/XXVII/495, 23 December 1789, creditors union contract, Luc-Augustin Langlois, jeweler

58 A.N., et/LXV/460, 7 December 1782, postponement, Laurent-Pierre Jourdain, tapestry and mirror-maker.

59 P.-C. Reynard noticed four kinds of arguments in the bankrupts' words in Languedoc. See P.-C. Reynard, "The Language of Failure: Bankruptcy in Eighteenth-Century France," *Journal of European Economic History* 30 (2001): 355–90, esp. 364–74.

60 W. Reddy, *The Rise of Market Culture: The Textile Trade and French Society, 1750–1900* (Cambridge 1984), 20–1.

61 [L]es crédits qu'il a été obligé de faire et les pertes qu'il a essuyées par ses crédits depuis plusieurs années ayant considérablement diminuer son commerce et sa fortune l'ont mis luy même dans la nécessité de manquer aux engagemens qu'il avoit pris avec eux, qu'il s'y est cru d'autant plus forcé dans ce moment que les créances à luy dues et sur lesquelles il avoit quelques eperances sont d'un recouvrement difficile et douteux [...]. Et lesdits créanciers susnommés après avoir pris connoissance de la situation dudit sieur Fagard ayant parfaite connoissance des pertes qu'il a essuyé par les crédits qu'il a été obligé de faire, [...] il a été unanimement arrêté et délibéré de venir au secours dudit sieur Fagard.

A.N., et/XCI/1135, 23 January 1776, postponement, Nicolas Fagard, watchmaker

62 Il ose même se flatter que la facilité que lui procureront les remises qui viennent de lui être consenties lui permettent de donner plus d'etendue à son commerce lui facilitant les crédits des fournisseurs, et le débit, il pourra par la suite faire honneur à la totalité de ses créances, et par là satisfaire à sa conscience et son exacte probité.

Joseph Bonein, haberdasher, postponement, 14, 15, 16, 18 and 20 July 1783, et/XXIX/566

63 J.E. Shaw, "Liquidation or Certification?" 277–95.

64 "[L]a loi de l'Atermoiement," J.-N. Guyot, *Répertoire universel*, Pt. I, 697, art. "Atermoiement."

5 Financial networks, migration and the transformation of the merchant elite in 18th-century Stockholm[1]

Klas Nyberg and Håkan Jakobsson

Introduction

Over the past 15 years, a growing number of researchers have presented new results on the social, genealogical, ethnic and financial networks among early modern merchants. Attention has been paid among other things to the extensive transnational kinship- and credit-networks that developed among immigrant merchants and producers in strategically important commercial cities and areas. During the early modern period, mercantile colonies were first formed in the principal countries of Europe and Asia, and subsequently in Europe's peripheries, Southeast Asia and North America. The colonies were often, but not always, unified by religion.[2]

Besides investing in their respective merchant houses, many immigrant merchants also played an important role in negotiating foreign credit for their new countries. Researchers have often assumed that large merchant houses played a decisive role in providing capital for the development of industrial society before the second half of the nineteenth century.[3] This view has also been applied in Scandinavia and Sweden. In Sweden the crucial role of merchant houses in Stockholm and Gothenburg has frequently been stressed.[4] The affluent members of the so-called "Skeppsbro Nobility" in Stockholm, and members of the British merchant colony in Gothenburg, in particular, have been considered central to the handling and financing of the iron export trade and industry.[5]

The mostly one-sided focus by Swedish researchers on the large exporters from Great Britain and Germany has, however, long concealed the fact that wholesale trading in Stockholm comprised a myriad of trading forms and activities of various scale and extent in the eighteenth century. The list of titles defining various kinds of traders, often compiled for statistical purposes, hides the complexity of activities pursued by the individuals in question, such as financial transactions, traditional export- combined with import-trade, and investments in handicraft and textile manufacture. We generally know very little about how trade and production were financed, and how financial networks were constructed using local, regional, public and international capital.[6]

The aim of this chapter is to highlight the financial networks of early modern migrant merchants, by studying how wholesale traders handled crises and

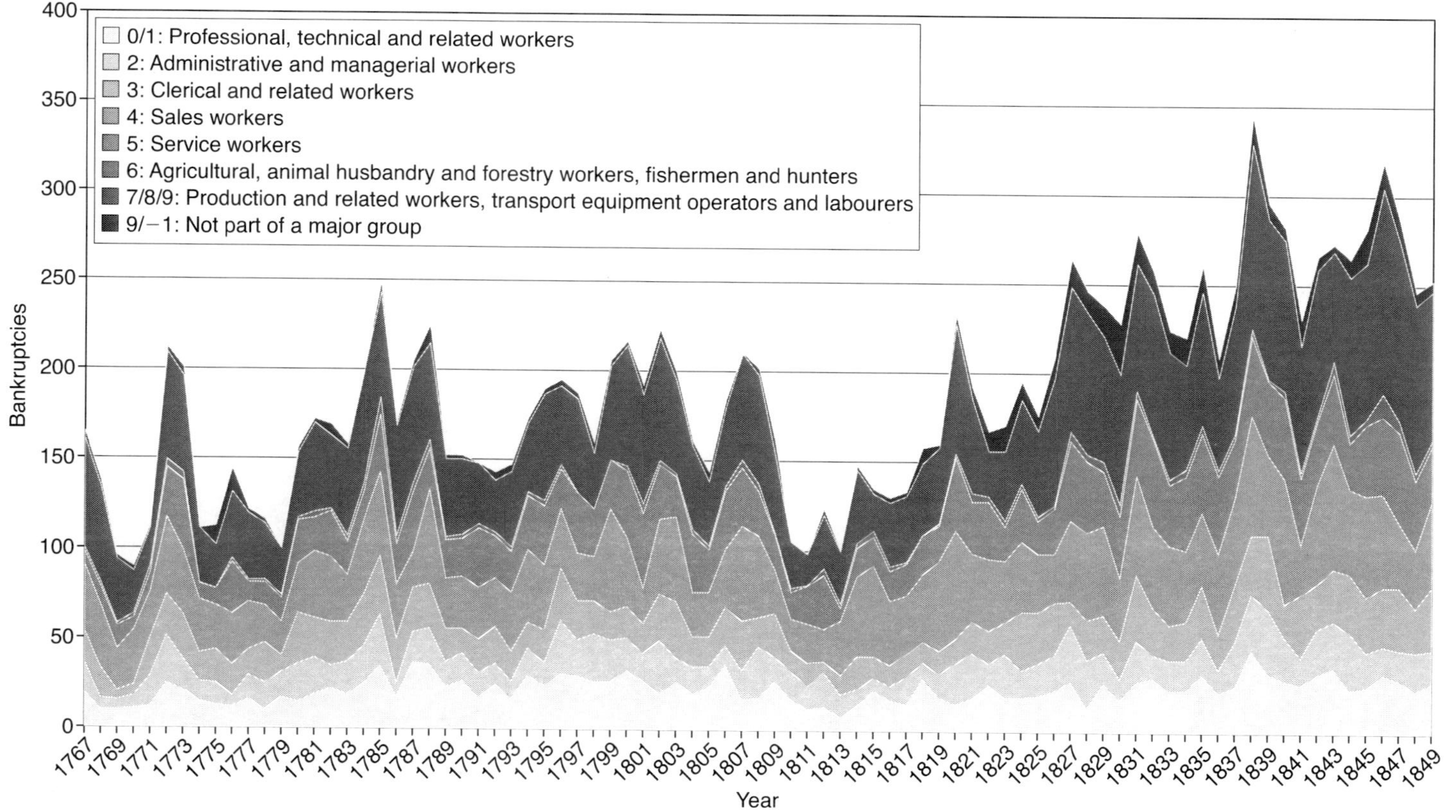

Figure 5.1 Number of reported bankruptcies in Stockholm 1707–1849, classified according to HISCO head groups.

Note

0/1 = professionals and technicians, 2 = administrators, 3 = clerks and officials, 4 = merchants and vendors, 5 = service workers, 6 = farmers and farm workers, 7/8/9 = artisans and laborers, 9/–1 = not part of a group.

breakdowns during bankruptcy proceedings. The viewpoints presented in the chapter are based on studies of all preserved bankruptcy cases involving insolvent wholesale traders in Stockholm between 1740 and 1800, but also include bankruptcy material from a range of other industrial and professional groups.[7]

One of the key objectives of the analysis is to show that concepts such as credit, security and dowries should not be considered in strictly economic quantities. Financial relations between companies and individuals, based on promissory notes, cheques, bills of exchange, were on the contrary often embedded in social and professional networks developed around kinship, gender, ethnicity and confession.[8]

The chapter is organised as follows. First, we present how the concepts of credit and trust were embedded in early modern financial networks and how private individuals and civil servants interacted to administer the credit networks during bankruptcy proceedings. After that, we present the basic tendencies and features of merchant migration and trade in eighteenth-century Stockholm. This is followed by a presentation and analysis of the development and role of wholesale traders and trading houses in Stockholm during the period from 1740 to 1800. Finally we discuss the financial networks of the wholesale traders, based on bankruptcy cases, with a point of departure in the 1776 bankruptcy of the important trading house Appelroth & Spalding.

Credit and trust

Credit relations in the eighteenth and early nineteenth centuries were built around personal networks, rather than banks and other credit institutions. The complex network relations between private actors and institutions all tended to be built on trust. To have a good credit rating meant that others trusted you as a person, and your increased trustworthiness as a business owner came from the various networks in which you participated.[9]

Large parts of the assets of wholesale traders, manufacturers and sometimes also artisans took the form of claims on other companies. If the owner of a major economic enterprise filed for bankruptcy, or lost his creditworthiness, other actors' claims on his assets were likely to be considered uncertain and were at risk of being treated as worthless. As soon as the bankruptcy was announced, their good debts became bad debts, and were typically also listed in either category in the financial statements drawn up in connection to the bankruptcy proceedings.[10] As a consequence, financial success in the early modern period often required a raft of different strategies.[11]

One important strategy was to spread one's debts amongst different individuals. That way, there would be a greater chance of not being hit so hard in the event of a bankruptcy. Our analyses of the bankruptcy material in Stockholm shows that large financiers monitored the frequent minor bankruptcies, even though the sums involved were comparatively small.[12] The behaviour can be viewed in the light of the greater possibility to secure small claims following the development of a more effective Swedish bankruptcy legislation. The

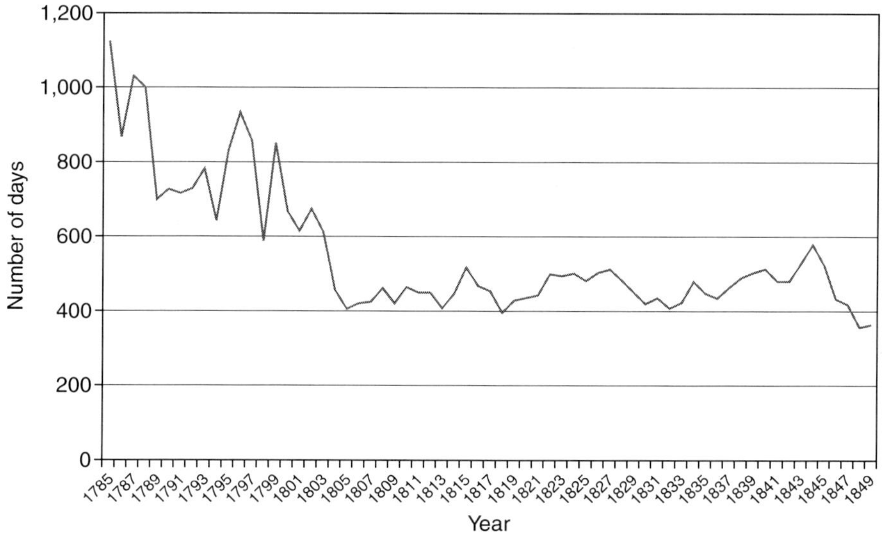

Figure 5.2 The average number of days for bankruptcy cases in Stockholm that started in a given year, 1785–1849.

development began with the revised bankruptcy laws of 1767, which provided for faster administration and played an important role in the reconstruction of credit networks and companies with the aim of reducing losses.[13]

As suggested above, financial networks should not just be seen as pure economic relations. Credit relations were embedded in social, economic and ethnic relations, and forged between individuals related by kinship or confession. These ties were consciously developed, for example through arrangements of godparentage, marriage, dowries and testaments.

In the event of bankruptcy, a wife's dowry risked being lost, and the couple risked destitution, even if a premarital settlement existed between the spouses. The children thus risked losing their inheritance. Dowries were part of a general problem related to the transfer of property between generations in early modern capital formation. Traders and manufacturers transferred capital to each other's businesses via daughters' dowries.

In bankruptcies in eighteenth-century Stockholm, debtors' wives commonly attempted to save the capital they had contributed by attempting to exclude it from the claimants' claim. Being legally incapacitated, women were owners of capital which they could not use. Access to the capital was granted to their male guardians: fathers, brothers or spouses. The women were only entitled to their capital as widows.[14] There existed a kind of underlying taboo, however, which prevented men from plundering their children's inheritances or their wife's dowry. If a spouse was declared bankrupt, women were able to cite the relevant section of the commercial code, the bankruptcy law and the marriage code in the

1734 general law, which defined the legal protection that married women's property enjoyed in the event of a bankruptcy.

Preliminary results suggest that the higher the social status of these women, the more likely they were to cite legal grounds in their arguments. Women from social groups in the lower middle classes were more likely to try to safeguard their dowries with emotion-based arguments.[15]

Once a bankruptcy became a reality, women from the middle classes often sought a judicial division of the estate. Typically, the claims were made with reference to the concept that the estate of the woman at the time of marriage should be unavailable to redeem any of her husband's possible future debts. To apply for a judicial division, in real terms a separation of property, was a common claim for a woman with a spouse who had abused his guardianship. A woman could also be released from her spouse's debts if it could be proved that the spouse had made decisions regarding her real estate without her approval.[16]

Many researchers have shown the existence and stressed the absolute necessity of extensive credit networks as a central part of early modern wholesale trade, and as an important part of the basic conditions of medieval and early modern entrepreneurship.[17] Being creditworthy had a further meaning, however, besides being a sound businessman with good liquidity. According to Fontaine, in the eighteenth century, the French word *crédit* meant that a person acquired respect through, for example, public office, had integrity, and was honest. *Crédit* was also linked to a person's reputation based on prosperity, power and authority, alongside the more commonly recognized economic aspects of good solvency and commercial credit.[18]

To minimize the damage from personal bankruptcy, institutional administration developed across early modern Europe. The underlying aim was partly to secure the estate's remaining assets and divide them between the claimants, and partly to ensure that none of the creditors was allowed to profit at the expense of the others through coercion or manipulation. A likely ambition was to minimise the potential damaging impact that an uncontrolled bankruptcy would have on local society and finance.

While the legal framework which regulated the bankruptcy procedure was developed and made more effective, we still know very little about how the practical administration of actual bankruptcy cases was handled in Sweden and the Scandinavian countries.[19] It is, for example, likely that different views on financial relations and credit in general, between different countries and even regions, also altered the effectiveness of the bankruptcy institution.[20]

The interaction between public and private actors in the handling of judicial and financial aspects of bankruptcy proceedings is a neglected aspect of the older history of the credit market. In Sweden, earlier research has often viewed the private and public granting of credit as separate phenomena. One of the aims of the investigations underway is to reveal their interplay.

Our investigations of bankruptcy cases and the bankruptcy procedure in eighteenth-century Stockholm shows that factors such as trust and repute played important roles in the interplay between private and public administrators during the handling of the economic instability following a bankruptcy. The city's civil servants managed the bankruptcy proceedings while special trustees, typically individuals with a vested interest in the bankruptcy and with thorough knowledge of the debtor's business, administered the bankruptcy resolution in line with increasingly detailed state regulations. Reputable local or state officials or private persons represented claimants who lived far away and, consequently, were unable to attend personally.[21]

In recent studies of the Paris credit market in the period 1690–1840, Hoffman, Postel-Vinay and Rosenthal have shown the huge significance of public notaries in Paris in ensuring that the private credit market worked properly. The notaries helped, among other things, to stabilise the credit networks, by applying strict regulations governing public loans.[22]

While the office of notary did not have the same impact in Sweden and the rest of Scandinavia, as it did in Italy, France, the United Provinces and Germany, an institutionalised system of public notaries was in place in Sweden. The Bills of Exchange Act of 1748 expressly stipulated that a protest on a bill of exchange should be set down in writing by a notary.[23]

The Swedish context

The migration patterns in Stockholm during the eighteenth century were influenced in particular by the commercial, maritime and manufacturing legislations of the time. Significant foreign elements settled in Stockholm during the eighteenth century, including new groups, such as Jews and individuals of Reformed and Catholic confession.[24] Certain groups were particularly sought after. Between 1739 and 1773, for example, around 2,000 specialist textile-workers and their families (altogether around 3,700 people) were recruited to build up a domestic textile expertise.[25] Almost one-half (around 1,600) came from the Verviers-Aachen area in the Vesdre region, which, at the time, was an important centre for the manufacture of woollen cloth.[26]

From the end of the Great Northern War in 1718 until the mid-1700s, the Stockholm economy fared relatively well, supported by legislation that included the Gulf of Bothnia Trade Restraint, which favoured Stockholm by denying northern Sweden and Finland the right to conduct foreign trade. In 1724, the Swedish Navigation Act, which supported Swedish merchants at the expense of foreign traders and regions, also came into force.[27] The regulations that unilaterally benefited the large exporters remained mostly intact until the international trading crisis of the 1760s and the emergence of the Cap Party. The Gulf of Bothnia Trade Restraint and the Navigation Act were repealed in the 1765/1766 session of the *Riksdag*, as were the full- and half-customs exemptions for Swedish ships, which had been renewed in 1722. The deregulation coincided with the birth of Stockholm's era of industrial stagnation.[28]

The establishment of merchant networks and the relationships between merchants and other groups in Stockholm during this period should be considered both in the context of the general shift in the economic climate and in the light of the transformation of the trading elite, because of growing immigration. Of particular importance in the latter respect was the establishment of the aforementioned group of large-scale merchants, the so-called "Skeppsbro Nobility" as a dominating group in the Stockholm middle class. These traders, who came from Great Britain, the United Provinces and Germany, primarily invested in the production and export of iron and copper from the Bergslagen region northwest of Stockholm. Following the end of the Great Northern War, the group became involved in trade and municipal government on a wider scale. Many of them had leading roles in the so-called Hat Party, which dominated the Swedish Age of Liberty. During the 1720s and 1730s, they pursued an active economic policy, which favoured their own special interests in Stockholm's trading activities at the expense of other social groups and regions.[29]

From 1720 to 1740, a growing economic divergence developed in Stockholm's middle class. During the period, the old class of textile importers for the most part disappeared, or were reduced to textile retailers, with a sharp drop in income as a result. At the same time, as already mentioned, a large number of skilled specialists immigrated, who were to have an important and, in part, new influence on the population. Some of the specialists, who were recruited from 1740 to 1765, later established as small-scale manufacturers. The main entrepreneurial groups in the manufacturing industry, however, were the large-scale wholesale merchants and, to a lesser extent, old textile importers.[30]

The establishment of financial networks among the new immigrants in Stockholm must be placed in a context that takes into account the historical background to Swedish integration in the larger European economy. The trade and production of high-grade copper and quality iron already in the late Middle Ages led to the establishment of permanent foreign merchant colonies in Stockholm and other Swedish staple towns. These early merchant colonies were almost exclusively made up of individuals of German origin. Although other groups, notably people from Scotland, the southern Netherlands and the United Provinces, entered Swedish society with greater frequency from the mid-sixteenth century onward, Germans remained the most numerous foreign group, also in the seventeenth and eighteenth centuries, with a particular presence among entrepreneurs and in the middle classes.[31]

Overall, the immigrants helped to integrate Sweden into international trade networks and helped to secure new migrants by tapping into new and exploiting established migration streams. They not only helped to finance the export of copper and iron, but they also communicated political, legal, economic and cultural impulses, including demands for religious freedom for non-Lutherans, for privileges and tax exemptions, and, often in conflict with the guild system, for the right to trade and produce goods. These influences and the general world of ideas carried by the international merchants often gave rise to social tension, when confronted with Swedish norms and legislation. International mercantile legal institutions as well as international mercantile practice often came into conflict with other social fields and interest groups in Sweden: members of the landowning nobility, who had strengthened their position in the seventeenth century;

the lower-middle class; and the practising Lutheran clergy. The migrants were, on the other hand, often supported by the Crown, government officials and the civil service, as well as by town magistrates.[32]

While by no means a uniform trend in Stockholm, the foreign influences doubtless played a part in the long-term disintegration of the key institutions of the *l'ancien regime* in Sweden. After the trade crisis of the 1760s, a transitional period, lasting until 1815 began in Sweden, which heralded the transition to modern times. During this period, the guild system and other corporative institutions started to weaken. The Swedish Tolerance Edict of 1782 granted freedom of religion to Catholic and, to a limited extent, Jewish believers. The privileges of the nobility were also increasingly questioned. While some politically active merchants played a leading role in this process, other immigrant groups joined the opposition. Those established in the textile sector in Stockholm, in particular, contributed to a corporative-based reaction, and textile manufacturers, retailers and craftsmen fought for the preservation of the guild system's principles.[33]

Wholesale trade represented a range of different company forms in eighteenth- and early nineteenth-century Stockholm. The economic activities, marital patterns and social, ethnic, financial and genealogical networks of the wholesale traders consequently varied considerably. During the period, 1740–1800, however, wholesale trade was typically conducted by small-scale, relatively short-lived trading houses.

It is important to consider the differences in scale and specialisation of the companies to correctly understand and interpret their function.[34] Recent research shows, for example, how a growing number of unmarried wholesale traders appeared in Stockholm from the middle of the century, coinciding with a long-term stagnation that afflicted the city from the 1760s onwards. Notably, the members of this group performed more poorly than the wholesale traders who were married.[35]

Earlier researchers have largely ignored diversity and instead mainly considered wholesale trade and trading houses as a unified category. By focusing attention on the largest traders and neglecting the more numerous minor trading houses, no systematic studies of the network relationships between merchants of various sizes and specialisation have been undertaken.[36] Research has, for example, been focused almost exclusively on the large exporters, even though the majority of the trading houses were active as importers, often also with involvement in small-scale trade in grain and foodstuff. The latter factor is significant, as it places wholesale trade in the same category as small-scale retail trade and, therefore, also connects it to the activities of various kinds of shopkeepers and merchants trading, for example, in silk and draperies.[37]

Between 1740 and 1800 the tendency was for the gap between wholesale and small wares trade in terms of average tax capacity to become further reinforced. The traders in small wares had the highest income level amongst retailers. Their income levels remained fairly stable during the second half of the eighteenth century, however. Traders in foodstuffs and, to a lesser extent, ironmongers strengthened their position but still had income levels which were 25 per cent below the small wares traders. Among the handicraft trades, linen traders strengthened their position while the position of flax traders weakened. The position of spice merchants and general dealers also weakened in terms of average tax capacity after 1760.[38]

The total number of wholesale traders in Stockholm was just under 100 per year before the mid-1700s, rising to just over 100 towards the end of the century. It should be noted that these numbers reflect the individuals who were categorised as wholesale traders in the ordinary tax registers.[39] This means that many of the largest and wealthiest wholesale traders are overlooked, since they were often classified separately, based on their other interests or official positions, for example as iron-mill owners or trade councillors, even though they had originally received privileges as wholesale traders. These additional individuals are not included in the analysis below, which only looks at people with the title of wholesale trader, registered in the so-called ordinary contribution, a record of the part of the tax levied as a reflection of the income from operations administered by the Stockholm Means Committee (*Bemedlingskommissionen*). It means that the number of really big wholesalers included in the following is lower than would be the case, if all taxpayers who previously had privileges as wholesale traders were included.

While a rough measure of the extent of the trading operations among reported wholesale traders can be obtained by using the ordinary contribution, it is important to determine the extent to which the tax level was adjusted after inflation, which was fairly high during the latter half of the eighteenth century. If the taxation values took into account the price changes, the sum of the ordinary contribution in fixed prices would give a more accurate picture of the total income trend among wholesalers compared to current prices. The accuracy is determined by how often the taxation levels were set after being adjusted in relation to the price trend. This probably happened, but it is difficult to know how often without extensive studies.[40]

Although roughly 100 trading houses existed in Stockholm for each year during the period of investigation, over 130 were reported in 1770. Calculations of taxation values, undertaken every ten years, show that the trading houses were fairly evenly divided into two size groups. The number of small trading houses – here defined as trading houses with a taxation value below the mean value of distribution – varied between 40 and 50 companies, while the number of large trading houses stood around 30, from the mid-1700s onwards.[41]

The smaller trading houses only accounted for a modest share of the financial profits of the entire group, frequently below 20 per cent. During the final quarter of the eighteenth century, the small trading houses only contributed around 10 per cent of the total taxation of the entire wholesale trade. Long term, the smallest of the smaller trading houses fared relatively well. The greatest losers were the medium-sized houses, while the greatest winners were the largest trading houses. Up until the mid-1700s, the latter group accounted for slightly more than half of the ordinary contribution of the entire group of wholesale traders. Thereafter, they strengthened their position so that, at the turn of the nineteenth century, they accounted for just below 80 per cent.[42]

The financial networks of wholesale traders

When the trading house of Appelroth & Spalding declared itself bankrupt in March 1776, it reported accumulated debts that amounted to just over one million copper dollars. At the time, the business was led by Carl Appelroth (1718–1797) and Karl Jacob Spalding (1702–1772).[43]

Appelroth & Spalding was one of the largest trading houses in Stockholm during the period and, hence, one of the largest which has been considered as part of the on-going investigations. It had been formed by two individuals from the group of textile importers whose members were supporters of the Caps at the start of the Age of Liberty, and which subsequently was almost wiped out as a professional group during the eighteenth century. Johan Spalding (1669–1738), the father of Karl Jacob Spalding, was one of the leading textile traders in the political opposition to the protectionist customs laws passed between 1727 and 1738. His business partner was the tailor Olof Appelroth (1678–1744).[44]

The Spalding family was of Scottish origin. Members of the family included Anders Spalding who immigrated to Mecklenburg in Germany and Johan Spalding who moved to Norrköping in Sweden. Jacob Spalding, a son of Anders Spalding, in turn, emigrated from Mecklenburg to Norrköping. In Sweden, the various branches of the family were considerably involved in trade and in the foundry business. The investments in the important industrial centre of Norrköping and the nearby rural industrial community of Gusum mainly concerned the production and refining of brass, typically in the form of the manufacturing of nails and drawing of wire. Johan Spalding and his nephew Jacob (1697–1745), who was working in Stockholm, also became involved in import trade.[45]

By 1776, the trading house had been formally active for about three decades, a comparatively long time for a Stockholm company. The other wholesale traders who declared bankruptcy during the 1770s had been active for an average of just 15 years, which corresponded well with the 14-year average for the period between 1740 and 1800 as a whole.

The total number of creditors in the 1776 bankruptcy was around 35. The number and size of the debts were large compared to the average wholesale trading bankruptcy during the period. Besides creditors in Stockholm, several foreign creditors were listed, as well as a number of individuals from Gothenburg, the second most important trading town in Sweden. The debt structure of the bankruptcy was very strongly connected to the complex family and kinship-based networks which had become established in the generation before Carl Appelroth and Karl Jacob Spalding, centred on their fathers Johan Spalding and Olof Appelroth.

All debts outside Stockholm were to individuals who had family relations to the trading house. The largest debt, just over 340,000 copper dollars, was owed to Abraham Spalding (a brother of Karl Jacob), a merchant who resided in London. Another debt of just under 66,000 copper dollars, dating back to the marriage between Johan Spalding and Anna Christina Brander, was to the trading house, Spalding & Brander, also in London. A debt of 12,000 copper dollars was to Daniel Pettersson, a Gothenburg mayor who was married to

Hedvig Schméer, a daughter of Hedvig Dorothea Spalding (a sister of Karl Jacob), in her marriage to Johan Henrik Schméer. Yet another debt of 12,000 copper dollars was to Ulrika Appelroth in Norrköping (married Willemoth), the daughter of Anna Maria von Yhlen in her second marriage to Olof Appelroth. Anna Maria von Yhlen had previously been married to the merchant Baltzar Daniel Schméer. This marriage had produced the above-mentioned Johan Henrik Schméer. The complexity of the family arrangement becomes clear when considering that Karl Jacob Spalding, one of the leaders of the trading house, was married to Hedvig Appelroth, the sister of his business partner Carl Appelroth and thus the daughter of his father's business partner, Olof Appelroth.[46]

Debts in Stockholm were also connected to a number of individuals who fit into the kinship-based social network. Of the debts to individuals outside this family group, most were held by traders who belonged to the Caps and had vested interests in the textile import business. No confessional features seem to have structured the credit network. While some members of the Spalding family belonged to the non-territorial Lutheran St Gertrud's Church in Stockholm, the so-called "German Church," others were registered in the territorial parishes. The claimants were mainly of Lutheran and to some extent Reformed confessions.

The Appelroth & Spalding bankruptcy happened at a point in time when bankruptcies peaked among wholesale traders in Stockholm. Indeed, nearly half of the bankruptcies studied (37 out of 80) occurred in the 1770s. During the 1780s only 17 cases occurred. In the last decade of the century, the number dropped to just over ten. The high number of bankruptcies during the 1770s must be considered in the light of the rise in the number of active wholesale traders, which took place during the 1760s. The roughly 100 wholesale traders who were reported in the tax registers in 1760 had risen to slightly more than 130 ten years later. In the following decades, the number once more fell. By the turn of the century, the numbers were back to the levels of the 1760s.[47]

The level of bankruptcies must also be considered in the light of the trade crisis of the 1760s. It is difficult to argue, however, that the decline of the Appelroth & Spalding business was caused by the trade crisis. The ordinary contribution, the tax levy reflecting the incomes of operations, shows that the trading house grew from 200 silver dollars in 1760, to 250 silver dollars ten years later. While the trading house was one of the highest taxed, it was not one of the ten most prominent in terms of turnover.[48]

Financial networks, bankruptcy, public representatives and private officials

The 80 wholesale traders who declared bankruptcy during the period of investigation fell into two main groups, when categorised based on the structure of their financial networks. One group included traders who were restricted to the local market in Stockholm. The second group included traders who had financial relations with towns in other parts of Sweden and in larger commercial centres in other countries. Appelroth & Spalding belonged to the second group.

A wholesale trader's credit, in the broad sense of the word as discussed here, was built up over a succession of years, from the early years of apprenticeship, until he was free to operate independently. Often traders had parents and/or siblings who were also involved in trade or other middle-class businesses. During the years in apprenticeship, and later when working as a business clerk, the typical second stepping-stone before independent operation, the financial dealings of the would-be trader were guaranteed by the trading house in which he trained and worked. To be able to win the freedom to operate independently, the trader had to be formally examined by the Stockholm Board of Trade and the Wholesale Trade Society. The examination process and the application were sponsored by well-reputed wholesale traders or other middle-class citizens. In practice, the sponsors guaranteed the ability of the applicant to pay tax for the next five years. In terms of credit and trust, however, the pledge had a further significance in that the sponsors guaranteed that they had a personal confidence in the applicant, in other words, that they trusted him.

As shown in the analysis of the Appelroth & Spalding bankruptcy, leading business families were often strategically intermarried in complex ways. The approach was crucial to develop personal credit. The period leading up to a marriage, which for wholesale traders often happened relatively late, also involved securing credit. This could be accomplished, for example, through sound business dealings and by building networks with parents and siblings. Another strategy was to enter into a partnership with an established trader, often the head of the trading house where the would-be trader had been employed as an office clerk or worked as an apprentice. This strategy could also be realised by marrying into the family of the senior trader. Once a person was established as an independent wholesale trader and perhaps got married, his credit could be further developed and strengthened by taking on municipal or institutional responsibilities or by being elected by peers, as a sign of trust, to occupy a specific post or position. Another way to develop a network was to apply for membership in a fraternal organisation or similar societal group.[49] Credit was also secured by moving in the areas where business undertakings were planned and played out. In Stockholm, such areas included the Stock Exchange, the system of Public Scales, where iron and grain was weighed for export, the courtyard of the Stockholm court of law and the many cellars and eateries scattered around town.

The role of personal credit was also important when a wholesale trader declared bankruptcy. Once a wholesale trader's insolvency was made public, either the debtor could declare himself bankrupt or the creditors could request that the court declared him bankrupt. It was common for the insolvency to be announced in connection with the death of the debtor, which resulted in the estate being declared bankrupt. In all cases, the debtor was declared financially incapable and his financial assets were turned over to be administrated by the court.

Our research shows that the system of trust inherent in the financial networks often was threatened following a bankruptcy. Even though most debtors lacked illicit intentions, and saw bankruptcy only as a last measure, the initiation of insolvency proceedings almost always forced both the debtor and creditors to behave in ways that strained their relationship. In the worst cases, all confidence and personal trust between the parties disappeared and were replaced by hatred and desperation. Countless creditors tell a similar story, when they petitioned to be prioritised or quite simply to have the debtor removed in the bankruptcy proceedings. The often theatrical tone of the petitions was the product of a harsh reality. The imploring tone of a creditor should be considered in light of the fact that the claim formed an integral part of his reputation and credit. Without the possibility of regaining his assets, his own credit was soon to suffer.[50]

This situation was to a degree stabilised by the institutional and social context which surrounded the bankruptcy. From the time of the issue of the proclamation until the passing of a judgement, various public officials and private representatives came together to protect, defend and reconstruct the financial networks that were threatened by or had been destroyed by the bankruptcy.

The public officials included individuals who functioned as representatives for local and state bodies, such as the municipal tax office or the national Board of Commerce. Other officials represented public financial institutions, such as the Swedish Central Bank, as well as various exchange offices and loaning agencies. It was also common for public officials to function as proxies for private creditors who were unable to personally attend the first meeting of the bankruptcy proceedings and, by so doing, be accepted as legitimate. The private representatives played a key role as administrators of the actual assets in the bankruptcy, when taking charge of the administration of the bankruptcy estate, after the bankruptcy was accepted by the court. They also often acted as representatives for private Swedish and foreign creditors, whose claims had been certified as legitimate but who were unable to attend the proceedings and guard their interests.

An important aspect of the role of the representatives concerns their function and position in relation to the various social and financial networks which existed as a result of the affairs of the debtor. This also raises some new and interesting questions. Did previous employers, sponsors or relatives, either with vested financial or social interests, take on roles in the administration of the bankruptcy, to minimise the damage of the bankruptcy? If so, were they part of the immediate family or distant relations, or did they share confessional networks?

Conclusions

This chapter has discussed the origins, structure and reconstruction of financial networks in trading houses and among wholesale traders in Stockholm during the period 1740–1800. A particular focus has been on the importance of credit, trust and creditworthiness.

One of the key points made in the chapter concerned the importance of trust and credit when building a financial and social network, the precarious nature of these concepts and the combined efforts to preserve them, when the network was threatened by difficult circumstances caused by bankruptcy. The point of departure was a fairly well-known concept, namely that most network relations between individuals develop over time with multiple purposes. This can be illustrated in the career of a typical wholesale trader.

When a wholesale trader in the eighteenth century received his right to operate independently, a long period of training and trading would have ensured that he had developed extended networks, which established creditworthiness as well as social capital. Such networks often came under threat following the breakdown of trust-based relationships during bankruptcies. Creditors, in particular those without strong kinship connections to the debtor, often showed determination in securing their assets in order to be able to maintain their creditworthiness in relation to their own business circles. This pursuit also meant that they introduced further distrust and conflict to a system, already destabilised by bankruptcy.

We have, however, suggested that this situation was, if not solved, then at least alleviated or defused through the legal framework, together with the work of public officials and private representatives. Together these various institutions worked to manage the bankruptcy to ensure a smooth transition of assets in a way that preserved financial structures and social networks and safeguarded the stability of private and public financial structures and local society.

Appendix

Table 5.a.1 Bankruptcies of 80 wholesale traders in Stockholm 1740–1800

Act	*Year*	*Title*	*First name*	*Surname*
55a	1746	Handelsman	Paul	Norling
397	1746	Handelsman	Martin Albert	Overkkampf
299	1750	Handelsman	Olof	Bång
6	1753	Grosshandlaren	Michael	Hising
6	1753	Grosshandlaren	Wolter	Petersen
510	1759	Handelsman	Carl	Sifvert
159	1760	Handelsman	Carl Frantz	Funck
828	1765	Grosshandlaren	Isaac	Ahlnoor
7	1767	Grosshandlaren	Hans	Wittfoth
7	1767	Grosshandlaren	Erik	Zettersten
8	1767	Grosshandlaren	Isaac	Clason
95	1767	Grosshandlaren	Carl Christopher	Pauli
205	1767	Grosshandlaren	Friedrich	Lundin
27	1768	Grosshandlaren	Johan	Fenvik (Fenwick)
2	1770	Grosshandlaren	Abraham	Winberg
56	1771	Grosshandlaren	Carl Emanuel	Lang
480	1771	Grosshandlaren	Olof	Wåhlberg
119	1772	Grosshandlaren	Alexander	Donner
196	1773	Grosshandlaren	Carl	Pohl
287	1773	Grosshandlaren	Jean Adolph	Kiellberg
292	1773	Grosshandlaren	Eric	Dufwenberg
106	1774	Grosshandlaren	Olof	Nilsson Sandberg
163	1774	Grosshandlaren	Nils	Forström

continued

Table 5.a.1 Continued

Act	*Year*	*Title*	*First name*	*Surname*
228	1774	Grosshandlaren	Jan	Jansson Cosswa and Anna Brita Palin
1028	1774	Grosshandlaren	Nils	Schwartz
159	1775	Grosshandlaren	Friedrich	Werderman
162	1775	Grosshandlaren	Johan Magnus	Lönbom
173	1775	Grosshandlaren	Jean Adolph	Kiellberg
26	1776	Handelsman	Nicolas	Öhrn
30	1776	Grosshandlaren	Hinric	Busch
37	1776	Grosshandlaren	Daniel	Müller
47	1776	Grosshandlaren	Petter	Siöstedt
124	1776	Grosshandlaren	Friedrich	Kahl
1266	1776	Grosshandlaren	Daniel	Zelling
1266	1776	Grosshandlaren	Abraham	Sundberg
42	1777	Grosshandlaren	Johan Hindrich	Müller
68	1777	Grosshandlaren	Zacharias	Wall
88	1777	Grosshandlaren		Appelroth and Spalding
136	1777	Grosshandlaren	Anders	Plongstedt
142	1777	Grosshandlaren	Erik	Robergs
272	1777	Handelsman	Abraham	Cassell
314	1777	Grosshandlaren	Johan Georg	Uhlen
73	1778	Grosshandlaren	Jonas	Hamn
103	1778	Grosshandlaren	Jacob	Kahl
256	1778	Grosshandlaren	Joachim	Ulmgren
272	1778	Grosshandlaren	Hindrich Reinhold	Grot
1414	1778	Grosshandlaren	Bengt	Olofsson Ström
30	1779	Grosshandlaren	Anders	Landsent Åkerman
103	1779	Grosshandlaren	David	Müller
212	1779	Grosshandlaren	Carl Gustaf	Thuring
8	1780	Handelsman	Carl	Danielsson Sten
11	1780	Grosshandlaren	Abraham	Arfwidsson
70	1780	Grosshandlaren	Samuel	Cöhler
191½	1781	Grosshandlaren	And	Broberg and Comp
22	1783	Grosshandlaren	Johan	Bays O.H.H. Juliana Holming
38	1783	Grosshandlaren	Johan	Melchior Sterbhus Änka N. C. Willman
187	1783	Grosshandlaren	Anders	Maulström Änka C. E. Crom
17	1784	Grosshandlaren	Carl	Sivert Sterbhus
192	1784	Grosshandlaren	Jonas	Lövgren
50	1785	Grosshandlaren	Sven	Hierton
156	1785	Grosshandlaren	Jacob	Winstedt
2524	1785	Grosshandlaren	Johan Eric	Schön
193	1787	Grosshandlaren	Jan Hindrich	Snicker
21	1788	Grosshandlaren	Lars	Clever
22	1788	Grosshandlaren	Moses	Nathan Judiska Handelshuset
221	1788	Grosshandlaren	Jacob	Galetski
126	1789	Grosshandlaren	Thomas	Hedberg Jr
166	1790	Grosshandlaren	Carl Fredric	Spann
18	1791	Grosshandlaren	Jacob	Neostadii
74	1791	Grosshandlaren	Carl	Fyrberg

Table 5.a.1 Continued

Act	*Year*	*Title*	*First name*	*Surname*
166	1791	Grosshandlaren	Philip Emanuel	Wasmouth
137	1792	Grosshandlaren	Samuel	Wickman
51	1793	Grosshandlaren	Jac. Lor.	D'ailly Johson
15	1794	Grosshandlaren	Sven	Holmström
37	1796	Grosshandlaren	Johan Ulric	Egge
47	1796	Grosshandlaren		Hultman
110	1796	Grosshandlaren	Olof	Engström
56	1797	Grosshandlaren	Joachim	Grabien
86	1799	Grosshandlaren	Frans Gustaf	Carré
119	1799	Grosshandlaren	Nils	Wennerberg
11	1800	Grosshandlaren	Jonas	Löhngren
213	1800	Grosshandlaren	Carlos and Clas	Grill

Source: City Archive of Stockholm, Stockholms magistrat och rådhusrätt, F6a, Konkursakter.

Note
"Handelsman" = merchant and "grosshandlare" = "wholesale dealer".

Notes

1 An earlier version of this chapter was presented at the 17th ESSHC Congress, Lisbon 2008, Session ECO10: The Economic, Legal and Social History of Bankruptcy II: Bankruptcy in Early Modern Western Europe. This earlier version and the present chapter are rooted in a number of earlier and ongoing research projects, which among other things investigate the character of the financial networks of Swedish and immigrant merchants, based on bankruptcy cases, and the influence of the origins and confessions of immigrant merchants. These are: K. Nyberg, *The "Skeppsbro Nobility" in Stockholm's Old Town 1650–1850: A Research Program on the Role and Significance of Trade Capitalism in Swedish Economy and Society* (Uppsala 2001), financed by Svenska Handelsbankens Research Foundations; with a greater emphasis on the role of bankruptcies: *Risk, Trust and Creditworthiness: The Institution of Bankruptcy in Stockholm, 1734–1862* and *The Stockholm Bankruptcy Database Project 1687–1849*, both financed by the Bank of Sweden Tercentenary Foundation. One of the results of the latter project, in collaboration the Stockholm City Archives is the creation and publication of an online database covering all recorded bankruptcies in Stockholm from 1687–1849, available online at www.tidigmodernakonkurser.se.

2 A. Schunka, "Glaubensflucht als Migrationsoption. Konfessionell motivierte Migrationen in der Frühen Neuzeit" *Geschichte in Wissenschaft und Unterricht: Zeitschrift des Verbandes der Geschichtslehrer Deutschlands* (2005); C. Lesger and L. Noordegraaf (eds), *Entrepreneurs and Entrepreneurship in Early Modern Times: Merchants and Industrialists within the Orbit of the Dutch Staple Market* (The Hague 1995); A. Das Gupta, *The World of the Indian Ocean Merchant 1500–1800: Collected Essays of Ashin Das Gupta* (Oxford 2001); C. Markovits, *The Global World of Indian Merchants 1750–1947: Traders of Sind from Bukhara to Panama* (Cambridge, UK 2000); S. Chaudhury and M. Morineau (eds), *Merchants, Companies and Trade: Europe and Asia in the Early Modern Era* (Cambridge, UK 1999); K. Fleet, *European and Islamic Trade in the Early Ottoman State: The Merchants of Genoa and Turkey* (Cambridge, UK 1999); R.P. Matthee, *The Politics of Trade in Safavid Iran: Silk for Silver 1600–1730* (Cambridge, UK 1999); K.A. Young, *Kin, Commerce, Community: Merchants in the Port of Quebec, 1717–1745* (New York 1995); J. Ojala, "Approaching

Europe: The Merchant Networks between Finland and Europe during the Eighteenth and Nineteenth Centuries" *European Review of Economic History* (1997).

3 R. de Roover, *Money, Banking and Credit in Mediaeval Bruges: Italian Merchant-Bankers, Lombards and Money-Changers. A Study in the Origins of Banking* (Cambridge, MA 1948); S. Chapman, *The Rise of Merchant Banking* (London 1985), ch. 1.

4 E.F. Heckscher, *Sveriges ekonomiska historia från Gustav Vasa*, Vol. I:2 (Stockholm 1936), 360–80; K. Samuelsson, *De stora köpmanshusen i Stockholm 1730–1815: En studie i den svenska handelskapitalismens historia* (Stockholm 1951), 38–45; K. Samuelsson, "International Payments and Credit Movements by the Swedish Merchant-Houses, 1730–1815" *Scandinavian Economic History Review* (1955): 163–202; R. Adamson, "Finance and Marketing in the Swedish Iron Industry, 1800–1860" *Scandinavian Economic History Review* (1968): 47–101. Current works include: C. Evans, O. Jackson and G. Rydén, "Baltic Iron and the British Iron Industry in the Eighteenth Century" *Economic History Review* (2002): 642–65; Lars Nilsson and Sven Lilja (eds), *Invandrarnas roll i lokalsamhället: Historiska aspekter på integrationen av invandrare i nordiska lokalsamhällen* (Stockholm 1998); I. Bull, *De Trondhjemske handelshusene på 1700–tallet: Slekt, hushold og forretning* (Trondheim 1998); C. Dalhede, *Handelsfamiljer på Stormaktstidens Europamarknad: Resor och resande i internationella förbindelser och kulturella intressen. Augsburg, Antwerpen, Lübeck, Göteborg och Arboga* (Göteborg 2001), parts 1–3.

5 For a summary of Swedish research and historiography, see Nyberg, *The "Skeppsbro Nobility"*. Current works include: L. Müller, *The Merchant Houses of Stockholm, c. 1640–1800: A Comparative Study of Early modern Entrepreneurial Behaviour* (Uppsala 1998); L. Müller, "The Role of the Merchant Network: A Case History of Two Swedish Trading Houses, 1650–1800" in: C. Lesger and L. Noordegraaf (eds), *Entrepreneurs and Entrepreneurship in Early Modern Times: Merchants and Industrialists within the Orbit of the Dutch Staple Market* (The Hague 1995), 147–63; B. Andersson, *Från fästningsstad till handelsstad 1619–1820. Göteborgs historia. Del I. Näringsliv och samhällsutveckling* (Stockholm 1996); Å. Eklund, "Iron Production, Iron Trade and Iron Markets: Swedish Iron on the British Market in the First half of the Eighteenth Century" (Licentiate Thesis, Department of Economic History, Uppsala University, 2001). For migration to Stockholm in general during the early modern period, see R. Sandberg, "Invandring och etnicitet i det tidigmoderna Stockholm: några reflektioner" in: K. Stadin (ed.), *I all anspråkslöshet: en vänbok till Lars Björlin* (Huddinge 2005).

6 Cf. with B. Andersson, *Göteborgs handlande borgerskap 1750–1805* (Göteborg 1988), chs 4–5. The main works which focus on the financing of Swedish exports during the period are: Samuelsson, *De stora köpmanshusen i Stockholm 1730–1815*, ch. 4; K.-G. Hildebrand, "Bruk och förläggare" in: *Fagerstabrukens historia*, Vol. 1 (Uppsala 1957); R. Adamson, *Järnavsättning och bruksfinansiering 1800–1860* (Göteborg 1966). For the financing of import and manufacture, see Samuelsson, *De stora köpmanshusen i Stockholm 1730–1815*, ch. 4; T. Gårdlund, *Svensk industrifinansiering under genombrottsskedet 1830–1913* (Stockholm 1947), 85ff.; P. Nyström, *Stadsindustriens arbetare före 1800-talet* (Stockholm 1955), 203–11, 309–13; S. Fritz, *Studier i svenskt bankväsen 1772–1789* (Stockholm 1967), 68–98, 253–5, tables E, F, G, H, J, K, L; C. Persson, *Stockholms klädesmanufakturer 1816–1846* (Stockholm 1993), ch. 5.3, 102–21; K. Nyberg, *Kommersiell kompetens och industrialisering: Norrköpings ylleindustriella tillväxt på Stockholms bekostnad 1780–1846* (Uppsala 1999), ch. 4; S. Carlén, *Staten som marknadens salt: En studie i institutionsbildning, kollektivt handlande och tidig välfärdspolitik på en strategisk varumarknad i övergången mellan merkantilism och liberalism* (Stockholm 1997).

7 Stockholms stadsarkiv (SSA), (Stockholm City Archives), Stockholms magistrat och rådhusrätt, F6a, Konkursakter. Cf. with Appendix 1.

8 M. Botticini, "A Tale of 'Benevolent' Governments: Private Credit Markets, Public

Finance, and the Role of Jewish Lenders in Medieval and Renaissance Italy" *Journal of Economic History* 60 (2000): 164–89; Peter Mathias, "Risk, Credit and Kinship in Early Modern Enterprise" in: J.J. McCusker and K. Morgan (eds), *The Early Modern Atlantic Economy* (Cambridge, UK 2000); F. Bedoire, "Kyrka, herrgård och bruk. Den fransk-reformerte kapitalisten som byggherre och kulturförmedlare i det svenska 1700-talet" *Konsthistorisk Tidskrift* 64 (1995): 147–62; Andersson, *Göteborgs handlande borgerskap 1750–1805*, 139–42.

9 L. Fontaine, "Antonio and Shylock: Credit and Trust in France, *c.*1680–*c.*1780" *Economic History Review* 1 (2001): 39–57; S. Ogilvie, "The Use and Abuse of Trust: Social Capital and its Development by Early Modern Guilds" *Jahrbuch führ Wirtschaftsgeschichte* (2005): 15–52; Y. Hasselberg, *Den sociala ekonomin: Familjen Clason och Furudals bruk 1804–1856* (Uppsala 1998), ch. 4. Compare with Balzac's novel on perfume trader C. Birotteau, *Histoire de la grandeur et de la décadence de César Birotteau*, set in Paris at the end of the 1810s, and published in several versions during the 1830s, discussed in G. Robb, *Balzac: A Biography* (London 2000), 427; S. Swahn, *Balzac i verket* (Stockholm 1987), 200–8.

10 SSA, Stockholms magistrat och rådhusrätt, F6a, Konkursakter.

11 P. Mathias, "Strategies for Reducing Risk by Entrepreneurs in the Early Modern Period" in: C. Lesger and L. Noordegraaf (eds), *Entrepreneurs and Entrepreneurship in Early Modern Times: Merchants and Industrialists within the Orbit of the Dutch Staple Market* (The Hague 1995), 5–24.

12 K. Nyberg, *Säljes: Ull, Köpes: Kläde. Yllemanufakturens företagsformer i 1780-talets Stockholm* (Uppsala 1992), 175. The results are based on in-depth studies of six industries covering around 30 different professions, including wholesalers, textile manufacturers, artisans and retailers. The claimants are normally listed for every debtor with a preserved bankruptcy file. The method of the study is presented in K. Nyberg, "Grosshandlare på Stockholms kreditmarknad 1750–1800: Presentation av undersökningens uppläggning" (Unpublished paper, Uppsala University, 2002). See also M. Hayen, B. Jordell and K. Nyberg, "Digitalisering av konkursärenden i Stockholms stadsarkiv, 1687–1849" (Unpublished paper, Stockholm University, 2006).

13 The main focus of the amended legislation was a gradual formalization with tightening of the debtor's payment requirements, including a limit on the extent of withdrawal, i.e. the right to be released from continued claims for repayment following bankruptcy. With the introduction of the 1773 bankruptcy law, the right to withdraw was granted only to debtors who had unquestionably suffered accidents. In the 1818 bankruptcy law, this right was further circumscribed. That same year, the provisions governing negligence and fraud were also tightened up. See *Sveriges Rikes Lag* [...] *med tillägg af de stadganden, som utkommit till den 20 december 1884 jämte bihang* (Stockholm 1884), 175–87, 568–97; L. Welamson, *Konkursrätt* (Stockholm 1961), 7–17; M. Ågren, *Jord och gäld: Social skiktning och rättslig konflikt i södra Dalarna ca 1650–1850* (Uppsala 1992), 55–8.

14 L.A. Pollock, "Parent–Child Relations" in: D.I. Kertzer and M. Barbagli (eds), *Family Life in Early Modern Times, 1500–1789* (New Haven, CT 2001), 210–13; A.L. Erickson, *Women and Property in Early Modern England* (London 1993), ch. 5; A. Göransson, "Kön, släkt och ägande: Borgerliga maktstrategier 1800–1850" *Historisk tidskrift* (1990): 525–43; M. Ågren, "Fadern, systern och brodern: Makt- och rättsförskjutningar genom 1800-talets egendomsreformer" *Historisk Tidskrift* (1999): 683–708; S. Cavallo and L. Warner (eds), *Widowhood in Medieval and Early Modern Europe* (London 1999); S. Ogilvie, *A Bitter Living: Women, Markets, and Social Capital in Early Modern Germany* (Oxford 2003), chs 4–5; C. Bladh, *Månglerskor: Att sälja från korg och bod i Stockholm 1819–1846* (Stockholm 1991), ch. 7.

15 Fourteen cases have been studied in S. Paulsson, "Ekonomiskt omyndig! Synen på kvinnlig egendom inom äktenskapet speglad i grosshandlarhustrurs försvar av sina hemgifter: Grosshandlarkonkurser i Stockholm 1781–1799" (Unpublished paper,

Department of Economic History, Uppsala University, 2004). The cases are: SSA, Stockholms magistrat och rådhusrätt, F6a, Konkursakter, nos 191½/1781, 22/1783, 38/1783, 192/1784, 156/1785, 104/1787, 221/1788, 126/1789, 166/1791, 51/1793, 47/1796, 56/1797, 119/1799.

16 K. Nyberg, "Finansiella nätverk: kredit och egendomsförhållanden" in: K. Nyberg (ed.), *Kopparkungen: Handelshuset Björkman i Stockholm 1782–1824* (Stockholm 2006), 155–80.

17 J. Kermode, *Medieval Merchants: York, Beverley and Hull in the Latter Middle Ages* (Cambridge, UK 1998), 242–7; E.S. Hunt and J.M. Murray, *Företagande och handel i det medeltida Europa 1200–1550* (Stockholm 1999), ch. 9; P. Spufford, *Pengar och makt: Medeltidens handelsmän i Europa* (Stockholm 2002), ch. 1; F. Braudel, *Marknadens spel: Civilisationer och kapitalism 1400–1800*, Vol. 2 (Stockholm 1986), 126ff.; J. Jonker, *Merchants, Bankers, Middlemen: The Amsterdam Money Market During the First Half of the 19th Century* (Amsterdam 1996).

18 Fontaine, "Antonio and Shylock", 39–43.

19 M.C. Finn, *The Character of Credit: Personal Debt in English Culture, 1740–1914* (Cambridge, UK 2003); L.V. Markham, *Victorian Insolvency: Bankruptcy, Imprisonment for Debt, and Company Winding-Up in Nineteenth-Century* (Oxford 1995); B.H. Mann, *Republic of Debtors: Bankruptcy in the Age of American Independence* (Cambridge, MA 2002); B. Hansen, "Commercial Associations and the Creation of a National Economy: The Demand for Federal Bankruptcy Law" *Business History Review* 72 (1998): 86–113; E.J. Balleisen, *Navigating Failure: Bankruptcy and Commercial Society in Antebellum America* (Chapel Hill, NC 2001); D.A. Skeel, *Debt's Dominion: A History of Bankruptcy Law in America* (Princeton, NJ 2001); K. Gratzer and H. Sjögren (eds), *Konkursinstitutets betydelse i svensk ekonomi* (Stockholm 1999); Welamson, *Konkursrätt*.

20 E. Fryde, "The Bankruptcy of the Scali of Florence in England, 1326–1328" in: R. Britnell and J. Hatcher (eds), *Progress and Problems in Medieval England: Essays in Honour of Edward Miller* (Cambridge, UK 1996), 107–20; J.W. Jones, *The Foundations of English Bankruptcy: Statutes and Commissions in the Early Modern Period* (Philadelphia, PA 1979); J. Hoppit, *Risk and Failure in English Business 1700–1800* (Cambridge, UK 1987); C. Muldrew, *The Economy of Obligation: The Culture of Credit and Social Relations in Early Modern England* (Basingstoke 1998); I. Agge, "Några drag av det svenska konkursförfarandets utveckling" *Minnesskrift ägnad 1734 års lag av jurister i Sverige och Finland* (Stockholm 1934); T.M. Safley, "Bankruptcy: Family and Finance in Early Modern Augsburg" *Journal of European Economic History* 29 (2000).

21 One of the aims of the project is to determine how bankruptcy cases were handled in light of the establishment and growth of Swedish bankruptcy legislation. Three periods of change can be identified: the period between the publication of the 1734 general law and the 1773 bankruptcy law; the period from 1773 until the publication of the bankruptcy laws of 1818 and 1830; and the following period leading up to the publication of the 1862 bankruptcy law. Cf. Agge, *Några drag av det svenska konkursförfarandets utveckling*; U. Johansson, "Stockholms magistrats och rådhusrätts arkiv 1720–1849: Ärendenas handläggning samt arkivets bestånd" *Berättelse över Arkivnämndens förvaltning och verksamhet under år 1969* (Stockholm 1969); K. Olivecrona, *Bidrag till den svenska konkurslagstiftningens historia* (Uppsala 1862). Cf. with note 13 above.

22 P.T. Hoffman, G. Postel-Vinay and J.-L. Rosenthal, *Priceless Markets: The Political Economy of Credit in Paris 1660–1870* (Chicago, IL 2000). Other publications by the same authors include "Private Credit Markets in Paris, 1690–1840" *Journal of Economic History* (1992): 293–306; "Redistribution and Long-Term Private Debt in Paris, 1660–1726" *Journal of Economic History* (1995): 256–84. See also G. Grantam, "Review of: *Priceless Markets: The Political Economy of Credit in Paris,*

1660–1870" *Journal of Economic Literature* 40 (2002): 559–61; B. Arruñda, "The Economics of Notaries" *European Journal of Law and Economics* 3 (1996): 5–37.

23 *Kongl. Majts Förnyade Wäxel-stadga, af Riksens Ständer wedertagen*, 21 January 1748. Printed in R.G. Modée, *Utdrag utur alle ifrån den 7 Decemb. 1718: utkomne Publique handlingar* [...], Vol. 4, 2526–41.

24 J. Hamilton, "Utlänningarnas roll i svenskt näringsliv under 1700-talet" (Unpublished paper, Department of Economic History, Stockholm University, 1942), 56ff.

25 S.T. Kjellberg, *Ull och ylle. Bidrag till den svenska yllemanufakturens historia* (Lund 1943), 454–63; Nyberg, *Säljes: Ull, Köpes: Kläde*, 257, 266, fn. 109; A. Hörsell, "Siden, sammet, trasa, lump: Importen av utländsk arbetskraft till Stockholms textilindustri 1759–1763" *Sveriges släktforskarförbunds årsbok* (1992): 105–58.

26 On the origin of the immigrants, see Hamilton, *Utlänningarnas roll i svenskt näringsliv under 1700-talet*, 84; Hörsell, "Siden, sammet, trasa, lump", 123. On the textiles in the Vesdre region, see P. Chorley, "The Shift from Spanish to Central-European Merino Wools in the Verviers-Aachen Cloth Industry (1760–1815)" in: E. Aerts and J.H. Munro (eds), *Textiles of the Low Countries in European Economic History* (Leuven 1990), 96–104; H. van der Wee, "The Western European Woollen Industries, 1500–1750" in: D. Jenkins (ed.), *The Cambridge History of Western Textiles*, Vol. 1 (Cambridge, UK 2003), 466–7.

27 The Swedish Navigation Act (*Produktplakatet*) is studied in depth by E.F. Heckscher, *Ekonomi och historia* (Stockholm 1922), although his perception of these negative effects has been re-evaluated, more recently in Carlén, *Staten som marknadens salt*, 247–69. For the Gulf of Bothnia Trade Restraint (*Bottniska handelstvånget*), see N. Friberg, *Stockholm i bottniska farvatten: Stockholms bottniska handelsfält under senmedeltiden och Gustav Vasa. En historisk-geografisk studie* (Stockholm 1983); Å. Sandström, *Mellan Torneå och Amsterdam: En undersökning av Stockholms roll som förmedlare av varor i regional- och utrikeshandel 1600–1650* (Stockholm 1990), ch. III.5; E.F. Heckscher, *Sveriges ekonomiska historia från Gustav Vasa*, Vol. II:2 (Stockholm 1949), 709–20; A.J. Alanen, "Stapelfriheten och de bottniska städerna 1766–1808" in: *Svenska Litteratursällskapet, litteraturhistoriska studier*, Vols 31–2 (Helsingfors 1956), 101–246. The trade policy after 1719 is addressed in E. Ekegård, *Studier i svensk handelspolitik under den tidigare frihetstiden* (Uppsala 1924).

28 For the effects of the changed trade policy, which was introduced at the 1765/66 session of the *Riksdag*, see M. Roberts, *The Age of Liberty: Sweden 1719–1772* (Cambridge, UK 1986), ch. 4; S. Högberg, *Stockholms historia*, Vol. 1 (Stockholm 1981), 335–6. For the industrial decline, see C. Persson, "The Decline of Manufacturing" in: J. Söderberg, U. Jonsson and C. Persson, *A Stagnating Metropolis: The Economy and Demography of Stockholm 1750–1850* (Cambridge, UK 1991), 31–45, which should be compared with Persson, *Stockholms klädesmanufakturer 1816–1846* and Nyberg, *Kommersiell kompetens och industrialisering*.

29 A modern presentation in English of the Age of Liberty (1719–1772), based on Swedish research, is given in Roberts, *The Age of Liberty: Sweden 1719–1772.* On the social struggles of Stockholm's middle class after 1719, see B. Boëthius, *Magistraten och borgerskapet i Stockholm 1719–1815* (Stockholm 1943), which still remains the standard work. For the situation in the 1760s, see P.-E. Brolin, *Hattar och mössor i borgarståndet 1760–1766* (Uppsala 1953); Nyberg, *Kommersiell kompetens och industrialisering*, 245–53.

30 L.-A. Aldman, *Protektionismens seger: Den svenska handels- och näringspolitikens omställning och dess effekt på Stockholm textila handel och importörer 1720–1738* (Licentiate thesis, Department of Economic History, Uppsala University, 2006). The careers of the immigrants can be assessed by comparing the dataset in Hörsell, *Siden, sammet, trasa, lump* with the dataset in Nyberg, *Säljes: Ull, Köpes: Kläde*.

31 C.C. Sjödén, *Stockholms borgerskap under Sturetiden med särskild hänsyn till dess politiska ställning: En studie i Stockholms stads historia* (Stockholm 1950), 21–4,

85–91; N. Ahnlund, *Stockholms historia före Gustav Vasa* (Stockholm 1953), 218–31, 300–1, 373–85, 489; G. Dahlbäck, *I medeltidens Stockholm* (Stockholm 1988/1995), 52–3, 71–2; G. Dahlbäck, "Invandring – särskilt tysk – till Sverige under medeltiden" in: Lars Nilsson and Sven Lilja (eds), *Invandrarnas roll i lokalsamhället: Historiska aspekter på integrationen av invandrare i nordiska lokalsamhällen* (Stockholm 1998), 11–30; M. Lamberg, *Dannemännen i stadens råd. Rådmanskretsen i nordiska köpstäder under* senmedeltiden (Stockholm 2001), 57–69; I. Peterzén, *Studier rörande Stockholms historia under Gustav Vasa* (Stockholm 1945), 67–94; B. Lager-Kromnow, *Att vara stockholmare under 1560-talet* (Stockholm 1992), ch. 3; L. Ericson, *Borgare och byråkrater: Omvandlingen av Stockholms stadsförvaltning 1599–1637* (Stockholm 1988), ch. 4, 336–340; A. Jansson, *Bördor och bärkraft: Borgare och kronotjänare i Stockholm 1664–1672* (Stockholm 1991), ch. 13; Samuelsson, *De stora köpmanshusen i Stockholm 1730–1815*, 38–45.

32 Cf. with N. Staf, "De främmande trosbekännarna i Stockholm under karolinsk tid: Några bidrag till karolinsk kyrkopolitik" in: *Studier och handlingar rörande Stockholms historia*, Vol. 3 (Stockholm 1966), 9–64.

33 F. Venturi, *The End of the Old Regime in Europe, 1776–1789. I: The Great States of the West* (Princeton, NJ 1991). The Swedish Tolerance Edict of 1782 is presented in H. Valentin, *Judarna i Sverige: Från 1774–1950-talet* (Stockholm 2004), ch. 8. See also H. Valentin, *Urkunder till judarnas historia i Sverige* (Stockholm 1924), 18–25. On the strong position of the guild system in Stockholm at the beginning of the 1800s, see E. Lindberg. *Borgerskap och burskap: Om näringsprivilegier och borgerskapets institutioner i Stockholm 1820–1846* (Uppsala 2001); Nyberg, *Kommersiell kompetens och industrialisering*, ch. 9. Nyberg links Stockholm's industrial decline to the existence of strong corporate institutions, and compares this to the development of industry in rural towns, where such institutions were weaker. See also S. Ogilvie, "Guilds, Efficiency, and Social Capital: Evidence from German Proto-Industry" *Economic History Review* 57 (2004): 286–333. In this article, Ogilvie describes the negative impact of preindustrial institutions on central European development, a view which she has put forward in several other works since the mid-1990s. The transitional period is dealt with in more depth in M. Melkersson, *Staten, ordningen och friheten: En studie av den styrande elitens syn på statens roll mellan stormaktstiden och 1800-talet* (Uppsala 1997), ch. 6; K. Nyberg, "Bengt Magnus Björkmans gärning i perspektiv" in: K. Nyberg (ed.), *Kopparkungen: Handelshuset Björkman i Stockholm 1782–1824* (Stockholm 2006), ch. 14.

34 Nyberg, *Kommersiell kompetens och industrialisering*, ch. 5.

35 M. Wottle, *Det lilla ägandet: Korporativ formering och sociala relationer inom Stockholms minuthandel 1720–1810* (Stockholm 2000), 226ff.; K. Ågren, *I nöd och lust: En studie av sambandet mellan äktenskapsmönster och ekonomisk status hos Stockholms grosshandlare på 1700-talet* (Licentiate thesis, Department of Economic History, Uppsala University, 2003).

36 Samuelsson, *De stora köpmanshusen i Stockholm 1730–1815*, 23–38; J. Norrby, *Jennings* (Köping 1991).

37 Wottle, *Det lilla ägandet*, Ch. 1; Lindberg, *Borgerskap och burskap.*

38 Nyström, *Stadsindustriens arbetare före 1800-talet*, ch. 5, Appendix VI; E. Söderlund, *Stockholms hantverkarklass 1720–1772: Sociala och ekonomiska förhållanden* (Stockholm 1943), 335.

39 Nyström, *Stadsindustriens arbetare före 1800-talet*, Appendix VI.

40 Studies of the price adjustments of the production values, as reported in the factory reports of the Stockholm Hallmark court, show that these were adjusted in line with inflation. The adjustments became infrequent and unsystematic over time, however, which resulted in a sort of administrative price rise. If the income levels reported in the ordinary contribution were adjusted in the same way, it would be wrong to calculate them in fixed prices. Cf. with Persson, *Stockholms klädesmanufakturer*

1816–1846, 41f. Hallmark courts (*hallrätter*) were municipal supervisory bodies for manufacture, which existed next to traditional guilds from 1739–1846. They had the right to give permissions to start manufactures (mainly woollen, worsted, silk, linen and cotton), inspect products, issue hallmarks and, in certain instances, act as a judicial authority. Hallmark courts were created as a special jurisdiction by politically motivated interest groups, consisting of members of the magistracy, large merchants and government officials, aimed against corporations and traditional textile importers. Nyberg, *Säljes: Ull, Köpes: Kläde*, ch. 1.

41 SSA, Bemedlingskommissionens arkiv, Taxeringslängder, ordinarie kontribution.

42 Cf. with Nyberg, *Kopparkungen*, 41–69, 364–6.

43 SSA, Stockholms magistrat och rådhusrätt, F6a, Konkursakter, no. 88/1777; A3a, Civilprotokoll, huvudserie, vol. 158 (1776), 677; vol. 159 (1776), 82, 90, 108, 196, 246, 278, 296, 397, 510, 527; vol. 162 (1777), 53, 119, 139, 144, 237, 285, 311, 456, 461, 507, 510, 850–911.

44 Boëthius, *Magistraten och borgerskapet i Stockholm 1719–1815*, 34, 52, 61, 76, 80, 89, 100–1, 107–9, 114, 116, 122, 126, 129, 1335, 272, 335; Brolin, *Hattar och mössor i borgarståndet 1760–1766*, 32, 52, 77, 207.

45 E. Ringborg, *Bidrag till Norrköpingsindustriens historia: Förra delen* (Norrköping 1922), 60–2, 144–5, 166–71, 270, 274; K. Forsberg, *Gusums bruks historia 1653–1953* (Stockholm 1953), 31–4, 55–86, 212.

46 SSA, Justitiekollegium och förmyndarkammarens arkiv, EIIa1:2, Bouppteckningar, huvudserien, 1702:355, 1704/1:294, 1712/1:570, 1726:1324, 1739/71:808, 1741/1:472, 1743/1:729, 1745/1/454, 1746/1:168, 1752/1:359, 1758/1/1:126, 1758/1/2:1134, 1767/4:36, 1769/1:293, 1771/1:717, 1773/1/2:697, 1777/4:96, 1783/3:1, 1788/3:749, 1789/1:305, 1791/2:415, 1794/1:30, 1797/4:268; Storkyrkoförsamlingens kyrkoarkiv, EIa, Lysnings- och vigselböcker, huvudserie, Vol. 1 (1712–1732), 270, 272, 305; Vol. 2 (1733–1747), 72, 96, 232, 239; Vol. 3 (1748–1772), 293, 358; Storkyrkoförsamlingens kyrkoarkiv, FIa, Död- och begravningsböcker, huvudserie, Vol. 1 (1725–1753), 25, 92, 113, 124, 125, 141, 165, 171, 186; Vol. 2 (1754–1783), 44, 47, 51, 147, 188, 210, 229, 243, 247, 441, 304, 306, 392; Vol. 3 (1784–1799), 107; Tyska S:ta Gertruds kyrkoarkiv, Vigselbok 1640–1700, 16, 33, 60, 62, 64, 79, 82, 90, 95; Vigselbok 1701–1734, 101, 107, 117, 138, 145; Tyska S:ta Gertruds kyrkoarkiv, Dödbok 1681–1747, 3r., 13v., 17v., 23r., 26v., 31r., 32r., 39r., 41v., 41r., 54r., 55r., 56r., 57r., 62v., 63v., 65v., 71v., 72v., 78r., 133v., 144v., 152v., 155v., 180v., 181v., 185v., 445v., 451v., 456v., 469v., 473v., 475v., 485v., 552v., 971v., 1221v; Tyska S:ta Gertruds kyrkoarkiv, Dopbok 1701–1734, 818, 828, 842, 869, 901, 920, 941, 961.

47 SSA, Bemedlingskommissionens arkiv, Taxeringslängder, ordinarie kontribution.

48 The ten biggest Stockholm trading houses every ten years between 1730 and 1820 are listed in Samuelsson, *De stora köpmanshusen i Stockholm 1730–1815*, 232–5.

49 S. Högberg, *Kungl. Patriotiska Sällskapets historia: Med särskild hänsyn till den gustavianska tidens agrara reformsträvanden* (Stockholm 1961), 65.

50 P.C. Reynard, "The Language of Bankruptcy: Explaining Commercial Failure in Eighteenth-Century France" *Journal of European Economic History* 30 (2001): 355–90.

Part II

Business practices

6 Bankruptcy in the Kingdom of Naples

The case of public banks (17th to 18th centuries)

Paola Avallone

Introduction

Study of the Neapolitan public banks is essential to understanding the economic and political life in the Kingdom of Naples. For over two centuries, financial life hinged on the banks; their organization and operation touched more than one part of society, affecting economic activities and influencing individual lives by conditioning their investments.

Public banks played the role of central banks *sui generis*, since their main operation was that of collecting metal coinage and issuing in its place a paper document, known as the "fede di credito" (credit certificate), that identified the depositor and the amount deposited. It was transferable by signature, giving its bearer the right to withdraw metal coinage in the value previously deposited in a bank vault on written order, known as a "polizza" (policy).[1] The government recognized credit certificates and policies as having legal value in its transactions with private persons. This recognition had its *raison d'être* in the fact that bank documents, besides facilitating transactions, also allowed the government to reduce the considerable expense incurred through the circulation of gold and silver coinage, given that the kingdom did not possess mines of either of these metals. This certificate offered the solution to the problem of constant scarcity of metal and its resultant high purchase price.[2]

Originally, in order to ensure that depositors did not run the same risks as with private banks in the past, metal coinage held in bank vaults had to correspond to the sum of the certificates and policies in circulation. In practice, however, it was different. The certificates issued by the banks were subdivided into *fedi libere* (free certificates), by which each bearer was able to redeem the deposit certificate at any time and withdraw all of or part of the total sum; *fedi condizionate o vincolate* (conditioned certificates), which could be redeemed only after satisfying certain conditions. Therefore, because cash deposits were legally considered irregular in nature, the banks calculated the average circulation time of their documents, invested the deposited cash assets and with the profits deriving from these investments not only maintained their organizations but also financed charitable works. This proved a successful strategy for all Neapolitan banks, except for the *Banco del Salvatore*.[3]

The use of this money was regulated by the Spanish viceroys, who restricted investments to the purchase of public annuities or interest-free loans to the court of the City of Naples in crises. The viceregal government thus protected the deposits of its citizens and ensured itself a sort of monopoly over these deposits, so as to be able to use them at any given moment.

These strict rules were rarely obeyed, however. The bank governors, who were entrusted with the management of charitable institutions, which were supported by their banks, discovered "the magic of credit." They succumbed to the temptation of making bold investments, unsecured loans and illegal financial instruments in order to ensure payments. They realized that, through greater investments, they could earn the funds necessary to meet the growing expenses of the charitable institutions. These costs had increased, on the one hand, because of demographic growth at that time (on the eve of the plague of 1656, Naples counted over 300,000 inhabitants) and, on the other hand, because of continuous price inflation.

The rise of the public banks and bankruptcies among private bankers

The close economic and monetary relationship between public banks and the viceregal court, on the one hand, enabled these institutions to maintain a pre-eminent role in the economy of the kingdom for a good two centuries. On the other hand, however, it did not save them from the consequences of the government's erroneous monetary policies, which forced them to declare bankruptcy. Precisely because of the important role played by the banks in the economy of the kingdom, they were dealt with in such a way as to avoid the definitive closure of the banks concerned. Even when failure due to government policy was compounded by mismanagement and embezzlement by directors or employees, a rescue package was worked out *in extremis* by the government.

The Neapolitan public banks, many of which suffered bankruptcy, were themselves born of bankruptcy. They were founded as a result of the failure of private banking houses that had monopolized Neapolitan banking activity since the time of the Norman domination. These were, for the most part, foreign houses from Genoa, Florence, Venice, Lucca, Sienna, Marseilles, Catalonia or Pisa.[4]

Most private bank failures occurred in the period between 1580 and 1623, which De Rosa singles out as the third stage in the rise and fall of the economy of southern Italy under Spanish domination.[5] During these years, the economy was unstable and government officials believed that only the removal of metal coinage from circulation in the kingdom would somehow allow the balance of payments debt to be settled, while avoiding a reduction in the standard of living of the country.[6]

In order to reduce the deficit, the Spanish viceregal government should have attempted to stimulate investments in the kingdom from external or foreign capital, either from émigré Neapolitans living abroad or from foreign bankers residing in the city, thus avoiding the drain of money from the south and stimulating production and intensifying exports.[7] Errors, however, were committed in the fields of both economic and monetary policies. In the first case, in order to find new sources of funds other than new and often unpopular taxes, they proceeded with the conversion of public revenue, reducing the rates of interest and causing damage to the holders of shares in the public debt. In the second case, in order to counteract the phenomena of counterfeiting and clipping,[8] they minted new coins, incurring more debt with private bankers. This occurred because the government borrowed from them in order to coin new currency without devaluating it so as to maintain a strong currency in commercial transactions, just as other states had done when they had found themselves in the same situation.[9]

The private bankers, whose loans had helped the viceroy to deal with the balance of payments debt, had been partially remunerated with shares from public revenue. These same private bankers also used their depositors' money to invest in those same shares during periods of economic downturn. Reductions in the rate of interest on shares of the public debt, carried out by a government that was unable to pay higher rates to investors, was a sure sign of imminent default. The bankers, who sought to resell their shares during the summer in order to gain liquid capital to invest in silk, wheat and other products, found themselves forced to sell cheaply at considerable loss. These damages were made worse by the fact that they also had to borrow money at high rates. Loss added to loss, a situation that ultimately immobilized them. The final blow came when private depositors began withdrawing their deposits.[10]

Many of the bankers fled the kingdom. The subsequent loss of confidence in private bankers was offset by an increased confidence in several lay charitable institutions. These had asked the viceroy for authorization to accept deposit accounts and to issue credit certificates. Between 1570 and 1600, seven philanthropic institutions founded public banks. The *Banco della Pietà* (1570) and the *Banco dei Poveri* (1600), which originated from the *Monte della Pietà* (1539) and from *Monte dei Poveri* (1563), institutions that issued interest-free loans upon pledge. The *Banco dell'Annunziata* (1587), the *Banco di S. Maria del Popolo* (1589), the *Banco di S. Eligio* (1592), the *Banco dello Spirito Santo* (1594) and the *Banco di S. Giacomo e Vittoria* (1597) were created by governors who managed hospitals and welfare institutions. In the mid-seventeenth century, an eighth public bank appeared, the *Banco del Salvatore* (1640), the only bank created by speculators. These would-be bankers, the flour-tax collectors of the kingdom, wanted to invest the proceeds of their excise.[11]

The functions of these banks were: (1) To accept and return money deposits on request, with no payment of interest; (2) to issue *credit certificates* to depositors who could endorse them to others, transferring all their credit to the bank; (3) to pay sums of money to third parties on written orders of the client;[12] (4) to pay third parties through account transfers. Apart from current account services, otherwise called "apodissario,"[13] the banks invested not only their own funds but also some of their account deposits in shares of the public debt, in loans to private individuals (sometimes in the form of revenue purchase), in futures from civil administrations and the government and, in the case of the *Banchi di Pietà e dei Poveri*, in pledged loans.

The first great banking crisis: the monetary reform of 1621–22

As mentioned before, the banks established by charitable institutions were the first to be taken to task when the government decided to deal with the monetary problem which had, for some time, been plaguing the economy. Because of counterfeiting and clipping, the real value of the money in circulation in no way corresponded to the nominal value. Despite the actions taken, which envisaged even the death penalty for those involved in fraud, coin-clipping led to about a 70 percent depreciation of the currency mostly used in small business. In 1609, only small denominations (*zannette* and *tre cinquine*) had legal tender status, while all the other denominations had to be withdrawn and collected by the Mint in order to be recoined with a different weight.

The possessors of damaged coins should have suffered the consequences but this provision was immediately revoked due to numerous protests from every side. Nevertheless, the situation had to be faced once and for all. Debased coinage, as it stood, could not be allowed to continue to circulate, damaging commerce and causing prices and exchange rates to rise. In March 1622, Viceroy Cardinal Zapata passed a law that decreed all low-value coins used for small purchases should be removed from circulation and replaced by new coins that were to be minted in the meantime. This new issue was due in part to the intervention of certain shopkeepers who had taken it upon themselves to bring silver into the kingdom at a value of 3,000,000 ducati.

Unfortunately, faced with the task of minting 6,000,000 ducati to be replaced in varying values, the kingdom produced only 1,500,000. This situation adversely affected the banks, which experienced runs by account holders, who presented their *fedi di credito* and wanted to exchange them immediately for the new money. Having been obliged by the viceroy to return metal coinage to the mint for replacement, the banks' strong-rooms contained minimal amounts compared to the value of certificates in circulation. This was because, after calculating the average circulation time of money, 75 percent of the deposits in banks had been put back into circulation.

The banks resisted their depositors as long as they could, but they ultimately were forced to close. Their function was, however, far too important for the economy of the kingdom and especially the government, which could need loans at any time. Therefore, the viceroy intervened in their favor, asking them to reopen and declaring a moratorium. It was established that creditors could not receive more than five ducati a day and only up to two-thirds of their total credit. To cope with this situation the banks set out to curtail all its investments, suspending all its community works including interest-free pledged loans.

Meanwhile, the incomplete minting of new currency, the devaluation of old money against new, the deficiency of an increasingly sensitive real numerary value, the inefficiency of legal provisions against the trade and the flight of new money according to Gresham's Law, all brought the cardinal's undertaking to real bankruptcy, with a consequent stagnation of small trade business, a lack of basic goods and suffering among the people. Innumerable legal cases were brought by creditors and debtors alike. The former maintained that they should be repaid in new money, whatever the borrowed sum may have been, on the basis of the stipulated nominal value. The debtors, on the other hand, replied that given the enormous difference between the value of the money borrowed and the value of the money to be repaid, it would not be fair to attribute a value of almost four times that of the original loan. They requested that the solution found for the banks be applied in their case, where the loss was shared. Finally, it was decided that in all the transactions made before 15 February 1622 in Naples and its provinces and before 20 February in other parts of the kingdom, the creditor should cover the shortfall. In all transactions after these dates, the debtors were responsible.

The banks had to be helped to emerge from this crisis, however, and the viceroy interceded with a long proclamation in April 1623, in which: (1) creditors who had deposited money in the last eight months would receive only 40 percent; (2) those who deposited money in the months of January and February 1622 would get back only two-fifths; (3) the staff in the banks would be reduced; (4) certain taxes would be imposed, the fruits of which would go toward covering the banks' shortfalls. Such measures notwithstanding, the monetary problem continued. This is proven by subsequent proclamations against counterfeiting and clipping, as well as written communications from the banks complaining about their inability to repay their account holders. Furthermore, even though the banks had downsized their human resources, there still was the problem of which funds to use to cover ordinary running expenses, precisely because incomes from interest payments on current accounts and from their charitable institutions were insufficient.

An alternative source of income was found in profits emanating from interest on pledged loans offered to the public. It was thus that a sum on the order of 30,000 ducati was written off current accounts, to be used for pledged loans, the interest from which would be used to cover management expenses. This latter strategy contributed, to a great extent, to the banks surviving the crisis. Difficult times, however, were still to come, even though they did not affect banking activities as the monetary crisis of 1621–22 had done.[14]

Risks of bankruptcies in the seventeenth century

Public banks faced major difficulties as a result of the 1647–48 revolution and the plague of 1656. The former, better known as Masaniello's Revolution, witnessed the "sacking" of the banks, not only by the viceroy, who was always desperately searching for alternative sources of income for the heavy expenditure incurred in the Thirty Years War, but also by the population, who struggled to recover the moneys they had deposited. The banks were forced to close their doors and to suspend payments. This proved no security, however, as some were still pillaged and robbed by the mob. Some banks collapsed, while others survived.[15]

No sooner had they recovered from the revolution than the plague struck the kingdom. Surviving banks fundamentally gained strength as a result, because about half of their employees either died or fled, which meant that there were fewer management costs to sustain. Moreover, during the destruction of the houses and belongings of plague victims, many certificates and policies as well as pledged loan documents were burnt. This helped the banks temporarily, because they were able to write off the undocumented loans. Many of the pawned items held in bank strong-rooms were sold on the streets.

Aware of the wealth held by the banks, the viceroy tried to take possession of it by asserting that *demortuo* money belonged to the court. To exert better control over these institutions and to be able to avail himself of their resources at any time, he installed a *Delegate* in each bank, an external observer who would report directly to him when required to do so. In addition, with the excuse that money continued to be counterfeited and clipped, he obliged every bank to employ an official weigher, appointed by the court, an office that was then sold in order to raise funds. The government thus gradually became ever more present in the banks based on the concept that their important public role justified direct control by political authorities.

Though the banks had survived the first monetary crises and Masaniello's Revolution, they could not escape the consequences of the new monetary reform that took place at the turn of the century. The kingdom never actually solved the monetary problems that caused the crisis under Cardinal Legate Zapata, despite proclamations and harsh penalties for counterfeiters and clippers, because the public authorities had not succeeded in coming up with any effective protection against the causes of such practices. The situation was nonetheless quite stable. A sort of equilibrium had been reached over the existence of counterfeit coinage, as a result of its gradual replacement with paper money, issued by the public banks.

With the passing of time, however, the continuous presence of counterfeit money and the decrease of the real value of small coinage against its nominal value because of clipping, brought about a situation similar to that of the 1620s. The banks managed to escape virtually unscathed from this new monetary crisis, both because past experience had taught them to keep a value equal to at least 50 percent of all obligations in their vaults, and because, unlike the previous monetary crisis, which the government tackled by minting new money without devaluing, this time the new money was devalued by 25 percent. The new money was paid for with new tax income, which was advanced by the banks with huge loans, repayable with shares in the public debt. If, on the one hand, this monetary policy increased the public debt, on the other hand, devaluation stimulated export commerce, which had been affected negatively for some time by a currency whose nominal value did not correspond to its real value.[16]

Despite these improvements, confidence in the public banks suffered in the late seventeenth century due to a series of internal and external problems. For example, the *Banco dello Spirito Santo* suffered a deficit of 280,000 ducati, because its Head Cashier, Pietro Monteforte, reportedly had provided off-the-book loans to various people. It is clear to the present author, however, after a close examination of court documents, that Monteforte was just a scapegoat for embezzlement at higher levels. It was precisely the discovery and attribution of guilt to Monteforte that allowed the bank to close only for two weeks, thus avoiding a run by depositors and to accept economic aid from the *Banco della Pietà*.[17]

The bankruptcy of the *Banco dell'Annunziata*

The reform of the 1690s had not solved the monetary problem. Counterfeiting and clipping continued despite the law, and money continued to flow out of the kingdom to pay its foreign debts and to support Spain's foreign policies. The situation worsened at the turn of the century when the kingdom was rocked by new political and military events resulting from the struggle for succession to the Neapolitan throne. The situation reduced the monetary reserves of the banks, making them unable to honor the policies of their depositors. These deposits were earmarked for the pledged loans, pledges that the beneficiaries were now unable to redeem for lack of money. This situation, which dragged on for years, the run on all the banks by depositors, the inability of the banks to pay out and, particularly, the inability to convert expired pledged items into cash, forced the *Annunziata* to close its doors.

At the beginning of the eighteenth century, a new risk of bankruptcy arose due to the news that King Charles II was seriously ill and would die without an heir, thus leaving the Neapolitan throne to Philippe of France. The barons of the kingdom opposed this succession. Fearing a revolt, depositors withdrew their funds. The viceroy had to intervene, requesting that the delegates of the bank tell the governors to persuade the depositors to leave their funds in place. The *Banco del Salvatore* and the *Banco dell'Annunziata* had the worst of it, because of rumors that there was no money in the coffers due to mismanagement. The *Banco di San Giacomo* and the *Banco dei Poveri* also suffered insufficient funds.

In 1702, the *Banco dell'Annunziata* closed forever with a deficit of over 4,500,000 ducati, of which half comprised unsecured certificates. In order to pay the creditors, the bank's governors decided to cut expenses at the *Casa Santa dell'Annunziata*, the bank's charitable institution for orphans, by lowering salaries and melting down church silverware. Such measures alone were not sufficient. It was still necessary to reduce by one-third the interest rate of 4.5 percent on capital, which amounted to no less than 60,000 ducati, paid in part with bank funds and in part with funds from the *Casa*. It was uncertain whether the goods of the *Casa Santa dell'Annunziata* could be utilized to pay off creditors without papal authorization, given the sacred nature of the institution. A legal dispute arose that concluded with a judgment that the estate of the *Casa Santa dell'Annunziata* should be considered a lay institution and could, therefore, be mortgaged for legal reasons without papal consent. Because the *Casa Santa dell'Annunziata* carried out its charitable works thanks to proceeds from current account holders, it ceded a large part of its assets to the creditors as part of the *Magna Concordia* of 1717. Seven years later, the governors tried to reverse this decision, arguing against the *Casa Santa dell'Annunziata* being associated with the bankrupt bank, but nothing changed.[18]

The apparent calm of the eighteenth century

The change of dominion permitted the seven remaining banks to continue their activity, always with the proviso of having to serve the state whenever it required assistance. Although they had lost some of their former wealth, they continued to fund the royal policy, financing the interminable wars between Phillip V and Charles VI, and to maintain the economy of the city of Naples.

After the definitive triumph of Bourbon armies, the autonomy of the kingdom was restored, but its economy and administration were in total disarray after centuries of bad government. Assisted by far-seeing ministers, King Charles embarked upon a reform that affected all sectors of the kingdom from the political to the economic to the religious.[19]

It is understandable that in this climate of reformist fervor even the banks should benefit. Monetary reform finally gave some semblance of order to a situation that had often been the cause of failure for the banks. Thus began a period of relative calm in which the state was always an "economic dependant" of the banks when it needed money.

There were moments of tension, however. Some banks risked closure had their true condition not been hidden. The king intervened to cover up embezzlement and malpractice. In the process, he also forced the banks to make new rules for themselves, which were stricter than those they had worked under a century-and-a-half earlier.

The episodes that induced the king to intercede in banking affairs were linked, perhaps for the first time, to fraudulent bank management.[20] People in the top echelons were involved in illegal activities to the detriment of depositors, but these episodes never led to the closure of any of the banks.[21] If on previous occasions the royal court had intervened in banking circles by imposing oversight and regulation that were consistent with the banks' own practices, Charles now intervened more drastically, giving the government the right to appoint its own representatives at the highest levels of management in order to exercise firmer control over bank activities. Such interference intensified during the reign of Ferdinand IV, partly to reinforce the political authority of the state, and partly to correct mismanagement by the banks. A "Committee against Bank Abuse" was set up in 1771, in the *Camera di Santa Chiara*, the highest financial body in the kingdom, in order to ensure that statutes were respected and not ignored.

No less important were the repercussions of the French Revolution in the Kingdom of Naples, due to its close ties to the deposed royal house of France. After taking a position against the revolutionary movement and joining the

Austrian-led coalition against France, the kingdom incurred great expense for armaments, an expense that had been relatively contained until that point. Large sums of money had to be found, and every means was examined. The banks came under such pressure at this point that they were threatened with closure.

They had flourished until 1792. From that year on, however, continuous requests for money became the norm, leaving the banks with smaller and smaller sums of money on deposit, requiring them to borrow in order to acquire the needed cash. Various proclamations had forbidden tallies between banks, even though they occurred in fact, but in 1794 the king ordered that such tallies be compulsory. The intent was to conceal the enormous shortfalls in some of these banks. Charitable institutions were required to pledge all their silver to the banks at 4 percent interest. The silver in turn would be sent to the Mint to be transformed into coinage.

Criminal activities on the part of cashiers of two banks, *San Giacomo* and *Salvatore* resulted in further crisis and reform. Two cashiers had agreed on their own authority to issue blank certificates worth over 300,000 ducati. So as not to threaten public confidence and create serious damage for the court, which had withdrawn so much money from the banks, the delegates were dismissed and all seven banks were placed under the surveillance of a new committee. It decided that the moment had come to merge them under one name, the *Banco Nazionale di Napoli*. The seven banks would become seven separate branches for the convenience of the public.

From this moment on, a different tale begins. Some of the seven banks closed definitively, giving rise to a period of great confusion. This ended with the creation of a single bank, built on the ashes of the old public banking institutions, the *Banco delle due Sicilie*.[22]

Conclusions

Bank failures were caused not only by general mismanagement but more so by the economic situation of a geographic area strategically important to foreign powers between the sixteenth and eighteenth centuries.

The Kingdom of Naples became an economic resource for Spain and, later, Austria. Through taxation of goods and people, they drained capital to be used to finance their various, usually military, policies. Private bankers had an important role as moneylenders to the government, a common practice in the other Italian states. As they were not only bankers but also merchants and businessmen, however, their objective was to invest in more profitable activities, which were not what the viceregal governments offered. Government activities caused serious losses to the bankers, who failed and closed as a consequence.[23]

The bankruptcy of private bankers was only one aspect of the economic crisis in the Kingdom of Naples in the second half of the sixteenth century. This crisis was quite complex as the causes were not only domestic but also foreign, linked to developments in the New World: the influx of precious metals, price inflation, rarefaction of money, declining exports, balance of payments deficits, increases in exchange rates. All of these created a need for a substitute for coins. The solution was the establishment and expansion of the *fedi di credito*, the founding element of the public banks

Neapolitan public banks managed to survive for two reasons. The first reason can be traced back to the role they played in the economy of a vast kingdom which always needed alternative sources of funds. Therefore, first the Spanish viceroys, then the Austrians and finally the king tapped into the great wealth deposited in their vaults through direct loans or forced purchases of the public debt. These tactics were made possible by the introduction of paper money in the form of *fedi di credito* and their derivatives, the second reason for the banks' survival. Unlike other states in the peninsula, Naples made widespread use of paper money. *Fedi di credito* and *polizze* also circulated outside the capital, in provinces of the kingdom and even in other states. Their acceptance depended on the confidence of depositors. They originated from charitable, lay institutions that, in the absence of a welfare state, supported a wide range of charitable works and were held in high regard by the Neapolitan people. The failure of those banks would have meant the failure of those charities, of which the people still had need.

The risks of bankruptcy incurred by the public banks were always contained by the government, as it had enormous interest in keeping these institutions open. They collected money from the kingdom and provided the government with funds when requested. Along with the military and political events that followed the Neapolitan Revolution in 1799, a gradual transformation of the banks took place in line with the economic development experienced across Europe. The banks eventually merged into a single bank, *Banco delle Due Sicilie* (1815–61), controlled by the government. After the unification of Italy, it became the *Banco di Napoli*, one of the issuing banks that contributed to the growth of the new kingdom.

Notes

1 When the *fede di credito* were cashed for a partial withdrawal of the amount specified, they became known as *madrefede*, similar to the present checking account. If more than one withdrawal (or policy) was made on the total amount deposited, the amount for which a *fede di credito* had been issued, it became known as a *polizze notate fedi*.

2 L. De Simone, *La fede di credito* (Naples 1922); on the legal implications of the *fede di credito*, see N. Palmieri, *La fede di credito del Banco di Napoli* (Naples 1905), 51ff.

3 On the history of the Neapolitan public banks, see M. Rocco, *De' Banchi di Napoli e della loro ragione* (Naples 1785–87), Vols. 1–3; G. Petroni, *De' Banchi di Napoli* (Naples 1871); P. Ajello, "I depositi, le fedi di credito e le polizze dei Banchi di Napoli," *Il Filangieri* (Naples 1882); A. Somma, *Trattato dei banchi nazionali del Regno delle due Sicilie* (Naples 1844); E. Tortora, *Il Banco di Napoli: Raccolta di documenti storici e statistici* (Naples 1883); R. Filangieri, *Storia del Banco di Napoli: I Banchi di Napoli dalle origini alla costituzione del Banco delle due Sicilie, 1539–1808* (Naples 1940); L. de Rosa, *Il Mezzogiorno spagnolo tra crescita e decadenza* (Milan 1987).

4 On the private bankers and their activities, see A. Silvestri, "Sui banchieri pubblici napoletani nella prima metà del '500: Notizie e documenti," *Bollettino dell'Archivio Storico del Banco di Napoli* 2 (1950); A. Silvestri, "Sui banchieri pubblici napoletani dall'avvento di Filippo II al trono alla costituzione del monopolio: Notizie e documenti," *Bollettino dell'Archivio Storico del Banco di Napoli* 3 (1951); A. Silvestri, "Sui banchieri pubblici nella città di Napoli dalla costituzione del monopolio alla fine dei banchi dei mercanti: Notizie e documenti," *Bollettino dell'Archivio Storico del Banco di Napoli* 4 (1952); A. Silvestri, "Sull'attività bancaria durante il periodo aragonese," *Bollettino dell'Archivio Storico del Banco di Napoli* 6 (1953).

5 de Rosa, *Il Mezzogiorno spagnolo tra crescita e decadenza*, 12.

6 de Rosa, *Il Mezzogiorno spagnolo tra crescita e decadenza*, 27.

7 de Rosa, *Il Mezzogiorno spagnolo tra crescita e decadenza.*

8 All gold and silver coins were cut on the edge. The result was the reduction of their weight and value.

9 de Rosa, *Il Mezzogiorno spagnolo tra crescita e decadenza*, 29–30.

10 de Rosa, *Il Mezzogiorno spagnolo tra crescita e decadenza*, 99.

11 Flour was a foodstuff that was in any case controlled by the state.

12 The policy, and in this case the credit certificate as well, was transformed into a *madrefede*, the current logbook of bank checks.

13 The word *apodissario*, as the deposit operation was called, comes from the Greek word αποδεικτικοσ=demonstrative, as the accounts and the books related to these deposits were arranged analytically (Palmieri, *La fede di credito del Banco di Napoli*, 2).

14 On the monetary market events during those years and their effect on all public banks, see M. De Stefano, *Banchi e vicende monetarie nel Regno di Napoli, 1600–1625* (Livorno 1940).

15 L. de Rosa, "Una struttura bancaria napoletana alla vigilia dell'insurrezione di Masaniello: il Banco dei Poveri dal 1641 al 1646," *Bollettino dell'Archivio Storico del Banco di Napoli* (1955).

16 L. de Rosa, *Il Mezzogiorno tra crescita e decadenza*, 212–34.

17 P. Avallone, "Delitti e castighi nei banchi pubblici napoletani tra XVII e XVIII secolo," in: L. Cajani (ed.), *Criminalità, giustizia penale e ordine pubblico nell'Europa Moderna* (Milan 1997), 171–98.

18 E. Tortora, *Il Banco di Napoli*, 219–28.

19 I. Zilli, *Carlo di Borbone e la rinascita del Regno di Napoli: Le finanze pubbliche 1734–1742* (Naples 1990).

20 For the mid-eighteenth-century events in the *Banco dei poveri* and in the *Banco della Pietà*, see P. Avallone, *Stato e banchi pubblici a Napoli a metà del '700: Il Banco dei Poveri: una svolta* (Naples 1995).

21 In 1771, the *Banco dello Spirito Santo* barely avoided the consequences suffered by the *Banco dell'Annunziata*, due to repeated till thefts by unreliable cashiers, high debts of the "Casa" (charity house) toward the "Banco" (bank), the debts incurred for the renovation of the Church and the enormous number of uneducated employees without any education hired when they were young children. The total debt was calculated to be about 740,000 ducati (80,000 for the renovation, 80,000 for the debt toward the "Banco," 280,000 for the thefts by the employees and the governors, besides 300,000 withdrawn upon pledge). They tried to save money by reducing expenses, by collecting the bank's credits debts and by managing the bank more efficiently. In 1772, the same happened in the *Banco della Pietà* (loans at interest, thefts by the pledge office employees, an inadequate inventorying had not been carried out for some time and the bookkeeping was very arbitrary). In 1780, the *Banco del Popolo* was accused of stealing 248,000 ducati from the City of Naples.

22 D. Demarco, *Storia del Banco di Napoli: Il Banco delle Due Sicilie, 1808–1863* (Naples 1958).

23 de Rosa, *Il Mezzogiorno spagnolo tra crescita e decadenza*, 71–88.

7 Learning from others' failures

The rise of the *Monte di pietà* in early modern Bologna

Mauro Carboni and Massimo Fornasari

Introduction

Business collapses have mostly been viewed as dramatic, negative and disruptive events. Yet, while failures meant disaster to some, they prompted change and offered opportunities to others. There is little doubt that bankruptcies and failures swept up not just capital but people from all walks of life and left behind a trail of broken social relations, litigations and negotiations that at times lasted decades. But in addition to misery and dislocation, failures promoted innovation and economic change, provided opportunities and helped institutional reforms.[1]

In the last quarter of the sixteenth century, the unfolding of a financial crisis of unprecedented pervasiveness nearly destroyed traditional merchant banking across Italy. The nearly frenetic tempo of credit operations via bills of exchange suffered a severe turnaround brought about by a sudden shift in the financial climate.[2] From the mid-1570s the growing difficulties that hit Lyons' financial fairs and the recurrent bankruptcies of the Spanish crown precipitated the peninsula into a sharp recession.[3] The web of financial obligations that had allowed states to have immediate access to large sums of money and had offered banks a golden opportunity for profits made it impossible for political and financial institutions to disengage.[4]

Since "le credit est au coeur des relations économiques et sociales,"[5] these financial blows had a deep and lasting impact, undercutting manufacturing and throttling the economy of Italian cities, just when they were showing signs of growing structural shortcomings. The ensuing deflation was so strong, in the midst of the Price Revolution, that it curbed the long-term upward trend of prices and paved the way for the severe subsistence crisis of the 1590s.[6] In some areas of the peninsula, such as the Po valley, the crisis had a most dramatic impact: it brought to a sudden halt the demographic expansion of the sixteenth century and it laid bare the fragility of the economic system, the competitiveness of which was gradually losing ground in European as well as Levantine markets.[7]

In the main Italian commercial and financial centers—from Venice to Milan, from Florence to Naples—a credit squeeze translated into a wave of bankruptcies that decimated the ranks of Italian private banks and brought depositors sudden and unforeseen losses.[8] Delumeau has documented the collapse of 18 banking companies between 1566 and 1606. In Venice no less than 96 private deposit banks collapsed.[9] The intensity of the credit crunch is clearly revealed by its most common feature: the lack of liquidity—the "strettezza" (stringency)—about which contemporary sources complained. The credit multiplier suddenly worked in reverse. The shortage of money induced cashiers either to pay "in ink"[10]—i.e., in the forms of checks or written endorsements—or to defer repayments, sending from one bank to the next customers who claimed their deposits back.

The disorders and the dissatisfactions brought about by the crisis prompted public intervention. "A switch from private to public banking" took place at the end of the sixteenth century and "was part of a broader trend leading to state domination over Europe's economic and financial life," according to Fernand Braudel, so that states became "the main entrepreneurs of the age."[11] The reaction of Italian states was twofold: on the one hand, they promoted the establishment of new credit agencies, licensed and supervised by public authorities either at the central or local level;[12] on the other hand, they introduced new commercial legislation. This revision led to several important innovations: the introduction both of stricter norms to limit the rights of creditors to the properties of bankrupts and of stiffer penalties to those unable to repay their debts; the subjection of financial operators to greater scrutiny and the requirement to provide more adequate guarantees. In addition new limited-liability forms of company financing began to take shape.[13]

The creation of new credit institutions aimed at regulating the banking sector, which had till then operated with very few restrictions, despite the fact that the custody and the management of savings was of crucial importance in the working of urban economies. In 1586, the *Banco di San Giorgio* resumed operations in Genoa; a year later the *Banco della piazza di Rialto* opened in Venice and the *Tavola della città* in Messina; in 1593 Milanese city authorities established the *Banco di S. Ambrogio* and in 1605 the *Banco di S. Spirito* was founded in Rome. Elsewhere this evolution was captured by the *Monte di pietà*, as was the case in late-sixteenth-century Florence. In Naples the establishment of the *Monte di pietà* (1539) was followed by a further wave of new banks, associated with charitable agencies: the *Monte e Banco dei Poveri* (1563); the *Banco della Ss. Annunziata* (1587); the *Banco di S. Maria del Popolo* (1589); the *Banco dello Spirito Santo* (1590); the *Banco S. Eligio* (1592); the *Banco di S. Giacomo e Vittoria* (1597) and later the *Banco del S. Salvatore* (1640).[14]

In Bologna—the second largest city of the Papal States[15] and one of Europe's leading silk manufacturing centers—the process of restructuring private banking crossed the rise of the local *Monte di pietà*.[16] Loosely controlled by the city itself, the *Monte*—first established in 1473—evolved into a *de facto* public bank, displaying a remarkable tendency to extend its functions to a vast array of credit activities. In the case of Bologna, as elsewhere, it was the waves of bankruptcies that decimated local merchant bank companies, sowed panic among depositors and businessmen, troubled local authorities and threatened public finance at the turn of the seventeenth century, that changed the late-medieval hierarchy of credit in Bologna.

The credit market in Bologna's "long sixteenth century": the institutional agents

At the outset of the sixteenth century, the credit market in Bologna was dominated by Jewish pawnshops and merchant banking firms. Aims, activities and clientele were largely different, as well as prestige and standing, in these two, different venues of money dealering in the city's credit topography.[17]

Seven Jewish pawnshops operated in Bologna during the fifteenth century, and their presence dated back to the mid-fourteenth century. These banks extended modest "distress loans" to poor people in return for pledges and worked according to the so-called practice of the *condotte* (grants of authorization): cities and princes licensed moneylending activities against the payment of annual fees. The system granted the city a regular source of income and regulated to a certain extent private lending activities. In fact, the *condotte* dictated the maximum interest rates that could be charged, routinely fixed between four and six denari per lira per month, i.e., from 20 percent to 30 percent on a yearly basis. Thanks to close ties established with the seigneurial regime of Giovanni II Bentivoglio, at the end of the fifteenth century Jewish banks had acquired a pivotal role, turning Bologna into a key hub and into "one of the capitals of Jewish moneylending in Italy."[18] In the early sixteenth century, Jewish banking kept expanding in numbers and depth, dominating the area of consumer credit, which attracted as borrowers a large clientele from the lower strata of a fast growing urban population.[19] In the meantime, though, after the ousting of the Bentivoglio, the stance of the Bolognese patriciate was undergoing a dramatic change.

Jewish moneylenders did not pose a competitive threat to Bolognese merchant bankers, who carried out credit activities on different levels, held key positions in society and enjoyed high social status. In late-medieval Bologna, leading political families, such as the Pepoli and the Gozzadini, emerged from the ranks of the *Società dei Cambiatori* (moneychangers), one of the oldest and most prestigious city guilds alongside notaries and merchants. Medieval statutes of the *campsores* (1245) were updated in 1481 and yet again in 1653. The presence of a large and affluent population of foreign students in need of credit services had rendered Bologna an attractive, competitive and vibrant market from an early date.[20] Merchant banks offered a variety of financial services: they accepted clients' deposits in their strong boxes, provided short-term credit by bank overdraft and offered a convenient means to transfer money by script without any cash changing hands, giving the same guarantee of a notarized act.[21] In this fashion they allowed a wide circulation of fiduciary money, i.e., bank money. Proximity—most banks were located under the arcade of the *Palazzo dei banchi*, next to *Piazza Maggiore*—helped as well, facilitating relations and ties among the banks and their respective clientele.[22] By the early sixteenth century, most banks had ventured beyond deposit banking and used financial expedients such as exchange contracts, repurchase agreement and bills of exchange. In addition, most banking houses did not limit themselves to financial services but combined banking with tax farming, trading and manufacturing activities.

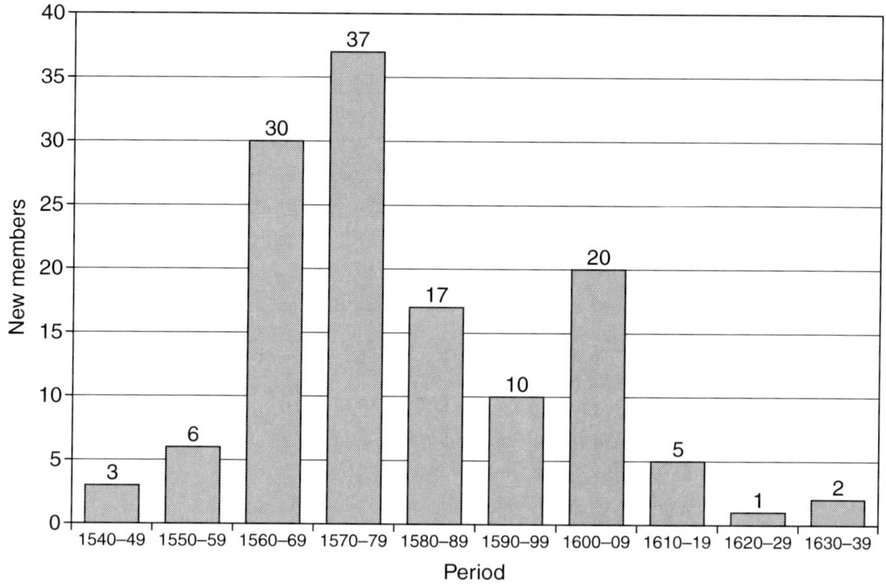

Figure 7.1 Enrollment to the *Società dei Cambiatori*, 1540–1639 (source: Lia Gheza Fabbri, *L'organizzazione del lavoro in una economia urbana: Le Società d'Arti a Bologna nei secoli XVI e XVII* (Bologna 1988), 39).

As a result, the number of registered members to the *Arte dei Cambiatori* expanded considerably alongside the overall number of active banking firms, which exceeded 60 in the 1570s. Such expansion was influenced by a variety of internal and international factors. At the local level, the growing financial needs of both private operators and public agencies once again offered moneydealers not just opportunities to accumulate wealth but even a welcome chance to climb the social ladder.[23] Local banking fortunes could be helped by political backing. Though possessing great entrepreneurial abilities, Ridolfo Bonfioli, Cornelio Malvasia and Mario Scappi rose in society because of the financial support they were able to provide to ambitious prelates and to the papal court. The ascent of the Malvasia, for instance, offers a paradigmatic example: Pope Julius III awarded Cornelio Malvasia a senatorial seat in 1554 in recognition of the generous financial backing he had received from him at the end of his tenure as Legate in Bologna. The opportunity seized by Cornelio Malvasia was fumbled by another local moneydealer, Matteo Amorini, whose decision to deny a personal loan to the future Pope proved disastrously shortsighted. In spite of the family's standing and connections the Amorini lost their chance to enter the patriciate. On the international scene Bolognese merchant bankers benefited from business ties they had managed to establish with Florentine and Genoese firms. These ties were instrumental in allowing Bolognese bankers to take part in the Lyons fairs, the importance of which peaked in the 1570s, and then in the fairs held in Piacenza.[24]

The mid-sixteenth century expansion of Bologna's banking sector, however, did not bring about any significant change in the merchant-banking tradition: the familial nature of capital formation, the fragile organization of the firm and the tendency to engage in other business activities. Bolognese firms did not reach the scale of operation or the geographical horizon of Florentine, Genoese or Venetian firms. The international scene reflected linkages to the silk market, which was emerging as the forward sector of the Bolognese economy, as well as connections to Genoese and Florentine banking houses and the exchange fairs at Lyons and Piacenza.[25] Bolognese moneychangers were a corporate organization, yet they did not possess any kind of larger institutional structure. No organization was imposed upon them by public authorities, and most firms were one-man/one-family operations with very limited evidence of interlocking business partnership. As a result, most firms were not very large, and mobility within the circle of bankers tended to be high. The fragility of the credit edifice was soon exposed by a string of failures spanning over 20 years.

From the late fifteenth century, the activity of a set of new credit agencies insinuated itself between Jewish and merchant-banking companies. The establishment of these new institutions was the result of decades of fierce preaching across central and northern Italy by Observant friars, who wanted to generate what Hermann van der Wee has labeled "a more socially responsible consumer credit":[26] the *Monti di pietà*. A *Monte* opened in Bologna as early as April 1473, but financial and political backing were shaky to say the least. The distrust of the local *Signore*—Giovanni II Bentivoglio—and the neglect of the families associated with his rule kept the *Monte* in political and financial limbo. Lacking political favor, the founders of the *Monte* had hoped that charity would induce people of means to make interest-free deposits that could be used for distress or pledged loans. But most wealthy Bolognese hesitated to place deposits. Since private funding remained sorely inadequate and public support did not shore up its dwindling fortunes, the *Monte* suspended operations as early as December 1474. The heart of the matter was that the Bentivoglio regime had close and lucrative ties with the Jewish pawnshops, to which the control of the lower end of the credit market was entrusted.

The *Monte*'s new start in 1504 was considerably more fortunate; it soon took advantage of the more favorable political climate brought about by the dismissal of the Bentivoglio (1506). The tables were turned: unlike the old *Signori*, the new ruling oligarchy backed the *Monte*, whose statutes were swiftly ratified in 1507 by Bologna's new overlord, Pope Julius II. Progress in the early decades of the sixteenth century was closely associated both with the support of public authorities and with the demise of Jewish pawn banks. Recognizing the usefulness of meeting the needs of the poor by controlling the lower end of the credit market, government officials came to confer the *status* of "civic" bank to the *Monte*. Regular assignment of public funds matched private resources to grant it adequate liquidity, while the standing and creditworthiness of the institution was further strengthened early on by entrusting the office of general treasurer to Antonio Legnani, a well-known banker and a member of the Senate.[27] In addition, authorities played a supportive role by encouraging charitable institutions and city guilds to place funds at the *Monte* during ad hoc public events designed to attract private donations.

In the meantime, the relationship between public authorities and Jewish lenders was reversed; the Jewish community's association with the ousted Bentivoglio regime made them suspect. The worsening religious and political environment doomed them. From the mid-sixteenth century, the growing negative stance of the Bolognese patriciate toward Jewish lenders coincided with a similarly negative attitude, emerging from the church hierarchy, toward all Jewish communities in the Papal States. The numerous ties and contacts, well beyond business relations, established between the Christian and the Jewish communities came under increased scrutiny. A complex set of economic, political and cultural factors, stemming from renewed Catholic religiosity, triggered the provisions leading to the Bull of Pope Paul IV "Cum nimis absurdum," which mandated on 14 July 1555 the segregation of Jewish communities, the sale of real estate owned by Jews, the prohibition of Jews from exercising mercantile activities and the reduction of the legal interest rate on loans to 12 percent.[28] It was the prelude to stricter provisions: the expulsion of the Jewish community from the city, decreed in 1569 and the expulsion of all Jews from the Papal States with the exception of Rome and Ancona, issued in 1593.

By the middle of the sixteenth century, the *Monte* was a towering presence in the pawn banking sector. In order to counter the superior presence of Jewish shops across the city and the countryside, it opened three new agencies within the city walls, placed in "key locations across the city"[29] and sponsored two subsidiary branches in the smaller townships of Budrio and San Giovanni in Persiceto. While Jewish banks faced increased scrutiny and even legal actions, the *Monte* activity grew in spectacular fashion.

Between 1504 and 1519, it handled about 7,000 transactions per year, lending almost 200,000 Bolognese lire. By mid-century, the number of transactions registered a fourfold increase to nearly 28,000 per year. In the decades between 1550 and 1589, the average number of transactions expanded rapidly to over 70,000 per year; the total value of loans increased even more rapidly from 115,877 lire in 1550 to 424,312 lire by the end of the century (see Table 7.2).

Table 7.1 Amount of loans and number of pawn operations at the *Monte di pietà* (1550–89)

	Amount of loans (Bolognese lire)	*Number of pledges*
1550–59	115,877	44,035
1560–69	187,173	67,907
1570–79	213,176	65,114
1580–89	291,563	74,132

Source: M. Fornasari, *Il "thesoro" della città: Il Monte di pietà e l'economia bolognese nei secoli XV e XVI* (Bologna 1993), 366–7.

Table 7.2 Amount of loans and number of pawn operations at the *Monte di pietà* (1590–1649)

	Amount of loans (Bolognese lire)	*Number of pledges*
1590–99	424,312	70,398
1600–09	592,572	93,504
1610–19	717,054	85,918
1620–29	939,528	122,615
1630–39	931,565	69,446
1640–49	1,126,725	99,225

Source: ASMPB, Campioni, *Libri Mastri*, L, M, N, P, Q, R, S, T,V, X, Y, Z, ++.

The operations of the *Monte* and the economic conjuncture followed inverse trends: pledged loans were in greater demand during periods of economic hardship. As a result the *Monte* acted as a social shock-absorber during the sixteenth century subsistence crises. In keeping with contemporary political theory, governments had the duty to ensure the provision of adequate quantities of foodstuffs to their subjects. Failure to do so had serious consequences from the point of view of public order. Yet no less important was the ability to grant subjects, through cheap credit, adequate purchasing power to weather hard times.[30]

Not surprisingly, the *Monte* was able, first, to challenge Jewish pawnshops and, later, to become the leading financial institution operating in Bologna. Command in the sector of pawnbroking turned swiftly into complete monopoly after the previously mentioned expulsion of Jews from the city in 1569. Dominance in the area of consumer credit was a fundamental step, yet the *Monte* emerged as the cornerstone of Bologna's financial edifice only after the crisis and subsequent downsizing of the system of merchant banking.

The collapse of Bologna's leading private banks

The negative cycle of Bolognese merchant banking started in the mid-1570s. The shift in financial climate was anticipated by a petition addressed to the city *Reggimento* by the guild of moneychangers in 1573. Guildmembers petitioned the Senate to grant a subsidy of 25 golden lire in order to give agents a chance "to keep exchange transactions operating to the prestige and advantage of the city, notwithstanding the current hardship."[31] The request was motivated by the financial turmoil, caused by the "ongoing wars in France and Flanders"; it was hoped that, as the confusion receded, it would be possible to resume "alli soliti negotii delle mercantie," without any need of further state support. The guild lamented losses suffered because of the damage recent political and military troubles were inflicting on the regular workings of the fairs at Lyons, in which Bolognese moneydealers took part. Shortly afterward, in 1575, the financial turmoil was made worse by the bankruptcy of the Spanish crown, the subsequent collapse of the money market and the decison of Genoese bankers, in 1579, to move the *Bisenzone* fair of exchange to Piacenza.[32] The credit contraction had severe repercussions in Bologna, where the scarcity of money led to a dramatic increase of interest rates, up to 30 percent on a yearly basis.

The late-sixteenth-century financial turnaround revealed the fragility of private banking: poor cooperation and coordination, insufficient capital accumulation, inadequate organization and dependence on tax farming. The weakness of Bologna's financial edifice was exposed by a string of failures spanning over 20 years. Unfortunately, the literature is rather limited due to the lack of suitable sources. Some of these bankruptcies have, however, left a trail of legal proceedings which fill the gap to some degree, allowing a glimpse of the size and operations of these firms, making up in part for the nearly complete loss of business accounts. Failure closed major as well as minor firms and resulted in a drastic downsizing of private banking, which had till then dominated Bolognese finances.

The string of failures started in November 1583 with the dramatic collapse of the *banco* of Gioseffo Gandolfi. Throughout the sixteenth century, the company had a wide geographical horizon and a good reputation both for its management and the scope of its operations. Private and public money flowed into the bank; it attracted large deposits from scores of clients—locals as well as foreigners—and had business dealings with local government agencies, to which it offered tax-farming services and short-term loans. The limits of sound banking must have been overstepped, and the Gandolfi experienced difficulties in meeting payments first in February then in August 1583. Things came to a head on 29 October when new rumors about the Gandolfi's solvency caused a run on its counting house, leading many to withdraw their money in just a few hours.[33] As the shortage of cash became acute, no assistance came from other firms, with which Gandolfi had business dealings. The entire system was already reeling from a liquidity crisis. Direct action from local authorities, lest their interest should suffer, made matters worse, turning fear into panic and accelerating the collapse. The feared "traboccamento" (overflowing) of the *banco* was communicated by Gioseffo's son, Paolo, to the Cardinal Legate on 4 November. In the meantime Gioseffo and Paolo's brother, Carlo Antonio, left Bologna for fear of imprisonment or worse.

The Legate's actions were swift and decisive. On 5 November, all Gandolfi's assets were seized, valuables were to be deposited at the *Monte di pietà*, and a balance sheet was hastily drafted. Concerns on the part of the authorities were justified by the prospect of serious losses of fiscal receipts. The Gandolfi bank had managed the Depositary of the office of the *Abbondanza*, which was responsible for the provision of grain, and the Depositary of both the Apostolic Chamber in Bologna and the municipal Chamber. The Gandolfi had collected revenues but were in arrears in their payments. Courts estimated the overall liabilities of the Gandolfi at nearly 500,000 lire, one-fourth of which was owed to public agencies. Delaying payments to private creditors in favor of "public" ones resulted in a lawsuit over priorities that pitted Bolognese and Roman authorities against one another. Pope Gregory XIII, trained in law at Bologna, found most unusual and improper that a depositary would be allowed to divert tax money.

Table 7.3 Assets and liabilities of the Gandolfi bank, 5 November 1583

Liabilities	*Bolognese lire*	*Assets*	*Bolognese lire*
Camera Apostolica	31,113.51	Urban properties	101,357.35
Other credits of the Camera Apostolica	6,099.81	Bonds	11,285.77
Camera di Bologna	89,476.75	Real estate	13,885.38
Palace in Bologna	5,975.70	Bakers	37,686.30
Private creditors	258,149.55	Domenico Baruta	15,948.51
Foreign creditors (approximately)	100,000.00	Old tax farmers	35,384.66
		Other debtors	171,794.36
Total liabilities	490,815.34	Total assets	387,342.34

Source: ASB, Ambasciata Bolognese a Roma, *Posizione degli affari trattati a Roma*, b. 201, f. 4.

He scolded Bolognese authorities for laxity and accused Gandolfi of having breached public trust by siphoning off tax receipts the bank collected and was supposed to retain in its safes. Although hardly legal, the practice of using public funds as a base to expand credit was certainly not uncommon (and not limited to Bologna) among moneylenders, who regularly acted as tax farmers or depositaries.[34]

The Gandolfi collapse was the result of both poor coordination and a liquidity crisis that the bank was unable to weather. Similar circumstances, in 1591, brought about the failure of two other local bankers: Cesare Vecelli and Ludovico Salani. Insolvency forced them out of business, but, according to chronicles, they faced misfortune in a very different fashion: The former "closed the bank and went into hiding"; the latter "did not hide himself" and faced creditors' lawsuits.[35]

A new string of failures marked the 1590s and did not spare larger, sounder and politically better-connected private banks. Actually, association with public finance turned from an asset into a liability. The dramatic economic downturn of the 1590s caused a severe reduction in the flow of tax revenues. As a result, banks that had participated in tax-farming contracts faced the dire prospect of incurring serious losses. In 1589, on the eve of the crisis, Antonio and Girolamo Lucchini, heirs to a family of Genoese merchant bankers who had resettled in Bologna in the first half of the sixteenth century, purchased in partnership with Girolamo Gnetti the right to collect the city's custom duties on the import and export of merchandises known as *Gabella Grossa*.[36] The contract stipulated a seven-year period and a net price of 85,588 lire 15 soldi per annum. The customs were considered a very profitable investment, and previous receipts provided a starting point. Unfortunately, the timing of the contract could hardly have been worse.[37] At about the same time another important banking firm, named after Mario Scappi, acquired the *Depositeria* of the *Gabella Grossa*. It is interesting to note that, by then, the Scappi and the Lucchini were not just business associates but had established solid family ties as well. An alliance had been arranged through the marriage of Francesca Scappi, daughter of Pietro Maria and sister of

Mario to Filippo Lucchini. Bankers Vincenzo, Bartolomeo, Girolamo and Giovanni Battista Lucchini were cousins to the *Gabella* contractors, Antonio and Girolamo.[38]

As the tax-farming contract ran its course, financial losses mounted. By October 1595, the farmers had an outstanding debt of 344,648 lire 14 soldi (see Table 7.4). The loss of the Lucchini forced the depositary to intervene and opened the prospect of a bitter struggle with the tax administration. In fact, the Scappi bank, now managed by the heirs of the deceased Mario, had to provide cash advances to meet the tax farmers' obligations. As a result, both firms teetered on the brink of receivership.

Yet again disaster loomed. On this occasion, perhaps prompted by the lessons learned a few years earlier at the Gandolfi's expense, decisive assistance came from public authorities. "To prevent lawsuits and limit losses" (*Per evitare liti e lenire le perdite*) an influential member of the Bolognese patriciate, Ridolfo Bonfioli, senator and financier, proposed an innovative transaction leading to a new 14-year contract and a debt rescheduling by means of the issuance of a 14-year, funded debt (*Monte*) with a capital of 500,000 lire at 6.5 percent interest. Bonfioli managed to secure the approval of both the local *Reggimento* and Pope Clement VIII for his plan, designed to avoid a dangerous financial meltdown. The *Monte*, which took the name of "Restauro della Gabella", received the papal *placet* in the Fall of 1595 at the slightly reduced sum of 450,000 lire.[39] Antonio Lucchini could float shares for the agreed amount, but had to secure the full backing of his cousins—"heir to Filippo Lucchini and his banks" (*eredi di Filippo Lucchini e loro banchi*)—as well as Scappi's participation and guarantee. The "public" bore the servicing costs of the debt; resources to pay interest to perspective creditors came from higher custom duties. Most of the capital raised went to settle the outstanding debt with the *Gabella* and the depositary. In the meantime, Antonio Lucchini and Girolamo Gnetti entered a new tax-farming contract, issued under much more benign conditions. To ease the financial straits tax farmers faced, the contract envisioned a duration twice as

Table 7.4 Profit and losses from the tax-farming of the Bolognese customs (1589–95)

Year	*Revenues (Bolognese lire)*	*Contract net price (Bolognese lire)*	*Other expenses (Bolognese lire)*	*Loss*
1589	102,356.2	85,588.75	40,730.25	23,963.2
1590	104,287.5	85,588.75	41,823.45	23,114.7
1591	85,312.9	85,588.75	44,490.15	44,766.0
1592	84,468.7	85,588.75	50,598.05	51,718.1
1593	73,657.9	85,588.75	56,254.15	68,185.0
1594	72,476.6	85,588.75	60,581.75	73,693.9
1595*	55,381.7	71,323.95	62,560.15	78,502.4

Source: ASB, Congregazione di Gabella Grossa, *Miscellanea*, b. 1024.

Note

* In 1595 revenues and expenses refer to a ten-month period only.

long, 14 years, while the rent was reduced by more than one-third to 56,008 lire from 85,588 lire.

Despite this favorable, new start, the negative economic conjuncture rendered the whole operation difficult. As a matter of fact, only intrafamily solidarity allowed the successful launch of the *Monte* itself. Since no subscribers at first stepped forward to purchase shares of the *Restauro*, Filippo Lucchini's company, headed by Vincenzo, filled the financial void. The son of Filippo Lucchini and Francesca Scappi, he was a successful manager, silk merchant and wholesale trader with an extensive network of business dealings that extended to Flanders.[40] He bought up *en bloc* the entire fund with the right to place shares on the secondary market afterwords. This allowed his cousins to settle their debt with the Scappi bank and to set aside a capital of about 150,000 lire that the Lucchini bank could invest in exchange operations at financial fairs. It was hoped that Vincenzo's ability to play with exchange rates—lending money through fairs and making a profit—would result in earnings adequate to retire the *Restauro* by 1609. Unfortunately the plan proved too ambitious: in 1603 the Lucchini company went bankrupt.[41]

Fatal was the combined impact of losses suffered in the commercial ventures in northern Europe, jointly operated by Vincenzo and his brother Girolamo, and those incurred in the exchanges to shore up the dwindling fortunes of his cousins. Court records of 1613, written a decade after the collapse, reveal that the Lucchini posted spectacular losses over the exchanges to the tune of 12 percent a year.[42] The insolvency amounted to a staggering 190,000 *scudi*, almost 1,000,000 lire. This was more than all the Bolognese fiscal agencies netted in a year. The reputation and fortunes of the Lucchini lay in ruins: their palace and all their country estates were seized and auctioned in the summer of 1604 (see Table 7.5). And court proceedings with *Restauro* creditors—mostly Genoese—continued for years afterward.[43]

Lucchini's increasing troubles related directly to Scappi's decision to abandon banking. In 1597, Pietro Maria and his brothers "ceased all banking activity at the end of May."[44] Patrician status and a senatorial seat may also have contributed to induce the Scappi to leave financial dealings for less risky activities. The appreciation of return versus risk may reveal both the adoption of an attitude and

Table 7.5 Seized properties of the Eredi di Filippo Lucchini Company, 1603

Properties	*Estimated value (Bolognese lire)*
Farms in the Bolognese countryside	884,000
Farms with mills and shops	124,000
Family palace in Bologna	80,000
Three silk mills (*filatogli*)	30,000
Banco headquarters in Bologna	14,000
House in Bologna	5,000
Total	1,137,000

Source: ASB, Congregazione di Gabella Grossa, *Instrumenti*, b. 156.

lifestyle closer to the *rentier* nobility and the increasing difficulty of "fare banca" at the turn of the sixteenth century. Indeed, in the very year the Scappi left behind banking, several provisions issued by Bologna's Vice Legate lamented the lack of liquidity, as 15 years earlier, warned against "sending creditors from bank to bank" (*far correre i creditori da un banco all'altro*) and denounced "the strictness of money and credit caused by Spain's decision to suspend payments a few months earlier." All this went to the detriment of bank activities and caused a loss of profitability.[45]

In 1602, a year before the collapse of the Lucchini bank, another banking firm held in high esteem, the *banco* Ghelli, went through an important but sudden societal transformation. Taddeo Ghelli, a well-known banker and silk merchant, was murdered under mysterious circumstances inside his family's palace.[46] Taddeo's wife, Livia Bocchi, decided thereupon to abandon banking: her sons were simply too young to take charge of the family business. The Ghelli's assets were liquidated and, as a result, the business was taken over by Ludovico Maestri and Annibale Fioravanti, the junior partners with whom Taddeo had shared his financial and commercial ventures till his sudden death. Taddeo's widow claimed an estate worth about 250,000 lire, half of which came from the bank patrimony. Its assets totalled about 300,000. Its ledger listed debtors and creditors from the main European financial centers, such as Cologne, Venice and Milan.[47] More than anything else, the hasty liquidation of Taddeo's assets revealed the hazard and vulnerability of one-man business operations. The lack of entrepreneurial talents able to follow in Taddeo's steps compromised the family's business prospects. The untimely death of the patriarch left family and business activities rudderless and prompted a hasty cessation of activity.

The rise of Monte

As successive crises engulfed local banks and public confidence was shaken, the *Monte* came increasingly to be perceived as a safe haven. Not surprisingly, depositors flocked to it in ever larger numbers. Already in the aftermath of the collapse of the Gandolfi banks, the four caretakers named by the board of creditors took the momentous step of placing all assets of the firm to be liquidated with the *Monte di pietà*.

It represented by far the most important institutional innovation on the Bolognese financial scene, and it is certainly significant that the arrangements that proved decisive in assuring the lasting fortunes of the *Monte* were introduced in the mid 1570s and put to the test in the decades that followed. The *Monte* developed a large professional bureacracy. The governing body was composed of 12 officials, called *presidenti*, one of whom assumed the role of chairman on a rotating basis. *Presidenti* were elected according to a complex procedure for a term of four years, renewable only once. By the end of the sixteenth century, the administrative staff consisted of more than 30 persons, about six in the central office and all others in four subsidiary branches. Central management was headed by a director (*economo*) with a general treasurer (*depositario*) and a small staff of accountants, headed by a bookkeeper (*campioniere*). Each branch had its own manager (*massaro*) and staff of accountants and clerks. This administration grew in size and specialization: by 1660, the staff included 48 employees. The *Monte* bureaucracy produced an increasingly sophisticated set of accounts, made up of separate but coordinated ledgers, with cross-references leading to the main ledger (*mastro*), a thick book that by the early decades of the seventeenth century was made up of about 1,000 folios.[48]

From the mid 1560s the ledgers of the *Monte* reveal a growing number of business transactions involving no less than 12 local *banchi*. It is interesting to note that while private banks initially deposited funds and were a welcome source of added liquidity to the *Monte*, the relationship slowly reversed. By the early 1580s, the *Monte* had taken increasingly the role of creditor, extending considerable loans to private banks.

The troubles that engulfed private banks in successive waves paid significant dividends not just in terms of reputation but also in terms of business. From the last decade of the sixteenth century onward, the ledgers of the *Monte* reveal that nearly all important agencies had opened a current account, from public institutions, such as the Municipal and Apostolic Chambers, to charitable institutions, such as the *Poveri Vergognosi* and the *Mendicanti*, to a variety of financial operators, such as the *Monte del Matrimonio* (a dowry fund), and private banking firms, such as Fioravanti, Cattalani, Marchesini and Davia and Fantetti and Cattani.

By the early decades of the seventeenth century, the *Monte* had become something like a public deposit bank, an enormous operation, dominating not just pawn banking but the entire credit market. In addition to the traditional pawn banking activities, it provided an easily accessible outlet for savings to people of moderate means and put capital to uses of varying economic importance. Besides distress loans, it provided direct loans to wealthy people, even if it is impossible to know to what extent loans to individuals went toward productive sectors of the economy. The *Monte* also became increasingly integrated into the machinery of Bolognese public finances, acquiring lucrative public offices and establishing firm financial ties with the local government through tax collection, short-term loans and public debt servicing.[49]

The change in the scale of operations becomes obvious upon confronting the ledgers. From the early decades of the seventeenth century, ledgers became so thick that they can hardly be handled, and the mass of data in the accounts far exceeds those of just a few decades earlier. Between 1590 and 1650, the number of *Monte* transactions vacillated in a remarkable fashion: the average annual number ranged from about 70,000 to about 122,000, but stabilized in the later part of the century around 100,000. Throughout the second half of the seventeenth century, the overall number of transactions, items pledged and redeemed, was frequently in excess of 200,000 per year. The financial scale of the *Monte* operations followed a much simpler and steeper upward trend: the flow of money lent against pledges soared from 424,000 lire in the 1590s to over 700,000 in the 1610s, to over 1.1 million in the late 1640s. Capital ballooned from 423,000 lire

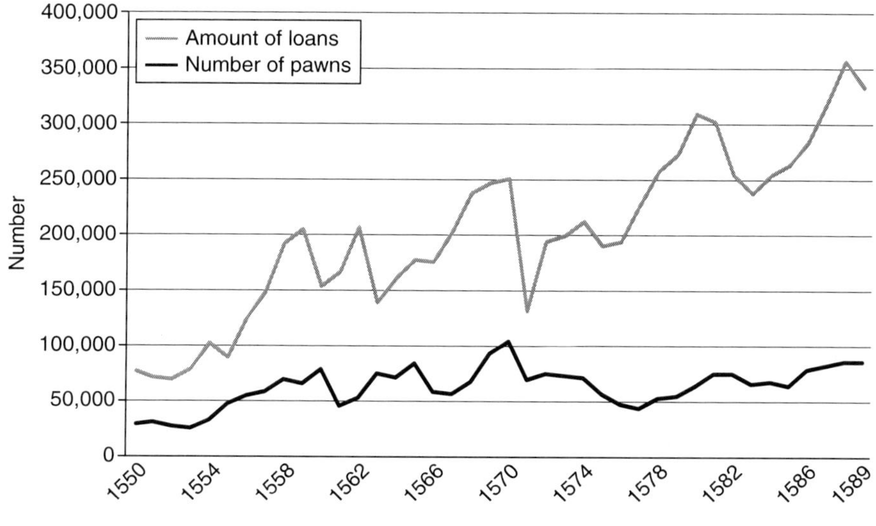

Figure 7.2 Number of pledges and amount of *Monte*'s loans (1550–89).

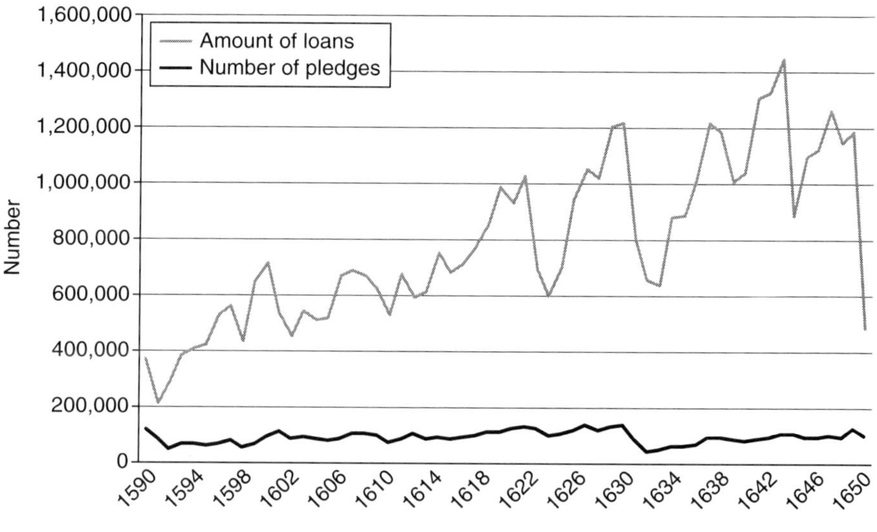

Figure 7.3 Number of pledges and amount of *Monte*'s loans (1590–1650).

in 1590 to 613,000 lire in 1610 to over 1.2 million in 1650. Clients with deposits increased from less than 400 to over 1,100. Overall assets shot from 560,000 lire in 1590 to nearly 1.1 million lire in 1610 to over 2.2 million by the mid-1640s.[50]

To put things into perspective, it is useful to compare *Monte* assets and activities to those of the main private banks. A review of the books of the *banco* Gandolfi shortly after its collapse in 1583 reveal assets of about 422,000 lire; the *banco* Ghelli had assets of 295,000 lire in 1602; while the *banco* Lucchini had assets in excess of 1.0 million lire in 1603. *Monte* operations increased even more sharply in terms of clientele. For the first time, Bolognese outside the circle of affluent elites had an accessible outlet for savings. Indeed, the *Monte* managed a much larger number of current accounts from private individuals in addition to those of private firms, charitable agencies and monastic houses. In 1610 the *Monte* held over 1,100 deposits, including sums less than one lira. By contrast, the *banco* Lucchini owed money to just 67 clients—mostly firms—and the *banco* Ghelli held deposits from 136 individuals and firms.

Conclusion

The wave of bankruptcies, which affected the credit sector of the economy in late-sixteenth-century Bologna, did not bring about formal changes in the internal organization or coordination of firms, nor did it introduce greater supervision from local authorities. Yet, the experience and concerns about the creditworthiness of financial institutions prompted in practice a major shift in the allocation of capital within the credit sector. Traditional banking, based on personal reputation, social relations and family capital, survived but was increasingly marginalized. More and more capital flowed elsewhere: political clout, collective responsibility, large assets and professional administration turned the *Monte* from a lesser player into the linchpin of the city financial system.

Financial activities came to revolve around the *Monte*, which institutionalized, consolidated, expanded and even refined the working of the local credit market. Its ledgers document the accumulation of financial means, the multiplication of current accounts and the increased familiarity with credit instruments of Bolognese from all walks of life. In addition, the institutionalization of lending practices resulted in the lowering of interest rates. It remains unclear how these advances, associated with modern banking, influenced economic development. Larger operation scales and lower borrowing costs seem to have produced little economic renewal. Rather, the supply of disposable wealth was not reinvested as capital in the forward sectors of the Bolognese economy, but was consumed to promote social stability.

Notes

1 P.C. Hautcoer, "Pour un approche quantitative des faillites," *Histoire et Mesure* 23 (2008): 3–17. The article is part of a collection of essays the above-mentioned journal has devoted to the issue of insolvency: "Justice commerciale et histoire économique." See also the recent special issue "Debiti e crediti" in *Quaderni Storici* 46 (2011).

2 C.M. Cipolla, *Money in Sixteenth-Century Florence* (Berkeley, CA 1989), 101–114; M.-T. Boyer-Xambeu, G. Deleplace and L. Gillard, *Private Money and Public Currencies: the Sixteenth Century Challenge* (Paris 1994), 160–197.

3 Delumeau has underlined the structural features of the late-sixteenth-century crisis in Italy: J. Delumeau, *Rome au XVIe siècle* (Paris 1975).

4 In recent years a considerable body of research has been devoted to the links that developed between governments and bankers during the sixteenth century: A. Orlandi,

Le Grand Parti: Fiorentini a Lione e il debito pubblico francese nel XVI secolo (Florence 2002); F.G. Bruscoli, *Papal Banking in Renaissance Rome: Benvenuto Olivieri and Paul III, 1534–1549* (Aldershot 2007); C. Marsilio, *Dove il denaro fa denaro: Gli operatori finanziari genovesi nelle fiere di cambio del XVII secolo* (Novi Ligure 2008); E.M. Garcia Guerra and G. De Luca (eds.), *Il mercato del credito in età moderna: Reti e operatori finanziari nello spazio europeo* (Milan 2009).

5 Hautcoeur, "Pour un approche," 4.

6 In a key commercial and financial center, such as Florence, Cipolla has noted that "at the height of the so-called Price Revolution one finds a drop of almost 10 percent between 1575 and 1590 in the price index calculated by Parenti"; Cipolla, *Money in Sixteenth-Century*, 115.

7 M. Aymard, "La fragilità di un'economia avanzata: l'Italia e le trasformazioni dell'economia europea," in: R. Romano (ed.), *Storia dell'economia italiana. II. L'età moderna* (Turin 1991); G. Alfani, *Il Grand Tour dei Cavalieri dell'Apocalisse: L'Italia del 'lungo Cinquecento' (1494–1629)* (Venice 2010).

8 Since the 1970s numerous works have been devoted to the "banking crisis" in Italian cities, the following lists include some of the most significant contributions: U. Tucci, *Mercanti, navi e monete nel Cinquecento veneziano* (Bologna 1981); G. De Luca, *Commercio del denaro e crescita economica a Milano tra Cinquecento e Seicento* (Milan 1997); Cipolla, *Money in Sixteenth-Century*; R. Sabatini, *I Guinigi fra '500 e '600: Il fallimento mercantile ed il rifugio nei campi* (Lucca 1979); Delumeau, *Rome au XVIe siècle*; L. De Rosa, *Il Mezzogiorno spagnolo tra crescita e decadenza* (Milan 1987).

9 Delumeau, *Rome au XVIe siècle*, 236–246; J. Day, *Money and Finance in the Age of Merchant Capitalism* (Oxford 1999), 38.

10 This colorful expression was used by the Florentine chronicler Bastiano Arditi and has been quoted by Cipolla, *Money in Sixteenth-Century*, 107.

11 Tucci, *Mercanti, navi e monete.*

12 G. Felloni, "Dall'Italia all'Europa: il primato della finanza italiana dal Medioevo alla prima età moderna," in: A. Cova, S. La Francesca, A. Moioli and C. Bermond (eds.), *Storia d'Italia. Annali 23. La banca* (Turin 2008), 93–149. De Rosa has claimed that "the successful consolidation of public banks in Naples was a key-factor in the economic decline of the Italian *mezzogiorno.*" De Rosa, *Il Mezzogiorno spagnolo tra crescita e decadenza*, 89.

13 The renewal of mercantile legislation dates from the mid-sixteenth century to the early seventeenth century. See, V. Piergiovanni (ed.), *The Courts and the Development of Commercial Law* (Berlin 1987).

14 *Banchi pubblici, banchi privati e monti di pietà nell'Europa preindustriale: amministrazione, tecniche operative e ruoli economici*, Atti del convegno, Genova, 1–6 ottobre 1990 (Genoa 1991); R. Goldthwaite, "Banking in Florence at the End of the Sixteenth Century," *Journal of European Economic History* 27 (1998): 471–525.

15 The Bolognese population was actually overtaken by Rome only in the later part of the sixteenth century. Within the walls, it oscillated between 60,000 and 70,000 throughout the early modern period. See A. Bellettini, *La popolazione di Bologna dal XV secolo all'unificazione italiana* (Bologna 1961), 25–26.

16 M. Fornasari, *Il "thesoro" della città: Il Monte di pietà e l'economia bolognese nei secoli XV e XVI* (Bologna 1993).

17 M. Fornasari, "Istituzioni, professionisti, privati: le reti del credito nella Bologna dell'età moderna," in: A. Prosperi (ed.), *Storia di Bologna, 3*, Bologna nell'età moderna secoli XVI-XVIII). I. Istituzioni, forme del potere, economia e società* (Bologna 2008), 791–856.

18 M. Luzzatti, "Banchi e insediamenti ebraici nell'Italia centro-settentrionale fra tardo Medioevo e inizi dell'Età moderna," in: C. Vivanti (ed.), *Storia d'Italia, Annali 11, Gli Ebrei in Italia* (Turin 1997), 203.

19 M.G. Muzzarelli, "I banchi ebraici, il Monte Pio e i mercati del denaro a Bologna tra XIII e XVI secolo," in: O. Capitani (ed.), *Storia di Bologna, 2, Bologna nel Medioevo* (Bologna 2007), 999–1016.
20 On medieval banking and politics in Bologna, see M. Giansante, *L'usuraio onorato: Credito e potere a Bologna in età comunale* (Bologna 2008).
21 U. Tucci, "Monete e banche nel secolo del ducato d'oro," in: A. Tenenti and U. Tucci (eds.), *Storia di Venezia, V, Il Rinascimento Società ed economia* (Rome 1996), 775.
22 M. Maragi, *Moneta e credito a Bologna dal Rinascimento all'Unità nazionale* (Bologna 1988), 76.
23 A cohort of banking families—Bonfioli, Legnani, Malvasia, Scappi—managed to join the ranks of the Bolognese elite during the sixteenth century: F. Massimo, "Credito e banca nella prima età moderna. Matteo Amorini, 'campsor Bononiensis,'" *Studi Storici Luigi Simeoni* 51 (2001): 29–42.
24 G. Felloni, "All'apogeo delle fiere genovesi: banchieri ed affari di cambio a Piacenza nel 1600," in: *Studi in onore di Gino Barbieri: Problemi e metodi di Storia ed Economia* (Pisa 1983), 883–901.
25 M. Amato, *Le radici di una fede: Per una storia del rapporto tra moneta e credito in Occidente* (Milan 2008), 143–154.
26 H. van der Wee, *Money, The Low Countries and the Early Modern World* (Aldershot 1993), 184.
27 Fornasari, *Il "Thesoro" della città*, 21–124.
28 A. Foa, *The Jews of Europe after the Black Death* (Berkeley, CA 2000), 138.
29 Fornasari, "Istituzioni, professionisti, private," 800.
30 D. Strangio, "Di fronte alla carestia in età preindustriale," *Rivista di Storia Economica* 14 (1998): 161–192.
31 Archivio di Stato di Bologna (ASB), Senato, *Instrumenti, scritture et altro*, B, l. 21, f. 13: *di poter mantenere il trafico del cambio ad honore et utile di questa cittade nonostante la mala qualità dei tempi.* On the financial fragility of the early modern Italian economy: Aymard, *La fragilità di un'economia avanzata*, 78–79.
32 M. Drelichman and H.-J. Voth, "The Sustainable Debts of Philip II: Reconstruction of Spain's Fiscal Position, 1560–1598," *Journal of Economic History* 70 (2010): 814–843.
33 Fornasari, *Il "Thesoro" della città*, 207–223.
34 Ibid., 222.
35 Biblioteca Universitaria Bologna (BUB), A.F. Ghiselli, *Memorie antiche manoscritte della città di Bologna*, MS 770, vol. XVIII (November 1591).
36 On the working of the Gabella Grossa, the management of which was entrusted to the Colleges of Bolognese *Studio*, see M. Carboni, "La finanza pubblica a Bologna in età moderna," in: A. Prosperi (ed.), *Storia di Bologna, 3*, Bologna nell'età moderna secoli XVI-XVIII). I. Istituzioni, forme del potere, economia e società* (Bologna 2008), 736–737.
37 ASB, Congregazione di Gabella Grossa, *Istrumenti*, b. 154, *Locazione della Gabella ad Antonio Lucchini, Annibale Gnetti e Compagni*, 30 December 1589.
38 BUB, Montefani Caprara, *Famiglie bolognesi*, t. 50, cc. 207–224.
39 ASB, Ambasciata Bolognese a Roma, *Posizione degli affari trattati a Roma*, b. 264.
40 BUB, Montefani Caprara, op. cit.
41 ASB, Congregazione di Gabella Grossa, *Instrumenti*, b. 156, *Procura di credito dello stato del fu Filippo Lucchini*, 22 December 1603; ASB, Ambasciata bolognese a Roma, *Posizione degli affari trattati a Roma*, n. 264.
42 ASB, Scappi Ariosti, II, *Processi*, n. 71.
43 Given the loss of the Lucchini archive, we have to rely on court proceedings and information assembled by public authorities.
44 ASB, Scappi Ariosti, II, *Processi*, n. 91: *in fini mensis maij desierint exercere bancum.*

45 ASB, Ambasciata bolognese a Roma, *Posizione degli affari trattati a Roma*, b. 15.
46 M. Fornasari, *Famiglia e affari in età moderna: I Ghelli di Bologna* (Bologna 2002), 130–142.
47 Ibid., 148.
48 M. Carboni, "La sfida della complessità: l'amministrazione del Monte di Pietà di Bologna nel Seicento," in: M. Carboni and M.G. Muzzarelli (eds.), *I conti dei Monti: Teoria e pratica amministrativa nei Monti di Pietà fra Medioevo ed Età Moderna* (Venice 2008), 75–92.
49 Carboni, *La sfida della complessità*, 76–77.
50 ASMPB, Campioni, *Libri Mastri*, nos. L, M, N, P, Q, R, S, T, U, V, X, Y, Z, ++.

8 Bankruptcy and the bank

The case of the "kaiserlich königliche Wiener octroyierte Commercial-, Leih- und Wechselbank" of Vienna in the 18th century[1]

Dana Štefanová

Introduction

The way banks treated customers who made mistakes with regard to their businesses or failed because of imperfect market structures (institutional failures, failure of contract enforcement, etc.) represents an under-researched area in business and social history. My chapter concentrates on insolvent or bankrupt businesses and how they were treated by their bank. Recent research points to the fact that 51 new laws of the period, 1808–1914, were designed to protect the interests of creditors in case of bankruptcy.[2] Such clear policy aims cannot be taken for granted, as the following case study from the period of enlightened absolutism in the Habsburg Empire illustrates. I shall try to show that much depended then on the social status of the individuals involved and on the political ambitions of state authorities.[3]

This chapter takes as its example the "kaiserlich königliche [hereinafter k.k.] Wiener octroyierte Commercial-, Leih- und Wechselbank," chartered in 1787 by Emperor Joseph II and granted privileges for a period of 25 years. In reality, it remained in business until approximately 1830. The reigns of Joseph II (1780–1790) and his mother, Maria Theresia (1740–1780), were characterized by many enlightened absolutist reforms in religion, politics, society and economy. Economic reforms combined mercantilist and physiocratic principles. In the context of this study, the efforts to limit the powers of rural landlords vis-à-vis their villagers seem particularly relevant, designed as they were to register and tax assets in landlord property. These only came into practice, however, with the next cadastral survey in the first half of the nineteenth century.

In order to grasp the bank's reactions and activities with respect to insolvent customers, it is crucial to understand the bank itself. The social background of the entrepreneurs as well as of the customers thus plays an important role in this period of reform as does the management organization of the institution. There follows a brief discussion of the bank. Then, two case studies—the Viennese–Greek merchant Johann Georg Paziazi and the woolen manufacturer Johannes Tost of Southern Bohemia—will illustrate questions surrounding the issue of bankruptcy.

The Vienna "k.k. oktroyierte Commerzial-, Leih- und Wechselbank"

When considering the foundation of the bank, which aimed at developing the realm's commerce and the manufacturing,[4] it appears paradoxical that the privilege was first given to a Danish merchant, Henning Friedrich Bargum, in 1787.[5] An earlier attempt, in 1786, failed, I think, because it lacked the participation of the nobility. In 1787, the founders included some of the best known and wealthiest aristocratic personalities of the Habsburg Empire: Johann zu Schwarzenberg, Franz Gundaker Colloredo-Mannsfeld and Friedrich Nostitz-Rieneck. Schwarzenberg was by far the richest member of the bank's board of owners, and Colloredo-Mannsfeld, as imperial chancellor, was the person with the greatest political influence.[6] Schwarzenberg's landed property was concentrated in Bohemia and Styria, Colloredo-Mannsfeld's in Lower Austria.[7] Friedrich Nostitz-Rieneck (1728–1796) was imperial field marshal, chamberlain, privy councillor and president of the war council. He held landed property in Bohemia.

The involvement of state authorities was particularly important to the bank, because only they could pass regulations that were valid in all parts of the monarchy. Rural landlords had some authority over the administration of their estates, and regional governments were responsible for the administration of particular provinces or territories. It is clear, therefore, that in order to be able to conduct business successfully in all parts of the Habsburg Empire, the bank required a special privilege and the support of the imperial government. It was a consequence of the particularistic and composite structure of a state made up by various semi-independent territories.

Even if the board of owners and Bargum concentrated on their own interests, they seemed to grasp the importance of the bank in a more general sense before the state administration did. They realized, if the services of the bank were used more widely, its full potential would become obvious. It seems that state authorities remained skeptical in this respect, because Bargum and company tended to argue the case repeatedly in great detail.

According to H. Freudenberger, the "Schwarzenberg Bank," as the "k.k. Oktroyierte Commerzial-, Leih- und Wechselbank" became popularly known,[8] was one of the first private banking houses of the Habsburg Empire.[9] The history of this bank and its role in the history of business and industrialization has been ignored until recently.[10] That the Schwarzenberg Bank was to become a private banking institution was not explicitly defined in the year when it was established, however, even though the first charter clearly separated the bank's business activities from state finances.

This became inevitable as a result of fraud. In 1791, the founding charter holder, Henning Friedrich Bargum, and his auditor, Schwarz, were implicated in the embezzlement of 200,000 gulden, an extraordinary amount. In the following year, the bank received a new charter[11] and regulations,[12] according to which the members of the board of owners were declared personally liable for the capital received in exchange for bank bonds (*Bankobligationen*). This was meant to reduce risk and regain trust from new customers,[13] both of which had been seriously affected by Bargum's crime.

The management of the bank had two levels of administration. The board of owners determined business strategies and bank regulations since 1792. The executive board, made up of the cashier, the bookkeeper and the auditor, ran the bank's day-to-day business and were in regular contact with the board of owners.

The question who could legally bind the bank was also resolved as a result of the scandal. Bargum had originally intended to take a position between the upper and lower administrations in order to exercise a strong influence over bank business. After his disgrace and the bank's reorganization, most contracts required the signatures of all three members of the executive board, while other matters, such as setting up bank bills of exchange, also required the signature of one of the noble members of the board of owners.[14] Bargum had intended that noblemen, apart from investing their own capital, should have only a representative role vis-à-vis investors and customers and, thus, help to increase public confidence in the institution. They should not participate in the concrete business, but this turned out within a few months to be an illusion.

Any transaction that had to do with income or expenses required the signature of all three members of the executive board and had to be entered into the protocols before it became valid.[15] The responsibilities of this board were outlined in bank regulations that show clearly its responsibility to represent an institutional unity, governed by the interests of the board of owners and of the bank. The executive board was responsible for all financial and commercial operations, each member having his own designated area of duties as well as mutual oversight of each other. Its members were also responsible for the daily operations of the bank and its employees, all of whom were to have the necessary qualifications. Of course, the executive board also had ideas of its own about business activities, such as the rates of interest and new ventures. Regarding everyday activities, they informed the board of owners about negotiations with customers and drafted decisions regarding account transactions, customer requests, labor relations (wages, employment) and so on. Management answered to the board of owners as well as to the bank.[16]

The new charter and regulations of 1792 tightened security measures and placed them in the hands of the board of owners. Transactions only became valid with the signatures of at least two of its members.[17] This was designed to secure the board's influence and control over the type and extent of transactions. At the same time, it signaled clearly that all members of the board had to develop an interest in the day-to-day business of the bank and take responsibility for decisions. Paragraph 15 of the regulations specifies that members of the board of owners had the right as individuals, but also as an institutional body—"in corpore"—to look into all bank activities and books. They could demand explanations regarding all affairs. To make this more efficient, the executive board prepared a weekly report for each member of the board of owners that listed daily income and expenditures. In a similar manner, all operational and other costs had to be presented to the board of owners for permission after audit investigations.[18]

By these and other measures, members of the board of owners realized very early that problems arose from the loans the bank had granted. To protect the bank's interests, they actively sought a privilege of litigation in order to be able to handle cases of non-payment or default. They argued that such customers caused enormous financial problems and that the bank, up to this point, had gained no advantage from holding goods, whether collateral or pawns, in exchange for a credit, but that, on the contrary, this added the costs of storage facilities to the bank's losses. The right to litigate would enable the bank to hold public auctions of goods held as collateral or security for loans. If the income was higher than the original debts, the surplus was to be paid to the goods' former owner. Because no laws existed to govern the resolution of bankruptcy, banks and financial institutions had to rely on individual privileges to be able to act. When the board first applied, there was an immediate suspicion that the bank just wanted to enrich itself at the expense of its customers.

Johann Georg Paziazi: a Greek merchant and bills of exchange

Soon after its foundation, the bank took up business relations with Johann Georg Paziazi and with a consortium of seven Greek merchants in Vienna, who formed a kind of association to do business with the bank.[19] Relations with the merchants were not limited to loans, but involved for the most part bills of exchange. The bank gave high priority to this activity, as it thought it would help it gain entry to financial markets. This can be illustrated by means of a 1796 application for credit on the part of the Greek merchant. The bank's executive board of directors advised that a rejection of the application could mean that the merchants would withdraw as potential customers altogether. The loss of the Greeks' business would also have meant the loss of an opportunity to invest bank capital in their enterprises. The board noted that, so far, all the Greek merchants had kept their promises in an exemplary manner.

No less important for the Greek merchants than loans were bills of exchange, but these posed liquidity problems for the bank. Clear procedures were established to make transactions less complicated and to enhance security for the bank. The executive board inquired how much cash could be advanced to local merchant houses, when they wanted to anticipate bills of exchange.[20] The board of owners suggested working out a system of five groups, into which individual merchant houses could be categorized. Membership in a specific group would determine the amount of cash advanced. To establish the maximum sum for bills of exchange, the following steps were to be followed. Should a Greek merchant who already received money for a bill of exchange want to cash a second bill, it would be permitted to do so only with the guarantee of three sound merchant houses.[21] Information had to be continuously acquired and updated. Any changes as to the composition of the groups had to be forwarded to the board of owners on a monthly basis.[22] Further measures stipulated that bills of exchange older than three full months could no longer be cashed, particularly when the most reliable group of merchant houses did not accept or send them.[23] Also bills for which the guarantees of three merchant houses had been required as sufficient security should no longer be anticipated, because the issuers, discounters and recipients often colluded among themselves to disguise their level of indebtedness and to give the impression of greater liquidity. The bank thus had to regard them as a single enterprise.[24] It wanted to protect itself from mutual obligations among the merchants, because these could endanger regularity of payments.

Naturally, the bank tried hard to maintain its security when classifying merchant houses according to their reliability as was fixed in the rules for anticipating bills of exchange. Even with these measures, the bank offered certain concessions. When a merchant company was declined permission to redeem a bill of exchange, the bank tried to find other helpful instruments for this customer that would allow him to cash the bill without violating the bank's need for security. This was the idea behind the old system of guarantees, by which three merchant houses took over responsibility for the bill of another. Noble members of the board of owners, whose economic activities were usually restricted to their rural estates and properties and who were themselves more anchored in relationships of patronage and clientele, assumed notions of honor and trust that were not necessarily consistent with or appropriate to such commercial or financial dealings. During the bank's functioning, attitudes toward "honor" and "profit" shifted evidently. This development was already visible in its earliest business activities, 1787–1792, when it became obvious that the originally planned system for bills of exchange would not work.[25]

The bank was not ready, either, to accept an agreement to pay an estimated flat sum against a bill of exchange, because even in this case the risk seemed too high. The board insisted that it would sign only contracts that involved the courts, most likely because the transactions were then legally sanctioned. A particular case will be analyzed, involving a trading company in (Buda)Pest that dealt in leather goods, operated by the Greek merchant Johann Georg Paziazi and his brother, that illustrates the problems this caused for the bank. Analysis will concentrate on the question of how the bank coped with recalling debts, which measures were taken and how responsibilities were shared between the two boards.

The bank's business with Paziazi's Greek merchant house first ran into difficulties in 1796. While the bank was heavily engaged in activities to rescue the trading firm, Paziazi's total debts with the bank increased from 76,000 gulden to 330,000 gulden at the end of 1797.[26] The problems reached a climax in the summer of 1798, as a result of which Paziazi's trade outlet in (Buda)Pest had to be closed (cf. below). By 1799, according to a report of that year, Johann Georg Paziazi had filed for bankruptcy.[27]

His company's debts with the bank forced it to assume control of its trade and, accordingly, to invest money in the company in the hope of returning it to profitability. The bank failed to achieve its goal, however, due to the improper conduct of its representative, a man named Rögler, who pursued his personal interests. The bank was concerned that "the bank's money would be involved with his own business [Rögler engaged in tobacco shipping, D.Š.], and the bank had no means for control," because he had only turned to banking activities "for reasons of ambition." This accusation was later confirmed. The bank found out that he embezzled 3,000 gulden in cash and goods worth a further 9,000 gulden. In addition, he owed the bank another 7,200 gulden for the ships he bought. His total debts were thus 19,200 gulden, a considerable sum, given that he was hired to recover debts for somebody else.[28] This was a challenge for the board, whose members discussed whether it should follow Paziazi's proposal to hire his brother to rescue the firm.

This case illustrates two problems. First, the bank management had to maintain a continuous control over its employees and their activities. Second, those controls were obviously imperfect if they could not prevent losses of this dimension.

The principles of trust that may have guided the noblemen of the board of owners in their relation vis-à-vis employees, which rooted in the *ancien régime* social structure, were not sufficient as relations between banks and their customers had a different quality from those between landowners and their tenants, between governors and subjects. For the board of owners, banking was a new form of enterprise. More generally, the board of owners viewed the Greek merchants' journeys abroad with skepticism, illustrating a certain mistrust and misunderstanding of the business activities of the merchant houses. A lack of trust also prevailed with respect to their ability to repay their debts. This can at least be inferred from a report sent by the executive board after they met Paziazi. It noted that the board calmly and politely discussed rumors that other Greek merchants had disappeared with other people's money. It stated further that Paziazi laughed and insisted that nobody was about to leave. He argued that travels abroad to destinations as far as Semlin (part of present-day Belgrade) were necessary for reasons of trade.[29]

At the beginning of 1797, another Greek merchant, Temeter Argiry, showed interest in Paziazi's trading house. The board of owners considered whether to inform him about the indebtedness of the business, to allow him to look into the balance books and to offer him "cheap buying options for a takeover."[30] At the same time, it was pointed out that Paziazi wanted the company to "finally be reserved for his brother" after the debts had been settled.[31] As a consequence, access to the books was denied.

How can this decision to prevent access to information about the development of a company that was under the control and administration of the bank be interpreted? It reflects a wish to maintain a certain degree of confidentiality; internal information about a customer, who was in danger of bankruptcy, should remain restricted. When the decision was discussed, whether Paziazi would be able to turn around his company, the board most probably considered his personal interest and assumed that, sooner or later, the merchant company would be transferred back into his property. The executive board seems to have been convinced that Paziazi's business would develop successfully. All members of the board signed such an evaluation of the company, signaling that Paziazi should be supported.[32]

Accordingly, the bank took further measures to rescue Paziazi's firm. Paziazi was forced to sign over two country estates in Hungary, which he owned, representing a value of 150,000 gulden. The bank abstained from seizing these assets, because it would mean that the properties would have been split up among all creditors. Instead, it received full title to the properties and decided that they would be leased until all debts and the interest of 6 percent were repaid. In addition, the bank received bonds worth 300,000 gulden from Paziazi and his brother-in-law. This capital provided security in excess of the 330,000 gulden that Paziazi's company owed at the end of 1797.

In consequence, the bank continued to support Paziazi and his company. It approved funds, so that he could travel on business. Paziazi actively shared with both boards new business ideas, by which he hoped to balance the debts. In 1798, he proposed to the board of owners to establish trade in Turkish cotton with an office in Semlin. He offered the bank a share of the profit and promised to bear the full risk. The bank evaluated this idea and reports seem to confirm that it was put into practice. The proposal was meant not only to intensify business relations between Paziazi and the bank but also to strengthen trust among the partners.

In endorsing the proposal, the board decided that an individual had to be approached who could be a trustworthy representative of the bank in Semlin and who could also be responsible for the finances there. At the same time Paziazi was to be assured that his proposal was not declined but under further consideration.[33] The bank was thus not only interested in finding ways to secure the debt but also signaled that it was interested in future cooperation. It offered to be a business partner provided the bank was not exposed to unacceptable risk.

The board of owners wanted further information in order to reach a consensus among its members. Meanwhile, pressure increased as a result of reports that the balance of the Pest company was worsening. Turnover seemed to have declined so strongly that fixed costs could no longer be covered, causing additional damage to the bank. The board of owners was asked to consider closing the company.[34] The correspondence between the two boards does not indicate clearly whether the board of owners believed the proposal to reorganize trade under the management of Johann or Spiridon Paziazi would really rescue the company in Pest. Its goal was the repayment of debt, which would also increase the trust in Paziazi's business. For the time being, it decided not to close the outlet in Pest. While the executive board continued considering his proposal to take up cotton trading,[35] Paziazi made efforts to find a third party who was willing to take over payment of his debts with the bank and who would accept bonds of the Bank of Vienna (*Wiener Stadtbanco*) as security. The executive board supported this measure, which Paziazi hoped would prove his willingness to make every effort possible.[36]

Over time, the balance sheet of the (Buda)Pest trade did not improve. The bank finally decided to dissolve the business, and the executive board criticized the bank's representative for acting too slowly and inefficiently. After a report in August 1798, concrete preparations were taken to sell the company. The bank took control of the larger part of wholesale transactions and discussed the best way to sell off the remaining leather products. It fired the last, remaining employees but, unwilling to risk a scandal, tried to reach a severance agreement with the affected people.

When judging the position of the bank with regard to the Pest company, the existing business risk was considered to be the most important problem. The efforts to avoid serious consequences for the bank led ultimately to the proposal to close the outlet.[37]

Johann Tost: a woolen manufacturer in Jihlava

Tost & Company, with which the bank started doing business in 1804, proved its most problematical customer. This relationship was established at the explicit wish of Johann Tost, who had just received a subsidy of 1,000,000 gulden from the Austrian War Department to build a woolen manufactory and produce military uniforms on a large scale. The bank acted as a guarantor of this sum and offered assistance with parts of Tost's business, such as financing bonds, purchasing raw materials and so on. His close relation to the state, which guaranteed sales, meant that Tost represented a relatively safe client for the bank. Despite the fact that the bank tried hard to gather additional information about his qualifications—he grew up in an environment with close links to textile manufacturing and was a member of the Lower Austrian regional administration—the deal ultimately went wrong.

By 1809, Tost's payment problems led to the signing of a convention between Tost & Company, supported by one of its investors, the Hungarian Count Nadasdy and the bank. At this point, the company's debts with the bank had risen to nearly 2,000,000 gulden. The reason for the relatively quick deterioration of Tost's business had to do with the general situation during the Napoleonic Wars as well as with difficulties with some individual customers, who, as Tost claimed, failed to pay for the goods they had ordered.[38] Tost's attempt to attract new investors had failed to reduce pressure from the bank.

In the course of handling a production contract for the Austrian War Department, Tost received an interest-free advance of 400,000 gulden from the department. This helped in the situation; the bank did not charge any interest for this sum.[39] For all other open loans, however, it charged a rate of 6 percent as well as a commission of 1 percent.[40] The bank was willing to wait until the due dates for installments,[41] but it decided to register its claims of 2,000,000 gulden with a court. It received permission to check the cost structure and the warehouse of the company at will,[42] in exchange for which Tost would remain in charge of the business, provided certain conditions were met.[43] He was to invest money sensibly, produce goods efficiently and sell them quickly.[44] To oversee the company, the bank again hired an agent, who sent reports about the price of produced goods,[45] the stock of raw materials and the company's monthly profitability.[46] Similar controls were established with respect to the purchase price of raw materials and the value of stock.[47] In case of inconsistencies, for instance, if the price of raw materials was too high, Tost's company would have to bear the consequences and his account would be debited the corresponding sum. Should the sums repaid exceed 50,000 gulden with interest, Tost could dispose of the excess amount as he wished, for instance, to buy wool or dyestuffs.[48]

If the business failed to generate enough profit, Tost's investor Count Nadasdy would be charged, because of the guarantees he had granted.[49] According to the 1809 convention between Tost and the bank, Nadasdy guaranteed the company's debts in the amount of 600,000 gulden; the value of Nadasdy's estate was estimated at 2,113,352 gulden and 52 kreuzer. The bank was to receive quarterly installments of 40,000 gulden, 160,000 gulden per year.[50] Should Tost fail to pay, the bank reserved the right to examine Nadasdy's estate administrators under oath or, as a further step, to seize the estate as surety and lease it to a third party. It was hoped that this would secure the bank's claims,[51] as the valuation of the estate was high enough. Interest was to be paid on time each quarter, and Tost and Nadasdy had to find new investors. The bank agreed to extend a lifeline to the company for another four years and seemed to be satisfied with the conditions and securities offered. It did not use the right to seize the assets (*Exekutionsklage*) for the time being but threatened to do so in case the interest installments were not paid according to the new agreement. After the four-year grace period, debts had to be repaid in annual installments of 200,000 gulden.[52]

Tost's debts with the bank increased to 2,626,087 gulden and 30 groschen between 1810 and 1811. He tried frequently to find new partners or owners. One of them was the company Emanuel Rosa & Company, which agreed to assume 1,600,000 gulden of Tost's debts. With this infusion of new capital, Tost's obligations were thus reduced to 1,026,087 gulden.

A misunderstanding arose in 1811. When Tost applied for money to pay wages and purchase wool, the bank refused under the impression that he wanted to buy new English spinning machines. It was only the intervention of Rosa & Company, which transferred the necessary installment of 200,000 gulden, that clarified the misunderstanding and prevented a lawsuit by the bank.[53] Heightened tensions remained, however. If other instalments were not met ("bey Verfall der ersten Rate und auf die Ausstellung der spaeter verfallenden Wechselbriefe"), a meeting with Tost & Company was to be arranged, but no further credits were to be issued.[54] Due to the permanent problems of the company, the bank's readiness to continue support, even if waning, seems surprising.

The bank hoped that such close control would turn the company around. By 1811, however, Tost's debts had risen to more than 2,600,000 gulden. The bank tightened and extended its control in order to save the manufactory. The intent to save explains the willingness to concede. When 70,000 gulden could not be paid at the beginning of September 1812, the bank still hesitated to seize the company's finished goods and raw materials. Rather, it mortgaged its real estate for

150,000 gulden, guaranteeing repayment with a further 200,000 gulden from Nadasdy.[55]

A report of the executive board suggests that the bank may have given Rosa & Company some time to establish themselves after they had taken over Tost's debts. When, two months later, a new report stated that bills of exchange had not been honored, the company was reminded of its obligation to the bank in a manner "tough and with all possible means."[56]

The case bears one more relevant dimension with regard to the debate in business history on the nature and success of family businesses. In this respect, the sources offer a rare glimpse on the role of Tost's wife, Theresa, in this conflict. She invested and provided support for the company with rather large sums drawn from her own property and raised with the help of her contacts. Thus, she was directly involved in the financial consequences of the bank's actions. Given this involvement of Tost's wife, the bank's relationships with the manufactory became even more complicated. In addition to making material investments, she confronted the bank with non-economic values such as "honor" and "family," pleading that she had three under-age children. She pointed out that the consequences of her husband's failure would impoverish them.[57] At the beginning of 1814, she sent a letter to Schwarzenberg, in which she declared that she was ready to help settle her husband's debts.[58] She actively tried to find alternative sources of credit to help rescue the company and her family and actually secured a loan of 110,000 gulden. She even tried to make the bank transfer all remaining debts to her person "in order to rescue the family."

Negotiations continued with regard to an arrangement that was not described in greater detail. Fearing that the Tost family might transfer their manufactory to an unknown third party, the board of owners asked to consult a third party of their own, who would infuse still more capital and, by so doing, would balance the bank's account.[59] Theresa argued that the bank should consider several different aspects of the situation. First, it had not suffered actual losses but, on the contrary, had made a profit of 96,000 gulden from her husband's business. Second, all the bank's demands were secured by the manufactory's real estate, leaving no reason to sell it to a different buyer.[60] Third, some of the debts were secured by her own wealth, such as her dowry of 20,000 and an annual rent of 3,000 gulden. These claims should have been set by her husband against the manufactories in Jihlava and Stecken as well as a house in one of the suburbs in Vienna and other properties in Hungary, all of which were debt free at the time when the company started business.[61] They should have guaranteed her legal claim that she herself was actually a creditor of her husband. Theresa had handed over to her husband jewelery worth at least 10,000 gulden, for which he gave her a bond. She hoped such complications and assurances would force concessions from the board of owners.[62]

It responded to her request that the company be transferred into the hands of the Tost family with conditions of its own. She had to raise 130,000 gulden within a specified period. A letter of 1815 shows that she and her husband tried to use certain social connections to find the necessary funds. She finally received

150,000 gulden in bank bonds from the Widows Society, but, despite the fact that these fetched good prices on the Vienna stock exchange,[63] the amount was not enough to satisfy the bank's claims. According to a letter of Theresa Tost, it required an additional 100,000 gulden to improve the enterprise's business situation. Despite insufficient surety, they declared the lower amount adequate.

Insufficient surety notwithstanding, the board of owners suddenly accepted the lower amount. It would seem that references to the loss of honor and property or its transfer to the children appealed to its noble members.[64] The enterprise was offered a lifeline. In April 1815, Theresa and Johann Tost reached an agreement regarding Theresa's intention to become the owner of the manufactories in Jihlava and Stecken.[65] The bank had taken over the property but was ready to transfer it to her, when certain conditions were met. The Musical Widow's Society (*Musikalische Witwengesellschaft*), which supplied Theresa Tost with a substantial loan, would receive a legal claim on the manufactories. Other contracts that Johann Tost had concluded with third parties would be changed accordingly.[66] Theresa Tost would have to compensate the bank after she had taken over the companies.[67] Finally, adequate security measures had to be provided in the event that Theresa Tost was unable to repay.

We can see from communication within the bank that repayment problems continued. An 1816 document reveals that a deadline was extended for three months in consideration of her situation.[68] In the end, the case resulted in lengthy court battles and strong antagonism between Tost and the bank.

An 1818 accountant's report to one of the bank's owners, Prince Colloredo-Mannfeld, mentioned one of Tost's statements. He threatened he would "sue the bank for usury and injustice with His Majesty," if his case was not resolved. In a later meeting, however, Tost seemed to confess his wrongdoing. He tried to describe himself as a victim of his other creditors. In the words of one of the bank's executive directors, Tost was a man "who [made] amateurish propositions and without any money." In 1820, Tost repeated his allegations and accused the bank of usury. The case was concluded only in 1831, when a sale contract was signed with Theresa Tost, who paid 160,000 gulden in cash for the manufactory and all other objects in Jihlava. In acquiring these properties, she also assumed all the debts with which they were burdened.

Conclusion

Both cases allow for several conclusions that show some patterns of business priorities among the board of noble owners. First, the bank firmly followed a strategy to require as much security as possible for the services it rendered. On the other hand, it showed a certain flexibility to enterprises that ran into debt; they were not simply seized, sold and, thus, ruined. The board carefully assessed the situation, searching for better solutions, and was particularly interested in measures that might help the bankrupts to return to profitability.

The two cases illustrate that the bank tried to make debtors pay. Terms such as patience, caution and opportunity seem characteristic of its relations with insolvent customers. If the financial situation of indebted companies did not improve, higher losses would result. For this reason, the bank sought—specifically, in each case—measures that would help restore profitability to the companies.

The board of owners avoided hasty decisions, by seeking constant information from the executive board about existing problems and extenuating circumstances. It is hard to determine whether these actions reflected a certain distrust of the executive board or a simple interest in business policy. Given their active concern for the financial activities and sound reputation of the bank, the involvement of the board of owners in decision-making can be interpreted primarily as a sign of a business-oriented attitude. The noble members of the board thus do not appear as passive investors but as active entrepreneurs.

In both of the cases of bankruptcy analyzed here, employees of the bank were installed as the bank's trustees in the companies. The Paziazi wholesale company and the Tost woolen manufactory had problems paying back loans from the bank but nonetheless maintained close business relations with it over several years. The bank and the companies actively sought ways to renew profitability and achieve repayment. If necessary, the bank would take over direct control of the companies.

As the debts were recalled, a very plain report was made, in which the bank described itself as a victim of both customers. Although its just claims and its customers' insolvency were clear, making legal intervention unnecessary in principle, the bank still turned to the courts and refused agreements that lacked legal ratification. Not all the bank's claims were compensated; direct conflicts arose between the bankrupts and the bank.

Sometimes, the board of owners confronted criticism that it did not consider seriously enough good opportunities available on financial markets or respond positively to the demands of customers. There was a particular inflexibility regarding the increase of interest rates in bill of exchange transactions, but this may have been the expression of a business policy that avoided maximizing profit at all times in favor of social considerations. The board stuck nonetheless quite consistently to its purpose of supporting entrepreneurs.

There was no chance of success in the case of Paziazi. When it became clear that he was unable to repay because of his financial situation, the bank granted him support to live on.[69] In the case of Theresa Tost, attempts to appeal to the moral values of the board of owners seem to have been successful, as the directors were ready to compromise. Several interesting features emerge from the two cases: securing the financial and legal claims of the bank, making the insolvent company profitable again, and considering the personal and family situation of the entrepreneurs involved. It should further be emphasized that, though it relied on legal instruments, the bank preferred extra-legal solutions that preserved both the bankrupts and the bank. The Schwarzenberg Bank's policies reflect thus the financial, social and moral aspects of bankruptcy in the early modern Habsburg Empire.

Notes

1 I would like to thank Thomas Max Safley for his suggestions on the first draft of this chapter and for his kind editing of the text.

2 J. Sgard, "Do Legal Origins Matter? The Case of Bankruptcy Laws in Europe 1808–1914," *European Review of Economic History* 10 (2006): 389–419, 389; for further research, see also M. Häberlein, *Brüder, Freunde und Betrüger- Soziale Beziehungen, Normen und Konflikte in der Augsburger Kaufmannschaft um die Mitte des 16. Jahrhunderts* (Berlin 1998); T.M. Safley, "Business Failure and Civil Scandal in Early Modern Europe," *Business History Review* 83 (2009): 35–60; T.M. Safley, "Bankruptcy: Family and Finance in Early Modern Augsburg," *Journal of European Economic History* 29 (2000): 53–77; P. Eigner and D. Štefanová (eds.), *Banken und Unternehmenskultur* (Vienna 2009); and the papers in *Österreichische Zeitschrift für Geschichtswissenschaften* 19 (2008).

3 Cf. Sgard, "Do Legal Origins Matter?" 390–2.

4 Státní oblastní archiv, pobočka zámek Český Krumlov (hereinafter SOA Český Krumlov), Fond Rodinný archiv (hereinafter RA) Schwarzenberků, Reglement der kaiserlichen königlichen oktroyierten Kommerzial- Leih- und Wechselbank 1787, Art. 23, 25 and 27, 7.

5 SOA Český Krumlov, RA Schwarzenberků, Privilegium der kaiserlichen königlichen oktroyierten Kommerzial- Leih- und Wechselbank vom Joseph II., 6 April 1787.

6 The Colloredo family had an annual income in excess of 50,000 gulden; Josef Schwarzenberg was the richest estate owner in Bohemia in 1770 and also Wrtby belonged to the ten wealthiest noblemen in Bohemia. See P.G.M. Dickson, *Finance and Government under Maria Theresia 1740–1780*, 2 vols. (Oxford 1987), 93–4; for the financial income of the nobility in 1741–1742, see also E. Hassenpflug-Elzholz, *Böhmen und die böhmischen Stände in der Zeit des beginnenden Absolutismus: Eine Strukturanalyse der böhmischen Adelsnation um die Mitte des 18. Jahrhundert* (Munich 1982), 335.

7 Ferdinand Colloredo-Mannsfeld (1777–1848) founded the first sugar refinery in Austria. *Österreichisches biographisches Lexikon 1815–1950*, Vol. 1 (Cologne 1957), 151.

8 H. Freudenberger, "The Schwarzenberg Bank: A Forgotten Contributor to Austrian Economic Development, 1788–1830," *Austrian History Yearbook* 27 (1996): 41–64; H. Freudenberger, *Lost Momentum: Austrian Economic Development, 1750s–1830s* (Vienna, Cologne, Weimar 2003), 224–32; F. Rager, *Die Wiener Commerzial- Leih und Wechselbank, 1787–1830* (Vienna 1918).

9 For the period 1780–1840, Youssef Cassis defined private banks as follows:

> the private bank in the nineteenth and during most of the twentieth century was a bank whose owners were also managers; and, more often than not, these were family firms, though people from outside the firm could also become partners. Their legal form was generally that of partnership and general partnership, with partners having unlimited responsibility; but there were also limited partnerships and even joint-stock companies, whose directors retained the major part of the capital.

See, Y. Cassis, *Capitals of Capital. A History of International Financial Centres, 1780–2005* (Cambridge, UK 2006), 8.

10 D. Štefanová, "Adelige als Bankiers in der Epoche der Aufklärung: Eine Studie zur Wiener 'k.k. oktroyierten Kommerzial-, Leih- und Wechselbank,' 1787–1830" (unpublished Habilitationsschrift, University of Vienna, 2008); H. Matis, *Die Schwarzenberg Bank, Kapitalbildung und Industriefinanzierung in den habsburgischen Erblanden 1787–1830* (Vienna 2005); Freudenberger, "The Schwarzenberg Bank," 41–64; Rager, *Wechselbank*, 19–108.

11 SOA Český Krumlov, RA Schwarzenberků, F.p.ü. Fasz. 261, Privilegium der kaiserlichen königlichen oktroyierten Kommerzial- Leih- und Wechselbank von Franz II., 24 July 1792.
12 See Štefanová, "Adelige als Bankiers"; SOA Český Krumlov, RA Schwarzenbergů, F.p.ü., Fasz. 260, not paginated.
13 SOA Český Krumlov, RA Schwarzenbergů, F.p.ü., Fasz. 261, Reglement der kaiserlichen königlichen oktroyierten Kommerzial- Leih- und Wechselbank 1792.
14 SOA Český Krumlov, Fond Ústřední účtárna (hereinafter ÚÚ), Deliberationsprotokolle, 33.
15 SOA Český Krumlov, RA Schwarzenbergů, Reglement, § 23, 8.
16 Ibid.
17 Ibid., §17, 7.
18 Ibid., §15, 6.
19 O. Katsiardi-Hering and M.A. Stassinopoulou, "The Long 18th Century of Greek Commerce in the Habsburg Empire," in: H. Hepner, P. Urbanitsch and R. Zedinger (eds.), *Social Change in the Habsburg Empire* (Bochum 2011), 191–215; further, V. Seirinidou, "Griechen in Wien im 18. und frühen 19. Jahrhundert: Soziale Identitäten im Alltag," *Das achtzehnte Jahrhundert in Österreich: Jahrbuch der Österreichischen Gesellschaft zur Erforschung des Achtzehntes Jahrhunderts* 9 (1994): 7–29, e.g., 8–14, 16–20.
20 SOA Český Krumlov, ÚÚ, Deliberationsprotokolle, 17 May 1793, 163.
21 Ibid., 164.
22 Ibid., 163.
23 SOA Český Krumlov, ÚÚ, Deliberationsprotokolle, 28 July 1793, 171.
24 Ibid., 28 July 1793, 171.
25 D. Štefanová, "Bankwesen als Unternehmenskultur: Das Beispiel der 'k.k. oktroyierten Kommerzial-, Leih- und Wechselbank, 1787–1830,'" in: P. Eigner and D. Štefanová (eds.), *Banken und Unternehmenskultur* (Vienna 2009), 24–40.
26 SOA Český Krumlov, ÚÚ, Hauptausweis aus der Revisionskontrollrechnung of the Chartered Commercial-, Loan- and Exchange bank in Vienna for the Years of 1797 as well as 1798, not paginated.
27 SOA Český Krumlov, RA Schwarzenberků, Fasz. 272, Lose Briefe zwischen 1799 und 1808, here 6 March 1799, 2.
28 SOA Český Krumlov, Referatsprotokolle, Letter of the executive board to the board of owners, 31 December 1797, 173–4.
29 SOA Český Krumlov, Referatsprotokolle, Letter of the executive board to the board of owners, April 1794 until November 1799, 10 March 1798, 197.
30 SOA Český Krumlov, Referatsprotokolle, Letter of the executive board to the board of owners, 18 February 1797, 90–2.
31 Ibid.
32 SOA Český Krumlov, Referatsprotokolle, Letter of the executive board to the board of owners, 14 May 1797, 105–6.
33 SOA Český Krumlov, Referatsprotokolle, Letter of the executive board to the board of owners from April 1794 until November 1799, 15 April 1798, 210.
34 Ibid., 206–8.
35 Ibid., Reply of the board of owners to the executive board, 8 April 1798, 209–10.
36 Ibid., Summary directive of the board of owners, 5 July 1798, 224–6.
37 SOA Český Krumlov, Referatsprotokolle, Letter of the executive board to the board of owners, 30 March 1798, 294–305.
38 SOA Český Krumlov, Referatsprotokolle, Letter of the executive board to the board of owners from 26 July 1810 until 20 June 1823, 20 December 1811, 51.
39 SOA Český Krumlov, RA Schwarzenberků, F.p.ü., Contract between Tost and the bank, concluded 20 April 1809, Fasz. 268, Art. 12, 3.
40 SOA Český Krumlov, RA Schwarzenberků, F.p.ü., Contract between Tost and the bank, concluded 20 April 1809, Fasz. 268, Art. 32, 7.

41 Ibid., Art. 14, 3.
42 Ibid., Art. 16, 3–4.
43 Ibid., Art. 17, 4.
44 Ibid., Art. 16, 4.
45 Ibid., Art. 19, 4.
46 Ibid., Art. 25, 5.
47 Ibid., Art. 26, 5.
48 Ibid., Art. 24, 5.
49 Ibid., Art. 26, 5.
50 Ibid., Art. 4, 1–2.
51 Ibid., Art. 13, 5.
52 Ibid., Art. 7, 2.
53 SOA Český Krumlov, Referatsprotokolle, Letter of the executive board to the board of owners from 26 July 1810 until 20 June 1823, 19 October 1811, 45.
54 Ibid., 44.
55 Ibid., 2 October 1812, 105.
56 Ibid., 5 January 1812, 115.
57 SOA Český Krumlov, RA Schwarzenberků, F.p.ü. Fasz. 264, Letter of 19 June 1816, 172.
58 Ibid., Letter of Theresa Tost, 19 January 1814, 1.
59 Ibid.
60 Ibid., 2.
61 Ibid., 2.
62 Ibid., 3.
63 Ibid., 1.
64 Literally: "we would achieve honor and wealth," SOA Český Krumlov, RA Schwarzenberků, F.p.ü. 264, Letter of Theresa Tost, 8 February 1815, 2.
65 SOA Český Krumlov, RA Schwarzenberků, F.p.ü. Fasz. 272, Conference protocol, 6 April 1815, Settlement with the Tost married couple, 2.
66 Ibid.
67 Ibid.
68 SOA Český Krumlov, Referatsprotokolle, Letter of the executive board to the board of owners from 26 June 1810 until 20 July 1823, 20 June 1816, 172.
69 Ibid., February 1818, 185.

9 Boom and crisis in financing the British transatlantic trade

A case study of the bankruptcy of John Leigh & Company in 1811

Mina Ishizu

Introduction

In August 1811, John Leigh & Company, Liverpool merchant, declared bankruptcy with over £139,000 owed to some 65 creditors of merchants and banking houses in London and Liverpool upon bills of exchange. Leigh emerged into the commercial life of Liverpool in 1803 and over the following eight years until his bankruptcy in 1811, he established a pattern of trade that linked together the West Indies, South America and Ireland, made possible by the banking houses of Lancashire and London. Leigh's bankruptcy was not the result of a person-specific reason. It is true that in a face-to-face society such as that of early-nineteenth-century Liverpool, an individual's social reputation and trust could sometimes cause his or her financial embarrassment. But Leigh's failure was caused by the more general economic climate of contemporary British commerce which also related to his decision-making in embarking on or expanding new trade or financial activities. Such new initiatives could increase both opportunities and risk which, by the turn of economic conditions, could cause business failures.

Leigh's bankruptcy in 1811 was no doubt largely part of the general economic crisis of 1810, which was the combination of banking and mercantile business failures. This is clear from the fact that 21 per cent of his debts were owed to merchants in Liverpool and London, who were engaged in South American and Irish trade, while 63 per cent were owed to various banking houses in London and Liverpool.[1] Some of his creditors also went bankrupt subsequently. The studies of early-nineteenth-century bankruptcies have identified the peaks of bankruptcy occurrences, and the years, 1810–11, were among the highest in numbers of bankruptcies together with 1815–16 and 1825–26.[2] They show a pattern of increasing bank failures in the first year leading to failures in non-banking sectors in the following year, which suggests it took several months before the initial shock of banking failure caused liquidity problems for business individuals and firms, especially in the provinces.

From the late eighteenth century, British overseas trade found its main export markets in Northern Europe, North America and, increasingly, the British West Indies and Southern Europe, while its major import markets were Northern

Europe, the British West Indies and Asia. The disruption of this pattern during the Napoleonic Wars was the long-term cause of the 1810 crisis. When the traditional markets for British textile goods in the continent and in the United States were closed by Napoleon's invasion in 1809, several merchants in London, Lancashire, Yorkshire and Glasgow ventured to explore new opportunities in South America and the West Indies.[3] The migration of the Portuguese Crown Court to Rio de Janeiro encouraged the British merchants to conceive that this would create a demand for manufactured goods in South America.[4] John Leigh of Liverpool was among these British merchants who ventured to explore the new markets during the wartime reorganisation of overseas trade. The Brazilian colonial market was soon flooded with British cargoes, and there were more well-loaded ships on their way. There was little way of knowing the consumption patterns and levels of early colonial society. By 1810, however, it was reported that Rio society was rapidly improving its taste in fashion and that there was constant demand for luxury items there.[5] Despite a temporary stagnation in the market, an experienced merchant with a good stock of capital should have been able to survive. Thus the stagnation of the South American market only explains a part of the general crisis of 1810.

The more direct cause of the crisis was the failure of a Lombard Street merchant bank, Brickwood & Company, in July 1810 with total debts of over £621,000.[6] As a bank in the City, their main business was dealing bills for country banks and merchants, and they were known as "perhaps as solid a house as any one in the City."[7] The general discount policy of Brickwood & Company was, according to Duffy, careful and involved little risk.[8] Their stoppage was attributed to "the failure for £300,000 of one of the first firms in general brokerage but more especially concerned with West India dealings."[9] The dealings mentioned here were those of Thomas Coles & Company of Mincing Lane, London, which had suffered a huge loss in April 1810 because of the recent restriction upon colonial goods imported from the continent. It was said that Coles & Sons had deposited with Brickwood & Company bills of exchange worth £70,000 as security for a loan which was not repaid.[10] In addition to this loan, Brickwood & Company regularly discounted Coles' acceptances for their brokerage business. Coles' failure damaged other merchants, including John Leigh, for whom Coles distributed their colonial produce in the domestic market.[11] Bills drawn, particularly at short date, on respectable London banks always bore the highest credit and were readily discountable at banks and merchant houses in any provincial town as well as in London. Once granted a drawing account with the bank, a merchant could draw a bill on Brickwood & Company, and he could without difficulty immediately discount it at any other banking house. Thus he could immediately get funds.

The high credit of Brickwood's acceptances is indicated by the wide range of their bill drawers. This wide range of bill drawers meant, however, that in times of tight credit they were exposed to failure.[12] At the time of their bankruptcies, non-banking firms and individuals claimed £195,663 in the form of bills of exchange, and £150,076 was claimed by various private bankers. In addition to that, country banks claimed £49,311.[13] The largest claimant among country banks came from Parr, Lyon and Hurst of Warrington, Lancashire, with £20,784. This sum was the fourth largest of all the Brickwood & Company's creditors after three London bankers including the Bank of England. Parr & Company's claim was made upon eight bills of exchange all drawn by John Leigh & Company of Liverpool dated in Liverpool between April and June 1810 and accepted by Brickwood & Company.[14] As I shall examine in what follows, John Leigh opened drawing accounts both with Parr & Company and Brickwood & Company during his active business years as he expanded his trade, and he regularly drew large volume of bills on them and had bills accepted by these banks. The specific arrangements and nature of Leigh's banking transactions will be discussed in the subsequent pages in the light of how they contributed to his bankruptcy in 1811.

The failure of another London bank, Devaynes, Noble & Company, in July 1810, although in much smaller scale, contributed to the widespread failure of businesses and individuals in the year. Devaynes & Company was regarded as one of the "West End bankers," whose clientele were traditionally thought to consist exclusively of members of the gentry and nobility, but Duffy has shown that the bank was also significantly involved in bill acceptance for mercantile customers.[15] As we shall see in this study, Leigh regularly drew on the London bank through Parr & Company because Devaynes & Company acted as their London agency. The agency system between country and London banks was emerging at the turn of the eighteenth century as the former required the access to the financial resources of the latter to accommodate the growing credit demand from local merchant customers. Parr & Company facilitated Leigh by providing him with drawing rights with Devaynes & Company, but this provincial–capital credit flow did not suffice Leigh's credit need and he sought a separate banking connection with Brickwood & Company.

Thus Leigh's bankruptcy in the summer of 1811 was strongly affected by the acute credit contraction of the previous year, and in this sense his failure was a part of the collapse of credit system originating from the failure of Brickwood & Company, the thesis that was advocated by Duffy in his 1985 case study of Brickwood & Company's failure and its subsequent damage to their merchant clients, including John Leigh.[16] Although Duffy's detailed study remains the best major account of the contagious nature of credit failures through bills of exchange in 1810 and 1811, it does not explain the business initiatives and decisions that individuals made in response to the opportunities and disturbances generated in the early nineteenth century transatlantic trade. Considering the importance of this branch of trade in the entire British economy during the period in question, the merchants' financial activities deserve more detailed and systematic investigation to shed light upon their reactions as causalities of bankruptcies. By drawing upon the archives of John Leigh & Company, which Duffy did not use in his study, this research is able to explore this.[17]

John Leigh & Company in the West Indies trade 1803–06

In October 1803, Leigh expressed his enthusiasm for the new commercial business in Liverpool and his ability to insert himself into the local "web" of credit in a letter to several merchants in London and Dublin.

> I have the pleasure to inform you I am in a situation to begin business having got my certificate as soon as it was possible when the commission was opened – I hope at some future time by my Industry to give all my Creditors that which they don't expect. I have begun business in this place [Liverpool] and have friends which will advance me money. If you'll favour me with your Consignment I shall feel very much obliged and will keep you regularly advised the state of this Market.[18]

Little is known about Leigh's early life, but it appears that he may have been engaged in some other business and that, as the above letter suggests, it may have failed before he commenced his new venture in the Atlantic trade under the name of John Leigh & Company. In the first year, he dealt chiefly in grain and colonial sugar shipments to Dublin and Sligo, but by 1804 he had established a pattern of trade that yoked together the West Indies with English and Irish markets.

Leigh engaged in the last decade of the British slave trade in Africa. Between 1804 and 1809, he planned nine voyages to the West Coast of Africa for the purpose of purchasing slaves.[19] In June 1804, he sent his first slave brig, *William*, with British manufactured goods from Liverpool to Bonny and New Calabar on the West Coast of Africa. The brig then transported and disembarked slaves in Suriname and returned to Liverpool on March 1805. Leigh successfully completed this venture and handsomely rewarded, as he suggested in the letter, his seven partners who had invested in the voyage. Before *William* returned to Liverpool, Leigh's second brig, *Sally*, sailed out from the port in February 1805 to Sierra Leone in West Africa then shipped slaves to Demerara and after exactly one year returned to Liverpool with colonial sugar. Leigh had two investors in this voyage.

Two voyages ended in capture by French and Spanish privateers, and another vessel was wrecked in a storm. The length of time from the start and to the end of each venture varied from nine months with *William* to 12 months with *Sally*. These illustrate not only the risky nature of the West Indies trade but also that the Atlantic trade involved multiple markets stretching over long distances which meant that it took considerable length of time for a merchant to realise profits.

The minimum capital requirement to set up in the Atlantic trade is said to have been between £5,000 and £10,000.[20] Profitability depended upon the ability of merchants to secure quick and regular payments. Sales of slaves in colonial plantations could be settled by payment in species or colonial products (sugar, cotton and so on), or bills of exchange drawing on Liverpool or London. During the eighteenth century, coins became less common as means of payment in the

British transatlantic trade; the risks of robbery and clipping on the way made the merchants reluctant to use them. Colonial products resulted in delays to the speed of remittance; it was not always easy to assemble the required amount of products available, sugar or cotton, to settle the slave sales. Thus, in order to secure quick and smooth payments, the transatlantic merchants resorted to various kinds of credit systems and credit instruments. The risks involved in slave purchase on the West Coast of Africa were managed by indigenous institutional arrangements. In Old Calabar, which was a popular destination for Liverpool slave merchants in mid-eighteenth century, human pawns were used as hostage to secure delivery of slaves. In another popular market, Bonny, local state authority facilitated credit, eventually making it a more appealing source of slaves than Old Calabar.[21]

In the West Indies, the British merchants suffered from a high risk of non-payment for slaves. The problem concerned the creditworthiness of the Caribbean planters' bills. Planters drew bills on the merchants, but the drawees occasionally doubted the bills' creditworthiness, rejecting them as "dishonoured" or "protested." Protested bills could affect the credit standing of all the people involved in the transaction, even if only one person in the chain had bad credit, because they placed doubt on the participants' ability to pay. Leigh had struggled with protested Irish bills in the earlier stage of his business. In a letter to his Irish correspondent firm, Gordon & Sayers, Leigh reported the recent loss of £800, suffered from West Indies bills that were "of no use." In another case, he sent back protested bills amounting to nearly £6,100 to Demerara.[22]

To avoid such problems of remittance and to secure profits from sales, British merchants in the eighteenth century invented a system in which they would not sell slaves in the West Indies unless the debt was underwritten or guaranteed by a merchant house (guarantor) in Britain, most often in London, it being the predominant capital market. British merchants also obtained guarantees for their corresponding houses in the West Indies to minimise their risk further. The wide use of this guarantee system may reflect the concern with the reliability of West Indies planters and factors, compared to those in other markets, such as the United States, where no such system was adopted.[23] The timing of the development of the guarantee system in the mid-eighteenth century is not yet fully understood,[24] but from *c.*1760 to 1807, virtually all British slave traders appear to have pursued remittances in post-dated bills of exchange. By the turn of the nineteenth century, there was "scarce a house" in Liverpool that did not obtain guarantees from "some of the first respectable houses in England" for trade with virtually all the British Caribbean islands.[25]

Leigh had no banking connection in the first two years of his business career, when he was mostly engaged in the Irish provisions trade, and occasionally had to struggle to realise bills. He lamented on one occasion, "If only I rather open my own Bank account."[26] By the time he entered the Caribbean trade, the lesson had been learned and better measures adopted. The guarantee system ensured smooth operation of bill transaction for the merchant, and a banking connection provided him with credit. On receiving the guaranteed bills from the Caribbean factors, the British merchant did not then have to wait for the drawee to honour the bill. He could, rather, endorse the accepted bill to a third party, who purchased it at its current discounted value, providing the merchant with immediate cash. Bill discounting became thus a means of granting extensive credit to the parties involved in business transactions. British merchants had already familiarised themselves with discounting bills of exchange in the early modern period.[27] If the merchant was an account holder of a local bank, he could get the bills discounted in the manner described above, but, instead of receiving immediate cash, he could arrange for his account to be credited.

In the early nineteenth century, interest was not given to deposits.[28] Rather, in order to keep his right to draw on the bank, he had to maintain his credit balance. From the bank's point of view, bills of exchange with mercantile origin were usually the most agreeable assets. When in need of more liquidity, the bank could pass the discounted bills to other banks or bill brokers for re-discounting. There was a specific discount rate at each time the bill was discounted in exchange for ready cash. Until brokers established their dominance in the (re-) discount market in the 1820s, London private bankers took the lead in re-discounting provincial bills. They formed agency contracts with the provincial banks and provided regular re-discounting services and other mediating facilities in London.

As Leigh began exploiting transatlantic markets more, he became a regular client of three banks (apart from occasional transactions with others), Parr, Lyon & Hurst of Warrington, Brickwood, Rainier & Bowles of London, both noted above, and Alexander Anderson also of London. Parr, Lyon & Hurst's founding partner, Thomas Parr, began his career in the sugar refining business and moved into banking around 1788.[29] His was considered one of the oldest country banks in England. Early country banks offered financial services on the basis of fortunes the partners had earned in commerce and trade. It was not uncommon for the early bankers to pursue another trade alongside banking, and, indeed, the main reason many merchants and manufacturers established banking houses was to attract local depositors, whose capital would underwrite the banker's other business interests. The connection to Parr, Lyon & Hurst may have been a matter of location. Warrington was the home of Thomas Leigh, John's father, who conducted an Irish grocery export business in the town. Through the connection of his father, or possibly his commercial interest in West India sugar imports, Leigh opened an account and began transactions in January of 1805. This was a few month before Leigh's first slave brig was due to return to Liverpool. Parr's Bank proved crucial to Leigh as he launched a more capital intensive transatlantic trade in addition to his Irish commerce.

The real importance of an account with Parr & Company was probably that it enabled Leigh to have bills accepted by Parr's London agent Devaynes, Noble & Company at a rate of ¼ per cent per pound. Founded by the descendant of a prestigious London goldsmith banker, Backwell & Company, around 1740, it became Parr's London agent in 1796.[30] Located in Pall Mall, it was regarded as a West End banker whose main business focused on the financial services for the nobility. The fact that the bank offered agency services to Parr & Company suggests, however, that it engaged in commercial finance on a regular basis, as did other City bankers. The separation between West End and City bankers became thus blurred. Figure 9.1 shows the volume of drawing on the London bank. Leigh regularly and increasingly sent bills of fairly large amounts for two or three months' usance for acceptance at Devaynes' bank.

John Leigh & Company in the Rio de Janeiro trade 1806–10

The abolition of the slave trade came into effect in 1807 but the bill had already influenced Leigh's West Indies trade in the previous year. In July of that year he instructed his ship captains and West Indies agents to return to England after discharging slaves in the islands, so that he could ship out the vessels to West Africa once again before the total abolition came into effect. Leigh calculated that the abolition would cause a shortage of slaves in Caribbean plantations that would, in turn, drive up prices. Historians argue that the abolition of the African slave trade seems to have had overall a positive rather than negative effect on Liverpool's growing trade. Hyde emphasises that prominent slave traders, aware

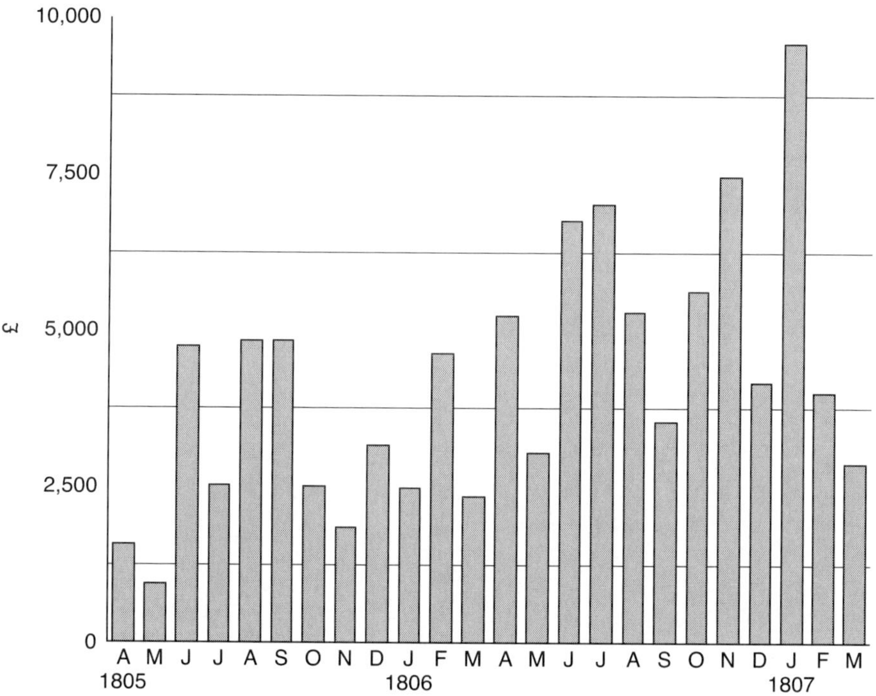

Figure 9.1 John Leigh's bill drawing on Devaynes & Company (sources: National Archives C108/212-4 Papers relating to the bankruptcy of John Leigh 1803–11).

of political and moral opposition to the slave trade, started to explore new markets from as early as the 1790s in order to hedge their risks. He wrote,

> This took the form of widening the scope of their trade with new markets particularly those in Central and South America so that, in the event of a curtailment of the African trade, their capital could still find profitable employment elsewhere.[31]

Leigh seems to have followed this overall business trend in Liverpool from 1806, as he began to explore new markets in Trinidad, Surinam and further southward into Brazil. Between October 1808 and March 1811, he commissioned 20 ventures to Trinidad and Surinam and 12 ventures to Rio de Janeiro. The largest shipment to Rio, which was carried by the brig *Belmont* that sailed in January 1810, amounted to a value of more than £19,800.

The few years beginning in 1806 were a crucially important turning point for British commercial dominance in Brazil. British merchants, like Leigh, exported manufactured goods (mainly textiles) and had traded slaves on the Angolan coast throughout the eighteenth century, and had formed an economic alliance with Brazil-born, Portuguese merchants on the other side of the Atlantic, particularly in the city of Rio de Janeiro. When Napoleon invaded Portugal in 1807, Britain moved the Lisbon court (Prince Regent Don Joao) to Rio de Janeiro under its protection.[32] The court was escorted by ships of the Anglo-Portuguese mercantile community. It was during this wartime market reorientation that Leigh launched his venture to Brazil. His efforts epitomise the wartime mercantile ambition of the British merchants.

Such a major and rapid diversion of commercial routes inevitably posed some challenges to Leigh's existing credit networks. I have argued above that bill discounting at local banks rested upon the guarantee system which was established in the Atlantic slave trade. Leigh would receive the bills of exchange from the colony, for remittance of the sale of slaves or manufactured goods in the West Indies. The creditworthiness of those bills was guaranteed by the respectable merchant houses. Parr's Bank did not oppose accepting Leigh's West Indian bills as long as they had originated from a factor house with guarantee status. Thus Leigh was able to get them discounted at Parr's Bank and to get his account credited so that he could draw on draft. He would draw against those bills to make payments for the purchase of manufactured goods for the next venture. Parr's Bank, despite not knowing the nature of the foreign bill drawer, was able to rest upon the guarantee in agreeing to discount. In other words, the guarantee system functioned as the basis on which the local bank could finance the British slave trade. When Leigh shifted his commercial interest into Trinidad, Surinam and Brazil, the bills from these new markets were not necessarily passed without question. Local recipients of the foreign origin bills were reluctant to accept them unless they were indirectly drawn on respectable houses in London or Liverpool. Leigh complained, "You cannot have any Idea how bad it is to make use of any Bills here excepting on Bankers or very respectable Houses."[33]

The series of bills in question here were draw by Clarke & Tods, merchants in Liverpool, who were Leigh's partner in all of his Rio trade. Clarke & Tods specialised in Brazilian trade, with one partner, Henry Clarke, residing in Liverpool and the other partner, Robert Tod, operating from Rio de Janeiro. They must have had an established reputation in the Brazilian trade as other British merchants also used them as their Rio agent.[34] Leigh had a high opinion of them, recommending their creditworthiness by stating that their bills were "as good as the Bank of England."[35] He also wrote to Parr's Bank explaining the trust of their bills: "Although we send you long Bills you know they are as good as Bank of England."[36] It was ironic that Leigh used the Bank of England as his measure of creditworthiness, because it was in the middle of a cash suspension. Leigh directly passed the Brazil merchants' bill to the Manchester manufacturers, Yates & Company, but Yates refused to send the invoiced goods on the grounds that the bill should have been drawn on a London merchant or a respectable banking house.[37] This suggests that Leigh's new commercial correspondents in Latin America had not yet established a system equivalent to the guarantee/acceptance system of the Africa–West Indian slave trade. Without authorised credit, a bill drawn in Latin America was too risky for a local manufacturer in the hinterland to accept.

The whole system of bill circulation was underpinned by trust. It required trust in the house on which the bill was drawn, the drawee. Some houses or some places were known for their better reputation. London's financial infrastructure and resources had ultimately the best reputation, which is why bills on London houses were the most desirable. Transactions between, for example, Liverpool and the West Indies could have been settled by a bill drawn on Leigh in Liverpool, but a bill drawn indirectly on London houses generally enjoyed a better reputation. Also, it required the trust and credit of the person who wrote/drew the bill, the drawer. Even if the drawee did not refuse to pay the bill and settle the transaction, there was still a risk that the house to whom the bill was addressed would refuse to receive it because trust in the drawer was insufficient.

Such reluctance towards Latin American bills was common not only among businessmen but also among bankers in South Lancashire. Their preference for particular bills was explained by Leigh as follows: "The Banks here will not take in any thing only direct on London, and on respectable Houses."[38] Presumably, by "the Banks here" he referred to Parr's Bank and others like it. As Leigh moved into the Latin American markets, the limited banking connections of the local Parr's Bank became increasingly inadequate. It is no surprise, therefore, that he looked to open accounts with London banks that would accept the colonial bills and was ready to offer a higher commission rate than he was paying to Parr & Company. He explained that he would receive bills of three to four months' date in payment of his sales which he would remit to his bank to be credited while he would draw bills at similar date on his brokers which he requests the bank to accept.[39]

In the autumn of 1806, Leigh succeeded in opening an account with Brickwood & Company through the introduction of his London agent. Leigh explained that the half-year transaction volume with Parr's Bank was expected to be £40,000. If Brickwood agreed to allow the same terms that Parr & Company had granted, Leigh would divide his transactions between Parr & Company and Brickwood & Company.[40]

As Leigh's trade expanded, his commercial and financial networks became more complicated, a fact reflected in the circulation of his bills. It involved a number of traders in Britain as well as overseas and a number of banking houses in Liverpool and London alike. The pattern of bill transactions can be described thus. First, the bills were drawn at three to 12 months[41] by the colonial factors on their guarantees in Britain for payment of sales in the colony; second, the bills were sent to Leigh by his ship captain on the return voyage; third, on receiving the bills, Leigh submitted them either to the manufacturers/merchants for goods purchase or to his banks to discount them; fourth, a second series of bills was drawn by colonial planters on their correspondents in Britain; fifth and finally, these bills were remitted by the factors, via Leigh, to their British guarantors to reimburse acceptance and payment of the first set of bills at the due date.

Figure 9.2 illustrates Leigh's extensive use of bill discounting at Devaynes' and Brickwood's for 20 months in 1808 and 1809, when he was engaged in West Indian and Brazilian trade. Looking at the individual bank transactions in detail,

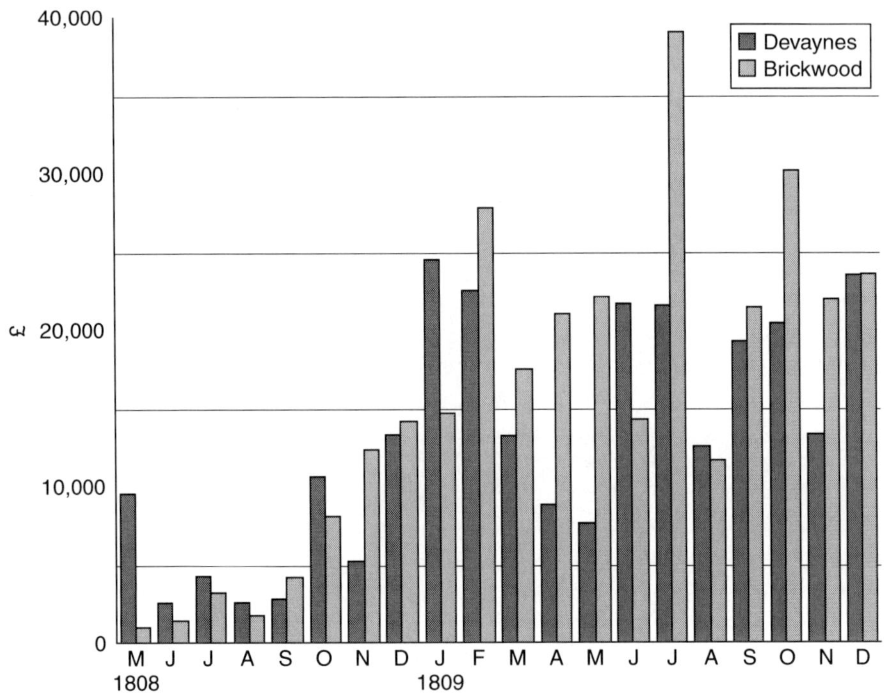

Figure 9.2 John Leigh's bill drawing on Brickwood & Company and Devaynes & Company (sources: National Archives C108/212-4 Papers relating to the Bankruptcy of John Leigh 1803–11).

it is notable that an enormous amount of bills was discounted by Brickwood's. In February and July 1809, for example, the amount reached as much as £35,000. Evidently Brickwood's grew to be the most involved with Leigh's bill transactions. Parr's Bank, which Leigh once complained was reluctant to discount non-London bills, appears to have become more actively involved with Leigh's bill transactions. It is as if they were induced to get more involved by Brickwood's active discounting. At the peak, the amount reached as high as £30,000, in June 1809. Leigh sent colonial bills for discounting, against which he drew on drafts at two to four months.[42] The content of the bills characterised Brickwood's active involvement with Leigh's commercial enterprise. The Brazil-addressed bills were more often drawn on Brickwood's Bank than on the others. Brickwood's allowed Leigh to draw on bills to Clark & Tod in Rio de Janeiro in contrast to the Manchester manufacturers, Yates & Company, who had refused the bills in the previous year.

John Leigh's bankruptcy 1810–11

While both imports and exports with South America and the West Indies rose in 1809, many British merchants began to feel the slowdown of the markets in the first half of 1810. Many British exporters had difficulties in grasping what commodities were in demand in the new markets and tended to over-supply inappropriate items. The exports of cotton goods to South and North America continued to grow at a relatively healthy rate in the first half of 1810. Many importers, however, held large stocks of colonial produce, for which demand decreased as early as the last quarter of 1809 and decreased even more sharply in the first half of 1810, when further bulk of produce arrived. This initial collapse of import prices was worsened by the shock of Cole & Company's failure and the subsequent bankruptcy of Brickwood & Company, which fundamentally shook the whole economy. Worst hit were those merchants, the acceptance of whose bills by Brickwood's ceased precisely as they were struggling to deal with slow returns in South American and the West Indies markets. Leigh was liable for £20,785 of Brickwood's acceptances, which he had discounted at Parr & Company. He wrote to the bank that he and his firm were doing all in their power to meet the cash advance that the bank had made for them.[43]

> With respect to receiving you have plenty, as Brickwood are likely to pay nearly all, but to ease your mind, we would make a sacrifice to take for [£]10,000 out of the acceptance you hold. It is to owe who knows Brickwood concern. Therefore it is likely to be a good concern.[44]

For this arrangement, Leigh gave up his claim for £10,000 acceptance which Parr's bank held for Leigh. In addition, Leigh & Company lost heavily on a series of bills accepted by the firms that failed during the crisis. Devaynes & Company, the agent bank of Parr's, stopped payment in July 1810 and went bankrupt. Shortly afterwards John Hodgkinson, the Liverpool merchant who regularly accepted Leigh's bills in Irish trade also failed. Lastly, Clarke & Tods stopped payment in May 1811. With a large amount of capital locked in Brickwood's and a series of failures among his regular acceptors, Leigh had difficulty in convincing his creditors to wait for payments. There was a general lack of confidence among the commercial community both in Liverpool and London. A witness, who offered testimony to the Select Committee investigating the cause of the recession, summarised the situation as follows:

> The capital of the banks is therefore taken up also and they are not able to give the regular accommodation which they had been used to do to their customer. In this situation, a want of confidence arises in the banks themselves, when there were people breaking down around them, they become timid and afraid of transacting any business; a want of confidence on the part of the banks, naturally creates distress among the upper classes of merchants who are thus deprived of the usual accommodation or means of negotiation that therefore persons who are possessed of solid property have not the same means of obtaining credit that they usually have had and very far from it.[45]

There was a general lack of confidence among banking houses and this psychology was prohibiting the market from recovering. There were many economically healthy merchants, even among those who had stopped their business in the crisis, many who would have undertaken to pay their creditors in full in a certain amount of time. The example of John Leigh illustrates some of the problems incurred in the chain of connection between the group of merchants and banks in the provinces and in London, who discounted and advanced upon the bills of exchange arising from the South American trade.

Conclusion

This chapter has drawn on the case study of John Leigh & Company's bankruptcy, which was a part of the general economic crisis in 1810–11. His failure came after most of business bankruptcies had occurred, which suggests that his business survived the initial collapse of the South American and the West Indies markets in the previous summer and that he was not one of the many ignorant speculators who ventured into the new markets without trading and financial knowledge. Those speculative merchants went under as soon as the import prices fell in the summer. Instead Leigh's failure was strongly affected by the stoppage of his London banks, Brickwood & Company and Devaynes & Company, in the summer of 1810. The former in particular posed fatal liquidity problems to Leigh's finance.

Of particular interest are the beginning and process of how Leigh opened accounts with those banks and extensively used their bill acceptance in expanding into the new markets. It has especially revealed the specific remittance problem in the new Rio market that encouraged Leigh to open accounts with

Brickwood & Company. The relatively immature state of the credit system in these new markets exposed Leigh's business to credit shortage when the merchant diverted to Brazil from the Caribbean as a result of both the slave trade abolition and the market reorganisation during the Napoleonic Wars. Many merchant firms concentrated much of their capital in a single bank, as did Leigh & Company, when they expanded their mercantile business. This rendered them dependent on their bank, and they became enmeshed in a chain of bankruptcies, when their bank failed. Widespread use of bills of exchange and interdependence of credit among tradesmen and banks had made the country's commerce very vulnerable to fluctuations in credit.

Notes

1 National Archives [hereafter NA] Bankruptcy file of John Leigh, Liverpool African merchant 1811.
2 I. Duffy, *Bankruptcy and Insolvency in London during the Industrial Revolution* (New York 1985), Table 2.2, 372; L. Neal, "The Financial Crisis of 1825 and the Restructuring of the British Financial system," *Federal Reserve Bank of St. Louis Review* (1985), Table 2, 69.
3 S.D. Chapman, *Merchant Enterprise in Britain: From the Industrial Revolution to World War I* (Cambridge, UK 1991), 69.
4 A.K. Manchester, *British Preeminence in Brazil: Its Rise and Decline* (London 1972), 87–91.
5 H. Heaton, "A Merchant Adventurer in Brazil 1808–1818," *Journal of Economic History* 6 (1946): 1–23.
6 NA B3/252-4, Bankruptcy file of Brickwood, Rainier, Morgan & Co.
7 At their bankruptcy, only £18,700 was claimed by non-commercial creditors (32 individuals) for their deposit balance with the bank. These non-traders were widows, "gentlemen," and "esquires." Although correct identification of the last two terms is difficult, it is usually considered that these were rentier customers who were more often served by the West End bankers. See L.S. Pressnell, *Country Banking in the Industrial Revolution* (Oxford 1956), 82–4.
8 Duffy, *Bankruptcy and Insolvency*, 244.
9 *The Times* cited by Pressnell, *Country Banking*, 466–7.
10 Duffy, *Bankruptcy and Insolvency*, 240–1.
11 Ibid., 244.
12 Ibid., 246.
13 NA B3/252-4, Bankruptcy file of Brickwood, Rainier, Morgan, Starkey & Co.
14 Ibid.
15 Duffy, *Bankruptcy and Insolvency*, 287–94. Ibid., especially Ch. 8.
16 Duffy used the bankruptcy file of Brickwood & Co in the analysis of the crisis of 1810: Duffy, *Bankruptcy and Insolvency*, Ch. 8. He did not, however, consult the bankruptcy file of John Leigh nor his business records. In fact, Duffy did not touch upon Leigh's trade with Rio de Janeiro at all and, as a result, dismissed the influence of South American commercial aspect in bill transaction around Brickwood & Company.
17 NA C108/212, John Leigh to Alexander Hume, 4 October 1803.
18 "Voyages: Trans-Atlantic Slave Trade" (www.slavevoyages.org/ accessed 20 July 2012).
19 The initial capital of mercantile firms trading to the North American colonies before 1775 ranged from 5,000 to 10,000 pounds on average. J.M. Price, *Capital and Credit*

in British Overseas Trade: The View from the Chesapeake, 1700–1776 (Cambridge, MA 1981), 36–8.

20 P.E. Lovejoy and D. Richardson, "Trust, Pawnship, and Atlantic History: The Institutional Foundations of the Old Calabar Slave Trade," *American History Review* 104 (2009): 333–55.; P.E. Lovejoy and D. Richardson, "'This Horrid Hole': Royal Authority, Commerce and Credit at Bonny, 1690–1840," *Journal of African History* 45 (2004): 363–92.

21 NA C108/212.

22 S. Haggerty, "Risk and Risk Management in the Liverpool Slave Trade," *Business History* 51 (2009), 827.

23 K. Morgan, "Remittance Procedures in the Eighteenth-Century British Slave Trade," *Business History Review* 79 (2005): 732–3.

24 Ibid.

25 NA C108/212, John Leigh to Alexander Hume, 15 December 1803.

26 E. Kerridge, *Trade and Banking in Early Modern England* (Manchester 1988), 66–7.

27 It was not until the 1830s, when local private banks began to pay interest on deposits. Pressnell, *Country Banking*, 243–52.

28 M. Dawes and C.N. Ward-Perkins, *Country Banks of England and Wales: Private Provincial Banks & Bankers, 1688–1953* (London 2000), 614–15.

29 The 1790s customer ledger of Parr, Lyon & Hurst includes "Thomas R Leigh, merchant." Possibly this was John's father. RBS PAB/1 Parr Lyon Ledgers.

30 H. Price, *A Handbook of London Bankers* (London 1890), 49.

31 Main ventures were made 24 October 1808 (Narcissus with £1,291), 6 April (Lady Warlington, £1,545), May (Super, £3,207), August (Little Venus, £10,447) of 1809, January (Belmont, £530) of 1810. NA C108/214, Invoice book of John Leigh & Co.

32 NA C108/213, John Leigh to William Hilton, 15 July 1806.

33 *London Gazette*, 26 June 1811.

34 NA C108/213, John Leith to Simon Cook, 9 September 1809.

35 NA C108/213, John Leigh to Parr, Lyon & Hurst, 31 December 1806.

36 NA C108/213 John Leigh to Yates & Co. of Manchester, 11 July 1808.

37 NA C108/213, John Leigh to Rimmer, 1806.

38 NA C108/212, John Leigh to John Kerwin, 29 August 1806.

39 NA C108/213, John Leigh to Brickwood & Bowles, 26 November 1806.

40 According to Price, sometimes the bills bore duration of as long as 30 months. J.M. Price, "Credit in the Slave Trade and Plantation Economies," in: B.L. Solow (ed.), *Slavery and the Rise of the Atlantic System* (Cambridge, UK 1994), 314.

41 At first, Brickwood's Bank appears to have shown reluctance on Leigh's three month drawing, and tried to charge higher commission on it. Leigh paid ¼ per cent commission to Parr's Bank for the same service, but Brickwood demanded more than that. Leigh could not agree to this and explained the solid nature of his bill transactions.

42 NA C108/214, John Leigh to Parr, Lyon & Co., 29 August 1810.

43 NA C108/214, John Leigh to Parr Lyon & Co., 29 August 1810.

44 British Parliamentary Papers 1811 Report from the Select Committee on the State of Commercial Credit 1810–1811 session 52, II, 367.

45 J. Hoppit, *Risk and Failure in English Business 1700–1800* (Cambridge, UK 1987), 130–9.

Part III

Institutional developments

10 The insolvent *Zuchthaus* as cameralist dystopia

Andre Wakefield

Introduction

Bankrupts were among the first inmates at Celle's *Zuchthaus*. In 1720, before construction of the building was even completed, a certain Ballauf was confined there because of his "dissolute lifestyle." Ballauf, who came to Celle from Hildesheim, had squandered his inheritance. One of his siblings then paid to have him confined in the *Zuchthaus*, because "otherwise my miserable brother would become too expensive for me." There was nothing especially novel about Celle's practice of admitting the dissipated members of wealthy families; the famous prison-workhouse in Amsterdam had long accepted such "bad seeds," promising to improve them through a regimen of work and discipline. In Celle, however, the motivation for taking such inmates appears to have been somewhat different, for here there was no claim about "improving" the degenerate offspring of the wealthy—bankrupts and debauched women among them. Celle's *Zuchthaus* simply promised to confine them indefinitely in return for regular payment. Like the nearby University of Göttingen, which opened its doors around the same time, Celle's prison-workhouse gladly accepted paying customers from wealthy families. They offered the best hope for surplus revenue.[1]

But if profitability was the dream of *Zuchthaus* officials, bankruptcy and ruin became their nightmare. Caught between the cost-cutting demands of the provincial *Stände* (estates) and the relentless calls for increased revenue by the *Kammer* (treasury), Celle's prison-workhouse officials resorted to extreme measures. They promised to feed the inmates for less; they promised to sell prison-workhouse products—linen thread and rasped wood—for more money; they promised to increase the number of inmates; they promised to do more with less. But it was never enough. Professors in Göttingen, with their fanciful visions of profitable prison-workhouses, did not help matters. They convinced fiscal officials that the problem must be poor administration, which led to more dissatisfaction and more audits. Desperate *Zuchthaus* commissars, under pressure from every side, began blurring the lines between public and private. Encouraged by authorities in Hannover and professors in Göttingen to make the *Zuchthaus* profitable, they imagined themselves as entrepreneurs. When their schemes failed, some of these entrepreneur-officials themselves went bankrupt.

"The management of prison workhouses," Pieter Spierenburg has claimed, "did not change very much between the introduction of the first such institutions around 1600 and the first half of the nineteenth century, when solitary confinement and the panoptic principle took center stage."[2] The emergence of new attitudes toward idleness and poverty around 1500, he argues, made the establishment of prison-workhouses around 1600 possible. After that, they remained essentially the same until the prison reforms of the nineteenth century.[3] Early prison-workhouses—Amsterdam (1596), Bremen (1608), Lübeck (1613), Hamburg (1622)—had close links to the utopian visions of writers like Thomas More and Dirck Volkertsz Coornhert; later nineteenth-century prisons to those of Jeremy Bentham and his followers.[4] But what happened between More and Bentham? Celle's *Zuchthaus*, constructed between 1710 and 1731, was not inspired by utopian visions of moral improvement; nor did it focus on Benthamite visions of efficient discipline. Rather, Celle's prison-workhouse commissars dreamt of creating a profitable institution. Some of those dreams would end in bankruptcy.[5]

The construction of Celle's new prison-workhouse coincided with a rise in bankruptcy prosecutions across central Europe, as territorial governments strove increasingly to classify different types of bankruptcy. A 1723 edict from Prussia, for example, distinguished between the various kinds of "malicious" (*böswillige*) and "deceitful" (*betrügerische*) bankrupts: some hid or withheld property as a way to avoid paying their debts; others pretended financial ruin as a way to avoid paying creditors; still others continued to loan money or accept deposits despite knowledge of insolvency. Nor was Prussia unusual in this regard. Similar regulations appeared in many towns and territories of the Holy Roman Empire.[6] Together with the usual prosecutions for such things as gambling debt and reckless speculation, authorities devoted increasing attention to disorderly bookkeeping and bad accounts.[7] But what to do with the bankrupts? At the time that Celle's *Zuchthaus* was built, the *Consitutio criminalis Carolina*, the 1532 penal code of Charles V, was still the foundation of criminal law. "The Carolina was a harsh code, prescribing a range of exacerbated capital punishments including burning, hanging, breaking on the wheel, quartering, burying alive, drowning."[8] By the early eighteenth century, however, authorities began to prefer confinement to the harsh physical punishments dictated by the Carolina. The move toward confinement meant that one needed prisons, and prisons were expensive to build and maintain. But in Hannover the authorities convinced themselves that the prison-workhouse in Celle could pay for itself. This would turn out to be a crucial and mistaken assumption. As it moved to confine more bankrupts, the territorial government created the conditions that would lead to the bankruptcy of its own officials.

The *Zuchthaus* as cameralist utopia

In 1782 Göttingen's Royal Society of Sciences posed the following prize question: What is the most profitable way to manage prison-workhouses?[9] The man behind the question was Johann Beckmann, Ordinary Professor of *Ökonomie* at the University of Göttingen. Göttingen's Royal Society eventually received a successful response from August Friedrich Rulffs, commissar of a workhouse in Einbeck, entitled "Among the Prickliest Thorns, I Seek the Prettiest Roses." Rulffs used Beckmann's work extensively—this probably did not hurt his chances at the prize money—arguing that Lower Saxony's workhouses should focus on linen production. Given the suitability of Lower Saxony's land and climate for flax cultivation, he maintained, the region's linen manufacture was not all that it could be.[10] By building prison-workhouses and incarcerating the idle poor, state officials could increase electoral Hannover's linen production. Increased flax spinning and linen weaving in the land's prison-workhouses would, in turn, encourage farmers to cultivate flax and, by improving the linen trade, help to keep money in the land. There would always be a market for linen, Rulffs argued, because of its universal appeal. If one discovered the secret of occupying criminals and poor people with profitable work, of making them "useful," then prisons and workhouses would no longer be a burden to the land. And if one could accomplish that,

> then these institutions will no longer be so rare, then such houses will no longer be places of pale hunger and pressing misery, then the spirit of industriousness will push out monstrous indolence and beggar-insolence, and the oft-asked question, "how can begging be prevented?", will resolve itself.[11]

Rulffs cited work by the Swedish cameralist Johann Bergius, one of Beckmann's favorite authors, as evidence for his claims.[12] He considered introducing a linen bleaching works based on the Dutch model. He also proposed that workhouses introduce the new two-spooled spinning wheels displayed in Leipzig and described in the *Hannoverische Magazin*. Children could master the new spinning wheels, which required special dexterity, in the workhouses. In this way, the territories of Lower Saxony could cultivate a new generation of skilled workers.[13]

In his references to cameralist authors like Bergius and Beckmann, in his awareness of new technologies and in his careful examination of numerous manufactures—tobacco, woolens, cotton, silk, camel hair, human hair, gold, silver, hemp, flax—Commissar Rulffs styled himself as a selfless entrepreneur. Like the clever merchant, he understood how to make a profit. But he also demonstrated the circumspect concerns of the wise fiscal official, making sure that prison-workhouse production would not harm existing manufactories and showing that it would discourage the purchase of foreign linen, something that had caused "great amounts of money to leave the land."[14]

"The author," wrote Beckmann, "a sensible and experienced man, hopes to produce enough profit through flax processing that workhouses will require no contributions."[15] Commissar Rulffs urged state officials to think more like merchants. Since "every merchant balances his accounts monthly," prison-workhouse officials could do the same. Any merchant, no matter how profitable his trade, would succumb to bankruptcy if he allowed "laziness, neglect and disorder" to infect his books. Similarly, any prison-workhouse in which "exact oversight, order, cleanliness and constant industry" failed to be observed would be ruined. Rulffs' essay appealed to Beckmann precisely because it blurred the line that separated public institutions from private enterprises. Beckmann envisioned public officials who behaved like entrepreneurs.[16] But the rewards of entrepreneurship came with risks: the entrepreneurial public official, like the private merchant, faced the dangers of bankruptcy if he ruined the enterprise.

Rulffs attributed the paucity of workhouses in Germany to a single cause: their high cost to the state. Bremen's new workhouse, for example, had largely eliminated beggars, but "the place is just too expensive." There were similar problems in Berlin, Hannover and Braunschweig. Prison-workhouses were burdening treasuries throughout the Empire, and the public seemed to have abandoned all hope of making workhouses profitable. Rulffs, however, had the solution. By stressing the distinction between prisons (*Zuchthäuser*) and workhouses (*Arbeitshäuser*), he would eliminate the stigma attached to the latter. The "upright people who like to work and who wish to support themselves and their families through work and with honor" would go to the workhouses; the naturally indolent, who "had been bred to shameful beggary since childhood," would go to prison. Having established these two classes of the poor, though actually mobilizing an established early modern distinction between the honorable and the dishonorable, the deserving and the undeserving poor, Commissar Rulffs outlined a plan of breathtaking ambition. In all towns and villages, authorities would arrest the begging poor. The healthy ones would be taken to the nearest workhouse. Those who refused would go to prison. Recalcitrant beggars could choose to move to the workhouse, where they could enjoy better food and housing. Otherwise, they would remain imprisoned. Rulffs's plan promised to rid the German lands of beggars while yielding profit from their work.[17]

It all depended on the skill, integrity and character of the *Zuchthaus* commissar. Only the chicanery of "ambitious and self-interested brokers and entrepreneurs," he argued, had ruined the Empire's prison-workhouses. If skillful and disinterested directors took control of the entire manufacturing process, planning and organizing every detail, Rulffs saw no good reason for losing money. More often than not, he claimed, unscrupulous and selfish entrepreneurs ruined such enterprises. Like any successful factory, the profitable prison-workhouse would require "exacting oversight and strict order" to discourage fraud and embezzlement. Everything depended on the integrity of the commissar. He would prepare meticulous account books. He would accept unannounced visitations by auditors and inspectors. He would be an unselfish man of business:

> He must not only be a skilled manufacturer, an experienced and order-loving merchant, but also an equally disinterested burgher, a warm philanthropist and a practicing Christian; also, where possible, already have conducted this kind of business. To such a man, the state can entrust its unlucky children without worry.[18]

By the same token the bad commissar—selfish and incompetent—conjured nightmares of bankruptcy and ruin. He would cheat the poor. He would permit disorder and filth. He might neglect the business of manufactures altogether. Bad commissars had single-handedly ruined expensive state enterprises. The successful commissar would need to be a public-spirited merchant, an unselfish profit seeker. It was the impossible dream.[19]

Less than two months after Rulffs's essay appeared in print, Hannover issued a special workhouse ordinance for Celle and surrounding villages.[20] The regulation incorporated many elements of Rulffs's proposals, providing for the appointment of eight bailiffs to scout for beggars and vagabonds in and around Celle.[21]

> Every beggar, as soon as he is encountered on the street or elsewhere, shall be led immediately to the workhouse. Depending on the circumstances, he shall be flogged and then provided with work. Should a pauper residing in the workhouse be found begging, however, such person will, according to the circumstances, be flogged, pilloried or even sentenced to the *Zuchthaus*.[22]

In the streets of Celle, police and soldiers were to help the bailiffs patrol for beggars and vagabonds. Residents of Celle were also expected to do their part. Those who gave out alms in the street, for example, would be fined one thaler; innkeepers could be fined ten thaler for taking in beggars.[23]

While Beckmann's academic visions conjured cameralist dreams of better, more efficient, and more profitable institutions, everyday prison-workhouse administration continued to produce cameralist nightmares of poverty, fraud and bankruptcy. Only two years after the publication of Rulffs's essay, a commission convened to investigate the misuse of funds by Commissar Cramer, the head of Celle's *Zuchthaus*.[24] When government auditors reviewed Cramer's books, they discovered a great "disorder of the accounts," making it almost impossible to ascertain exactly what had happened. Eventually the auditors managed an overview of the *Zuchthaus* budget and determined that funds were missing. The most serious accusations leveled against Commissar Cramer involved the misuse of public funds and the failure to keep good books, both commonly heard complaints against bankrupts. Commissar Cramer, argued the commissioners, had "taken funds meant for feeding and clothing the prisoners and lunatics … and employed them for his personal use." Investigators concluded that Cramer could no longer be trusted to keep accounts. He was to be dismissed from office.[25] The missing funds amounted to over 3404 thaler, or more than eight times Cramer's annual salary.[26] He could not pay it. The royal government appointed Captain von Spörken as the commissar's bailsman, with full authority to liquidate all of Cramer's possessions.

Commissar Cramer protested his innocence.[27] Because his debts were a private matter, Cramer explained, there would be no need for Bailsman von Spörken. Having no money of his own, the commissar had borrowed on credit to purchase clothing for the inmates, intending to repay the money later. The minutes of the meeting capture the heart of Cramer's defense:

> As *Zuchthaus* Commissar, he had to ensure that the inmates were clothed, but the office did not obligate him to trouble about the purchase of wares, or the manufacture of clothing; he could delegate this to any entrepreneur. If that one [the entrepreneur] had materials delivered, then he would be obligated to his suppliers, and these would have claims on the entrepreneur, but never on the *Zuchthaus* fund. This was also the case here, since the commissar had to be separated from the entrepreneur.[28]

Cramer saw a clear distinction between his role as *Zuchthaus* Commissar, who administered the prison-workhouse, and his role as entrepreneur, who sought the best suppliers for materials and the best markets for finished goods. Not the *Kammer*, or the provincial deputies or the investigating commission accepted his defense. As far as they were concerned, Cramer had misused public funds and kept bad accounts. The commissar had become the bankrupt. On 8 August 1785, about two weeks after Cramer's hearing, Lieutenant Christian August von Döhren was appointed as Celle's next *Zuchthaus* commissar. "We assume," came official word from the *Kammer* in Hannover, "that he is a man skilled and experienced in accounting."[29]

The dream: Celle's physical and regulatory architecture

Celle's *Zuchthaus*, originally completed in 1731, was an imposing structure. Before passing under the bell-tower and into a grassy courtyard, inmates and visitors would have been greeted by the inscription over the front gate:

> *Puniendis facinorosis*
> *custodiensis furiosis*
> *et mente captis*
> *publico sumtu dicata domus.*[30]

The *Zucht- und Tollhaus*, that is, would punish bad people and lock up crazy ones, all with "public" funds.[31]

The *Zuchthaus* had been constructed to house 200 inmates. Most of them would be incarcerated at public expense, but there were a certain number of "private" cells in the west wing, which housed the so-called "state convicts." These "elegant people" (those with personal or family wealth, who could pay for their own food and shelter) paid 12 thaler in "house moneys" annually, more than twice as much as the cost for the average working convict.[32] State convicts generally enjoyed better food and drink than the common inmate, and they paid considerably more than the normal fee of five thaler for that privilege.[33]

Entering the outer yards through the eastern gate, visitors would have noticed a second, shorter structure behind the main *Zuchthaus* building. This was the so-called "madhouse" (*Tollhaus*). The *Tollhaus* lay directly behind, and was separated from, the main prison-workhouse building. Its central feature was the long "mad corridor" (*Tollgang*), with 24 cells, which ran parallel to the *Zuchthaus* proper. Using special tin-plated copper bowls, which were chained to each cell, the food master delivered food to the corridor's residents through slots in the doors. There was no light in the mad cells, since prison officials worried too much about fire to let the residents anywhere near a lantern. The only available light came through the small barred window high up in the corner of each mad cell, and since officials did not trust the "lunatics" with glass, these small windows remained open throughout the year, even in winter.[34]

The real innovation and technical marvel of the madhouse was the elaborate sewer canal that ran under the building. Each cell had a permanent toilet; actually, a hole in the floor that opened directly into the canal. The canal, which passed under the long mad corridor and along both wings of the *Tollhaus* building, was connected to toilets in the main *Zuchthaus* building by a special tunnel system. Sluiceways linked the canal system to the Aller River and, twice a week, water would be pumped into the canal system, the locks would open, and sewage would drain into the Aller. That, at least, was the labor-saving idea behind its construction. In practice the system failed to work as planned. The main canal, which ran under the mad corridor, tended to back up. Unpredictable river levels, trouble with the pumps, and other technical problems combined to leave a stinking residue in the canal. The stink, which emanated from under the mad corridor and penetrated every part of the *Zuchthaus*, became one of the defining characteristics of the institution. Visitors noted the profound stink of the place, and the *Zuchthaus* commissars, in their regular reports to Hannover, frequently commented on it.[35]

The physical structure, as completed in 1731, embodied a familiar vision of punishment and confinement, of work and improvement. The architecture of the place, with workrooms flanking a church in the center, linked industriousness to piety. Like other prison-workhouses in Holland and the Holy Roman Empire, Celle's designers had followed a well-established model of moral improvement through work. The squat madhouse building, which was separated completely from the improvement-oriented work of the prison-workhouse proper, conformed to a different model. Here, communal work gave way to isolation. As evidenced by the iron-plated doors and oak-walled cells, the architects feared the raging and insane more than the most dangerous of criminals. Or perhaps, more to the point, they had no idea what to do with them. In a *Zuchthaus* focused on work and profit, there was no place for the insane. The sewer canal itself contributed to isolation, since it obviated the need periodically to remove buckets of urine and feces from the cells of the madhouse.

The *Zuchthaus* Ordinance of 1732, which aimed to regulate life at Celle's prison-workhouse, was as much a part of the institution as its cells, workrooms and sewer canal. By 1732, when the *Zuchthaus* Ordinance was drafted, the primary goals and purposes of the place had already begun to change. The grand baroque structure that had cost so much to build, with its massive walls and spacious workrooms and expensive sewer canal, became a source of concern. Officials in Hannover and the provinces worried more and more about account deficits, less and less about improving the lazy, confining the insane or disciplining the wicked. Over the course of decades, the bulk of official correspondence—between the royal government and the provinces, between the *Kammer* and the commissar, between the deputies of the provinces and the commissar—concerned itself with income and expenditure, with maximizing income through paying inmates and profitable labor and minimizing the losses of an expensive institution. During this period, the vision of a balance, or even a surplus, structured every aspect of daily life at the *Zuchthaus*, shaping the lives of inmates and their overseers.[36]

Everyday life in Celle's *Zuchthaus* was supposed to be organized around work, like that at the prison-workhouses in Holland and the Hanseatic cities on which it was modeled.[37] The regular tolling of the bells established the rhythm of the workday. At 5 a.m. (6 a.m. in the winter) the bells would toll to signal the beginning of the day. Throughout the following hours bells punctuated the intended pattern of work and rest until bedtime at 9 p.m.[38]

The Ordinance distinguished sharply between royal officials (*Bediente*) and subalterns (*Unterbediente*). Higher officials included the royal inspectors, the commissar, the physicians and surgeons and the pastor. Subalterns included the schoolmaster, the scribes, the "food master" (*Speisemeister*), the "discipline master," the "spin mother," the gatekeeper and the night watchman. While higher officials enjoyed some measure of autonomy as representatives of the royal government, the subalterns were to be strictly subordinated to the commissar and the royal inspectors. All officials, however, were expected to maintain distance from the prisoners. Subalterns especially were supposed to avoid "lengthy conversations" or disputes with the prisoners. Should they become involved in theft or illegal trade with the inmates, *Zuchthaus* officials could themselves be condemned to lifelong imprisonment.[39]

The royal inspectors were, above all, guardians and enforcers of the 1732 Ordinance. With orders to ensure that the house maintained "good order and discipline," they were the eyes and ears of the royal government in Hannover. Inspectors would visit the prison-workhouse once a month. They also had the right to make surprise visits, or "extraordinary" inspections, at any time. They were required to consult regularly with the commissar and to submit regular reports to the royal government about the status of the house. "Specifically," the 1732 Ordinance declared, "they [inspectors] are to make inquiries from time to time about whether and how the officials are following their orders."[40]

The ruler and head of Celle's *Zuchthaus* republic was the commissar. He was to ensure that the house be kept in good order i.e., that the schedule be strictly observed, that all of the officials and subalterns fulfill their obligations, that the account books be balanced and that the Ordinance be strictly observed. Specifically, he had to see that the inmates, insofar as possible, would earn their keep. For the men, he was to find "more profitable work." For the women, he was to make sure that they fulfilled their spinning quotas and, if they failed to do so, to "coerce" them into greater productivity. In the workrooms of the women, he would check the so-called "spin-boards" on which the daily amount of spun flax or wool was noted. The commissar was also expected to be present at the end of every week, when the scribes received and measured finished work from the inmates, so that he could "note who has been idle." He was to guarantee that the subalterns performed their duties carefully and unselfishly. He had to send lists of "prisoners and lunatics" to the *Kammer* and the royal inspectors four times a year. The insane remained under the care of the physicians and could only be released with their written approval. He had to keep a meticulous inventory of everything in the house—furniture, instruments, etc.—and to do everything possible to protect it. Most importantly, he had to safeguard all *Zuchthaus* funds and keep strict accounts.[41]

In supervising the work of the inmates, the commissar would be assisted by the two scribes, who were charged with committing the productive life of the prison-workhouse to paper. They had to note and safeguard all materials, such as flax and wool, stored in the house. They had to keep strict records of how much had been spun and to safeguard all finished materials. If wool, flax or other materials had to be purchased, they were to notify the commissar and to help him ensure that one got "good, faultless wares" and that these were delivered according to the full weight or volume that had been ordered. If outsiders brought their flax, wool or yarn to the house for processing, the scribes were required to accept it, make an "accurate catalogue" and, once the things were finished, to account for everything without taking the "smallest profit or gain" for themselves. The essential task was to keep strict records of raw materials, processed materials and income from the work. Scribes would keep a monthly account and deliver any surplus money to the commissar. This money, in turn, went to the *Speisemeister* to defray the cost of food for the inmates. The scribes were to police the *Speisemeister* by making sure that he did not scrimp on food for the inmates. They would also be expected to police the inmates by keeping strict track of their productivity and noting it on the boards in the workrooms. Any prisoner who could not work because of an illness had to be certified as "sick" by the physician. Every Monday, in the presence of the commissar, the discipline master and the spin mother, the scribes were directed to measure the finished work and take it into their possession, specifying the exact amounts in a special register.[42]

The early generation of prison-workhouses had developed techniques, sometimes very expensive ones, to "improve" its inmates by making them diligent and industrious.[43] Amsterdam had its infamous water cell, and Hamburg its "wooden horse," to impose industriousness on convicts. Celle was different. Wasteful punishment would not be tolerated. Instead, all punishment would be useful; that is, it would serve to reduce costs and increase revenue. Shiftless prisoners would be beaten and, "in cases of continued laziness, they will be punished with bread and water for a few days, or also with complete starvation."[44] Those condemned to bread and water would be isolated in a special "hunger cell" to prevent fellow inmates from giving them extra food. Should their idleness be grounded in "stubborn viciousness," they would be whipped in front of the others and shackled hand to foot "for as long as their health can sustain it." Moreover, troublesome men and boys would clean the canals.

We should be wary of reading the 1732 Ordinance as a mirror of practice. Records of everyday administration reveal, to the contrary, that officials routinely ignored its dictates. Nevertheless, the Ordinance is revealing for what it says about Hannover's vision for its new prison-workhouse in Celle. With its expressions of concern for the health of inmates and the systematic elimination of gruesome spectacles, the 1732 Ordinance has seemed to some a harbinger of humane prison reform.[45] But the substitution of starvation for water cells, and of sewer cleaning for wooden horses, had no such philanthropic grounds. Rather, these changes were driven by a desire to limit costs. Water cells and wooden horses were expensive to build, costly to maintain and wasteful to oversee. Why waste resources on punishment when one could use it to save precious thaler? With its carefully calculated daily rations of food and beer—down to the last penny—each inmate-day of starvation meant more money for the royal and provincial coffers. One could also use the extra food to reward the productive while starving the indolent. And the same held for sewer cleaning. Why hire townspeople, or offer the subaltern staff incentive pay, when one could employ prisoners? At the same time, prisoners who produced more than their quota, or even those who earned their keep, would be rewarded. They might get better food, or special advantages or even a reduced prison sentence. In short, the 1732 Ordinance was devoted to the notion of making Celle's *Zuchthaus* pay for itself. The institution never lived up to those expectations.

Everyday realities

Though the *Zuchthaus* had originally been constructed to house 200 inmates, by 1739 it already held 286 people. By 1750, there were 294 inmates: 209 "convicts" and 85 "lunatics."[46] It was one of the most expensive and impressive institutions of its kind.[47] But Hannover's royal government and the provincial *Stände* were unhappy. It was not so much that there was overcrowding, or that the cells were filthy, or that there were escapes, or that the inmates were lazy. Rather, after 18 years of operation the place had simply become too expensive to maintain.[48] Hannover's fiscal officials and provincial deputies were annoyed. They would have known, from the many reports solicited from officials in Holland and across the Empire, that prison-workhouses tended to be expensive. They had assumed that Celle would be different; that it would support itself.

The focus of criticism was Commissar von der Hude. As head of the *Zuchthaus*, he was its accountant (*Rechnungsführer*) and, from the perspective of fiscal officials in Hannover and the provinces, this was his most important function. Due to the "large sums" demanded by the *Zuchthaus* every year, and the heavy burden of annual contributions, the revenue *Kollegium* from Calenberg (one of the provincial estates) directed its treasurer to visit the prison-workhouse to acquaint himself with the budget "and to see whether one could arrange things in such a way that the provincial treasuries would be less burdened than they have been."[49] His report, presented before the provincial deputies at the annual *Zuchthaus* audit, proposed major changes.

There had been many suggestions, the treasurer noted, about finding the kind of work that would at least support the house and its inmates. Before visiting Celle, he confessed, he had had similar notions, but his opinion had changed after visiting Celle. "A large proportion of the inmates, almost half, are afflicted with epilepsy or other diseases." Not only were these inmates incapable of earning their keep, he explained, but many of the healthy inmates could not work, because they had to care for the sick and insane. Moreover, many inmates stayed at the *Zuchthaus* for only a few months, leaving before they could ever really learn the work and before they could ever realize any advantages from it. Even worse, he explained, "the duplicity and wickedness of some convicts" was so great that they could not be forced to work productively, even with the "strongest means of coercion." As a result, he concluded, the provincial coffers would be best served by making sure that authorities who sent people to the *Zuchthaus*—patrimonial courts, district offices, private people, the royal government, etc.—took full responsibility for supporting them.[50]

Calenberg's treasurer saw much more potential for improvement on the expense side. In accordance with the *Zuchthaus* Ordinance of 1732, the food master received 21 thaler per inmate per year for food.[51] The treasurer, however, noted that this was often too much, since the inmates could be fed for 19½ thaler. With 200 inmates, "the annual income would be increased 300 thaler through this means alone." This surplus might be increased even more by reducing the quantity and quality of food provided by the house. One could, for example, cut back on the amount of meat consumed. In this way, the *Zuchthaus* would save one thaler per inmate, or another 200 thaler.[52]

"In order to reduce the expenses as much as possible," explained the treasurer, "I went over all the rubrics with the *Zuchthaus* Commissar." These "rubrics" corresponded to the headings of the many income and expense tables that the commissar, as bookkeeper of the prison-workhouse, had to maintain. Proceeding through the tables category by category, the treasurer found many opportunities to reduce expenses. The copy fees, which covered the costs of record-keeping (mail, paper, ink and other materials), averaged almost 70 thaler each year, and the combined salaries of the two scribes cost the house 256 thaler each year. Calenberg's treasurer suggested that these costs could be reduced and that the *Zuchthaus* might get by with a single scribe, "though one has assured me that the work cannot be done by one person." He also claimed that many prison officials and subaltern staff were either unnecessary or overpaid. The surgeon's annual salary of 72 thaler "seemed too much to me." The 100-thaler salary for the house physician could be reduced to 50. The royal inspectors, with their annual salary of 100 thaler, seemed too expensive. *Revisor* Kretschmar, the special examiner of "alimentation" accounts, was altogether unnecessary. The beadle got paid twice as much as he deserved. Perhaps worst of all, though, were the many special expenses, the rewards and gratuities. "The physician gets a *douceur* when a lunatic is cured. ... If the pastor troubles himself over a lunatic, he gets *douceurs*, even though it is a duty of his office."[53]

Calenberg's treasurer ordered Commissar von der Hude to submit his own suggestions about how to reduce costs and to "free the provinces somewhat from the increasing burden of rising contributions." The commissar marveled at the costs himself, and he promised to make every possible "menage" to reduce them. Perhaps, he suggested, the *Zuchthaus* could attract more "foreign" customers. "The income for the *Zuchthaus* fund," he explained, "could, in my opinion, be increased if outside [*auswärtige*] persons paid no more in house moneys than people from those provinces that supported the construction and maintenance of the prison-workhouse."[54] The so-called "house moneys," which amounted to five thaler annually for common inmates, went to defray the costs of maintaining the house. But "foreigners" (i.e., inmates from provinces other than the ones that funded the house) had to pay 21 thaler in house moneys.[55] In von der Hude's opinion, this high fee tended to "scare off foreign authorities and private persons" who might otherwise send their criminals and lunatics to Celle. By lowering that fee, he suggested, Celle would attract more inmates and generate greater income in house moneys. Better yet, the house might attract more foreign "dignitaries" who would pay 12 thaler in house moneys each year for one of the private cells. "Although there are 300 people in the *Zuchthaus* right now," he declared, "the place is big enough to take another 100 or more people into custody." In this way the *Zuchthaus* coffers could take in another 500 thaler each year. It would, of course, mean more work for the prison's officials and subalterns, but that did not really matter.

Perhaps Commissar von der Hude was joking; it is hard to imagine that he was serious. The *Zuchthaus* had been constructed to house only 200 inmates and could not comfortably support more than 250. Von der Hude was, however, less than sanguine about cutting salaries and eliminating gratuities. "If I attack a lower official now," he explained, "then I will have them all at my throat" and this, he warned, might upset the delicate balance of the "*Zuchthaus* republic" over which he governed.

Over the next three decades things would only get worse. By the 1780s, as the number of inmates burgeoned to well over 300, the *Zuchthaus* experienced a crisis of space and available resources.[56] This crisis, as we have already seen, led to the trial, dismissal and bankruptcy of Commissar Cramer. Cramer had blurred the line between public and private. But where state officials saw this as a crime, Cramer perceived it as part of his job. He was, as we have seen, expected to be entrepreneurial in his approach to creating profits from inmate labor. According to his own account, therefore, Cramer sought out better suppliers and new markets. But in doing so, he treated public funds as his own money. The auditors who reviewed his accounts saw this, quite clearly, as a crime. They also recognized that Cramer's approach, which blurred the distinction between public and private moneys, would permit private bankruptcies to ruin public institutions.

Things did not get any better for Christian von Döhren, Cramer's replacement. We have a vivid picture of life in the *Zuchthaus* under von Döhren's leadership from the writer Carl Friedrich Pockels:

> From the outside, it is true, the building is like a palace and has a pleasant, open appearance; but inside it is the gathering place of countless sufferings and horrible scenes, because the people incarcerated here are almost all contemptible, depraved criminals who have been expelled from human society ... or otherwise the most deplorable lunatics, who will probably never recover their understanding in this miserable house.[57]

The windows and corridors of the *Zuchthaus* had been opened in an attempt to disperse the foul odors and vapors that emanated from the crowded workrooms and cells of the inmates. Nevertheless, a "disgusting smell" and "evil-smelling vapor" suffused every part of the building.[58] As he entered the large halls of the prison, Pockels encountered scenes of "unspeakable misery." In the first large hall for criminals, the quieter lunatics had been mixed in with the criminals, "as in other German prison-workhouses." Immediately in front of them, by the door, stood a "formless, stinking, male mass of flesh only half covered with rags." The man stuffed food in his mouth like an animal, and could not be made to sit, "so that his feet were horribly large and swollen to a bloody red." Several other lunatics sat nearby, squatting like apes with "true Orangutan faces."[59]

From the large workhouse rooms of the men, Pockels moved on to the separate spinning rooms of the women. Here, as elsewhere, the quieter lunatics mixed with the criminals. Although begging was forbidden, "a hundred hands" stretched out for alms. Pockels moved on to the "mad cells" in the west wing of the madhouse. He noted how different it was here, how food and drink were passed through openings in the doors, and how the only light emanated from a small window high up in each of these "nooks of despair." From there, and accompanied by Commissar von Döhren, Pockels entered the mad corridor.[60]

> Finally we arrived at that corridor of the *Zuchthaus* that no one should enter ... who lacks the resolution to observe his fellow creatures in the highest state of misery; namely, to see a true maniac in the worst condition. Here it seems that one has sunk into the deepest abyss of hell. And before this passage through hell [*Höllengang*] was even opened we heard ... first the rattling of chains, now the awful screaming and cursing, now the mad singing and howling, which caused a terrible echoing in the long mad corridor and almost never stopped.

In this "black gallery of the highest human misery," Pockels found himself confronted by an awful smell emanating from the long corridor. The air was poisoned with the vapors that rose up out of the stinking sewer canal, through the cells and out into the corridor. The screaming inmates, with their "shrieking songs" and "raging curses," became so crazy that Pockels could no longer hear his own words.[61]

Conclusion

Celle serves as a nice metaphor for the anxiety and uncertainty that plagued cameralists and fiscal administrators in eighteenth-century Germany. The fiscal troubles and bank failures of the 1750s and 1760s are only the most obvious effects of the chronic state deficits that dogged central European governments around the time of the Seven Years War. Regional and local authorities also went bankrupt.[62] For local authorities in and around Celle, and for the royal government in Hannover, the failure of institutions such as prisons or mines or universities threatened to trigger larger fiscal problems. That is why Commissar Cramer's personal bankruptcy, which threatened to ruin Celle's *Zuchthaus*, endangered the state as well. The chronic failure of Celle's *Zuchthaus* to realize promises of productivity also called into question cameralist visions of the state. If Johann Beckmann and his colleagues were so wrong about prison-workhouses, how could they be trusted to create policy for whole territories and populations? The ruin of one institution spelled trouble for the whole system. It was the mad corridor of Germany's well-ordered police states.

Notes

1 Niedersächsiches Hauptstaatsarchiv Hannover (hereinafter HStArchHann), Dep. 7 B, Nrs. 461 and 2041; K. Emmermann, "Das Zuchthaus zu Celle" (unpub. Ph.D. diss., Universität Göttingen, 1921), 63–4.

2 P. Spierenburg, "The Body and the State: Early Modern Europe," in: N. Morris and D.J. Rothman (eds.), *The Oxford History of the Prison* (New York 1995), 68; and P. Spierenburg, *The Spectacle of Suffering: Executions and the Evolution of Repression, from a Preindustrial Metropolis to the European Experience* (Cambridge, UK 1984).

3 P. Spierenburg (ed.), *The Emergence of Carceral Institutions: Prisons, Galleys, and Lunatic Asylums, 1550–1900* (Rotterdam 1984), 3–39; P. Spierenburg, "The Body and the State," 65–7. See also N. Finzsch, "'Competing Apples and Oranges?' The History of Early Prisons in Germany and the United States," in: N. Finzsch and R. Jütte (eds.), *Institutions of Confinement: Hospitals, Asylums, and Prisons in Western Europe and North America, 1500–1950* (Cambridge, UK 1996), 216–17.

4 P. Spierenburg, "Four Centuries of Prison History: Punishment, Suffering, the Body, and Power," in: N. Finzsch and R. Jütte (eds.), *Institutions of Confinement: Hospitals, Asylums, and Prisons in Western Europe and North America, 1500–1950* (Cambridge, UK 1996), 20–3; R. McGowen, "The Well-Ordered Prison: England, 1780–1865," in: N. Morris and D.J. Rothman (eds.), *The Oxford History of the Prison* (New York 1995), 92–5; M. Foucault, *Discipline and Punish*, translated by A. Sheridan (New York 1979), 200–9.

5 See Spierenburg, "The Body and the State," 68–72; and Emmermann, "Zuchthaus zu Celle," 15–16.

6 H. Hammerl, "Die Bankrottdelikte. Zur strafrechtlichen und kriminologischen Problematik des einfachen und schweren Bankrotts (§§ 239, 240 KO)," (Inaugural Dissertation, Johann Wolfgang Goethe Universität Frankfurt am Main, 1970), 34–5.

7 R. Köstlin, "Darstellung der Lehre vom strafbaren Bankerott überhaupt und besonders nach der neueren deutschen Gesetzgebung," *Archiv für preußisches Strafrecht* 5 (1857): 721–44.

8 K.H. Wegert, "Contention with Civility: The State and Social Control in the German Southwest, 1760–1850," *Historical Journal* 34 (1991): 349–69, esp. 355.

9 Celle's *Zuchthaus* had a reputation for high costs. See H.B. Wagnitz, *Historische Nachrichten und Bemerkungen über die merkwürdigsten Zuchthäuser in Deutschland* (Halle 1792).

10 Beckmann estimated that the linen trade brought one million thaler into the lands of electoral Hanover each year. Meanwhile, the much smaller territory of Osnabrück gained 1.5 million thaler by it. See J. Beckmann (ed.), *Beyträge zur Oekonomie, Technologie, Polizey und Cameralwissenschaft*, nr. 5; F.A. Rulffs, *Ueber die Preisfrage der Königl: Societät der Wissenschaften zu Göttingen: von der vortheilhaften Einrichtung der Werk- und Zuchthäuser* (Göttingen 1783), 18.

11 Rulffs, *Werk- und Zuchthäuser*, 1–2.

12 Bergius had a great influence on Beckmann, who edited some of Bergius' work. See J. Beckmann and J. Bergius, *Sammlung auserlesener teutscher Landesgesetze, welche das Policey- u. Cameralwesen zum Gegenstande haben* (Frankfurt, 1781); Rulffs, *Werk- und Zuchthäuser*, 17.

13 Rulffs, *Werk- und Zuchthäuser*, 12–17.

14 Ibid., 18.

15 Johann Beckmann, preface, in Rulffs, *Werk- und Zuchthäuser*; see also [J. Beckmann], *Göttingische Anzeigen von gelehrten Sachen* (1783): 1265. Rulffs was not able to collect the prize money because his essay arrived after the deadline for official responses had passed.

16 Rulffs, *Werk- und Zuchthäuser*, 43–4.

17 Ibid., 4–5, 66–8.

18 Ibid., 10.

19 Ibid., 9–11, 37–8.

20 "Erneuerte und durch Anordnung eines besonderen Arbeitshauses verbesserte Armenordnung der Stadt Celle und deren Vorstädte." Hannover, 7 November 1783.

21 Armenordnung der Stadt Celle," §6, §19.

22 "Armenordnung der Stadt Celle," §17.

23 Ibid., §18–20, §23.

24 StArchHan Dep. 7 B, Nr. 466, 76–121. The protocols of the Cramer investigation appear in the same bundle as the new "Instruction" for Commissar von Döhren.

25 StArchHan Dep. 7 B, Nr. 466, 171–2.

26 Subsequent negotiations and explanations reduced the amount to about 2493 thaler.

27 StArchHan Dep. 7 B, Nr. 466, 180.

28 StArchHan Dep. 7 B, Nr. 466, 190–1.

29 StArchHan Dep. 7 B, Nr. 466, 72.

30 To punish the wicked,
to guard the raging
and insane,
with public funds a house is dedicated.

31 See Wagnitz, *Zuchthäuser in Deutschland*, 67–8; C.F. Pockels (ed.), *Denkwürdigkeiten zur Bereicherung der Erfahrungsseelenlehre und Characterkunde* (Halle 1794), 149. The structure, which is still used to this day as a prison, does not—at least so it seemed to me—look much different from the outside now than it did in the eighteenth century. I was not allowed to tour the inside.

32 "House money," which amounted to five thaler annually for common inmates, was meant to defray the costs of maintaining the house. As a rule, the authority—patrimonial court, royal government, private person—responsible for sending the inmate to Celle was responsible for remitting house money (this in addition to the annual "alimentation money" for each inmate) to the *Zuchthaus* commissar.

33 Emmermann, "Zuchthaus zu Celle."

34 Emmermann, "Zuchthaus zu Celle," 15–16; Pockels, *Erfahrungsseelenlehre und Characterkunde*, 150–2.

35 StArchHan, Dep. 7 B, Nr. 2038.

36 StArchHan, Dep. 7 B, Nr. 2037. Cf. Spierenburg, *The Emergence of Carceral Institutions*; and R. Evans (ed.), *The German Underworld: Deviants and Outcasts in German History* (London 1988).
37 Wagnitz, *Zuchthäuser in Deutschland*, 151.
38 "Die Ordnung," Cap. II, § 4; Emmermann, "Zuchthaus zu Celle," 67–8.
39 "Die Ordnung," Cap. IV, § 1, 6 and 7.
40 "Die Ordnung," Cap. IV, § 2.
41 "Die Ordnung," Cap. IV, § 6; StArchHan, Dep. 7 B, Nr. 2038.
42 "Die Ordnung," Cap. IV, § 8.
43 See S. Schama, *The Embarrassment of Riches* (New York 1987), 15–24. On Hamburg, see Wagnitz, *Zuchthäuser in Deutschland*, 176–8.
44 "Die Ordnung," Cap. II, § 9.
45 Emmermann, "Zuchthaus zu Celle," 39.
46 StArchHan Dep. 7 B, Nr. 462, 14.
47 Wagnitz, *Zuchthäuser in Deutschland*.
48 At the annual audit of prison accounts in 1750, provincial deputies and fiscal administrators offered extensive advice about reducing the costs of operation. See StArchHan Dep. 7 B, Nr. 2043.
49 StArchHan Dep. 7 B, Nr. 2043, 45.
50 StArchHan Dep. 7 B, Nr. 2043, 45–6.
51 "Die Ordnung, wie es bey dem Zucht-Hause zu halten, betreffend. Den 27. Octobr. 1732," Cap. II, § 3.
52 StArchHan Dep. 7 B, Nr. 2043, 47–8.
53 StArchHan Dep. 7 B, Nr. 2043, 50–3.
54 StArchHan Dep. 7 B, Nr. 2043, 57.
55 These "foreigners" included residents of Bremen, part of electoral Hannover since 1715, since that territory had not funded the building and maintenance of Celle's prison-workhouse.
56 StArchHan Dep. 7 B, Nr. 2038, 64.
57 Pockels, *Erfahrungsseelenlehre und Characterkunde*.
58 Ibid., 150–1.
59 Ibid., 154–5.
60 Ibid., 154–66.
61 Ibid., 167.
62 See J.G. van Dillen, *History of the Principal Public Banks* (The Hague 1934); P.T. Hoffman and K. Norberg (eds.), *Fiscal Crises, Liberty, and Representative Government, 1450–1789* (Stanford, CA 1994).

11 Bankruptcy in early modern German territories

Paul Fischer

Introduction

The German territories offer particularly interesting evidence for the evolution of bankruptcy law and procedure in the early modern period. To illustrate these developments, this chapter gives special attention to two legal texts about bankruptcy[1] proceedings, both of which originated in the city of Augsburg, the first in the year 1447, the second in the year 1749.

The *Augsburger Gantordnung*[2] (1447) to the *Augsburger Fallitenordnung* (1749)

The *Augsburger Gantordnung* of 1447 has no distinct structure; there are no titles, chapters or articles that separate or distinguish its content. It states that, first of all, a creditor has to bring an action to the city court of Augsburg if there is no chance of voluntary satisfaction by the debtor.[3] Then, the debtor has the opportunity to come to court and ensure by a so-called "bet-contract"[4] that he will pay off the debts within eight days. If he neither appears nor "bets," then the creditor is allowed to go to the debtor's home and to levy execution against him by seizure of his goods. If the creditor is not able to satisfy his claims within eight days, he can request that the court "proclaim" the debtor, which gives him a last deadline of eight days to satisfy his creditor. If the debtor fails to meet this final deadline, he is banished from the city under oath never to return. Whoever thereafter harbors the debtor becomes personally liable for the full debt owed by the defaulter.

In contrast to its predecessor, the *Augsburger Fallitenordnung* of 1749[5] is structured with Roman numerals and contains articles and subchapters. It endeavors to form concise rules by using technical legal terms borrowed from Roman law, but it does not, however, set any rules about the basic bankruptcy proceedings.[6] Rather, it reflections about the debtor's liability, distinctions about the guilt of the "faillite" and guidelines for the dealings with the creditors.[7] The text also mentions more than one creditor[8] and the possibility for the debtor to negotiate for a reduction of the debt with them.[9] Moreover, it regulates the treatment of the family of the "faillite"[10] and sets a special rule for the bankruptcy of merchants.[11]

This brief comparison of these two ordinances might surprise readers and could raise questions about the reasons behind their differences. This chapter tries to give answers to these questions by looking at the influences on and the developments of bankruptcy law and procedure in early modern German territories. It will examine in brief the legal situation of bankruptcy in the middle of the fifteenth century and outline the influences on and developments of bankruptcy and the significant codifications that emerged from that era.

The choice of the sources should be addressed in brief. Aside from the fact that the chosen dates, 1447 and 1749, "frame" the early modern period, Augsburg is a logical focus of study. The city experienced vigorous economic growth in the fifteenth and sixteenth centuries under the influence of an energetic merchant community, headed by such renowned trading houses as the Fugger and Welser. It became a major European banking and commercial centre.[12] As a free imperial city, it also hosted a series of Imperial Diets: 1518, 1530, 1548 and 1555.[13] Its wealth made it also a center for humanist learning and home to a vigorous printing industry. As such, it experienced a variety of economic, political, intellectual and legal developments.[14] Finally, in the course of the sixteenth century, it witnessed a surprising number of business failures. Augsburg is, therefore, especially well suited to illustrate the development of bankruptcy law in early modern Germany.

Its advancement does not, however, run linearly, but rather in "waves."[15] Legal problems in a given polity demand a solution and, if that solution proves successful, it sooner or later becomes legal praxis. A clear regional separation of legal developments is not possible, because solutions may be drawn not only from local legal sources and traditions but also from those of other polities, be they city or territorial states. Augsburg, as a prosperous commercial center, was exposed to legal challenges, and its legal and political authorities were familiar with a variety of different ways to respond to them even if a concrete connection between their knowledge and their statutes cannot always be established. Therefore the development of bankruptcy law, as codified in the regulations of other German cities and territories, will be considered with that of Augsburg to illustrate change in this field of law.

Bankruptcy in early modern German territories

The *Augsburger Gantordnung* of 1447 regulates the executive process from the action for debt to the liquidation of assets. It basically summarizes the rules for bankruptcy in the city of Augsburg as they existed through the thirteenth century.[16] A coherent regulation of bankruptcy proceedings it offers nonetheless no information about the procedure with more than one creditor.[17] Every step of the procedure had to be brought before and approved by the court, which made the process quite lengthy. That the creditor had a claim to the goods and not merely to the person of debtor himself, made the Augsburg law fairly progressive.[18] Other contemporary sources for bankruptcy proceedings in Augsburg outlined severe personal consequences, if the debtor could not satisfy the creditor's claims.[19] Given these strict regulations, the flight of the debtor was understandable and even expected but not yet considered a threat to economic continuity. As such it was not yet a matter seen as requiring regulation.[20]

If we look beyond the city walls of Augsburg, we see that most medieval German legal systems based their bankruptcy proceedings on the principle of priority of the creditors.[21] Of course, individual local laws differed. In the codes of some Hanseatic towns at the end of the thirteenth century, rules already established the distribution of a debtor's estate to multiple creditors by proportion of the debts owed, but only if the bankrupt had indeed escaped or died.[22] The laws of cities, such as Augsburg, Nuremberg or Lubeck, were all dominated by a concern for prevention:[23] to avoid the danger of non-payment, the debtor could be arrested and his estate confiscated. Arrest could be executed by the creditors themselves[24] and was applied to any debtor, domestic or foreign, who was suspected of fleeing the city.[25] In fact, any bankrupt was liable to do so.[26] The debtor's personal liability was still applied as a last resort. Putting him in chains and forcing him into servitude for a period of time was a common part of the procedure.[27] There is no doubt that the reception[28] of Roman law in the High Middle Ages influenced the law of bankruptcy procedure, but the clear legal shift from personal distraint to property distraint, which Roman law established,[29] had to be newly acquired.[30]

"Ad fontes"—back to the sources—is a leitmotiv that formed a basis of the educational movement of Humanism that took up the thought and culture of classic antiquity and decisively influenced the intellectual life of the Renaissance. In the field of law, jurists sought to reconstruct a historically legitimate, humanistically educated and linguistically demanding jurisprudence.[31] This movement was supported by the invention of moveable-type printing, which made it possible to reproduce and, so, spread the antique sources, contemporary literature and existing laws to an increasing number of people.[32] Roman-canon law began to be taught at universities and to influence legal administration and practice as early as the eleventh century.[33] Educated, secular jurists occupied important positions as advocates, councilors, judges or diplomats. Clerical jurists held important administrative and legal positions in the Roman Church. The Imperial Chamber Court Ordinance of 1495 stated that half of the justices of the court had to be trained in Roman-canon law with the result that cases were decided in concordance with those codes.[34] Roman-canon law became thus integrated and incorporated into local legal customs in the form of "common law," which, of course, also affected bankruptcy laws.

In German territories of the late fifteenth and sixteenth centuries, reform efforts in the field of bankruptcy were—despite all regional differences—mainly guided by the proposal to prevent private execution and to detach from execution the rules about procedures with more than one creditor. Private, individual execution violated the principle of a fair satisfaction and equal treatment of all creditors. These regulations could be found in *Gantordnungen* and similar statutes that regulated bankruptcy proceedings, which became over time detached from the rules governing executions and the bankrupt himself.[35] The movement[36] of these reform efforts got started in Italy; from there it spread northward over the salt road to the German territories.[37] In the following, the reform efforts of the cities of Nuremberg, Freiburg im Breisgau and especially Augsburg, will stand as examples of the new developments in the dealings with bankruptcy.

The Nuremberg legal reform of 1479,[38] with its systematic regulation of bankruptcy, acted as a model for other city and territorial laws. The procedure was entitled "Vollung," which allowed the creditor to first seize personal property, then real property and, finally, for the first time, debts owed. As a last resort, creditors could seize the person of the debtor and imprison him from five to ten years. Alternatively, the bankrupt could be banished from the city.[39] The *Reformation of Nuremberg* resulted in a streamlining of the procedures and in a protection of the debtor, who could only be arrested as a last resort, rather than immediately upon proclamation of insolvency. Out of the rules about the debtor's arrest also evolved regulations about the fair treatment of all creditors. From the moment the debtor tried to escape, their claims were listed and placed in the hands of an official administrator, who pursued both the equal treatment of all creditors and the personal protection of the debtor.[40]

The 1520 *Stadtrecht* of Freiburg im Breisgau,[41] supposedly created by the noted jurist Ulrich Zasius,[42] possessed concise, clear articles and a systematic structure.[43] It included a highly developed bankruptcy law, which officially regulated the proceedings in a progressive manner: the creditor of an approved debt had to apply to the city officials to get an administrator who accompanied him to the debtor's house; default initiated the seizure first of personal property, then of accounts receivable and, last, of real property. There are detailed rules regarding the liquidation of property.[44] Moreover, the proceedings with a number of creditors were adjusted: claims were listed and categorized; property was sold at auction; and the proceeds were split in proportion to the amounts owed.[45]

The *Augsburger Gantordnung* of 1447 shared the same name with the above-mentioned later regulations but fixed in detail bankruptcy proceedings with only one creditor. It presumably started from the principle of priority and understood "Gant" simply as the auction sale of the debtor's goods to satisfy the creditor's claims.[46] In spite of Augsburg's geographical proximity and the busy commerce relations with Italy, there are—in contrast to Nuremberg and Freiburg im Breisgau—initially no verifiable sources that prove the influence or utilization of the thoughts of Roman-canon law in the reform of bankruptcy proceedings.[47] In the end, early modern reform efforts did not bring about a complete transformation of city law. Nor were the reforms authorized by the city council, unlike those to Nuremberg, Freiburg im Breisgau or Frankfurt am Main.[48] That might lead to the conclusion that the citizens of Augsburg modified and improved regulations in single statutes and special laws while keeping the established *Stadtrecht* as a basis or that the city lacked a jurist of the stature of an Ulrich Zasius of Freiburg im Breisgau, to catalyze a new codification.[49]

There are, however, sources that prove the reform efforts and legal innovations in the bankruptcy law of Augsburg. The private work of Franz Kötzler, an Augsburger court reporter, contains a compilation of customary law, judicial decisions and council orders, which are gathered in two initial issues of 1529 and 1540 and also in many manuscripts. However, his work lacks any systematization: it is chronically arranged.[50] One document of 1529 provides evidence of the equal treatment of the creditors, if the debtor asked civic authorities to summon the creditors to a mutual court session, which had the effect of hindering execution by a single creditor.[51] This practice was used famously in the "Höchstetter bankruptcy" in 1529[52] without any explicit legal basis. The practical possibility of a procedure with a number of creditors necessitated an officially adjusted regulation about it. One could say that the experiences from the "Höchstetter bankruptcy" acted as a role model and inspired reform actions.[53]

Over 60 bankruptcies occurred between 1529 and 1580.[54] The force of events compelled further reforms in the second half of the sixteenth century. Bankruptcy proceedings in Augsburg were put on a new legal basis: the city's legal counselor, Georg Tradel (1530–1598),[55] Doctor of Canon and Civil law, drafted a new code with strong connections to Roman law. This unmodified and unratified draft became legal practice in Augsburg.[56]

It is clearly structured with chapters, fully systematized with legal terminology that demonstrates Tradel's education, even as it lends the statutes more accuracy and clarity in contrast to the *Augsburger Gantordnung* of 1447. At the beginning of the chapters about bankruptcy, Tradel explains that a reform in the field of bankruptcy is needed because of the length and expense of procedures under the old law and because of the conflicts related to the priority and number of creditors.[57] So he declares that creditors have to adhere to three deadlines: first, they have to name their claims and protocol them; second, they have to decide among themselves the priority of their claims; and, third, they have to bring in a writ that sets the order decided and, so, commit to ending the process.[58] The time gap between each of the deadlines is four weeks. This period is peremptory; a creditor, who does not appear is procedurally excluded.[59] Certain exceptions were granted,[60] procedures were expedited,[61] priorities were set and *pro rata* payments ruled.[62] Creditors acting in common were thus assured of at least a portion, if not all, their due.[63]

Tradel's draft confirms the fact that the principle of priority had yielded to the principle of proportional distribution and debt classification, evidence for which can be seen in Augsburg as early as 1529.[64] In another draft, entitled "Consuetudines almae Reipublicae Augustanae,"[65] Tradel and Mattheus Laimann further regulated the treatment of bankrupts themselves.[66] By the end of the sixteenth century, the developments in bankruptcy proceedings came to a temporary end.[67]

In addition to reforms concerning dealings with a number of creditors and the general course of procedure, there are efforts made to change the legal treatment of the bankrupts themselves. The basis for these rules was still the ancient presumption, or rather prejudice, that bankrupts were faithless and unscrupulous. All in all, such persons were considered dangers to the commonweal of the community.[68] But self-administrated justice, as practiced and regulated in medieval times, was officially obsolete and illegal, an offense that could be brought to the Imperial Chamber Court.[69] So, it was the duty of the sovereign to preserve the commonweal by setting strict procedural rules that limited the dangers ensuing from such behaviors. The 1577 Constitution of Electoral Saxony, for example, abolished private personal distraint, but replaced it with sovereign personal distraint in the so-called "Schuldturm."[70] On the one hand, it offered protection against the arbitrariness of the creditors, while they tried to satisfy their claims; on the other hand it criminalized the debtor.[71] The Imperial Discipline Ordinance (*Reichspolizeiordnung*) of 1548, adopted by the Imperial Diet at Augsburg in that year, was another sovereign regulation. It emphasized that bankruptcy caused heavy damage to the commonweal and ruled that fraudulent bankrupts must not be harbored by anyone, but had to be arrested and held liable for the sanctions,[72] including death by hanging.[73] Whether hanged or not, the bankrupt suffered a social death, because bankruptcy caused infamy and disqualification from public office.[74] Although the bankrupt was still assumed to be malicious, exceptions were afforded the unfortunate: they were to be treated according to common law, and it was not forbidden to help them.[75]

Enforcement of these Imperial regulations failed, however, due to the territorial particularities of the Empire and, so, relied for their efficacy on a connection to city or territorial law codes: the 1564 *Fallitenordnung* of Augsburg echoed the imperial distinction between honest and dishonest bankruptcy and mandated a full accounting of all properties.[76] Furthermore, the *Fallitenordnung* of Augsburg of 1574 stated that the burgomasters had to order the town magistrate to confiscate immediately the estate of a debtor when they got wind of his bankruptcy.[77] It was forbidden to support the "faillite," and the escape of the debtor was criminalized. These measures sought to combine the objectives of the Imperial Discipline Ordinances with local law. The 1580 *Fallitenordnung* intensified the sanctions by emphasizing the punishment of economic crime and by insisting that all creditors should submit their claims to the civic-appointed representatives.[78] This was the third bankruptcy regulation in Augsburg in under 30 years and could, therefore, have been a reaction to the increasing frequency of failure. The idea behind these rules was, on the one hand, to prevent the flight of the bankrupt and, on the other hand, to make him negotiate with his creditors.[79]

It is evident that the dealings with bankrupts during the first decades of the early modern period were still characterized by the distrust of such persons and the disgrace of bankruptcy itself. The laws of the sixteenth century basically intended to ensure the satisfaction of the creditors' claims.[80] A clear separation of the proceedings had not yet been worked out, but, increasingly, dealings with the "faillite" were enforced by sovereign authority that limited independent actions by the creditors. A tendency emerged as well to consider the causes of bankruptcy and the guilt of the bankrupt and to shape legal action accordingly.

As outlined above, the reform efforts at the beginning of the early modern period laid the basis for a complex response to bankruptcy, including the differentiated treatment of the debtor and the procedures necessary for a number of creditors. The Bavarian territory law of 1616 contained these aspects and gave evidence of further progress in the development of bankruptcy proceedings. It regulated the minimum general conditions of bankruptcy law but left the detailed drafting of the procedure to local customs. Its intention was to prevent arbitrary proceedings in the entire state of Bavaria by placing execution against the bankrupt's property and person in the hands of an official administration.[81] Henceforth, "Gant" referred not only to the official sale at auction of the debtor's goods, but also extended to the "legal procedure of bankruptcy with a number of creditors." The 1616 Law treated real and personal distraint under different titles. In the so-called "edict procedure," it set the classification of the creditors only with regard to a single property of the debtor and not to all of his property. But, it also established specific bankruptcy procedures concerning the claims of individual creditors. Their order of priority was publicized, but it became possible to appeal against that imposed order. The closure of the edict procedure initiated the detailed procedure of execution and distribution of proceeds.[82] The execution aimed to realize the maximum available compensation to the creditors and the protection of the debtor. Therefore, it included no threat of punishment.[83] It provided acceleration of the procedure in low-value cases,[84] and there was no process at all, if the debtor cooperated or the state of evidence was clear.[85] In another title, dealings with the bankrupt were also regulated in a differentiated way. The innocent "faillite," for example could petition for the "cessio bonorum,"[86] that is, he ceded all his property to his creditors, and, by so doing, kept a minimum means of subsistence. If bankruptcy resulted from his own actions, whether honest or dishonest, however, the "cessio bonorum" was not allowed, all his property was confiscated and he was arrested or banned from the city.[87] It is not absolutely certain that Bavarian bankruptcy law had a direct impact on legislation in neighboring Augsburg, but it shows the general advancement of legal thought on the problem of bankruptcy, very much in terms of a history of ideas, as will become apparent in the consideration below of the bankrupt's culpability under the *Augsburger Fallitenordnung* of 1749.

Bankruptcy law in the eighteenth century

As mentioned above the order of priority and the course of execution were finalized by the end of the sixteenth century. The *Augsburger Fallitenordnung* of 1749 took up other matters.[88] It adjusted rules for dealing with the bankrupt person, now depending on the degree of provable guilt. Furthermore, it linked the personal consequences of bankruptcy to the percentage of debt the debtor could repay. The malicious bankrupt still had to expect personal consequences, but bankruptcy came also to be seen as a heavy burden for the family, which was taken into account with rules that dealt specifically with the wife[89] or the children[90] of the bankrupt. The innocent "faillite," whose failure was not the result of fraud, was not banished from official positions and could negotiate with creditors (the so-called "Akkord") on a reduction of the debts.[91] The debtor's free disposal of his property still ended with the start of the bankruptcy proceedings, but the trigger was no longer the flight of the debtor, but rather his insolvency.[92]

Further developments in German territories showed tendencies to detach the proceeding with multiple creditors from the subsequent execution and adjusted a more administrative procedure to satisfy the creditors and to minimize the cost of the process. The *Hamburger Fallitenordnung* of 1753 ruled that an administrator should inspect the debtor's estate, examine the debts and pay off existing creditors. Then, further claimants should negotiate a consensual procedure to settle the debts owed them. Only if they did not reach a consensus did a more rigorous bankruptcy proceeding begin.[93] Additional sanctions against the debtor depended on his behavior and the graduation of his debt. The innocent "faillite" received assistance and was eventually reintegrated into society after the proceedings. This statute expressly delineated and regulated the actual method of bankruptcy resolution, to which earlier laws had made only vague indication.[94] Here again, the Hamburg ordinance represents an advance in legal thought—especially with regard to the separation of proceedings from execution—that would eventually be mirrored more generally in Augsburg and elsewhere.

If one looks at further development of reform efforts in the field of bankruptcy, one has to outline the work of the Spaniard Salgado de Somoza, who was influenced by Roman, Spanish and Italian law and created a system for a more administrative mode of bankruptcy proceedings.[95] The influence of his thinking is revealed by the fact that the German term for bankruptcy, "Konkurs," arose from Somoza's work.[96] It significantly influenced German codifications, such as the Prussian "Hypotheken- and Konkursordnung"[97] (1722), the "Codex Juris Bavarici Judiciarii"[98] (1753) and also the aforementioned "Hamburger Neue Fallitenordnung"[99] (1753).

Achievements in the field of bankruptcy in early modern Germany

The developments under the motto "ad fontes" triggered vital processes in the development of early modern bankruptcy laws that no longer linked failure to shame and infamy. Dealings with the "faillite" and his family depended on the degree of his culpability. Bankruptcy proceedings separated the execution levy and the property liquidation. The procedure itself became briefer, more efficient; in certain cases there was no process at all to avoid costs. Regarding bankrupt persons, flight was no longer the only option: they could also invite a "cessio bonorum" and negotiate with their creditors about a reduction of the debts. Bankruptcy proceedings now constituted a process, in which the debtor's estate was inspected and the creditors' claims were approved and listed, all under official administration. Moreover, the legal texts in general endeavored to present a clear structure, a systematization and concision, borrowed from Roman law. Further developments would emerge under the influence of enlightened thought and natural law.[100]

Notes

1 In today's Anglo-Saxon legal system, bankruptcy is the term that is used to describe the legal proceeding on behalf of creditors, if their debtor is unable to pay his debts. The modern German equivalent is "Konkurs" or "Insolvenz." Bankruptcy originates from the Italian expression "banca rotta," which described the demolition of the stands of medieval merchants who could not pay their debts. See P. Hertner, "Bankrott," in: *Handwörterbuch zur deutschen Rechtsgeschichte*, Vol. I (Berlin 2008), 428. In this chapter the term, "bankruptcy," is used in its shifting meaning (depending on the contemplated context) from the inability of the debtor to satisfy his creditors and the consequential procedure to the registration and classification of all creditors as a thing apart from the sale at auction of the bankrupt's property.

2 The Upper German term "Gant" (from Latin: *in quantum*) describes the judicially ordered sale at auction of goods of the debtor. See W. Forster, "Gant," in: *Handwörterbuch zur deutschen Rechtsgeschichte*, Vol. I (Weimar 1932).

3 For the following description of bankruptcy proceedings, see M. Spann, *Der Haftungszugriff auf den Schuldner zwischen Personal- und Vermögensvollstreckung* (Münster 2004), 163 et seq.

4 About this bet at the court, see T.M. Safley, "Die Frage einer frühneuzeitlichen Standardisierung des Rechtsprozesses in Bankrottfällen am Beispiel des Höchstetter-Konkurses 1529," in: T.M.J. Möllers (ed.), *Vielfalt und Einheit: Wirtschaftliche und rechtliche Rahmenbedingungen von Standardbildung* (Baden-Baden 2008), 108; for further details, see Spann, *Der Haftungszugriff*, 86.

5 "Falliten" (from Latin: *fallere*=to betray, to cheat, to evade) is a description of persons who are unable to satisfy the claims of their creditors. The etymologic origin by itself gives the description a negative connotation. See, *Eines HochEdlen, und Hochweisen Raths Verordnung Die Falliten Betreffend* (Augspurg 1749); C. Becker, "Bancarottierer," *Konkurs, Treuhand, Sanierung: Zeitschrift für Insolvenzrecht* (hereinafter *KTS*) (2008): 3–14.

6 F. Hellmann, *Das Konkursrecht der Reichsstadt Augsburg* (Breslau 1905), 152 et seq.

7 Preamble of the *Augsburger Fallitenordnung* from 1749, 7 et seq.; §§ 1 et seq.

8 §§ 2, 7 *Augsburger Fallitenordnung*.

9 § 2 *Augsburger Fallitenordnung*.

10 §§ 13 et seq. *Augsburger Fallitenordnung*.

11 § 8 *Augsburger Fallitenordnung*.

12 *The New Encyclopedia Britannica*, 15th ed., Vol. I (Chicago, IL 2002), 698.

13 *Meyers Neues Lexikon*, Vol. I (Mannheim 1994), 376.

14 Evidence is derived from the documents of the Augsburger notary, Johann Spreng (1524–1601). These demonstrate richly the interaction of city and common law in a "European commercial center." See C. Becker, "Die Akten des Augsburger Notars Johann Spreng (1524–1601): Ein Einblick in das Rechtsleben eines frühneuzeitlichen europäischen Wirtschaftszentrums," in: H.-G. Hermann (ed.), *Von den Leges Barbarorum bis zum ius barbarum des Nationalsozialismus: Festschrift für Hermann Nehlsen zum 70. Geburtstag* (Cologne 2008), 477.

15 C. Paulus, "Entwicklungslinien des Insolvenzrechts," *KTS* (2000): 239 et seq.

16 Spann, *Der Haftungszugriff*, 163.

17 Ibid., 163 et seq.

18 Hellmann, *Das Konkursrecht*, 16.

19 Ibid., 27 et seq.

20 Ibid., 29.

21 C. Becker, *Insolvenzrecht* (Cologne 2010), 15 et seq.

22 W. Ogris, "Konkurs," in: *Handwörterbuch zur deutschen Rechtsgeschichte*, Vol. II (Berlin 1978), 1, col. 1084 et seq.

23 W. Uhlenbruck, "Insolvency," in: Stanley N. Katz (ed.), *The Oxford International Encyclopedia of Legal History*, Vol. III (Oxford 2009), 249.
24 C. Becker, "Konkurs," in: *Handwörterbuch zur deutschen Rechtsgeschichte*, Vol. II (forthcoming).
25 Becker, *Insolvenzrecht*, 16.
26 Concerning the inherent distrust of bankrupts, cf.: Becker, "Bancarottierer," 3 et seq.
27 Ogris, "Konkurs"; Becker, "Konkurs"; Hellmann, *Das Konkursrecht*, 28.
28 Cf. H. Schlosser, *Grundzüge der Neueren Privatrechtsgeschichte* (Heidelberg 2005), 36 et seq.
29 Becker, "Bancarottierer," 3 et seq.
30 Becker, *Insolvenzrecht*, 15 et seq.
31 Schlosser, *Grundzüge*, 71 et seq.
32 C. Becker (ed.), *"Consuetudines almae Reipublicae Augustanae" von Matthaeus Laimann und Georg Tradel mit "Notwendigs Bedenckhen" von Georg Tradel. Eine Zusammenstellung Augsburger Stadtrechts mit einer Denkschrift zu seiner Reform vom Ende des sechzehnten Jahrhunderts* (Berlin 2008), xii et seq.
33 K. Luig, "Germany," in: Stanley N. Katz (ed.), *The Oxford International Encyclopedia of Legal History*, Vol. III (Oxford 2009), 118.
34 § 1, "Reichskammergerichtsordnung of 1495." Cf. Schlosser, *Grundzüge*, 60. See also Spann, *Haftungszugriff*, 174, who argues that the influence of the Imperial Chamber Court is overestimated.
35 Becker, *Insolvenzrecht*, 16 et seq.
36 Christoph Paulus describes it as a "wave." See C. Paulus, "Entwicklungslinien des Insolvenzrechts," *KTS* (2000): 239 et seq.
37 Ibid., 241.
38 The city law of Nuremberg was reformed again in 1564 to include regulations on bankruptcy: on the one hand, there were only minor adaptations; but, on the other hand, substantive and systematic reform efforts were fixed. This demonstrates that bankruptcy was a highly relevant matter and required rules for its regulation. See Spann, *Der Haftungszugriff*, 178–9.
39 Ibid., 173 et seq.
40 Ibid., 177 et seq.
41 U. Zasius, *Nüwe Stattrechten und Statuten der loblichen statt Fryburg im Prißgow gelegen* (Freiburg i. Br. 1520).
42 Paulus, "Entwicklungslinien," 241. About the life of Ulrich Zasius and his influence on bankruptcy law, see H. Knoche, *Ulrich Zasius und das Freiburger Stadtrecht von 1520* (Karlsruhe 1957), 9 et seq., 45.
43 Ibid., 151 et seq.
44 Ibid., 72 et seq.
45 Ibid., 74.
46 Compare the above-mentioned description of the "Augsburger Gantordnung" of 1447. There are fragmentary statutes that describe procedures with multiple creditors in the city laws of Augsburg in 1439 and of Nuremberg in 1431. See, Hellmann, *Das Konkursrecht*, 42 et seq.; Spann, *Der Haftungszugriff*, 168 et seq.
47 E. Liedl, *Gerichtsverfassung und Zivilprozess der freien Reichsstadt Augsburg* (Augsburg 1958), 53.
48 Becker, *Consuetudines almae Reipublicae Augustanae*, xiii et seq.
49 Ibid., xiv. Konrad Peutinger (1465–1547), a towering classical scholar, was town clerk of Augsburg from 1495–1534 and decisively guided the city's political policies. He registered amendments into the old city law, but he concentrated on economical issues and his literary-historical projects. See Becker, "Die Akten des Augsburger Notars Johann Spreng (1524–1601)," 489; G. Grünsteudel, G. Hägele and R. Frankenberger (eds.), *Augsburger Stadtlexikon* (Augsburg 1998), 708 et seq.
50 Liedl, *Gerichtsverfassung*, 53.

51 Hellmann, *Das Konkursrecht*, 66 et seq.
52 Hellmann, *Das Konkursrecht*, 68; for details about the "Höchstetter bankruptcy," see Safley, "Die Frage einer frühneuzeitliche Standardisierung," 107 et seq.
53 Ibid., 121.
54 T.M. Safley, "Bankruptcy: Family and Finance in Early Modern Augsburg," *Journal of European Economic History* 29 (2000): 56.
55 Georg Tradel studied Roman law at the universities of Padua and Bologna. See P. Kreutz, "Matthaeus Laimann und Georg Tradel: Ein Lebensbild zweier Augsburger Juristenpersönlichkeiten zu Beginn der Frühen Neuzeit," in: Becker, *Consuetudines almae Reipublicae Augustanae*, xxi et seq.
56 Hellmann, *Das Konkursrecht*, 71. Transcript of the draft called "Notwendigs Bedenckhen" including rules about bankruptcy, printed in: Becker, *Consuetudines almae Reipublicae Augustanae*, 32 et seq.
57 Ibid.
58 Ibid.
59 Ibid.
60 Ibid.
61 Ibid.
62 Ibid.
63 Safley, "Bankruptcy," 69.
64 Hellmann, *Das Konkursrecht*, 101 et seq.; even if, in the Höchstetter case of 1529, the order of priority was set by rolling the dice, as Safley suggests. Cf. Safley, "Die Frage einer frühneuzeitlicher Standardisierung," 109.
65 For a transcript of the draft "Consuetudines almae Reipublicae Augustanae" see Becker, *Consuetudines almae Reipublicae Augustanae*, 1 et seq.
66 Ibid.
67 Hellmann, *Das Konkursrecht*, 138.
68 Becker, "Bancarottierer," 3 et seq.
69 Spann, *Der Haftungszugriff*, 174.
70 Literally translated: "Tower of guilt." It was the prison the debtor was brought to while his creditors tried to satisfy their claims against him.
71 Becker, "Bancarottierer," 3 et seq.
72 Art. 22/2, "Imperial Discipline Ordinance" (*Reichspolizeiordnung*) 1548, in: M. Weber, *Die Reichspolizeiordnungen von 1530, 1548 und 1577: Historische Einführung und Tradition* (Frankfurt am Main 2002), 167 et seq.; cf. Becker, "Bancarottierer," 3 et seq.
73 Safley, "Die Frage einer frühneuzeitlicher Standardisierung," 120.
74 Art. 22/2 Imperial Discipline Ordinance 1548; cf. Becker, "Bancarottierer," 3 et seq.; Becker, *Insolvenzrecht*, 17.
75 Art. 22/2 Imperial Discipline Ordinance 1548; cf. Becker, "Bancarottierer," 3 et seq.
76 Safley, "Bankruptcy," 67.
77 Hellmann, *Das Konkursrecht*, 74 et seq.
78 Safley, "Bankruptcy," 67.
79 Safley, "Die Frage einer frühneuzeitlichen Standardisierung," 122.
80 Becker, "Bancarottierer," 3 et seq.
81 Spann, *Der Haftungszugriff*, 187 et seq.
82 Ibid., 191 et seq.
83 Ibid., 202.
84 Ibid., 208.
85 Ibid., 188.
86 About it, see Becker, *Insolvenzrecht*, 15.
87 Spann, *Der Haftungszugriff*, 212 et seq.
88 Hellmann, *Das Konkursrecht*, 138.
89 §§ 13 et seq. *Augsburger Fallitenordnung*.

90 §§ 18 et seq. *Augsburger Fallitenordnung.*
91 Hellmann, *Das Konkursrecht*, 152 et seq.
92 § 8 *Augsburger Fallitenordnung* uses the term, "insolvent," to describe the state of a debtor that leads to bankruptcy proceedings.
93 Becker, *Insolvenzrecht*, 18.
94 Becker, "Bancarottierer," 3 et seq.
95 Uhlenbruck argues that the work of Somoza led to delayed proceedings because of superfluous bureaucractic activity. See Uhlenbruck, "Insolvency," 249. See also S. de Somoza, *Labyrinthus creditorum concurrentium ad litem per debitorem communem inter illos causatam* (Valladolid 1645).
96 Becker, "Konkurs."
97 In English: Mortage and Bankruptcy Law.
98 In English: Bavarian Code of Judiciary Law.
99 In English: New Bankruptcy Law of Hamburg. See also Uhlenbruck, "Insolvency," 249.
100 Luig, "Germany," 118.

12 Bankruptcy, insolvency and debt collection among merchants in Antwerp (*c.*1490 to *c.*1540)

Dave De ruysscher

In the later years of the fifteenth and in the early years of the sixteenth century, Antwerp emerged to become a leading hub for international business. Merchants from southern Europe settled in Antwerp to pursue new commercial opportunities and to take advantage of the thriving popularity of the Brabantine fairs.[1] In the decades thereafter, these fairs, which were held in Antwerp and in the nearby Bergen op Zoom, gradually transformed into a permanent market that was exclusively located in Antwerp.[2] This accompanied developments within the Antwerp market. In the first years of the sixteenth century, when credit relations among the rising number of traders residing in Antwerp became more intertwined, their strategies for collecting debts and the rules imposed by the city government to regulate that collection fundamentally changed.

Even as late as the 1460s and 1470s, Antwerp law and merchant culture had placed much emphasis on the culpability and defamation of debtors with persistent payment problems.[3] Their debts were executed rather than renegotiated. Creditors favoured imprisonment and expropriation above remedies supporting their debtors' recovery. It was only after 1515, when the commercial scene in Antwerp had become more international, and when credit and business networks had connected more merchants belonging to different nationalities, that favouring the extensive rights of creditors started to give way to a different approach towards bankruptcy.

These novelties were imposed by Antwerp's leaders, and also by royal legislation, which followed many of the former's initiatives and ideas and were, in turn, also supported by merchants. The authorities indeed acknowledged the convictions of the merchants who were doing business in the city, and the merchants followed those regulations in their pursuit of overdue debts before the City Court.[4] The law laid out the contours of negotiations that could take place between creditors and debtors. It provided a set of measures and remedies that creditors could take when debtors did not manage to honour their contractual obligations.

This chapter analyses the period between *c.*1490 and *c.*1540, which includes several transitions closely related to these different developments. Changes in the legislation that governed credit–debt relations responded to new economic and mercantile trends, but also to cultural phenomena, such as the authorities' growing knowledge of and affinity with academic law (*ius commune*), and political developments, such as state-building and centralization of the royal government.[5] A reshuffling of rules regarding bankruptcy and debt collection took place in distinct steps, mirroring these changes. Legal-economic novelties, near the end of the fifteenth century, were general collaterization and the growing popularity of swift credit in the form of bearer notes, which made imprisonment of debtors less rewarding for creditors. The intensifying application of the learned, academic procedural style in the Antwerp City Court, around 1500, brought about lawsuits in which creditors combined efforts and shared expenses. The confrontation of the Antwerp rulers and resident merchants with many more cases of insolvency served as a catalyst to reform in 1516. In that year, the Antwerp law regarding bankruptcy liquidation was altered, and it was henceforth based on collectiveness and on equality among non-privileged creditors. This new legislation was soon followed by a trend towards more indulgence for debtors and an aim to reach settlements based on their cooperation. Debt collection became more equitable, which was beneficial both for individual debtors and for the market; negotiations between creditors and their debtor under the authority of royal councils of justice led to agreements of postponement and discharge of debts, which became common in the 1520s; leniency towards debtors was considered as pertaining to the "justice and grace" of the monarch. Hence, the shift towards more rights for debtors was imposed in large part by the sovereign, through judicial decisions and royal legislation, but in close interaction and consultation with the Antwerp leaders.

An early emphasis on liability and imprisonment (first half of the fifteenth century)

Antwerp had been a commercial centre throughout the fifteenth century, mainly because of the success of its fairs, which alternated with the ones held in Bergen op Zoom, which is some 40 kilometres north of the city. In the weeks surrounding Whitsun and *Bamis* (Saint Bavo, on 1 October), merchants flocked to Antwerp to sell their merchandise.[6] In spite of the success of these fairs, the mechanisms of debt collection applied there were based on out-moded principles and, so, were not adapted to contemporary commerce. In the first decades of the 1400s, the law of contract in Antwerp was too unwieldy for business on an international scale. The assets of a debtor, who defaulted on informal agreements and private contracts could be expropriated against his will, but only after lengthy proceedings before the City Court. As for the rules regarding evidence and attachment, a distinction was made between privileged debts, those that had been written into an official deed, and all others. Antwerp aldermen issued so-called "aldermen's letters" and certificates, confirming the statements and provisions that were agreed between persons who appeared before them. Such authenticated contracts and declarations required no oath to be rendered legally valid and binding, which by contrast was the common rule for private and informal agreements, even if they had been registered with a notary.[7] Only those contracts written in deeds of the aldermen permitted attachment of collateral in the event of default, even before a judgment providing for its expropriation.[8] Informal contracts, by contrast, involved no rights of attachment upon default of a debtor and require the creditor to ask for the surrender of a movable asset as surety for his debt.[9] If the debtor refused to do so, the only option was to bring a lawsuit in court. Assets could then only be attached and expropriated upon a favourable judgment, which followed lengthy proceedings and delays.

Most mercantile contracts were informal, and thus did not contain provisions of collateral, as they had not been presented to the aldermen for registration.[10] Under these circumstances, in commercial disputes, imprisonment for arrears was a common measure, because it was believed to put pressure on the debtor, his family and his business contacts, so as to have them present sureties or payments. Incarceration of a debtor also helped the creditors to gain rights on the belongings of their debtor. Detained debtors could abandon their estate, after which the aldermen released him from prison.[11] This action was often sought by creditors, if no contracts granting collateral rights on property had been made.

As a technique of debt collection, imprisonment was commonplace but also harsh, because it ruined the reputation of the arrested party.[12] Early on, therefore, some restrictions were imposed in order to avoid excesses. In 1438, for example, the Antwerp City Council explicitly provided that detentions of "strangers" in the public prison were henceforth required to last for a minimum of six weeks, and that the salaries and expense of the warden during the confinement were to be paid by the plaintiff, if a judgment of the aldermen ruled the incarceration illegitimate or unnecessary.[13]

Debtors were nonetheless not usually inclined to comply with the rules when facing serious and persistent financial problems. It was not in their interest to cooperate, if compliance equalled imprisonment and the loss of their status and reputation. Even after release from prison, the damage would hinder them when trying to obtain new credit.[14] Also, there was no possibility of discharge. Even when debtors were set free from prison, creditors could have them imprisoned again, or file a lawsuit for any part of their debts that had not been repaid.

These rules did not acknowledge the specific characteristics of insolvency, for they hinged on a philosophy of deterrence. Admittedly, the 1438 measure that imposed a minimum period of detention and charged the plaintiff with the costs would most certainly have prevented creditors from making hasty decisions in this respect. Because such practices as moratoria and renegotiating debts did not yet exist,[15] however, a debtor with lasting shortages would still be encouraged to abscond rather than to face the defamatory consequences of his creditors' actions.[16] Following payment problems, "flight" out of jurisdiction or asylum in churches were typical responses in this period. The Antwerp government responded to this trend with another discouraging measure, by proclaiming that any citizen who hid from his creditors and who did not return to pay his debts, would be banned from the city and lose his rights of citizenship.[17]

General collateral, attachment and the reduced importance of imprisonment for debts (after 1450)

Over the course of the fifteenth century, it slowly became accepted that private contracts, which had not been copied into an official deed of the aldermen, would affect a debtor's movable property, even if the contract did not contain a provision of collateral. At first, it became possible to attach assets for arrears on the basis of such agreements in exceptional circumstances, for example, when debtors committed a crime and, in particular, when they hid themselves or concealed assets from their creditors. Still, authorization of the Antwerp city government, in the form of a judgment, was required in order to have the attached goods publicly sold.[18] Near the end of the fifteenth century, creditors could claim that a debt had become due and lay an attachment on properties of their debtors, even though expropriation thereafter required approval of the aldermen. An attachment involved the locking of movable assets, often in the City Hall, which forced debtors to settle the debt quickly, in order to retrieve their belongings.

This broadened possibility of attachment profoundly influenced debt collection in Antwerp in the early years of the sixteenth century. According to the new principle, overdue debts based on any type of contract could be compensated with attachment and later expropriation. It served as a stick. Creditors could have all or part of the properties of a defaulter seized, after which they could start a proceeding before the urban court in order to obtain authorization of expropriation and sale. The proceeds were then given to the creditors.

The new approach was expanded further with a relaxation of the rules protecting visitors to the Brabantine fairs. In the middle of the fifteenth century, the so-called "freedom of the market," prohibited arrest and seizure of visitors and their merchandise during the weeks of the fair.[19] Around 1500, however, it became the rule that this "freedom" did not apply to unpaid sums that had been negotiated at a previous fair.[20] Because of the growing attraction of the fairs and the expansion of credit relations among visitors, most debts contracted in Antwerp had to do with the fairs, and their payment was commonly linked to the periods in which the fairs occurred. Also, under "freedom of the market," expropriation for "fair debts" became swifter than under the regular proceedings.[21] After 1490, the popularity of private acknowledgments of debt, to which a bearer clause had been added that made them negotiable (*obligaties*),[22] further enhanced these developments, because they commonly included the so-called "general clause," which provided that all properties of the debtor served as collateral for the debt in the bill.[23]

As a result of the new practices and views regarding collateral and attachment, incarceration of debtors became less urgent and useful, was even considered illegal, if sufficient assets could be found.[24] Imprisonment of debtors in the prison of the city now served mainly to attract sureties and payments, if no properties sufficient to pay all their contracted debts could be found. Rights on property were presumed in any contract as surety for its fulfilment, and the locking away of debtors was thus no longer required in order to force them to surrender their belongings.

Incarceration remained, as before, a feasible measure against debtors without fixed resdience in the jurisdiction in Antwerp,[25] or when it was feared that they would disperse their properties or hide them.[26] Consequently, many of the negative features of the system of the early fifteenth century could persist. Expectations of fraud were enough to break a merchant's reputation, when he was locked away for some time. As before, many of them, having no serious prospect of renegotiating their debts, thought the only way out was to leave the city. Still, because of the above-mentioned developments, in the later 1400s and early 1500s, arrest and incarceration of a debtor became less common,[27] and if it was being sought and imposed, it was nonetheless – and certainly with regard to merchants – considered a "rigorous" measure because of its consequences for the debtor's reputation.[28] Detention generally did not last long. The prisoner could contest his arrest and imprisonment within 24 hours, and, in any case, the aldermen had to check the conditions and lawfulness of the creditors' actions within three days. A judgment imposing release often came soon as a result,[29] and the earlier prescribed minimum period of detention was no longer applied. For creditors, aiming at generating a shock effect, a short imprisonment could nonetheless still be a remedy of last resort.

Attachment regulation and creditor competition (*c.*1470–1516)

It is a fair characterization to say that in this period after approximately 1470 attachment became the prime method of debt collection in Antwerp, both during and after the fairs, and among merchants. However, even so, attachments in the context of expanding networks and credit relations were not always ideal. An attachment sometimes set off a chain reaction of further attachments by other creditors, when they suspected that the actions of their colleagues meant that their debtor was in financial difficulty. Often this fear proved to be a self-fulfilling prophecy, as a generalized distrust of creditors, all of whom pursued their debts with attachment, made it difficult for a debtor to mobilize new credit. It was indeed still the reputation of debtors that largely determined their fate, as it had been the case in the first half of the fifteenth century.

In cases of insolvency, multiple attachments required new rules, in particular with regard to their priority. If the value of the belongings that were found with the debtor were insufficient to cover all his debts, then it had to be determined what proportion would be repaid to each creditor. In the period before 1516, the problem of distribution had been solved by recourse to the distinction between privileged and non-privileged debts. Debts that were mentioned in official deeds of the Antwerp aldermen and in judgments of the City Court were given priority over those debts that had been agreed on informally or privately. The latter debts commonly encompassed debts out of mercantile contracts, which frequently were not written into deeds of the aldermen. Among the privileged debts, a ranking was made according to their date, and priority was given to the eldest.[30] For non-privileged debts, the creditor who had first made an attachment had to be paid before the one who had come later, and so on.[31]

The latter rule had some important negative consequences. First, it stimulated "a run on the debtor," since creditors risked not receiving part of their debtor's assets were they to wait with their own attachment. Second, attachment required no publicity and created information asymmetries, placing foreigners and others, who did not know a local merchant's insolvency, at a competitive disadvantage. When the latter became aware of their debtor's situation, they could join the collective proceedings, but because of the urban law their claim was honoured only after those of the other plaintiffs.

This fostered conflict and litigation with regard to the nature of debts and the date of attachment. In the first years of the 1500s, the argument that an attachment had been laid first, was typical in proceedings among creditors going after the estate of their debtor.[32] For example, when in the Spring of 1503 Couckard van Elzas died, his creditor Dirk Cruse swiftly attached the inheritance. Another creditor of the deceased, Hans Kuent, heard of the death of van Elzas sometime later and had parts of the estate attached as well. Because each creditor contended that he had priority over the other, the Antwerp City Court adjudicated the dispute. Cruse's advocate insisted that his principal had been the first to lay an attachment, whereas Kuent's representative argued in court that Kuent was, by virtue of his previous attachment, already owner of the assets, which should be handed over to him.[33]

Contentions of the latter sort frequently posed difficulties. It could be that a debtor had acquired merchandise or other goods that had not been paid at delivery, and for which the seller had given credit. The ownership of such goods was for a long time a legal conundrum. According to Brabantine law of the fifteenth century, which had supposedly been applied in Antwerp, property was transferred only and always at delivery, even if the price remained unpaid; whereas a provision in the learned law, which became more important in Brabant and Antwerp around the turn of the sixteenth century, stated the contrary solution that the seller remained owner of the goods, if he remained unpaid after the delivery and the credit given had not been linked to a specific date of payment. Possibly because the learned law had not yet gained influence, in 1503 the Antwerp aldermen judged in favour of Cruse, probably following the Brabantine rule. In the following years, Antwerp judges heard similar arguments, and their decisions would gradually bend to the academic solution.[34]

Because of these and other uncertainties as to law, and because in matters of debt collection the urban rules stimulated competition among creditors, litigation between creditors pursuing debts against the same debtor was not uncommon in the first years of the sixteenth century. Such lawsuits were a serious burden for any creditor wanting to recover his money. The law was not always clear, and proceedings among creditors demanded time and money. Even if a favourable decision was obtained in such a trial, the expropriation procedure against the debtor still had to be initiated thereafter.

At around the same time, merchants commonly collected debts by means of a lawsuit before the Antwerp City Court. Mediation by merchants became more practised as well. The latter was closely linked to litigation, since merchants were appointed by the City Court as commissioners in discussions that turned around the size of debts or the probity of evidence. Under such circumstances, plaintiffs commonly asked the judges for a commission of "good men," most often merchants doing business in the city.[35] Many of the trials among merchants involved traders from different nations,[36] since disputes among compatriots were administered by the consuls and the councils of their nation. Such trials became more common as credit and business relations extended over the usual networks of nations. In many cases, discussions did not end with an agreement mediated between the parties, but returned to the court as a result of breach.

After approximately 1505, this new recourse to the court encouraged creditors more often than before to combine their efforts.[37] Proceedings before the aldermen were costly, especially since advocates familiar with the academic procedural style more commonly handed in written pleadings in support of their arguments. With its insistence on precise arguments and allegations of doctrine, the learned law became common practice in the Antwerp City Court around this time. When many creditors started a lawsuit together, the costs could be split and shared. There were other early signs of a trend toward more collectiveness among the creditors of the same debtor. Those who had payment problems started petitioning the royal councils (the Great Council of Mechelen and the Council of Brabant) for *lettres de justice*, which granted privileges because of the exceptional circumstances in which the petitioner found himself. The most popular of these, the *lettres de répit*, required that all creditors of a petitioning debtor be invited to negotiate postponement or discharge of his debts. In some lawsuits between 1505 and 1515, such letters were used as arguments against creditors suing their debtor.[38] After 1515, the use of *lettres de justice* would become normal practice and collectiveness among creditors the general rule.

Towards equitable bankruptcy proceedings and attachments: spreading the risk of failures and the emergence of a new culture of composition (*c.*1515 to *c.*1540)

In the 1510s, the idea that (fear of) flight allowed for exceptions on general principles became more widespread. Also, the trend towards collectiveness among creditors became stronger and was ultimately imposed by law. In January 1516, a collective bankruptcy proceeding was imposed in an ordinance of the City Council. In case of "flight" or concealment of assets, all creditors of the debtor (*fugitivus*) were henceforth invited by means of a public proclamation to submit claims to the court within 40 days. Except for privileged debts, which had priority, claims were paid *pro rata*, if all debts could not be compensated in full from the proceeds of the public sale of the debtor's assets. In the ordinance, the *amman*, who was an officer and representative of the Duke of Brabant, was given the power to seek and retrieve those movables that had been placed beyond the reach of the creditors, with third parties, such as relatives, associates and agents. These goods were fused with the so-called *massa creditorum*, the sum or mass of all property available to discharge debt.[39]

Before 1516, collectiveness in expropriation of a debtor had been possible, but not mandatory, and non-privileged debts had not been treated on an equal basis, which made the dates of attachments so important in many cases. The legal reform in 1516 intended to adjust fundamentally the earlier rules and procedures, in order to make them better fit an international business environment, which the Antwerp market had become after 1490. This is also evident in a 1518 ordinance, which extended from six weeks to three months claims submitted by creditors residing outside the Netherlands.[40] This measure attempted to reduce the competitive advantages of those creditors having a business agent on the spot, who kept them well informed about what went on in Antwerp.

As a result, the rules regarding the collection of arrears became somewhat more equitable, at least as regards the treatment of creditors and the options available to debtors. The idea behind the ordinance had been that criminal insolvency was a risk that should be shared among all those having contracts with the perpetrator, in order to make the market absorb the shock as well as possible.

In many respects the new rules still hinged on ideas that had been popular in the fifteenth century. The bankruptcy procedure applied only to "fugitives," those debtors who deliberately absconded. Negotiations about the payment or postponement of debts, or a possible discharge, were not envisaged. Again, as had been the case before, these limitations did not encourage debtors to be clear about their financial situation, and creditors were still impatient to start the expropriation proceedings in case of doubt. The new principle of equality only applied after it had become clear that the debtor was insolvent, and thus discussions over priority, also for non-privileged debts, continued in matters of multiple attachments that had been laid with one debtor. This state of affairs would soon change, however, and foremost because of the economic crisis of the later 1510s and of the 1520s.

In the 1510s, more attention was already being paid to the honest insolvent, who had not committed bankruptcy, whose insolvency was the result of misfortune rather than fraud. In the previous years, as was mentioned before, royal councils such as the Council of Brabant, had begun occasionally to grant *lettres de justice*, postponing or discharging debts or declaring protection from imprisonment and expropriation, but it now granted such letters only to debtors who were deemed to have been unfortunate. At his "Joyous Entry" as monarch of the Netherlands, in 1515, King Charles (later, Emperor Charles V) declared that such letters could be awarded only to applicants of good intent.[41] Since the royal councils often could not fully assess the declarations made in an application or the trustworthiness of an applicant, fraudulent statements sometimes resulted in exemptions from expropriation. The 1516 Antwerp ordinance addressed this concern as well. It provided that debtors be criminally prosecuted, if their insolvency had not been caused by misfortunes such as the loss of ships, fire and flood. Even though the condemnation of bankruptcy as theft remained regular in the course of the following decades, in practice no bankrupts were criminally condemned, let alone executed, as had been their occasional fate.[42] Furthermore, in the 1510s and thereafter, imprisoned debtors could be released from prison, even against the will of the creditors who had them locked away, on the condition that they had not absconded and that they transferred to their creditors whatever property they still possessed. This measure of "cessie van goede" (*cessio bonorum*) brought about the loss of citizenship, but prevented lifelong incarceration of poor and *bona fide* debtors.[43] "Cessie van goede" did not discharge debts, and if the released debtor acquired new capital, he had to repay any debts that remained.

At around 1520, insolvents could apply for royal letters that required a composition between the debtor and his creditors, in which debts had at least to be postponed and preferably be paid. A new focus on the debtor's good faith had made cooperation possible. As a result, and with the possibility of discharge and moratorium, many more debtors brought their payment problems to light. To encourage further cooperation and composition among creditors and debtors, it became normal practice in the late 1520s for an insolvent to file a request with the Council of Brabant to commission the Antwerp aldermen to attempt to mediate an agreement between the creditors and their debtor. The aldermen had to check the veracity of the applicant's statements and discover the causes of his insolvency. If it became clear that the applicant had committed malicious acts, his request was denied. If no such problems arose, first an inventory of the debtor's property was made, then the creditors submitted evidence of their claims. Thereafter, negotiations began under the guidance of the Antwerp City Council. When an agreement had been reached, the case file was returned to the Council of Brabant, which confirmed and registered the contract.[44] Such a composition could take the form of a five-year moratorium.[45] In spite of these measures, however, creditors often left the table and brought suit before the City Court to have their debts paid. Petitions for royal letters were occasionally submitted at this point, when negotiations before the Antwerp aldermen had broken down, or when it had become clear that important creditors with the largest claims would not accept new terms of payment.[46]

These developments were closely linked to the financial and economic crisis, brought about by the Frisian war (from 1517 onwards) and the Italian Wars, which had resumed in 1521.[47] Rising prices and interest rates shook the economy of the Netherlands and of Antwerp in particular. Large Florentine banking firms with branches in Antwerp went bankrupt, including the Frescobaldi and Gualterotti houses, in 1518 and 1523 respectively.[48] The Frescobaldi failure was the first international bankruptcy case to confront the Antwerp leadership, and it left many traces in the archives of the Antwerp urban government.[49]

It is clear that this crisis, which caused liquidity and credit problems for many others, set developments in motion that further generalized the features of the 1516 Antwerp bankruptcy ordinance and the resort to royal "letters of justice." One important innovation was the extension of the rules of equality among nonprivileged creditors in all proceedings upon attachment of a debtor's property.

These norms were also applied when two or more creditors attached property that was to pay their debts.[50] Another novelty regarded the further collaterization of debts. In the 1520s, it became possible to lay attachment "on all goods" of a debtor, and thus not only on assets that were found with him or were known to the creditors. If an application of this kind was made to the Antwerp *amman*, he was entitled to search for and attach properties that could not be found with the debtor.[51] Such third-party attachments involved the arrest of assets that were found with other people, but were allegedly the property of the debtor.[52] They hinged on the idea, drawn from learned law, that ownership of property did not transfer upon delivery in cases of fraud. The Antwerp aldermen remained reluctant to order a public sale of assets attached in this manner, however, because the rights of parties other than the ones involved in insolvent contracts were at stake.[53] Such attachments were formidably efficient tools for creditors intent on pressuring their debtors. The third-party victim of the attachment, with whom the creditors had no contractual relations but who was nonetheless damaged by the debtor's insolvency, would also press the debtor to undo the attachment as fast as possible.

As a result of these further developments, creditors resorted less frequently to imprisonment of their debtors. The prisoner could always petition for a "letter of cession," which was a *lettre de justice* that would allow him to go free upon negotiation with his creditors and abandonment of his properties to them.[54] The creditors retained one unilateral weapon, namely the public announcement of bankruptcy. There are some examples of creditors applying to the Antwerp aldermen for a public statement that mentioned criminal action before starting a collective proceeding.[55] There were few opportunities for debtors to deny such allegations, once the public statement had been made. In the years following 1540, insolvency came to represent a loss of trust among creditors, with all problems arising therefrom.[56] Debtors could still apply for *lettres de justice* and force their creditors into negotiations, but the opportunities to engage in new ventures or borrow new capital were severely limited.

Conclusion

By the end of the 1520s, debtors with persistent payment problems could to a certain extent influence proceedings regarding their arrears. This did not, however, result in a procedural and legal framework that was exclusively directed at the interests of debtors. Because negotiations now took place before courts of law, arguments for both sides could be examined, evaluated and weighed against one another. Of course, the litigants underscored those facts that were to their advantage and used terminologies intended to achieve the best possible result. Applicants for royal letters stressed how unfortunate, poor and miserable they were;[57] creditors insisted on the debtors' fraud, flight and concealment. In the fifteenth century, "flight" had been an elastic concept,[58] and even in the middle of the sixteenth century it remained customary for applicants of royal letters to mention that they themselves had not been paid by "debtors who had become fugitive." In this way, creditors marked insolvency and even temporary illiquidity with defamatory implications.[59] Even so, and notwithstanding arguments of this kind, the involvement of the authorities ensured a more equitable proceeding, which was no longer biased solely towards the rights of the creditor.

By 1540, the Antwerp system of debt collection had come a long way. Despite difficulties and adaptations, it was very progressive when compared to English bankruptcy legislation, which allowed for discharge only in 1705 and 1706.[60] Even the French system, with which Antwerp had much in common, including *lettres de justice*, allowed less latitude to debtors.[61] Though Antwerp bankruptcy procedures and the Amsterdam system, which was built in part upon the Antwerp example, have long been considered relatively "debtor-friendly," this conclusion should not be exaggerated. They provided debtors with more rights than elsewhere, but their purpose after 1520 was a weighing of the interests involved, and they did not erode bankruptcy or the concession of absolute rights to a "fresh start."[62] Reputation remained essential to business, but vulnerable to creditors' accusations and denunciations.[63] In this way, the law of Golden Age Antwerp retained features both medieval and modern.

Notes

1 B. Blondé, O. Gelderblom and P. Stabel, "Foreign Merchant Communities in Bruges, Antwerp and Amsterdam," in: R. Muchembled (ed.), *Cultural Exchange in Early Modern Europe. Volume 2: Cities and Cultural Exchange in Europe, 1400–1700* (Cambridge, UK 2007), 160–1; J. Maréchal, "Le départ de Bruges des marchands étrangers (XVe et XVIe siècle)," *Handelingen van het genootschap "Société d'Émulation" te Brugge* 51 (1951): 26–74.

2 H. Van der Wee, *The Growth of the Antwerp Market and the European Economy (Fourteenth-Sixteenth Centuries)*, Vol. 2 (The Hague 1963), 166. Stabel emphasizes that the Bergen fairs had been less important than the Antwerp ones, and even as early as the middle of the fifteenth century. See P. Stabel, "Italian Merchants and the Fairs in the Low Countries (12th–16th Centuries)," in: P. Lanaro (ed.), *La practica dello scambio: Sistemi di fiere, mercanti e città in Europa (1400–1700)* (Venice 2003), 151–2.

3 In this chapter, the notion of "bankruptcy" is limited to criminal default (*banqueroute*), which could consist of concealment of assets or flight of the debtor from his creditors, or of preparations to do so. "Insolvency" comprises long-term shortages of a bona fide debtor who did not abscond from his creditors.

4 On the Antwerp City Court, see: D. De ruysscher, "From Usages of Trade to Default Rules: Practices of Trade: *Ius Commune* and Urban Law in Early Modern Antwerp," *Journal of Legal History* 33 (2012): 6, 15.

5 For a general overview of the relations between the *ius commune* and Antwerp urban law on commercial arrangements in this period, see De ruysscher, "From Usages of Trade to Default Rules," 12–17.

6 O. Gelderblom, "The Decline of Fairs and Merchant Guilds in the Low Countries, 1250–1650," *Jaarboek voor Middeleeuwse Geschiedenis* 7 (2004): 216–17; Y. Kortlever, "The Easter and Cold Fairs of Bergen op Zoom," in: S. Cavaciocchi (ed.), *Fiere e mercati nella integrazione delle economie europee secc. XIII–XVIII* (Florence 2001), 628.

7 The *Keurboeck* has been published in G. De Longé (ed.), *Coutumes du pays et duché*

de Brabant: Quartier d'Anvers. Coutumes de la ville d'Anvers, Vol. 1 (Brussels 1870), 82, s. 4 (hereinafter *Keurboeck*); Ph. Godding, *Le droit privé dans les Pays-Bas méridionaux du 12e au 18e siècle* (Brussels 1987), 433–4. Even in 1515, private mercantile contracts regarding commerce were not considered to have the same evidential value as aldermen's letters. See Antwerp City Archives (FelixArchief, hereinafter ACA), Privilegiekamer (hereinafter PK), 914, f. 69 (24 November 1515).

8 This is evident in the few sections of the fourteenth- and fifteenth-century *Keurboeck* providing for exceptions to this principle, for example with regard to innkeepers, who could enforce rights on assets of their debtors within short periods, even before an expropriation judgment and without having a (formal or official) contract. *Keurboeck*, 2–89, see section 53/3, at 20.

9 *Keurboeck*, 46 (s. 125).

10 Analysis of the ledgers of the aldermen into which official contracts were written (the so-called *schepenregisters*), of the years 1425, 1458 and 1490, shows that mercantile contracts, and contracts between merchants, were less common in the former two than in the latter. See ACA, Schepenregisters (hereinafter SR), 11, 56 and 97.

11 W. Van der Tannerijen, *Boec van der loopender practijken der raidtcameren van Brabant*, edited by E.I. Strubbe, Vol. I (Brussels 1952), 262–3.

12 Admittedly, merchants belonging to chartered *nations*, which were organizations that had obtained charter privileges from the Duke of Brabant to administer the interests of merchants of a single nationality residing or visiting Antwerp and the Duchy of Brabant, were protected from arrest and imprisonment. For the most part of the fifteenth century, however, only the *nations* of the Hanseatic League and the English Merchant Adventurers were chartered. For Hanseatic merchants, see ACA, PK, 1063/2 (30 April 1409). For the English, consult O. De Smedt, *De Engelse natie te Antwerpen in de XVIde eeuw (1496–1582)*, Vol. 1 (Antwerp 1950), 93. Other merchants visiting the Antwerp fairs were protected under the Duke's *saufconduit*, which made their merchandise and persons immune from arrest. In spite of these privileges, even Hanseatic and English merchants were occasionally arrested and detained, in which case the charters were brought up only in the course of the proceedings before the City Court. Arrest and imprisonment were thus feasible methods of debt collection by means of pressure also against privileged traders. See, for example, ACA, V, 1231, f. 105 (5 February 1491 (n.s.)) and ACA, Vierschaar (hereinafter V), 1233, f. 13v (4 July 1503).

13 ACA, PK, 1371, ordinance of 22 February 1438 (n.s.).

14 This compliance problem is inherent to bankruptcy systems that focus on punishment and imprisonment. For comparable remarks regarding the similar English bankruptcy system after 1543, see E. Kadens, "The Last Bankrupt Hanged: Balancing Incentives in the Development of Bankruptcy Law," *Duke Law Journal*, 59 (2010): 1233–4.

15 The practice of mediation by "good men," who were often merchants, was not very common in the first half of the fifteenth century. Between *c.*1450 and *c.*1515, this technique served mainly to discuss the existence and extent of claimed debts, and not to mediate agreements between debtors and their creditors as to postponement or discharge. See, for example, ACA, V, 1231, f. 36 (4 November 1489).

16 For late-medieval Italian cities and for sixteenth-century England respectively, see: U. Santarelli, *Mercanti e società tra mercanti* (Turin 1998), 70; and Kadens, "The Last Bankrupt Hanged," 1246–7.

17 *Keurboeck*, 54 (s. 146).

18 See, for example, a query for an authorization upon flight of debtors: "Het 2de Oudt Register in 't parkement gebonden, 1438–1459," *Antwerpsch Archievenblad*, 1st series, 30 (*s.d.*): 316–18 (24 May 1448).

19 *Keurboeck*, 84 (s. 9).

20 The "freedom of the market" had been imposed with various conditions by the duke of Brabant and by the aldermen of Antwerp since the 1490s. See Kortlever, "The

Easter and Cold Fairs," 629–30. The exception for "fair debts" is first mentioned in ACA, V, 2, s. 141. This manuscript (the so-called "Golden Book") dates from the early 1530s, and contains rules that had been established at *turbe*-inquiries. For this particular rule no *turbe*-record could be found. Yet, it is likely that it dates from the early years of the 1500s.

21 See, for example, ACA, V, 2, f. 35. This section provides that, during the "freedom of the market," stolen goods could not be recovered from a person who had bought them without being aware that they had been stolen. It is implied that such a recovery was, in principle, speedy. It seems that an attachment being laid by a merchant during the fairs was likewise handled expeditiously.

22 On these bearer documents, which became negotiable paper around 1500, see H. Van der Wee, "Anvers et les innovations de la technique financière aux XVIe et XVIIe siècles," *Annales: economies, societés, civilisations* 22 (1967): 1074–81; H. Van der Wee, "Antwerp and the New Financial Methods of the 16th and 17th Centuries," in: H. Van der Wee (ed.), *The Low Countries in the Early Modern World* (Aldershot 1993), 151–3. Also, with references to their use as transferable paper in the late fifteenth century, see D. De ruysscher, "Innovating Financial Law in Early Modern Europe: Transfers of Commercial Paper and Recourse Liability in Legislation and *Ius Commune*," *European Review of Private Law*, 19 (2011): 508–9.

23 This is suggested in ACA, V, 68, f. 23v (1 December 1507), and in ACA, V, 69, f. 41v (21 August 1562). For a debt out of a sale contract, it could be provided in the acknowledgement of debt handed to the bearer that the delivered goods were collateral for the debt. See, for example, ACA, SR, 97, f. 39 (5 July 1490).

24 Citizens of Antwerp were given protection against imprisonment after 1450. In the early 1500s, such a rule did not apply to resident non-citizens. See ACA, V, 1232, f. 248v (3 October 1500). Before that time, it was also possible, when the debtor refused payment or denied the existence of the debt. For a reference to this Brabantine principle, see E. Strubbe, "Het Rechtsboek van Lier (ca. 1415)," *Bulletin de la Commission royale pour la publication des anciennes lois et ordonnances de la Belgique* 16 (1950): 167.

25 See ACA, V, 1232, f. 237v (31 June 1500). This judgment was pronounced following the arrest and detention in Antwerp of the mayor of Brouwershaven, located in Zeeland. See, for another example, ACA, V, 1233, f. 13v (4 July 1503).

26 This older Antwerp rule was corroborated by learned opinion, which became more common around this time. Willem van der Tannerijen, who had been secretary of the city of Antwerp in the 1450s, mentioned in his treatise on Brabantine forensic practice (1474–76) that, if no surety had been provided in a contract, the creditor could not imprison the debtor for arrears, unless there was suspicion of preparations for abscondence. See Van der Tannerijen, *Boec van der loopender practijken*, 566 (ch. 177).

27 This is clear in the fact that in this period, in order to achieve greater success for creditors, whose arrests and detentions were contested, agreements provided that the debtor would pay "or go to jail on his own expenses." See, for example, ACA, SR, 56, f. 3v (27 April 1515). A comparable provision was inserted into an agreement reached by "good men," between a creditor and his debtor, in 1505. See ACA, V, 1233, f. 82v (27 August 1505).

28 See, for example, ACA, PK, 228 (*provisie van cessie*, *c.*1515).

29 See, for example, ACA, V, 1233, f. 81 (14 August 1505).

30 "Oudt Register, mette berderen, 1336–1439," *Antwerpsch Archievenblad*, 1st series, 29 (s.d.): 144–6 (26 June 1437); E. Strubbe and E. Spillemaeckers, "De 'Antwerpse rechtsaantekeningen' van Willem de Moelnere," *Bulletin de la Commission royale pour la publication des anciennes lois et ordonnances* 18 (1954): 67.

31 ACA, V, 68, f. 12v (around 1508); ACA, V, 1233, f. 281v (20 October 1509).

32 For example, ACA, V, 1233, f. 67v (23 January 1505 (n.s.)).

33 ACA, V, 1233, f. 11v (30 June 1503).

34 For a comparable case, in which an explicit reference was made to "the written laws" (i.e. the *ius commune*), see ACA, V, 1235, f. 265v (10 July 1520). The unrestricted academic rule was finally adopted in the Antwerp urban law of 1608.

35 See, for example, ACA, V, 1235, f. 27 (8 August 1517) and f. 202v (22 October 1519).

36 See, for early examples, ACA, V, 1231, f. 31v (22 September 1489) and f. 36 (4 November 1489). After 1500 such lawsuits rose in number.

37 From those years onward, references to "the creditors of" started to appear in ledgers containing the "extended sentences" of the Antwerp City Court. See, for early examples, ACA, V, 1233, f. 73 (6 March 1505 (n.s.)), and f. 85v (1 October 1505).

38 An early example is ACA, V, 1233, f. 38 (15 January 1504 (n.s.)).

39 On these points, see: D. De ruysscher, "Designing the Limits of Creditworthiness: Insolvency in Antwerp Bankruptcy Legislation and Practice (16th–17th Centuries)," *Legal History Review (Tijdschrift voor Rechtsgeschiedenis)* 76 (2008): 309–13.

40 ACA, V, 4, s. 7–8.

41 A. Anselmo, J.B. Christyn and J.M. Wouters (eds), *Placcaerten, ordonnantien, edicten … in dese Nederlanden*, Vol. 8, (Brussels *s.d.*), 136 (26 April 1515, s. 4–5).

42 No traces of criminal prosecution or execution for this crime were written in the accounts of the *écoutète*, the officer in charge for criminal affairs. See Archives of the Realm in Brussels, Audit Office (*Rekenkamer*), accounts 12905 and 12906. In one case, the *écoutète* brought charges, but the lawsuit was not continued, probably because none of the creditors insisted. See ACA, V, 144, f. 18v (27 January 1542 (n.s.)).

43 ACA, V, 1233, f. 85v (1 October 1505), f. 89 (6 November 1505) and f. 110v (9 July 1506); ACA, V, 1235, f. 51 (12 November 1517); ACA, V, 68, f. 33 (1 June 1520). I would like to thank Jeroen Puttevils (University of Antwerp) for bringing the first two references to my attention.

44 ACA, PK, 271, 1 (1 June 1527); ACA, PK, 299. This practice was formalized in a 1536 royal law. See *Recueil des ordonnances des Pays-Bas*, Vol. 4, 328 (30 August 1536).

45 ACA, PK, 271, 43.

46 ACA, PK, 271, 1 (1 June 1527). It was only in the beginning of the seventeenth century that majority rules were imposed. Before that time, any creditor had the right not to sign a moratorium and to try to recover his debt individually. See L. Guicciardini, *La Description de la Cité d'Anvers*, edited by M. Sabbe and S. Strauss (Antwerp 1920), 108–9. This 1567 description of the law of the city accorded with royal legislation of 1540, 1541 and 1544. See *Recueil des ordonnances des Pays-Bas*, 2nd series, Vol. 4, 234, 328 and Vol. 5, 55 (s. 34).

47 Van der Wee, *The Growth of the Antwerp Market*, Vol. 2, 141–53.

48 R. Ehrenberg, *Das Zeitalter der Fugger: Geldkapital und Creditverkehr im 16. Jahrhundert. Erster Band: die Geldmächte des 16. Jahrhunderts* (Jena 1922), 280–1.

49 ACA, V, 1235, f. 92 (23 June 1518), f. 99 (20 July 1518) and f. 106v (19 July 1518).

50 See De ruysscher, "Designing the Limits," 321.

51 Ibid., 320.

52 See, for example, ACA, f. 28v (25 September 1535).

53 Only if it could be proven that the assets seized from third parties had been alienated intentionally to the detriment of the creditors, or only after the debtor's flight, could those assets be sold publicly. In other cases, this was considered to be impossible, even though in the course of the sixteenth century, there was discussion of the hypothesis concerning goods that had been sold around the date of bankruptcy and insolvency, and whether the good faith of the acquirer could be deemed annulled by the bad intentions of the bankrupt. See, for example, ACA, V, 69, f. 50v (16 May 1565).

54 Such letters were granted (exceptionally) by the Privy Council, by the Council of Brabant and by the Great Council of Mechelen, until the latter lost its jurisdiction around 1515.

55 ACA, PK, 675, f. 258v (22 December 1595). In this request, creditors petitioned for measures following "a big and ugly bankruptcy." After 1516, similar petitions were directed to the aldermen in order to obtain a public ordinance on the bankruptcy of the creditor. For an early example of such an ordinance, see ACA, PK, 914, f. 75 (8 November 1516).

56 De ruysscher, "Designing the Limits," 317–18, 325–26.

57 ACA, PK, 312, request by the merchant Hendrik Dries to the Council of Brabant, attached to a letter of the Council, dated 17 February 1535 (n.s.).

58 It is not possible to be sure, due to the lack of evidence, but allegations of flight may not always have corresponded to actual flight, but rather may have involved denunciations from the community of merchants. "Flight" may have been as flexible a concept, as much metaphorical as real, as was "sodomy" in late-medieval Bruges, where prosecution for that crime served mainly to underscore royal and princely authority and power. For the latter, see M. Boone, "State Power and Illicit Sexuality: The Persecution of Sodomy in Late Medieval Bruges," *Journal of Medieval History* 22 (1996): 135–53.

59 ACA, PK, 312, requests to the Council of Brabant, attached to letters of the Council dated 16 November 1534 and 19 April 1536.

60 Kadens, "The Last Bankrupt Hanged," 1252–70.

61 J. Hilaire, *Introduction historique au droit commercial* (Paris 1986), 321–4, labelling *lettres de répit* as a symptom of a "laxist approach towards debtors."

62 This was suggested in J. Whitman, "The Moral Menace of Roman Law and the Making of Commerce: Some Dutch Evidence," *Yale Law Review*, 105 (1996): 1877–83. On the more beneficial nature of bankruptcy law in the Netherlands compared to other locations, see M. Steele, "Bankruptcy and Insolvency: Bank Failure and its Control in Preindustrial Europe," in: *Banchi pubblici, bancchi privati e monti di pieta nell'Europa preindustriale. Amministrazione, tecniche operative e ruoli economici*, Vol. 1 (Genoa 1991), 199–200.

63 De ruysscher, "Designing the Limits," 326–7. Lack of clarity would persist after 1540, for example, in unfortunate and unpractical definitions of insolvency, and in the lasting uncertainties as to ownership after delivery. All this proved beneficial for creditors who wanted to label their debtor as "bankrupt."

13 The reception of the *actio Pauliana* in Scots law

John MacLeod

Introduction

In premodern and modern bankruptcy adjudication and resolution, the actions of insolvent debtors to diminish their assets were recurrent and fraught. They were widely viewed as wrongful, because they favoured certain creditors over others or secured the debtor's property from the satisfaction of his debt. As a result, insolvency often spread from the debtor to some or all of his creditors, upsetting the professional and social solidarity of the mercantile community. This chapter takes up the legal response to this problem in early Scots law.

Both civilian and common law systems allow creditors to attack transactions whereby insolvent debtors diminish their assets.[1] The classic applications of the rule (often referred to as the *actio Pauliana*) are well known. A debtor recognises that he or she is irrecoverably insolvent. Knowing that the assets will be sold to pay creditors, and preferring them to go to friends or relatives, the debtor gives them away. The gift may be intended to allow the debtor continued use of the property, as where a merchant in embarrassed circumstances transfers the family home to their spouse. Whatever the purpose, the result is the same: a pool of assets which was already insufficient to meet debtor's obligations is further diminished. Creditors' interests are thus prejudiced. Either the creditors or an insolvency official acting on their behalf can recover property so alienated and apply it to the satisfaction of creditors' rights.

Alternatively, an insolvent debtor might grant a security right to a favoured but hitherto unsecured creditor. For instance, a plumber or electrician might provide services to the debtor and initially be content to give credit without any security. Once the debtor becomes aware of the impending insolvency, the debtor and the tradesman may try to protect the latter's position. The debtor might pledge some stock to the tradesman. This security right is granted so that that the favoured creditor does not have to share the proceeds of the sale of the pledged stock with other creditors. Payment in full is more likely, but this is achieved by diminishing the pool of assets available to the others. In certain circumstances, they or their representative may be able to set the right in security aside, restoring equality of creditors in respect of the pledged assets. The range of transactions subject to challenge goes beyond these examples but the focus of this chapter will be on grants made by the debtor because they form the core cases to which all other cases may be considered analogous.

While *actio Pauliana* rules were common across Europe and can be traced back to Roman law, the decisive moment in Scots law was the passage of the Bankruptcy Act 1621.[2] The act's preamble makes it clear that the drafters understood themselves to be drawing on the civilian tradition. However, it is somewhat surprising that legislation was thought necessary. Scots lawyers in this period drew freely on civilian sources. By the nineteenth century, common law rules allowing challenge were recognised alongside statutory rules. Writers in that period suggested that the Roman rule was received prior to 1621 and that the act was primarily concerned with matters of proof.[3] This account has been generally accepted since.[4]

The 1621 Act makes provision regarding proof, and such questions generated a significant amount of litigation under the act.[5] There are some hints of recognition of the Roman law rules prior to its enactment. Examination of the pre-1621 sources and of the act itself suggests, however, that it had a substantive as well as a procedural impact and that the common law rules post-date the legislation. This chapter also examines the interaction of legalisation and common law sources that formed Scots law's *actio Pauliana*.

Scots law prior to 1621

Transfers were being attacked on the basis that they were "in defraud and hurt of creditors" as early as 1492.[6] The case would not be explained on that basis today: the creditors who challenged the transfer had already comprised[7] the relevant property. This would be regarded as enough to give the compriser priority over the transferee without fraud. This case is significant, however, because it is evidence of early use of the formula "in defraud of creditors" to describe transactions which disappoint creditors' attempts to seek satisfaction from the debtor's assets. The phrase echoes the opening words of Digest 42.8 "quae in fraudem creditorum facta sunt ut restitutuantur."[8] Prior to the numbering system introduced in the Berlin Stereotype edition of the *Corpus Iuris Civilis*, these words or some contraction of them were used to refer to the major collection of texts discussing the Roman law rules on challengeable transactions by debtors. The phrase is therefore likely to have brought these rules to the mind of Scots lawyers educated in the civilian tradition.

The details of the classical Roman law on this topic remain a matter of some controversy.[9] There is more general agreement about the position presented in the *Corpus Iuris Civilis*, which formed the basis of the treatment of fraud on creditors across Europe. The basic rule was that a transaction was challengeable if four requirements were fulfilled: diminution of the debtor's estate; resulting loss to the creditors; intention to defraud on the part of the debtor; and knowledge of that intention on the part of the counterparty.[10]

These requirements do raise one major question: What was it that rendered a scheme fraudulent? Roman jurists were famously ambivalent about abstract concepts and general definitions, so it is no surprise that the texts in the *Corpus Iuris* give a multitude of examples of fraudulent conduct but no definition of fraud. Radin suggests that *fraus* in the relevant sense means merely "prejudice" or "disadvantage," pointing to the fact that *dolus* is the Latin word for fraud in the sense of deceit.[11] It is certainly true that *fraus* involves prejudice to creditors but it is impossible to separate it from the debtor's intention. A careless act by the debtor, which diminished the value of one of the assets, could not be regarded as *fraus* in the sense in which the term is used in Digest 42.8. Further, in order to qualify as fraud on creditors, the act of the debtor required to harm creditors in their role as creditors rather than in some other capacity. A debtor who stole from a creditor would certainly be acting intentionally to the creditor's prejudice but, while they would be liable for theft, it would not be a case of fraud on creditors. Therefore, Kaser, Krüger and Ankum seem closer to the truth in suggesting that *fraus* had two elements: harm to the creditors and intention to do so on the part of the debtor.[12] A fraudulent transaction might be characterised as one which was calculated to frustrate satisfaction of the creditors' rights.

It is perhaps surprising that the transaction did not require to be gratuitous or at undervalue. How, it might be asked, can the debtor's patrimony be diminished if the transaction is for full value? The situation becomes clearer when we bear in mind that what matters are the assets available to creditors rather than the patrimony the instant after the transaction. Someone who buys assets from a debtor knowing that the proceeds of sale will be used to fund the debtor's absconding can be understood as an accessory to a fraudulent scheme to disappoint creditors although the transaction itself is onerous. One who takes a disposition of assets subject to a secret obligation to hold them for the benefit of the debtor might be regarded in similar terms. The primary situation addressed by the Roman rule was fraudulent collusion. The remedy might be characterised as undoing the wrong done by the granter and transferee in their common plan to frustrate satisfaction of the creditors' rights. The general rule was subject to two qualifications that would have a major influence on later development.

First, the requirement that the recipient knew of the debtor's fraudulent scheme was waived where the transaction was a gift. However, in that case, the donee's liability was limited to his or her enrichment.[13] In Scotland, due to the 1621 Act, the former exception would tend to overwhelm the rule,[14] with non-gratuitous cases on the analytical periphery. When the focus is on gratuitous alienations, it can be rather difficult to see why lawyers linked the rule so closely to fraud. This approach makes a lot more sense, however, if they saw the Scottish rules as merely the local version of a European rule which was firmly grounded in fraud.

The second qualification was that those who merely received what was due to them could not be regarded as acting fraudulently.[15] This meant that a creditor who had been paid or received a conveyance or right in security, which the debtor was specifically obliged to grant, was safe from challenge. This principle would be a significant controlling factor in the development of the law of fraudulent preferences.

The description of transfers of property subject to diligence as being "in defraud of creditors" was not unique to *Ramsay* v. *Wardlaw*. A statute of 1592, described purported transfers by debtors at an unrelaxed horn as "maid in defraud of the creditour."[16] Early discussions of inhibition (a type of diligence which prohibited debtors from alienating property and gave third parties notice of this) showed a similar pattern. Transfers in breach of the prohibition could be set aside by the party who instigated the inhibition on the grounds that they were "of nane avail, as done *in fraudem creditoris*."[17] The old form of letters of inhibition,[18] narrated that the inhibited party "does therefore intend, in defraud and prejudice of the complainer ... to sell, annailzie, wadset, dispone, resign, burden or otherwise dilapidate" their assets.

By the beginning of the seventeenth century, inhibition no longer affected moveable property so its scope was narrower than that of the *actio Pauliana*.[19] The formula, however, does suggest that it was regarded as Scots law's response to the problem of fraudulent debtors. Similarly, Stair notes that inhibitions were introduced because debtors were "dilapidating their estates" and "are much more ancient and extensive than the remedy by reduction *ex fraude creditorum*, which is determined by that excellent statute of Session, ratified in Parliament, *anno* 1621."[20] In his *Jus Feudale*, Craig uses the *actio Pauliana* as a comparative counterpoint in his discussion of inhibitions.[21] He suggests that inhibitions are preferable because they are less ambiguous and are a matter of public notice. Craig took the idea that inhibition was a remedy against fraud on creditors sufficiently seriously to consider whether a transfer in breach of inhibition by a solvent debtor was nonetheless valid.

The perception of inhibition as a rule which dealt with fraud on creditors might be expected to discourage adoption of the *actio Pauliana*. There were, however, some cases in the sixteenth century in which transfers were held null on the basis that they were "in defraud of creditors" despite the absence of any diligence. The most striking is *Kennedie* v. *Somervill*. It concerned a debtor who, prior to the summons in the relevant case, had alienated so many of his assets that he was incapable of complying with the judgment when it was obtained. Balfour explains that the court held that the transfer "aucht and sould be reducit, as done and maid efter the dait of the decrete, in defraud and hurt of the creditour obtenar thairof."[22]

Despite the terseness typical of records from this period, Balfour's note tells us quite a lot. It presupposes a rule under which an alienation which was made after the judgment was handed down and which rendered the debtor unable to comply with it was null on the basis of fraud.[23] That rule was of no assistance here: the alienation was made before the judgment. The Lords were willing to employ a legal fiction, however, deeming the transfer to have been made after the decree. This extended version also seems to have been applied in *Innes* v. *Oliphant*[24] but that case indicates some reticence: Balfour's account stresses that the alienation was made after the date of summons, suggesting an inclination to limit the extension. Balfour stresses that there is no requirement of a close relationship between the debtor and the recipient, although the disponee in *Innes* was the debtor's "tendir kinsman."[25] He gives no indication of whether either bad faith on the part of the transferee or gratuity was requisite. Some other cases suggest, however, that these factors were being taken into account. The first appears only in the manuscript record of the Acts of the Lords of Council and Session. In 1512, John Inglis sold lands to his brother Gilbert. At the time, he was liable to Margaret Allan and did not have other lands sufficient to meet the obligation. She challenged the sale, alleging that Gilbert knew both of the liability and of the absence of other lands. There was also a suggestion that the sale was a sham because Gilbert had not paid the agreed price: effectively an allegation of gratuity. Gratuity was also alleged to support a plea for nullity in *Spens* v. *Anstruder*.[26] Once again, the pursuer sought to cast the transfer as "simulat" (i.e., a sham) because it was made "to ane conjunct person without any reasonable caus [*sic*]."

Sixteenth-century Scots lawyers regarded simulated or sham transactions as a species of fraud. This understanding was common in the *ius commune* until Bartolus. He argued that sham transfers (where the parties did not really intend to transfer) should be distinguished from transfers which were truly intended to take effect but which were none the less designed to defraud creditors. The former class was automatically null while others were merely challengeable at the instance of creditors. Bartolus' distinction is a persuasive one, and one which was generally accepted across Europe.[27] In a sham transaction, a prerequisite for transfer is missing. In the latter case all the elements for a valid transfer are in place. The problem is that the transfer itself amounts to a wrong against the creditors. It seems, however, that the Bartolist analysis did not take hold in Scotland.

These materials suggest that Scotland was on the way to developing a common law rule along the lines which the 1621 Act would eventually establish. Key elements such as the insufficiency of assets to meet obligations were beginning to emerge. Unfortunately, the laconic nature of the records from this period means that there is no indication of the sources being relied on.

One contrast with later law is worthy of note. The majority of the decisions turn on the sufficiency of the debtor's assets to meet a particular decree rather than on absolute insolvency.[28] This is not surprising. In the absence of a collective procedure (which was first introduced in 1772),[29] absolute insolvency would be very difficult to establish.[30] It did mean, however, that many transfers caught by the later law would not have been captured by the rules in these early cases. A debtor may well have enough assets to pay any single creditor without having enough to pay all of them. This focus also makes it difficult to see the rules as being directed at equal treatment of creditors. Rather, they aimed to prevent frustration of particular creditors' attempts to obtain satisfaction.

While there are some hints, the sparse nature of the sources, the uncertainty surrounding their precise ambit and the slight difference in focus suggest that a common law *actio Pauliana* cannot be said to have developed in Scotland prior to the passage of the 1621 Act.

The matter was not left for the courts to develop. In 1567 a parliamentary commission was instructed to consider "ane artickle for thame that puttis thair sonnis or freindis in thair landis or makis assignatiounis of thair gudis in defraude of the executioun of decreitis."[31] The issue is framed in traditional Scottish terms, focussing on particular decrees rather than creditors in general. The desire for legislation reflects a preference for statutes over other sources of law in this period,[32] a general concern with the state of the statute book during the reign of James VI[33] and legislation on this topic elsewhere in Europe.[34]

The commission did not produce the envisaged legislation. In 1582, however, the Lords of the Court of Session made an act of sederunt[35] concerning the execution of decrees. The act's narrative discloses that it was motivated by concern that delays in execution opened the way for "simulatt and fals assignationis of [the debtors'] movable guidis, fraudfull and private alienationis of thair possessionis, landis and heretageis." The remedy, however, was not challenges to the grants but expedited execution. It was ratified by parliament in 1584[36] but the validity of fraudulent grants was not addressed. Of course, this legislation presupposes the validity of the fraudulent grant.

The 1621 Act

Eventually the judges took the matter up with a further act of sederunt in 1620. This was ratified by parliament the following year. It is reproduced here with added section markers:[37]

> *A ratificatioun of the act of the lordis of counsell and sessioun made in Julii 1620 aganis unlauchfull dispositiones and alienationis made be dyvoures and banckruptis*
>
> [a] Oure soverane lord, with advyse and consent off the estaittis convenit in this present parliament, ratiefies and apprevis and for his hienes and his successoures perpetuallie confermes the act of the lordis of counsell and sessioun made aganis dyvoures and bankruptis at Edinburgh, the tuelff day of Julii 1620, and ordanis the same to have and tak full effect and executioun as ane necessarie and proffitable law for the weill of all his hieghnes subjectis, off the quhilk act the tennoure followes:
>
> [b] The lordis off counsall and sessione, understanding by the grevous and just complayntis of many of his majesties gude subjectis that the fraude, malice and falshoode of a number of dyvoures and bankruptis is becum so frequent and awowed and hathe alreddy taikin sick progres to the overthairow of many honest menis fortounes and estaittis that it is liklie to dissolve trust, commerse and faythfull dealing amang subjectis, quhairupoun must ensew the ruine off the whole estate gif the godles deceatis of those be not preventit and remeidit, who, by there apparent welth in landis and guidis and by thair schow of conscience, credite and honestie drawing into thair handis upoun trust the money, merchandice and guidis of weilmeaning and credoulous persounes,

do no wayes intend to repaye the same, bot ather to leiff ryioutouslie by wasting of uther menis substance, or to enriche thame selffis by that subtile stealthe of trew menis guidis, and to withdraw thame selffis and thair guidis furth of this realme to elude all executioun of justice; and to that effect, and in manifest defraud of thair creditouris, do mak simulate and fraudfull alienationes, dispositiounes and utheris securities of thair landis, reversiounes, teyndis, guidis, actiounes, dettis and utheris belanging unto thame to thair wyiffes, childrene, kynnismen, alleyis and uther confident and interposed persounes without anye trew, lauchfull or necessarie caus and without anye just or trew pryce intervening in thair saidis barganis, wherby thair just creditoures and cautioneris ar falslie and godleslie defraudit off all payment off thair just dettis and manye honest famelies liklie to cum to utter ruine.

[c1] For remeid quhairoff, the saidis lordis, according to the powar gevin unto thame by his majestie and his most noble progenitoures to sett doun ordouris for administratioun of justice, meaning to follow and practize the guid and commendable lawis, civill and cannone, maid aganis fraudfull alienatiounes in prejudice of creditouris and aganis the authoures and partakeris of suche fraude, statutes, ordanis and declairis that in all actiounes and causes depending or to be intentit by any trew creditour for recoverie of his just debt or satisfactioun of his lauchfull actioun and right, they will decreit and decerne all alienatiounes, dispositiounes, assignatiounes and translatiounes whatsoevir made by the dettour of ony of his landis, teyndis, reversounes, actiounes, dettis or guidis quhatsoevir to anye conjunct or confident persoun without trew, just and necessarie causes and without a just pryce realie payit, the same being done efter the contracting of lauchfull dettis frome trew creditoures, to have bene frome the beginning and to be in all tymes cuming null and off nane availl, force nor effect at the instance of the trew and just creditour be way off actioun, exceptioun or replye, without farder declaratour.

[c2] And incace anye of his majesties gude subjectis (no wayis pertakeris of the saidis fraudis) have lauchfullie purchesit anye of the saidis bankeruptis landis or guidis by trew barganis frome just and competent pryces or in satisfactioun of thair lauchfull dettis frome the interposed persounes trusted by the saidis dyvoures, in that cace the right lauchfullie acquyrit be him quha is nawayes partaker of the fraude sall not be annulled in maner foirsaid, bot the ressaver off the pryce of the saidis landis, guidis and utheris frome the buyer salbe haldin and obleisit to mak the same furth cuming to the behuiff of the bankruptis trew creditouris in payment of thair lauchfull dettis;

[c3] and it salbe sufficient probatioune of the fraude intended aganis the creditoures if they or onie of thame salbe hable to verefie by wreate or by oathe of the pairtie receaver of anye securitie frome the dyvoure or bankrupt that the samen wer made without anye trew, just and

necessarie caus or without anye trew or competent pryce, or that the landis and guidis of the dyvoure and bankrupt being sold by him who bocht thame frome the said dyvoure, the whole or the maist pairt of the pryce thairoff wes converted or to be converted to the bankruptes proffite and use, prowyding alwayes that so muche of the saidis landis and guidis or pryces thairof so trusted by bankruptis to interposed persounes as hathe bene reallie payit or assignet by thame to anye of the bankruptis lauchfull creditoures salbe allowed unto thame, they making the rest forthcuming to the remanent creditoures who want thair dew paymentis.

[d] And if in tyme cuming anye of the saidis dyvoures or thair interposed partakeris of thair fraude sall mak anye voluntarie payment or right to ony persoun in defraude of the lauchfull and more tymelie diligence of ane uther creditoure haveing servit inhibitioun or useit horning, arreistment, comprysing or uther lauchfull meane dewlie to affect the dyvoures landis or guidis or pryce thairoff to his behuiff, in that cace the said dyvoure or interposed persone salbe holdin to mak the same furthcumand to the creditour haveing used his first lauchfull diligens, who sall lyikwayis be preferrit to the concreditour, who being posteriour unto him in diligence hathe obtenit payment by partiall favoure of the dettour or of his interposit confident, and sal have gude actione to recover frome the said creditour that whiche wes voluntarlie payit in defraude of the persewaris diligens.

[e] Finallie, the lordis declairis all suche bankruptis and dyvoures and all interposed personis for covering or executing thair fraudis and all utheris who sall gif counsell and wilfull assistance unto the saidis bankruptis in the dewysing and praktiezing of thair saidis fraudis and godles deceittis to the prejudice of thair trew creditoures salbe reputed and holden dishonest, fals and infamous persones, uncapable of all honoures, dignities, benefices and offices or to pas upoun inquestis or assysses or to beir witnes in judgement or outwith in anye tymes cuming.

It falls into five parts: [a] ratification by parliament, [b] preamble to the act of *sederunt*, [c] provision on transfer to conjunct or confident persons, [d] protection of partially completed diligence and [e] imposition of *infamia*, penalising those engaged in the transactions.

The first surprising point is that the legislation took the form of an act of *sederunt*. The statute ratifying the institution of the Court of Session had expressly conferred on the judges a power to make "sic actis, statutis and ordinancis as thai sall think expedient for ordouring of processes and haisty expeditioune of justice."[38] However, this act of sederunt concerns substantive rights rather than procedure.[39]

Discomfort about competence may explain why the Lords felt it necessary to make explicit reference to the basis in Roman law.[40] Mackenzie seems to take this approach, arguing that, had they been faced with a case in which a disposition had been made in fraud of creditors, they would have been justified in adopting the Roman rule (and indeed expected to do so). It was not problematic that they decided the case "in *Hypothesi* [rather] than in *Thesi*."[41] Any deficiency was cured by the statutory ratification but the origins of the act might go some way to explaining the judges' later willingness to adopt a flexible interpretation of the act.

If it had been simply concerned with proof as Bell would later suggest, Mackenzie might have presented it as within the Session's procedural jurisdiction but this argument is not proposed. Similarly, if he had taken the view that the Roman law rule had already been received into Scots law, he might have been expected to make reference to this as well as to the Roman law precedent. He made neither argument. It may be, however, that nineteenth-century perceptions about the proper sphere of acts of sederunt contributed to Bell and M'Laren's view that the act was merely concerned with proof.

The act focuses on two relatively narrow cases: transfer to conjunct[42] or confident persons for which there was no "trew, just and necessarie" cause; and voluntary payment or transfer in prejudice of diligence which had commenced but not been completed. In contrast to the approach in the *Corpus Iuris* and the English statutes,[43] there is no general provision striking down acts done to defraud creditors.[44] This narrow scope would prove to be a major defect. A great number of the cases which came before the court did not fit into either of the two categories. This led to pressure for a flexible interpretation of the act[45] and to recognition of common law rules alongside the statutory provisions.

The scope of the act is muddied somewhat by part [c3]. It provides that fraudulent intent shall be presumed where it is proved that either (i) the transfer was made without a just price really paid or (ii) that the receiver sold the assets on and that the debtor got the benefit of the price obtained. Strictly speaking, such a presumption was not necessary because the condition for nullity expressed in part [c1] is not fraud but the absence of "trew, just and necessarie" cause.

The drafters may have felt it necessary because the *ius commune* background of Scots lawyers meant that they would conceive of actions by debtors which defeated their creditors in terms of fraud. Part [b] shows that those behind the act considered fraud by the debtor to be the relevant mischief. They were also aware, however, of the difficulty of proving fraudulent intent. One response to this problem is a presumption of fraud, triggered by proof of certain objectively discernible facts. The other option is to craft a rule which turns on these criteria *tout court* rather than using them to establish fraud. Particular objective conditions would be chosen because they were circumstances where fraud is thought likely to be present.

In conceptual terms, there is a substantial difference between the two approaches: one operates at a procedural level and ensures that the relevant boxes will be treated as ticked; the other operates at the substantive level, controlling which boxes require to be ticked. In practical terms they feel very similar. In both cases, the grant can be challenged by establishing certain objectively discernable facts. It is not surprising, therefore, that the distinction between the two has not always been strictly maintained.[46]

If the starting point for development is a rule based on fraud, a system might initially deal with problems of proof by means of presumptive fraud and develop from there to the substantive approach.[47] It may be that parts [c1] and [c3] of 1621 Act reflect a lack of clarity about where Scots law was in this process. The ambiguity persisted for some time. Writing in the mid-eighteenth century, Bankton describes the effect of part [c] as "Statutory Presumptive fraud,"[48] despite having earlier observed that this part of the act "concerns Gratuitous rights granted by a bankrupt in prejudice of prior creditors"[49] where no fraud was needed.

Parts [b] and [c3] follow the pre-1621 case law and the approach of the English statutes in conflating simulation and fraud on creditors. Part [b] simply describes the acts of debtors as "simulate and fraudfull." Part [c3] gives a clear example of simulation, where the disponee sells the assets and applies the proceeds for the benefit of the debtor. The transfer is effectively a sham to protect the proceeds of the sale from the creditors.

It also casts some light on the nature of the creditors' right against the disponee. A bad faith purchaser who has sold the property on is liable to pay the proceeds to the debtor's creditors, subject to a deduction for any part of the price already applied to the insolvent's debt. If part [c] of the act was simply concerned with the validity of the transaction, such a provision would be difficult to explain. The fact that the transfer was challengeable when the asset was in the transferee's hands would not explain why the price should be paid to the creditors. The price paid for an asset is distinct from the asset itself and Scotland had no developed law of tracing which would allow the price to substitute for the asset.

If, however, the rule was essentially concerned with compelling the fraudulent grantee to make reparation for their role in diminishing the pool of assets available to the creditors, then it makes sense that where natural reparation (return of the asset) is no longer possible, pecuniary compensation should be payable instead. Such an analysis would also explain why there was a deduction for funds paid out to creditors. To the extent that the funds had been paid to lawful creditors, no wrong was done and therefore the right to reparation could only cover the residue. While rights to reparation are frequently subject to such modification, it is more difficult to marry such thinking with the "on–off" analysis implicit when we ask if a transfer is valid or not. This approach, which effectively treats the "nullity" as flowing from a personal right against the grantee for reparation would also explain how it was possible to limit the innocent donee's liability to their enrichment.[50]

Part [c] makes no reference to the solvency of the granter at the time of the impugned act. It merely requires that a lawful debt had been contracted prior to the act and that it was prejudicial to the creditors' interests. This marked a departure from the earlier Scottish approach because it focusses on prejudice to creditors in general rather than to a particular decree. It left two questions open for later litigation to settle: must the creditor bringing the challenge have been a creditor at the time of the grant; and must the debtor have been bankrupt at the time of the grant or just at the time of the challenge?

The rules on protection for good-faith purchasers are evidence of the relative immaturity of thinking about voidness (where a transfer is ineffective *ab initio*) and voidability (where a transfer may be set aside by a particular party or parties) in this period. Part of the confusion arose from inadequate terminology. The term voidable does not appear to have been received into Scots law until the mid-eighteenth century.[51] Until then, "null" tended to be used to denote both situations.

Modern law explains the protection of the good-faith purchaser very simply. The transfer is valid until the creditors attack it. That means that, until the attack, the acquirer has the power to make someone else the owner. The terms of part [c2] might be taken to suggest something different, particularly in light of part [c1], which provides that the relevant deeds are null by exception. The procedural term nullity by exception was associated with transactions which were void *ab initio*.[52] On that model, any subsequent transfer would be void, but a good-faith purchaser might be protected by a special rule introduced to protect security of transactions.

Despite the terms of the act, however, the court quickly replaced nullity by exception with nullity by action (a procedure which was more closely associated with voidability) where a right to land had been granted.[53] Further, as has been noted, other aspects of the act suggest the creditor's right arises from a duty of reparation rather than a problem with the validity of the transfer.

When Scottish writers sought to present the protection of good-faith purchasers in a conceptual framework, they characterised the challenge as being based on a personal right rather than a question of the fundamental nullity of the impugned transaction. That meant that the protection of good-faith third parties followed as a natural consequence, since the third parties were not bound by the same duty of reparation.

When Mackenzie discussed [c2], his first resort was to the characterisation of the *actio Pauliana* by "the Doctors." He noted that the Gloss and certain other interpreters considered the *actio Pauliana* to be a personal rather than a real action because the receiver's liability depended on conduct rather than the mere fact of possession and observes that "Our Law agrees in this with the Civil Law."[54] His approach was not altogether consistent, however.

In an earlier passage, he cast doubt on the standard justification for allowing challenges under the 1621 Act or (in the *ius commune*) the *actio Pauliana* to be brought by creditors with "incomplete" rights: those to whom payment is not yet due or subject to an as yet unfulfilled condition.[55] The common view was that such creditors needed to be protected from the risk of the transferee's insolvency. This view flows naturally from the personal right analysis. Mackenzie objected that "Reductions are *in rem*" and so are not affected by insolvency. This is inconsistent with the obligations-based analysis that he gives in his treatment of part [c2]. It seems, however, that his earlier treatment was closer to the majority view in his own day. It is certainly the one which is reflected in discussion by other Scottish writers.

Hope describes part [c] as rendering acts in defraud of creditors as "null at the instance of true and just creditors."[56] If the transfer was void *ab initio*, there would be no question of the nullity operating at anyone's instance. The phrase implies an innocent party's option of the type described by Stair in his general discussion of the remedies for fraud.[57] Stair himself explains the protection by observing that "Fraud is no *vitium reale* affecting the subject, but only the committer of the fraud and these who are partakers of the fraud."[58] Furthermore, Stair discusses the act in his title on the obligation to make reparation for wrongs done.[59] This aspect of Stair's structure is followed by the eighteenth-century writers, Forbes[60] and Bankton.[61] The reparation analysis is also supported by the fact that a grantee could defeat a challenge by offering to pay the debt owed by the creditor. By doing so, they made reparation for any wrong done, thus removing the creditor's interest in challenging the grant.[62]

The move away from nullity by exception and its implications shows the willingness of the court and legal writers to adapt the statute when they found its terms inconvenient and the continued role of the *ius commune* understanding of fraud in their discussion of the Act. The 1621 Act was the starting point, rather than the conclusion of the Scottish analysis.

Post-1621 developments

As observed above, the scope of the two bases of challenge in the 1621 Act was, on its face, very narrow. This is illustrated by Bankton's summary:

> it consists of two principal parts: the first concerns Gratuitous rights granted by a bankrupt in prejudice of prior creditors who had done no diligence; the second, Rights granted by a bankrupt to one creditor, in prejudice of another's lawful diligence.[63]

Many transactions by fraudulent debtors were either not purely gratuitous or not made with conjunct or confident persons. The creditors prejudiced had often not commenced their diligence. Therefore, they fell outside the terms of the act. These situations encouraged a flexible approach to its interpretation. Where the case at hand was too much of a stretch, the common law of fraud was allowed to resurface and fill the gap. The end point of this process was an independent common law challenge to transactions in fraud of creditors, which sat alongside the 1621 Act.

The most immediate challenge in applying the 1621 Act, however, was establishing which transferors were caught by part [c]. As noted above, part [c] made no mention of the solvency of the granter. The rubric of the act indicated that it was concerned with deeds by "dyvoures and banckruptis" but there was considerable uncertainty as to whether these words should be read as limiting part [c]'s sphere of application. Even in those cases where it was taken to do so, there was some uncertainty as to who could be considered a bankrupt or dyvour. A number of early cases on the act focus not on the sufficiency of the debtor's assets to meet debts but on events such as flight or its contemplation or charges to pay which would later be considered conditions of notour (i.e. notorious) bankruptcy.[64]

The requirement that the debtor be absolutely insolvent at the time of the grant first established itself as a defence.[65] If the donee could demonstrate a sufficiency of assets, even after the gift, to pay all creditors' debts then no creditor could be said to have been prejudiced. What was done with the rest was none of their business. The focus was on absence of prejudice rather than solvency per se, as is evidenced by the suggestion that certain assets which would be difficult for creditors to find out about or get access to could not be relied on for establishing solvency.[66] Of course, the requirement of prejudice to creditors was a key element in the Roman law rule, but it is not mentioned in the 1621 Act.

Over time, absolute insolvency began to mature into a positive requirement. Steps in this direction are evident in cases where there was a significant lapse of time between the disputed grant and the challenge. There, those seeking to uphold the transfer were discharged of any burden in establishing the granter's solvency.[67] Bankton's analysis in the mid-eighteenth century reflects a further shift. He suggests that the granter was required to be a "bankrupt" and that, for the purposes of this part of the act, that meant insufficiency of assets to which "creditors might have had free access."[68] He went on to argue, however, that, while solvency was generally presumed, the opposite was the case under this act. Thus, while in theory those challenging the deed were required to establish insolvency, the presumption operated immediately to throw the burden of proof on to the grantee.

The court took a narrow view of the other major question raised by the wording of part [c], restricting the right to challenge to creditor's whose rights were constituted prior to fraudulent act.[69] Where the Lords felt that an arrangement was nonetheless fraudulent in respect of posterior creditors (typically because of simulation or latency), however, they were willing to entertain a challenge on the basis of fraud at common law.[70] This approach persists, without much further analysis, into modern treatments[71] and reflects the continued conflation of simulation and fraud, contrary to the Bartolist tradition, and a conflation between simulation and latency.[72] It also shows that, where the court saw a gap to which the statute could not stretch, they allowed the common law to grow up and meet the need.

Seventeenth-century case law also established that a sale at undervalue could be challenged under part [c] although the transfer was not entirely gratuitous.[73] Mackenzie justified this position by arguing that there was no "true" cause for the transfer with reference to the equivalent rule in the *ius commune*.[74] This in turn meant there was no "true, just and necessary cause" and therefore the grant fell foul of part [c]. Without such a rule, the protection offered would have been very easily evaded. Indeed, the rule is best thought of as an anti-avoidance measure. Both Mackenzie and Stair stress that the price need not be the highest that could have been obtained with the former suggesting that the challenger must show either that the low price was intended as a device to cheat the creditors or that it was "extraordinary [sic] low in itself."[75] It might have been argued that any sale below the market value would amount to an enrichment of the purchaser. That argument was not invoked, however. This suggests that the rule was not intended to strip away an unjustified enrichment. Rather, the extraordinarily low price might be taken as an objective circumstance which would almost certainly be accompanied by fraud, although the fraud was very difficult to establish, echoing the reasoning discussed above in relation to part [c3].

By the time Mackenzie was writing his *Observations* on the 1621 Act,[76] it was clear that any gratuitous deed by an insolvent debtor could be attacked on the basis of part [c].[77] Mackenzie and Stair saw this move as a change in the interpretation of the statute based on judicial practice,[78] although Mackenzie, in particular, appears to have found the position troubling. In a late work, he rationalised the extension as an *actio utilis*, justified by parity of reason with the rule explicitly set out.[79]

This line of reasoning held sway for a long time.[80] Other circumstances were making it more and more vulnerable, however. First, the developing case law regarding challenges by posterior creditors and challenges to transactions with existing creditors meant that, by the end of the eighteenth century, it was well established that actions by insolvent debtors in fraud of their creditors were challengeable at common law. This offered an alternative justification that did not require the words of the statute to be stretched. Second, attitudes to statutory interpretation were becoming less flexible.

Despite these pressures, there is no evidence of the shift before the nineteenth century. It first appears in the first edition of Bell's *Commentaries*, published in 1804. After his treatment of part [c] of the 1621 Act, Bell devotes a separate section to "Fraudulent Embezzlement of Funds, as reducible at Common Law."[81] Here he deals with gratuitous grants to strangers. He begins by suggesting that "it was held by some of our lawyers, that, if the grantee was not a conjunct or confident person, under the statute, the deed was not liable to challenge as gratuitous."[82] Somewhat bizarrely, he supports this by quoting the passage from Mackenzie's *Observations* where the narrow terms of the act and the broader practice are discussed.

Bell does not address the other authorities considered above which make it very clear that the broader practice was seen as being based on an extended reading of the statute. Instead, he moves on to attack Erskine's suggestion that in a grant to a stranger, a claim in the narrative of a deed that it is onerous can only be rebutted by writ or oath.[83] Bell argued that, if this was truly the case, fraud would be very easy indeed. A few extra words in the deed would secure it from challenge.[84] This is true, and Erskine's statement of the distinction between grants to conjunct persons and to strangers probably went too far. What is more interesting, however, is Bell's other argument.

Erskine had relied on *Trotter* v. *Hume*[85] to support his position. In *Trotter*, a grant to a stranger had been challenged under the 1621 Act, but the challenge was unsuccessful because their narrative of the grant disclosed that it was in consideration of "money paid and undertaken, conform to an inventory." Bell rightly points out that the court merely held that the narrative threw the burden of proof on to the pursuer rather than necessarily limiting his options for discharging it.[86] He also argues, however, that the reason for the citation of the statute in *Trotter* and cases like it was that the ambit of the act was not clear and that pursuers were invoking the act in cases where it was not appropriate "with the view of throwing the burden of proving the onerous cause on the holder." The assumption behind this argument is that the challenges could have been brought on the basis of the underlying common law and that part [c] of the 1621 Act was concerned with proof rather than the substantive law. The argument also provided Bell with some sort of explanation for the multitude of cases in which the 1621 Act had been invoked although the grantee was not a conjunct or confident person. There can be little doubt, however, that Bell's approach was a departure from the previous analysis.

Although it was novel, Bell's approach found support in the nineteenth-century case law. Mackenzie's analysis was rejected by the Lord Ordinary in *Wilson* v. *Drummond*,[87] a decision which was upheld by the Inner House and Bell's approach received explicit support in the Inner House in *Obers* v. *Paton's Trustees*.[88] It provided the bedrock common law challenges to gratuitous alienations in the modern era.[89] The sources prior to Bell suggest, however, that common law challenges grew up in the gaps left by the act and, where at all possible, Scots lawyers preferred an extended reading of the act to a common law ground. This suggests that they regarded it as the foundation of the substantive law on the topic.

Transactions with existing creditors: fraudulent preferences

Part [d] of the 1621 Act was devoted to transactions between the debtor and existing creditors, but it was very narrow. Creditors did not qualify for its protection until they had commenced diligence. Once diligence was complete, they did not need its protection: they could rely on their priority of diligence. This cautious approach is understandable. The development of this area in the *ius commune* exposed fundamental tensions that were not yet resolved.

As mentioned above, a text in the *Corpus Iuris* suggested that payment of a debt that was due was not fraudulent.[90] This principle had strong support in the European tradition, bolstered by the consideration that payment of a debt has a neutral effect on the debtor's assets since it operates to discharge a liability equal to its value.[91] Such an approach does, however, neglect the fact that this creditor will receive full payment while the others must be content with a proportion of their entitlement. If the payment is reversed, the favoured creditor will rank alongside them for a proportion of the debt, while the pool of assets available to all will be increased by its full value. It is very difficult to say that a transaction, whose reversal would be beneficial to creditors, is not prejudicial to them.

These concerns are expressed in the *Corpus Iuris*.[92] Although Scaevola's concluded views on the matter are not entirely clear, he does seem to hint that those who have diligently enforced their rights are entitled to retain their advantage in a question with those who neglected to do so. Problems arise where the debtor favours one creditor over others *ex propio motu*. This line of thinking was developed by certain medieval lawyers who took the view that a payment to one of many creditors was vulnerable to challenge under the *actio Pauliana*. In the civilian tradition, however, it was largely overwhelmed by the view that creditors were entitled to look to their own interests and accept payment debts owed to them.[93]

Creditors' freedom to take what they can get was generally more limited if what they get is not cash payment but a right in security.[94] This approach was rejected, however, in the eighteenth century by Voet, Wissenbach and some of the *usus modernus* writers on the basis that it made no sense to allow a creditor to accept total satisfaction in the form of payment but not a right in security, which was something less than full satisfaction.[95]

While these considerations may have led to a narrow approach in drafting part [d], the general attitude of Scottish judges was hostile to preferential conduct by insolvent debtors. Even prior to the 1621 Act, they were willing to set aside diligence on the basis that the debtor had assisted the creditor using it while not offering the same help to others. This continued to be penalised after the Act was passed.[96] It reflected an attempt to strike a balance between the creditors' right to look to their own interests and the debtor's duty to be neutral in respect of them. The court's desire to prevent preferences by the debtor was also evident in a liberal attitude to the requirement in part [d] that the creditor had commenced diligence against the debtor, accepting horning[97] as sufficient although it did not, in itself, attach any particular assets[98] and by recognising a horning as sufficient even when it was open to a technical procedural objection.[99]

Another technique employed in extending the capacity of the 1621 Act to catch fraudulent preferences was to read the requirement, in part [c], of a true, just and necessary cause cumulatively. On this basis it could be argued that a transfer made in discharge of a debt which was not under pressure of diligence was without necessary cause. However, the reception of this line of argument was, however, mixed at best.[100]

Beyond the 1621 Act, the cases are inconsistent, suggesting some uncertainty about the right balance between equality of creditors and their right to look to their own interests. Thus, in *Scougal* v. *Binnie*[101] the Lords suggested that even a payment would have been struck down had the creditor been a participant in the debtor's fraud,[102] although no other creditor had done diligence prior to the payment. Five years later, in *Jack* v. *Gray*,[103] the court held that, in the absence of prior diligence, a creditor could accept either payment or security even from a debtor they knew to be contemplating absconding.

In many cases, the concept of notour bankruptcy was deployed. In some, the condition (in part [d]) that the debtor be a dyvour at the time of the grant in frustration of diligence was taken to require notour bankruptcy.[104] In others, notour bankruptcy was used to establish the parties' fraudulent intent and thus a common law challenge although there may have been no prior diligence. A number of these cases involved dispositions *omnium bonorum*: where a disposition disclosed that it covered all of the debtor's assets. Such preferees must have been aware that the debtor was left with nothing to meet other creditors' claims.[105] These cases established a principle that one who was notour bankrupt (and thus, presumptively, known to be insolvent by all and sundry) could not prefer one creditor over another even where there was no prior diligence.[106] The justification here is very close to that noted above in relation to fraudulent transfers. If both parties know of the debtor's insolvency, then the grant of a security can be considered a scheme designed to (further) frustrate other creditors' attempts at satisfaction.

There was, however, considerable dispute about the precise criteria for notour bankruptcy and whether something less, such as "material bankrupt[cy]," was sufficient for a challenge.[107] The former question would be settled by statute in 1696,[108] which established clear criteria for notour bankruptcy. It also declared that all acts in favour of creditors were "voyd and null" if undertaken within the 60 days prior to notour bankruptcy or at any time thereafter.[109] The 1696 Act itself caused confusion as some doubted whether it was necessary to satisfy its requirements in order to bring a challenge under part [d] of the 1621 Act.[110] The majority of cases suggested that this was not the case,[111] but they did require that the preferee was a participant in the debtor's fraud.[112]

Whatever its effect on the 1621 Act, the 1696 Act's express provision might have been expected to bring common law challenges to an end. As the with the 1621 Act, however, the conditions for notour bankruptcy established by the 1696 Act were quite restrictive. Creditors continued to bring common law challenges to preferences in situations falling short of these, and the court was receptive to them. Some of these involved dispositions *omnium bonorum*,[113] but others simply involved intention to prefer by the granter.[114]

In the vast majority of the cases, the creditors receiving the preference knew what was going on: either there was express collusion, the transfer was of all of the debtor's assets or the debtor was notour bankrupt. It is easy to see why the preferee would be liable to other creditors in these cases. The transaction was impossible without the preferee's participation. Therefore, the preferee facilitated the debtor's wrongful conduct just as much as someone who buys goods from the debtor knowing that the funds will be used to abscond. In *Grant* v. *Grant*,[115] however, a successful challenge was brought against security rights although the Lords proceeded on the basis that the preferees were innocent of the debtor's scheme. The justification was that an attempt to hold on to the preference made a preferee a participant in the fraud. Collusion came after the fact rather than at the same time. The case would become particularly influential in the later development of the common law relating to fraudulent preferences.[116] McBryde suggests that it established that a preference could be challenged as fraudulent despite the good faith of the preferee.[117]

As the foundation of the modern law of fraudulent preferences *Grant* can be taken as the end point of the present investigation. As with gratuitous alienations, the narrow scope of the protection in the 1621 Act left space for a more extensive common law rule to develop alongside it. Even further legislative intervention in the form of the 1696 Act did not constrain this development.

Conclusion

The Scots law development concerning fraudulent transactions shows the dynamic interaction of statute and case law in the early modern period. Legislative intervention was key, most notably in shifting the focus from frustration of particular decrees to general solvency, but the rules in the statutes proved too narrow, necessitating continued common law development which was informed by Scots lawyers' *ius commune* learning, initially in stretching the statute but finally in setting up common law grounds alongside it. Although the modern substantive rules do not depend on fraud, it played a key role in their development.

Notes

1 See generally B.M. Goodman, "The Revocatory Action," *Tulane Law Review* 9 (1934–5): 422; W Gerhardt, *Die systematische Einordnung der Gläubigeranfechtung* (Göttingen 1969); A. Boraine "Towards Codifying the *actio Pauliana*," *South African Mercantile Law Journal* 8 (1996): 213; J.J. Forner i Delaygua, *La protección del crédito en Europa: La acción pauliana* (Barcelona 2000).

2 1621 c. 18, *RPS*, 1621/6/30: available at www.rps.ac.uk/.

3 G.J. Bell, *Commentaries on the Law of Scotland*, 7th ed., edited by J. M'Laren (Edinburgh 1870), Vol. II, 171. See also *Obers* v. *Paton's Trs* (1897) 24 R 719 at 734 per Lord M'Laren.

4 Scottish Law Commission, *Report on Bankruptcy and Related Aspects of Insolvency and Liquidation* (SLC No. 68, February 1982) paras. 12.5 and 12.16; W.W. McBryde, *Bankruptcy* (Edinburgh 1995), para. 12.04; *Henderson* v. *Foxworth Investments Ltd* [2011] CSOH 66.

5 E.g. *Monteith* v. *Anderson* (1665) Mor 1044; *Crawford* v. *Ker* (1680) Mor 1012; *Spence* v. *Creditors of Dick* (1692) Mor 1014; *Leslie* v. *Creditors of Lauchlan Leslie* (1710) Mor 1018; *Guthrie* v. *Gordon* (1711) Mor 1020 and *Gibb* v. *Livingstone* (1766) Mor 909.

6 *Ramsay* v. *Wardlaw*, 27 June 1492: J Balfour, *Practicks* (Edinburgh 1754), 184.

7 A form of diligence against land.

8 C.f. the title of part II.xiii of J.A. Clyde (ed.), *Hope's Major Practicks, 1608–33*, Vol. I (Edinburgh 1937): *De creditoribus et his qui in fraudem creditorum.*

9 The most recent contribution to discussion is G. Grevesmühl, *Die Gläubigeranfechtung nach klassischem römischen Recht* (Göttingen 2003).

10 B.T. Windscheid, *Lehrbuch des Pandektenrechts*, 9th edn, edited by T. Kipp (Aalen 1963), § 463; H. Dernburg, *System des römischen Rechts*, 8th edn, edited by P. Sokolowski (Berlin 1912), § 400; J.A. Ankum, *De Geschiedenis der "*Actio Pauliana*"* (Zwolle 1962), 396; and Gerhardt, op. cit. 56.

11 M. Radin, "Fraudulent Conveyances at Roman Law," *Virginia Law Review* 18 (1931–2): 111. Radin's view was anticipated in the German literature: See H. Krüger and M. Kaser, "Fraus," *Zeitschrift der Savigny-Stiftung für Rechtsgeschichte: Romanistische Abteilung* 63 (1943): 118–19 for a summary.

12 Krüger and Kaser, op. cit.; M. Kaser, *Das römische Privatrecht: Erster Abschnitt* (Munich 1971), 628 and Ankum, op. cit., 392. See e.g. D.42.8.1pr and D.42.8.6.8.

13 D.42.8.6.11.

14 Goudy discussed the subject under the headings "Gratuitous Alienations at Common Law," "Fraudulent Preferences at Common Law," "Act 1621, c. 18 – Gratuitous Alienations" and "Act 1621, c. 18 – Alienations in Defraud of Diligence": H. Goudy, *Treatise on the Law of Bankruptcy*, 4th ed., edited by T.A. Fyfe (Edinburgh 1914).

15 D.42.8.6.6.

16 Act 1592 c. 147, *RPS*, 1592/4/88. Horning was the first stage in diligence. It led to the debtor's moveable property being forfeited to the Crown and used to pay of the executing creditor: 1579 c. 75, *RPS*, 1579/10/28.

17 Balfour, op. cit., 185.

18 Recorded in J. Dalrymple, Viscount Stair, *The Institutions of the Law of Scotland*, new ed., edited by D. Walker (Edinburgh 1981), IV.xl.4.

19 T. Craig, *Jus Feudale* (Edinburgh 1934), I.xii.31. It was published posthumously in 1655 but is likely to have been written in the 1590s: J.W. Cairns, "The *Breve Testamentum* and Craig's *Jus Feudale*," *Tijdschrift voor Rechtsgeschiedenis* 56 (1981): 317.

20 Stair, op. cit., IV.xl.3.

21 Craig, op. cit. I.xii.31.

22 30 March 1503/4: Balfour, op. cit., 184.

23 E.g., *Fleming* v. *Drummelzear* 4 August 1525; *Mouat* v. *Kynnaird* 4 May 1531; *Waterstoun* v. *Laird of Teiling* 22 April 1553 and *Spens* v. *Chalmer* (undated): Balfour, op. cit., 185.

24 19 March 1529/30, Balfour, op. cit., 184–5, A.M. Godfrey, *Civil Justice in Renaissance Scotland* (Leiden 2009), 349–50.

25 See Godfrey's paraphrase of the record in the Acts and Decreets.

26 (1569/70) R. Maitland, *The Practiques of Sir Richard Maitland of Lethington* (Edinburgh 2007), Item 312.

27 Ankum, op, cit., 399–400.

28 That is, that the debtor's total liabilities outweigh their total assets.

29 Goudy, op. cit., 1–3.

30 C.f. Ankum, op. cit., 392 and Grevesmühl, op. cit., 110 making the same point in respect of Roman law.

31 *RPS*, A1567/12/24. The Commission was renewed in 1581: *RPS*, 1581/10/28.

32 E.g. Craig, op. cit., I.viii.12–17. See also J.D. Ford, *Law and Opinion in Scotland during the Seventeenth Century* (Oxford 2007), 57–8, 129–30.

33 E.g. Commissions in *RPS*, A1575/3/7, 1578 *RPS* 1578/7/18 and *RPS*, 1633/6/47. The Compensation Act 1592 c. 143, *RPS*, 1592/4/83, the Prescription Act 1617 c. 12, *RPS*, 1617/5/26, and the Registration Act 1617 c. 16, *RPS*, 1617/5/20 are the best known products of this process.

34 Gerhardt summarises provisions in municipal laws in Germany and Italy: op. cit., 62–79. For Italian and French legislation of the period, see Ankum, op. cit., 417. For England, see 34 and 35 Henry VII c. 4 (1543) Statute of Elizabeth 1571 (13 Eliz c. 5) and 1 James 1 c. 15 (1604).

35 Acts of sederunt were legislation passed by the Court of Session, and primarily concerned with regulation of court procedure.

36 1584 c. 139, *RPS* 1584/5/21.

37 The statutory text is the most reliable record of the Act of Sederunt because the Book of Sederunt for the period 1608 to November 1626 was lost in 1674. See I. Campbell (ed.), *The Acts of Sederunt of the Lords of Council and Session* (Edinburgh 1811), 64.

38 1540 c. 93, *RPS*, 1540/12/64.

39 There are other examples of essentially substantive acts of sederunt which were later ratified by parliament: e.g., 1579 c. 75, *RPS* 1579/10/28 and 1584 c. 139, *RPS* 1584/5/21. For a discussion of changing attitudes to the proper scope of Acts of Sederunt see Campbell, op. cit., xv–xvii.

40 None of the Scottish materials (and indeed none of the European materials consulted) refer to Canon law texts. It seems likely that the phrase "lawis, civill and cannone" is used as a catch all term for the *ius commune*.

41 G. Mackenzie, "Observations upon the 18th Act of the 23d Parliament of King James the Sixth against Dispositions made in Defraud of Creditors," in: G. Mackenzie, *The Works of that Eminent and Learned Lawyer, Sir George Mackenzie of Rosehaugh*, Vol. II (Edinburgh 1722), 5–6.

42 I.e., related.

43 See 34 and 35 Henry VIII c. 4 and 13 Eliz c. 5 s. 2. Bell suggests that it the latter provision was clarified by 1 James I c. 15 s. 5, providing that grants by the commissioners of bankruptcy prevail over voluntary deeds given without onerous consideration: op. cit., 171. It should be borne in mind, however, that the latter statute (in contrast with the Statute of Elizabeth) only applies to deeds by one who has committed an act of bankruptcy (similar to the requirements for notour bankruptcy) as defined in s. 2 of the statute.

44 This approach was also that adopted in France in a 1609 Edict of Henry IV and in the *Code marchand* promulgated by Louis XIV in 1673 (for which see Gerhardt, op. cit., 83).

45 Which was at odds with the general approach to statutes with penal elements (as this act did in part [e]).

46 See e.g., Gerhardt, op. cit., 78 suggesting that the presumption of fraud in the period running up to bankruptcy laid the foundation for the objectivisation of the requirements for challengeability in the Italian city states. See also N. Hoffmann, "Die Actio Pauliana im deutschen Recht: Gläubigeranfechtung nach dem Anfechtungsgesetz und der Insolvenzordnung," in: J.J. Forner i Delaygua, *La protección del crédito en Europa: La acción pauliana* (Barcelona 2000), 155, 161.

47 This pattern of development is evident in a number of systems, although the fraud-based rule often remains as a fall back: Gerhardt, op. cit., 75, 77–8, 82–8 and 108.

48 Op. cit., I.x.85.

49 Op. cit., I.x.73.

50 D.42.8.6.11.

51 A. McDouall, Lord Bankton, *Institute of the Laws of Scotland* (Edinburgh 1993), I.viii.74.

52 Mackenzie, op. cit., 23–4.

53 E.g., Mackenzie, op. cit., 24; Stair, op. cit., I.ix.15 *Secondly*; Bankton, op. cit., I.x.108 and Bell, op. cit., 181–2.

54 Mackenzie, op. cit., 24–5. The European position was not quite as clear cut as Mackenzie suggests. On the debates on the characterisation of the *actio Pauliana*, see Ankum, op. cit., 402–5.

55 Mackenzie, op. cit., 11.

56 Hope, op. cit., II.13.18.

57 Op. cit., I.ix.14.

58 Stair, op. cit., I.ix.15 *Seventhly*. A similar approach is taken by Bankton, op. cit., I.x.85.

59 Stair, op. cit., I.ix.15.

60 W. Forbes, *Institutes of the Law of Scotland*, Vol. I (Edinburgh 1722), 204.

61 I.x.73.

62 J. Steuart, *Dirleton's Doubts and Questions Concerning the Laws of Scotland Resolved and Answered*, 2nd ed. (Edinburgh 1762), 331; and W. Forbes, "Great Body of the Laws of Scotland," Vol. I, 987 (unpublished, available at: www.forbes.gla.ac.uk/).

63 Bankton, op. cit., I.x.73.
64 Flight: *Finlaw* v. *Park* (1621) Mor 895; *Richardson* v. *Eltone* (1621) Mor 1047; *Scougal* v. *Binnie* (1627) Mor 879. Charge to pay: *Craw* v. *Persone* (1623) Mor 1047.
65 *Pringle* v. *Ker* (1624) Mor 931; *Lady Borthwick* v. *Goldilands* (1629) Mor 914; *Garthland* v. *Ker* (1632) Mor 915; *Clerk* v. *Stewart* (1675) Mor 917; *Creditors of Mouswell* v. *Children of Mouswell* (1679) Mor 934; *M'Kell* v. *Jamieson & Wilson* (1680) Mor 920; *Guthrie* v. *Gordon* (1711) Mor 1020; *M'Kenzie* v. *Fletcher* (1712) Mor 924; *Executor Creditors of Meldrum* v. *Kinnier* (1717) Mor 928; and *Creditors of Hay, Competing* (1742) Mor 929. Stair, op. cit., I.ix.15 *Thirdly*.
66 *Garthland* v. *Ker* (1632) Mor 915; *Callander* v. *M'Kell* (1680) Mor 932; *Lord Queensberry and Creditors of Mouswell* v. *Children of Mouswell* (1682) Mor 936; *Children of Mousewell* v. *Duke of Queensberry* (1688) Mor 932; and *Deas* v. *Fullerton* (1710) Mor 921.
67 *Spence* v. *Creditors of Dick* (1692) Mor 1014; *Brown* v. *Creditors of Kennet* (1696) Mor 1055; and *Street* v. *Mason* (1672) Mor 4911.
68 Bankton, op. cit., I.x.73: citing *Lourie* v. *Dundee* (1663) Mor 911 and *M'Kenzie* v. *Fletcher* (1712) Mor 924.
69 *Pollock's Creditors* v. *Pollock and Son* (1669) Mor 1002; *Street and Jackson* v. *Mason* (1673) Mor 4911 (c.f. *Street* v. *Masson* (1669) Mor 1003); *Reid* v. *Reid* (1673) Mor 4923, summarised and endorsed in Stair I.ix.15 and *Watson* v. *Malloch* (1681) Mor 883. See also Forbes, "Great Body," 982–3, with reference to further cases.
70 *Pollock's Creditors* v. *Pollock and Son* (1669) Mor 1002; *Kolston* v. *Weir* (1682) Mor 902; Bankton I.x.89, op. cit.; and J. Erskine *Institute of the Law of Scotland*, (Edinburgh, 1773), IV.i.44.
71 E.g. Goudy, op. cit., 33, and McBryde, op. cit., para. 12.49, adopting Goudy's analysis.
72 Sometime collusion was thrown in as well. There is no necessary conflict here since collusion refers to the process by which a scheme is executed while simulation or latency refer to what is done.
73 *Glencairn* v. *Brisbane* (1677) Mor 1011 and 911.
74 Mackenzie, op. cit., 21–2.
75 Mackenzie, op. cit., 22; Stair, op. cit., I.ix.15 *Fourthly*. Cf. *Murray* v. *Drummond* (1677) Mor 1048.
76 Published in 1675.
77 A distinction continued to be drawn between conjunct and confident persons and others: the latter, but not the former, were entitled to rely on the narrative in a deed to establish that the grant was onerous: Forbes, "Great Body," Vol. I, 984. See also *Hume* v. *Smith* (1673) Mor 889; Bankton, op. cit., I.x.76; and Erskine, op. cit., IV.i.35.
78 Mackenzie, op. cit., 18; Stair, op. cit., I.ix.15.
79 Mackenzie, *Treatise of Actions* in *Works*, Vol. II, 492, 495. This treatise was published for the first time in the second volume of the collected works in 1722. See *Works*, Vol. I (1716), x.
80 Forbes does not really discuss the point, but the placement of his comment suggests that he followed Mackenzie's approach: *Institutes*, 205, "Great Body," Vol. I, 988. Mackenzie's justification is repeated by Bankton, without reference to *actio utilis* as a character: I.x.75 and by Erskine, op. cit., IV.i.35.
81 Bell, *Commentaries on the Municipal & Mercantile Law of Scotland*, 1st ed. (Edinburgh 1804), Vol. I, 98.
82 Bell, ibid., 99.
83 Erskine, op. cit., IV.i.35.
84 Bell, op. cit., 100.

85 (1680) Mor 12561.
86 Bell, op. cit., 101.
87 (1853) 16 D 275.
88 (1897) 24 R 719 at 734 per Lord M'Laren.
89 McBryde, op. cit., para. 12.19 but the challenges do not bear on the idea that gratuitous alienations are challengeable at common law.
90 D.42.8.6.6. Early payment was considered fraudulent: D.42.8.10.12.
91 See Ankum, op. cit., 409–10.
92 D.42.8.24.
93 Ankum, op. cit., 409–10.
94 D.42.8.10.13. D.42.8.13 was explained in the *ius commune* as concerning a right in security granted or promised before the debt was constituted: Ankum, op. cit., 410.
95 Ankum, op. cit., 410–11.
96 See the cases reported under Collusion in Morison's dictionary, starting at page 2427. The earliest is *Kinloch* v. *Haliburton* (1618) Mor 2427. See also *Creditors of Hunter, Competing* (1695) Mor 1023; Stair, op. cit., I.ix.13; and Bankton, op. cit., I.x.72.
97 When a debtor failed to comply with a court order to pay, he was declared a rebel or outlaw because he had disobeyed an order given in the king's name. This was done by proclamation at the main burgh (town) in the region where the debtor lived. The proclamation was preceded by the blowing of a horn, from which the procedure took its name: horning. Horning was an initial step in execution against the debtor's assets. On horning, see further Stair, op. cit., III.iii.
98 *Richardson* v. *Eltone* (1621) Mor 1047; *Veitch* v. *Pallat* (1675) Mor 1029; *Murray* v. *Drummond* (1677) Mor 1048; *Bathgate* v. *Bowdoun* (1681) Mor 1049; *Bateman & Chaplane* v. *Hamilton & Co* (1686) Mor 1067; *Hamilton* v. *Campbell* (1709) Mor 1059; *Chaplain* v. *Drummond* (1686) Mor 1067; *Dalrymple* v. *Lyell* (1687) Mor 1052; and *Wordrop, Fairhom and Arbuthnot & Co Competing* (1744) Mor 1025.
99 *Kilkerran* v. *Couper* (1737) Mor 1091.
100 *Birkinbog* v. *Grahame* (1671) Mor 881; *Creditors of Tarpersie* v. *Laird of Kinfawns* (1673) Mor 900.
101 (1627) Mor 879.
102 I.e. aware of intention to abscond.
103 (1632) Mor 897.
104 *Veitch* v. *Executors of Ker and Pallat* (1675) Mor 1073.
105 *Kinloch* v. *Blair* (1678) Mor 889; *Cranston* v. *Wilkie* (1678) Mor 889; *Pollock* v. *Kirk Session of Leith* (1679) Mor 890; *Brown* v. *Drummond* (1685) Mor 891; *Duchess of Buccleugh* v. *Sinclair* (1728) Mor 893.
106 *Shaw* v. *M'Millans* (1685) Mor 105; *Moncrief* v. *Creditors of Cockburn of Lanton* (1694) Mor 1054; *Scrymzeor* v. *Lyon* (1694) Mor 903. *Moncrief* would become the key authority on the point.
107 *Spence* v. *Creditors of Dick* (1692) Mor 1014; *Moncrief* v. *Creditors of Cockburn of Lanton* (1694) Mor 1054; *Moncrieff* v. *Lockhart* (1696) Mor 884.
108 1696 c. 5, *RPS* 1696/9/57.
109 As with the 1621 Act, the statute reflects foreign influence. Suspect periods prior to the moment of bankruptcy during which acts by the debtor are presumed to be fraudulent were known in both Italy and France in this period: Gerhardt, op. cit., 77–8 and 82–3. The idea of establishing bankruptcy on the basis of particular events which strongly suggest that debtor's inability to pay his creditors closely resembles the English concept of an "act of bankruptcy." On "acts of bankruptcy," see W.J. Jones, "The Foundations of English Bankruptcy: Statutes and Commission in the Early Modern Period," *Transactions of the American Philosophical Society* 69 (1979): 24–5.

110 *Miln* v. *Nicolson's Creditors* (1697) Mor 1046; *Deans* v. *Hamilton* (1703) Mor 1062; *Bank of Scotland* v. *Kennedy* (1708) Mor 1057; *Hamilton* v. *Campbell* (1709) Mor 1059.
111 The exception was *Deans* v. *Hamilton* (1703) Mor 1062.
112 *Tweddie* v. *Din* (1715) Mor 1037.
113 *Weems* v. *Murray* (1706) Mor 912; *Crammond* v. *Bruce* (1737) Mor 893.
114 *Cochrans* v. *Couts* (1747) Mor 947; *Grant* v. *Grant* (1748) Mor 949; *Brown* v. *Murray* (1754) Mor 886.
115 *Grant* v. *Grant* (1748) Mor 949.
116 See Lord Justice Clerk Hope *M'Cowan* v. *Wright* (1853) 15 D 494 at 500–1.
117 McBryde, op. cit., paras. 12.16 and 12.34.

14 Bankruptcy, fresh start and debt renegotiation in England and France (17th to 18th century)

Jérôme Sgard

Introduction

Bankruptcy is the ultimate market sanction. When markets fail to impose a change of course, a public institution should do the job and make sure that the distressed firm exits the market, that assets are restructured and that losses are shared among its creditors. Since medieval times, lawmakers have endlessly redesigned and reformed this intricate mechanism while also providing, occasionally, organizational support.

Lawmakers have sought to strike a balance between two wholly different publics that are potentially affected by bankruptcy law: the merchants and firms inside or outside market exchanges. If the whole population of market participants, say the solvent ones, is considered the most important, then bankruptcy should probably work, first of all, on an *ex ante* basis; i.e. it should make clear that bad decisions will involve high costs, so that managers think twice before adding more risk to their balance sheets. The harsher the expected treatment of bankrupts, the better: market discipline would be stronger, microeconomic decision closer to optimum, and welfare higher; or so the argument runs.

Alternately, lawmakers have also pursued a laissez-faire approach that leaves individual debtors and creditors in charge of resolving insolvencies. They are allowed to bargain *ex post* and adopt the solution to their own default that best suits their interests. After all, their own money is at stake and, besides, they have private information that should guide the decision on whether to liquidate or restructure the business. The downside risk is that the expectation of an easier way out of default may cause moral hazard, hence a weakening of market discipline and a looser pattern of capital allocation.[1]

Viewed in these terms, lawmakers appear historically to have moved between two options: what is for the agents to decide; what belongs to the public realm. The present contribution compares how early bankruptcy law in England and France stabilized on two opposite trade-offs as regard the *ex ante* versus *ex post* dilemma or, in other words, between market discipline as opposed to renegotiation. Specifically, the French tradition has always accepted the judicial confirmation of majority votes among creditors as a means to control holdout investors and reduced transaction costs when bargaining *ex post*. Statutes, in other words, assumed that supporting continuation arrangements was positive both in private and collective terms. As a consequence, this very peculiar forum that is being established by bankruptcy statutes has developed, since early modern times, as a judicial platform for private bargaining.

In England, on the other hand, this option was closed in the early seventeenth century, so that bankruptcy became a single entry/single exit process. Once it began, it led exclusively to liquidation. It worked, therefore, as a debt collection instrument, often a harsh one, that did not support businesses that had suffered a liquidity shock while remaining intrinsically solvent. Entrepreneurs had to be careful and limit risk-taking.

A historical sketch

Modern bankruptcy laws emerged in the trading cities of northern Italy, Florence, Pisa and Venice, among others, in the thirteenth and fourteenth centuries.[2] The opening of a bankruptcy procedure at that point already imposed on agents its sharp, defining brake with normal time contractual interaction: the capacity of creditors to trade-off alternate investments strategies was curtailed and the debtor's status was severely impinged. He was generally imprisoned and occasionally tortured, he could not trade anymore, his assets, books and correspondence were seized and his family was generally affected. The aim was first to control end-game problems in strategic interaction – creditors may seize assets, the debtor may flee the situation or adopt high-risk strategies to restructure or restart his business. Then, the debtor's property was seized and, quite often, sold, and the proceeds were shared among creditors on a *pro-rata* basis.

In the Italian tradition, however, the overall process could end either in straightforward liquidation or in a *concordato*, that is, a private continuation agreement, that typically allowed the debtor to recover his assets and restart trading with reduced or rescheduled debts. The critical point – where again the collective bears heavily on individual rights – is that a majority of qualified creditors (those whose debts had been recognized as legitimate) could bind dissenters; if needed, judicial confirmation would guarantee enforcement of the majority agreement. In other words, after the debtor had been legally expropriated, the creditors could have their individual contracts contravened. In both instances, confirmation by a sovereign authority was critical, though the actual decision typically remained in private hands.

These core Italian principles were then exported to the rest of Europe and absorbed in the statutes of the larger trading cities (Barcelona, Lyons, Antwerp, Bruges, Hamburg, etc.). As in Italy, the procedures were generally conducted by largely self-regulated, commercial courts, manned by judges elected by the merchants from their own ranks, sometimes assisted by learned lawyers. During the sixteenth century, emerging modern states started to introduce specific penal sanctions against failed debtors. These statutes were their first attempt at influencing the way market participants perceive failure and the associated threat of market exit.[3] More comprehensive, far-reaching developments took place during the seventeenth century: Italian institutions and cross-European commercial customs, known as the *lex mercatoria* (Law merchant), were progressively confirmed, absorbed and restructured into the new legal and judicial institutions.[4] Regulations that had worked in specific places and at specific times became the founding stones of emerging national legislation, enforced by new, territorial, mercantilist states. As such they came to apply to all traders, in all places within the realm.

Lyons and its renowned traders' court – *la Conservation de Lyon* – is generally considered the main place in France where the Italian and *lex mercatoria* traditions were aggregated and rewritten. Being a major European financial hub in the sixteenth and early seventeenth centuries, it attracted many Italian traders and bankers, who brought with them both private and public, economic institutions. These customs and rules were then confirmed by the monarchy before they became the main basis for the 1673 *Ordonnance du Commerce*. This summary version of the *lex mercatoria* was, in fact, the first modern commercial code, and a rather light and liberal one. Its long-standing influence in continental Europe was compounded by a series of additional, piecemeal royal decisions, as well as by a large body of case law and learned comments.[5] After the Revolution, its mark remained very strong on the 1808 *Code de commerce*, which would shape the legal field for at least another century. In this long run history, bankruptcy, which was addressed comprehensively in the 1673 text, presents the strongest elements of continuity.[6]

One of the most remarkable features of this French institution is how, under the *ancien régime*, two successive lines of defence protected the merchants' interests against rent-seeking forces that could have either forced their way on to the bargaining table or pre-empted the spoils of failed businesses, for instance by way of taxation. First, the jurisdictions in charge of bankruptcies, especially in the larger cities, were most often the *Cours Consulaires*: judges were elected by traders among themselves for two-year terms; justice was free of charge; rules of discovery and proof were simple; and an appeal did not usually suspend execution.[7] Second, even when the old civil jurisdictions were in charge of bankruptcies, they had to follow the *Ordonnance*, which made very clear that no judge, commercial or civil, had a say in the parties' decisions and that cash would never pass through the hands of bailiffs, notaries, police officers or "autres personnes publiques" (title 11, article 9). In other words, the risks that come with a statute that allows *de facto* intervention in private property were balanced by tangible guarantees that private parties would remain in control of the process. This was clearly not the case for most other jurisdictions, which at that time remained closely controlled by the King. When comparing the Italian–French tradition with the English one, it seems that an early, most significant bifurcation was caused by the gradual marginalization of the English medieval traders' courts (Piepowders and Staple courts) and, consequently, them being superseded by the common law courts. By the sixteenth century, the traders' courts were clearly on their way out at a time when their counterparts were blossoming on the continent.[8] Hence, in England, absorption of the *lex mercatoria* into the broader legal order would not be advanced by a specialized commercial jurisdiction, but primarily by the common law courts, with Equity courts and the Parliament playing a secondary role.[9] Certainly, there would be nothing like an *Ordonnance*, a comprehensive edict or *code*, adopted and enforced by the monarch.

Starting in 1543, bankruptcies were administrated by so-called "Bankruptcy Commissions," created on a case-by-case basis by Chancery after one or more creditors had petitioned the Lord Chancellor. Each commission was, therefore, a short-lived public authority, whose members were chosen from local notables and fellow traders. It received control over a debtor's assets, and it had the power to imprison or audit him, control debt titles, collect and sell assets and share the resulting dividends. Contrary to the comparatively well-established *Cours consulaires*, however, the judicial character of bankruptcy commissions was at best partial and their weaknesses regarding procedural guarantees were quite clear. At least until the eighteenth century, guidelines for decision-making were not explicit, recruitment was not strong and corruption is often mentioned. This relative weakness made an unpromising forum for open-ended bargaining among the parties, not to mention the possibility of confirming majority arrangements.

David Smith accounts for the long trial-and-error process, from the 1590s until the 1620s, whereby Equity courts tried to develop a viable procedure for confirming qualified majority votes among creditors.[10] But these attempts remained continuously under attack from both the Common Law courts and the Parliament, which perceived majority arrangement as an intolerable intervention into private rights. This conflict ended in Parliament, in 1624, when any attempt to force an involuntary accord on creditors was entirely forbidden and even penally sanctioned. From that point until the late nineteenth century, English bankruptcy procedures would only liquidate businesses, leaving no room for negotiation. The whole structure of the institution as well as the incentives that it created would thus develop along lines quite different from those observed in France and Italy.

Two legal architectures

Under the *ancien régime*, French law offered no less than four different options to address financial distress or default. They schematically derived from commercial, constitutional, civil and penal law, respectively; and these four entry gates then lead to a minimum of eight different possible exits.

First, the *faillite* was the standard commercial procedure, directly inherited from the Italian, medieval *fallimento*, a continuity that extends beyond the 1808 codification to the present. As in Italy, the *faillite* could end up first in liquidation (or *contrat d'union*): the proceeds of the auction were then distributed on a *pro-rata* basis among non-senior creditors, with senior rights being by definition protected.[11] The residual post-liquidation debts remained binding after the procedure had ended, so that individual creditors could again pursue the debtor and his possible new assets, whether they had been acquired by inheritance, marriage or work. Lastly, the debtor would not regain his civic and professional rights unless he reimbursed all his debts, as César Birroteau did at the end of Balzac's novel, immediately before dying. Hence, liquidation did not result in debt discharge and fresh start.

Alternately, the *faillite* could lead to a continuation arrangement, also called a *concordat* after 1808. The actual content of these accords was left for the private parties to bargain and agree upon: there was no notion that the law or any official could restrain their choice. If no unanimous support from the creditors could be reached, then a qualified majority of creditors and judicial confirmation would have to be obtained. In a typical agreement the debtor would then commit himself to new schedule of debt payments against concessions by the creditors or could receive a mandate to sell out his assets over a given period of time. This would be less shameful than liquidation and possibly more profitable.

Second, after the *faillite*, the *Lettre de Répit* was the second route towards financial restructuring. It was granted upon the demand of the debtor and it gave him some temporary relief in order to negotiate an arrangement.[12] Contrary to the *faillite*, which was shaped as a private, collective contract to be confirmed by the judiciary, the *Lettre de Répit* came from the sovereign and at his discretion. It was clearly shaped as an instrument to coerce the creditors, so that asking for a *Lettre* clearly indicated that direct negotiation had failed. Accordingly, reputational costs were much greater than in the *faillite*. Although the *Lettres* became increasingly regulated, especially under the 1673 *Ordonnance*, they raised considerable and apparently increasing resistance over the course of the eighteenth century; they were seen as a major source of fraud and dissimulation.[13] For this reason, long after they had been abolished in the 1808 *Code*, the entire legal profession remained thoroughly opposed to any method of settlement that would unfold out of court.

The third option, the cession, was a direct legacy of an antique form of collective action against debtors that originated in ancient Rome and re-emerged in the Middle Ages within the civil law.[14] The cession was the most common instrument of debt relief for non-traders, who did not have access to the *faillite*. The logic was that the debtor surrendered *voluntarily* all his goods and assets to his creditors, who then proceeded with selling them and sharing the return on a *pro-rata* basis. The main benefit for the debtor was that he avoided being adjudicated as a bankrupt and that all individual proceedings against him were cancelled, especially imprisonment for debt. Typically, he would be freed from jail and not threatened with further arrest or seizure, so that he would actually set about a "fresh start."[15]

Fourth and last, *la banqueroute* was the penal procedure associated with commercial failures that involved suspicion of fraud. It originated in the early, exclusively repressive statutes adopted during the sixteenth century. The 1673 *Ordonnance* then opposed *la faillite*, which remained a purely commercial procedure, administered by civil or trade courts, and *la banqueroute*; the 1808 *Code* then further distinguished, as a matter of degree, between *banqueroute simple* and *frauduleuse*.

Note also that the Italian and French tradition in matters of bankruptcy extends to virtually all continental Europe, over the whole period under review. Critically, during the early modern and modern periods, all continental statutes and codes included the possibility of confirming majority arrangements. Table 14.1 lists a series of statutes or legal treatises that explicitly make the point.[16]

When compared with the baroque French landscape, the English scene was much simpler: as noted, from the 1620s until the 1880s, once a bankruptcy procedure had been opened, liquidation was inevitable. Before 1705, the sole issue of common interest for creditors was the distribution of the proceeds. Room for collective information, deliberation or decision-making among the creditors was thus very limited. And if any unpaid debt remained after the procedure was closed, any new resources earned or inherited by the debtor could be seized. He could also be imprisoned again by any creditors for as long as they wanted. Fresh-start provisions were lacking in early English bankruptcy: Daniel Defoe, among many others, has described the dire fate of English bankrupts.[17] Business risks were further compounded by the absence of limited liability in partnership, of the *commenda* type.[18]

The 1705 *Act of Anne* brought more balance into the institution. Provided the debtor had transferred all his assets and a qualified majority (four-fifths in sum) of creditors had agreed, the debtor would be discharged of his residual liabilities and his old creditors would not be able to imprison him or seize his assets.[19] The main beneficiary of this reform was of course the proverbial "honest but unlucky trader" as opposed to the criminal one. This fresh-start rule had major social benefits. In the much-quoted commentary by Blackstone: "Thus the bankrupt becomes a clear man again; and … may become a useful member of the commonwealth" (1811, p. 488).[20] Since then, this reform has been hailed as the true birth of modern, pro-market bankruptcy law in England.[21]

Still, early English bankruptcy law retained an in-built preference for *ex ante* market discipline against *ex post* negotiation and fresh-start. Even in its post-1705 version, the whole regime resembled very much the old, restrictive Roman *cessio*.[22] In practice, when firms had to be restructured and their going concern

Table 14.1 Majority arrangements in continental Europe

Italy	Bologna (1509), Florence (1322, 1415, 1585), Siena (1619), Venice (1395), Genoa (1589)
Flanders (Antwerp)	Statute (1615)
Republic of Geneva	*Statuts de la République de Genève* (1713)
Hamburg	Statute on bankruptcy (1753)
Nuremberg	Statutes (1517, 1634)
Prussia	Code Prussien (1794)
Austria	Statute 1734, 1781
Spain	*Ordenanzas* of Bilbao (1737)
Low Countries	Amsterdam 1659 statute (*Kamer van der Desolate Boedels*)
France	Bounyn (Paris, 1586), Mareschal (Paris, 1625), *Le stile de la jurisdiction royale établie dans la ville de Lyon* (Lyon, 1657), *Ordonnance sur le commerce* (Paris, 1673)

value preserved, agents had to bargain out-of-court, proceeding on a voluntary basis under private deeds. While this approach was more respectful of private property rights, it was also confounded by obvious problem of collection action.[23] The common law courts proved quite helpful at this point, however, as they supported the gradual development of a legal framework that mitigated these obstacles to negotiating arrangements. This parallel route to restructuring emerged during the later half of the eighteenth and the early decades of the nineteenth century. By the 1780s, a large body of precedents had given strong legal foundation to this private law institution, which was now a major feature of the overall English insolvency regime.[24] Indeed, at that time, there was apparently a strong consensus whereby a liquidation-only bankruptcy law, plus voluntary private arrangements, plus discharge, offered a satisfactory response to the *ex ante* versus *ex post* dilemma.

Two economic logics

These opposite roads taken by English and French laws are then prolonged by a series of secondary patterns. While they have typically been studied in the literature as self-standing issues, they should in fact be brought into a broader, comparative perspective.

First, the initiation of bankruptcy was associated in England with an observable "Act of Bankruptcy," originally a reprehensible one that allowed one or some creditors to petition for a commission.[25] From there on, as noted, liquidation was inevitable. French law, on the other hand, envisaged the opening of a procedure as a response to the underlying economic state of a firm and what the consequences of that state might be. "Un commerçant est en faillite, ou tombe en faillite," as the contemporary language still has it. Of course, insolvency was the issue at stake, whatever the major difficulties that were encountered when attempting to qualify this unenviable "state." Judges also looked for directly observable, if elusive, signs or acts that would reveal insolvency. Typically, if the debtors flew away, or if a series of individual procedures were opened by independent creditors, the situation was clear. Still procedures founded on a human act or an unobservable state of nature are doomed to be structured very differently, critically as regards incentives.

Second, the adjudication of bankruptcy as a consequence of the observation of certain "acts" implied, in England, that procedures were opened only on an "involuntary" basis. Before 1705, the threat of life-long prison made implausible the alternate "voluntary" road initiated by the debtor. Later, the possibility of discharge only added new reasons for leaving control in the hands of creditors. Alternately, in France, where the procedure was framed as a platform for negotiation, there was no reason at all to restrict entry: mutual control would take place, provided the internal architecture of the institution was adequate. And indeed, historically, there is almost no debate in France on the principle that bankruptcy might be voluntary, whereas this is a most important issue in the Anglo-American historical literature.[26] By the same token, the opposition between pro-debtor and pro-creditor statutes is also very much an Anglo-American concern; open-ended negotiation tends to shift the focus on relationships among creditors, hence on the balance between pro-liquidation and pro-continuation interests, or between senior and juniors interests.

Third, the French notion of an *état de faillite* also invites an inquiry into the reason for the failure and the prospect of recovery. Its sheer ambiguity makes explicit the need to address an in-built informational problem. Moreover, the institution's primary objective of supporting private renegotiation also demands that all available information should be collected, centralized and shared among all parties. Accounts and correspondence are to be open, the debtor should be interrogated, the cause of his failure queried, experts consulted, as the 1673 *Ordonnance* made clear. In the English framework, there was certainly a need to identify all assets and to check, for instance, that false creditors did not attempt to join the distribution of dividends. Successive statutes included regulations to this effect. Yet, because the enterprise closed once a commission had been created, the examination of reasons for failure and prospects for recovery was a secondary concern. An institution that was wholly bent on *ex ante* market incentives faced much fewer requirements in terms of *ex post* discovery.

Fourth, a corollary of its single-exit approach is that disentangling the penal and civil dimensions in bankruptcy proved much more difficult in England. Because there was no way for the debtor to negotiate an arrangement and regain the management of his assets, no internal logic pushed for a differentiation between statuses. In the French case, the very possibility of continuation made it necessary to differentiate early on between merchants who should be allowed to negotiate and resume trading, and those who had acted in a reprehensible manner. This modern principle was already stated in a 1629 reform proposal,[27] and it became a defining principle of the 1673 *Ordonnance.* As mentioned, *la faillite* (title 11, articles 2–9) was explicitly designed as a civil framework for renegotiation, while *la banqueroute* (title 11, articles 10–13) implied crime and prosecution.[28]

Fifth and last, of course, is the contrast between the two traditions as regards the scope of out-of-court settlements. Certainly, as in all commercial countries, avoiding bankruptcy has always been the first-best option of all merchants and bankers. The difference here is about the support received, more generally, from the law and the enforcement agencies. In France bargaining on a private basis remained very much informal and narrow in scope. Significantly, such agreements would take the form of a series of bilateral accords between the debtor and each creditor. No "legal envelope" was available that could help them bring together their interests. English merchants, on the other hand, received much more support from case law. Critically, from the eighteenth century onward, they could pool their assets into a trust that would formalize and preserve their joint interest in the successful recovery of the firm.

Table 14.2 Two institutional logics

	England	*France*
Bankruptcy statutes		
Possible outcomes	Liquidation only	Liquidation or renegotiation
Institutional structure	Administrative	Judicial
Signal/criteria	Acts of bankruptcy	*État de faillite*
Initiation	Involuntary only	Involuntary and voluntary
Role for discovery	Limited	Important
Qualified majority vote	Impossible	Standard
Debt discharge and fresh start	After 1705	Always there
Distinction between penal and civil dimensions	Late and difficult	Intrinsic
Main expected benefit of the law	*Ex ante* market discipline	*Ex post* absorption of exogenous shocks
Main downside risk of the law	Undue liquidations	Moral hazard
Out-of-courts arrangements		
Private agreements	Most common	Most common
Capacity to design permanent, post-negotiation, collective arrangements	Large (from late-eighteenth century onwards)	Nonexistent
Willingness of the courts to sanction private innovation	Substantial	Limited

Conclusion

The parallel developments of bankruptcy laws in England and France, between the seventeenth and the nineteenth centuries, highlight their joint origin in the early mercantilist period. Both were part of the early attempts at building national trade legislations on a par with the law of debt instruments or company statutes. For the same reason, bankruptcy procedures became in both countries a major issue in the struggle among various courts for the jurisdiction over commercial issues.

In France, an unruly, despotic state entered *de facto* into a side-commitment with merchant communities that allowed them to settle contractual disputes on their own. The *lex mercatoria* was thus enforced and interpreted by elected commercial courts, or *Cours consulaires*, before being confirmed by the King. In order to prosper, commerce had to be insulated from rent-seeking interests that were powerful before the Revolution. This suggests that the remarkably lean and modern features of the 1673 text reflected ultimately the archaic character of the *ancien régime*: tight insulation of merchant interests against rent-seeking interests apparently allowed the design of a rather clear-cut, pro-business institution. Because it only affected a small segment of the population, it was allowed to take a highly abstract, impersonal, context-free character that cut through all the multiple jurisdictions and local legal regimes that were common in pre-1789 France. Hence the enduring influence of the *Ordonnance* over the following centuries. In other words, this was codification at its best: clearly rooted in the international practice of merchants and bankers, though also rational, simple and clear.

Whereas the success of English common law courts in gaining jurisdiction over commerce reflected, arguably, the superior guarantees that they offered generally to litigants. Absorbing commercial issues and concerns for market efficiency proved a most complex, convoluted process. Among other legal institutions, an archaic bankruptcy framework was a significant side-cost of this institutional pattern. The disincentives to entrepreneurship and risk-taking are striking at this point. Furthermore, what is most remarkable is how the common law courts developed, over several decades, a secondary set of private law rules that eventually offered much support to the parties, as they bargained out of court.

Whereas today's *Tribunaux de Commerce* remain remarkably similar in France to their *ancien régime* forbearers, the large role still given to out-of-court settlements in England offers a similar echo of the early modern experience. In the former, continental case, institutional resilience reflects a long-standing (and still active) strategy of insulation against infringements by competing jurisdictions. In the English case, rigid statutes protect the parties from the intrinsic weaknesses, if not the corruption, of bankruptcy commissions simply by limiting their discretion. Then, the courts developed a powerful framework for private arrangements as an alternate means to restructuring and continuation.

In both cases, therefore, path-dependency reflects alternate strategies, developed centuries ago, in order to control the risk of regulatory capture by rent-seeking interests, at a time when they exercised vital threats on fledgling market interests.

Notes

1 The expectation that *ex post* renegotiation may have adverse *ex ante* effects on contract implementation is primarily associated with the works of Janos Kornaï. Its core concept of soft *versus* hard budget constraints was built on the account of the widespread inefficiency of resource allocation, in soviet-type, centrally planned economies. The standard model was formulated by M. Dewatripont, E. Maskin, "Credit and Efficiency in Centralized and Decentralized Economies," *Review of Economic Studies* 62 (1995): 541–555. For an overview of the literature, see J. Kornaï, E. Maskin and G. Roland, "Understanding the Soft Budget Constraint," *Journal of Economic Literature* 41 (2003): 1095–1136.

2 U. Santarelli, *Per la storia del fallimento delle legislazioni italiene dell'età intermedia* (Padua 1964); Kohler, *Lehrbuch des Konkursrecht* (Stuttgart 1892); J. Hilaire, *Introduction historique au droit commercial* (Paris 1985).

3 These first such statutes were enacted respectively in 1543 and 1571 in England, and in 1536 and 1560 in France.

4 The exact legal quality of the law merchant and the history of its absorption into state-sanctioned legal orders are two topics on which consensus knowledge is still limited. This is especially the case in France, where a large part of available research still dates from turn of the twentieth century. Neither is the literature unanimous when accounting the influence of the *lex mercatoria* in England. Jones considers its impact as negligible in W.J. Jones, "The Foundation of English Bankruptcy: Statutes and

Commissions in the Early Modern Period," *Transactions of the American Philosophical Society* 69 (1979). Holdsworth and Treiman, on the other hand, endow it with much more influence. See, W.S. Holdsworth, "The Rule of Venue and the Beginning of the Commercial Jurisdiction of the Common Law Courts," *Columbia Law Review* 14 (1914): 551–562; I. Treiman, "Majority Control in Compositions: Its Historical Origins and Development," *Virginia Law Review* 24 (1938): 507–527. On the *lex mercatoria* in England, see also W.S. Holdsworth, "The Development of the Law Merchant and Its Courts," *Select Essays in Anglo-American Legal History*, I (1907); C. Gross and H. Hall (eds.), *Select Cases Concerning the Law Merchant, Volume I* (London 1907); L.S. Sutherland, *The Law Merchant in England in the Seventeenth and Eighteenth Centuries* (London 1934); C. Donahue, "The Empirical and Theoretical Underpinnings of the Law Merchant," *Chicago Journal of International Law* 5 (2004): 21–38.

5 Savary's *Parfait Négociant* (1675) is by far the most famous commentary and was re-edited and translated until the end of the eighteenth century. Other treaties include: J. Toubeau, *Les institutes du droit consulairs, ou la jurisprudence des marchands* (Paris 1682), Ph. Bornier, *Ordonnance de Louis XIV sur le commerce, enrichie d'annotations et de decisions importantes* (Paris 1749); M. Rogue, *Jurisprudence consulaire, et instruction des négotiants* (Angers 1773).

6 Immediately before the new *Code* was adopted, Boileau published an elegant summary of the practice of bankruptcy in France, as it had evolved since 1673. See L.J. de Boileau, *Code des faillites* (Paris 1806). For a more detailed study, see J.-L. Laurens, *Traité des faillites et banqueroutes* (Paris 1806). Renouard offers a representative nineteenth-century view of the pre-1808 legislation and a comment on the Code and its first reforms. See A.-Ch. Renouard, *Traité des faillites et banqueroutes* (Paris 1857).

7 On the eighteenth-century Parisian *Cours consulaire*, see A. Kessler, *A Revolution in Commerce* (Paris 2007). For a fine monograph on Lille, see J.-P. Hirsch, *Le deux rêves du commerce* (Paris 1992). Also a number of contributions published in *Les Tribunaux de Commerce* (2007).

8 Many scholars agree that traders' courts were marginalized early on, but they also admit to not having a satisfactory explanation of this fact. See W.S. Holdsworth, "The Rule of Venue," *Columbia Law Review* 14 (1914): 551–562; Sutherland *The Law Merchant in England*; M.J. Holden, *The History of Negotiable Instruments in English Law* (London 1955); J.H. Baker, "Merchant and the Common Law Before 1700," *Cambridge Law Journal* 38 (1979): 295–322.

9 The literature is far from unanimous in assessing the medieval *lex mercatoria* in England. Some scholars hail it as a self-standing legal order with a specific and enduring influence. See, for example: Holdsworth "The Development of the Law Merchant and Its Courts," 289, 292–293; Gross and Hall, *Select Cases*, Vol. I; F.M. Burdick, *Contributions of the Law Merchant to the Common Law* (London 1909); and Treiman, "Majority Control in Compositions." Recent literature is far more circumspect, see: Baker, "Merchant and the Common Law Before 1700"; J.S. Rogers, *The Early History of the Bills and Notes* (Cambridge, UK 1995); M.E. Basile, J.F. Bestor, D.R. Coquillette and D. Donahue, Jr., *Lex Mercatoria and Legal Pluralism* (Cambridge, MA 1998); Donahue, "The Empirical and Theoretical Underpinnings of the Law Merchant." Note also that in general the comparative dimension in this debate is weak. Continental scholars often consider England an economic sideshow until the late sixteenth century, while their English-language counterparts generally ignore the continental literature, most patently the Italian. See, however, F. Galgano, *Lex Mercatoria* (Bologna 1976) or Padoa Schioppa's many writings.

10 D.A. Smith, "The Development of the Bill of Conformity, 1603–1624," *Mimeo*, American Society of Legal History Annual Conference (Baltimore 2006). It is not clear to what extent the Italian *concordato* was practised in England before the late

sixteenth century. The main authority supporting this proposition is Malynes, but few other authors concur.

11 Under the *Ordonnance*, a majority of creditors, representing three-quarters of the total junior debt, was needed in order to receive confirmation.

12 The *Lettres de Répits* were issued by the *Chancellerie*, and the *Lettres de Défense Générale* by courts; the *Arrêt de surséance*, finally, was issued by the *Conseil du Roi.*

13 See, for instance, *Le nouveau commentaire des loix du commerce*, 1787; or Bornier, *Ordonnance de Louis VIC sur le commerce* and J.B. Denisart, *Collection de décisions nouvelles et de notions relatives à la jurisprudence actuelle* (Paris 1771).

14 The cession would then find its way in the 1804 *Code Civil*, rather than in the 1808 *Code de Commerce*, the third book of which was entirely devoted to *faillites et banqueroutes*.

15 This actually describes the voluntary version of the cession that took the form of a contract between debtor and creditors. A judicial version, mandated by a court and imposed upon creditors, was considered highly infamous and implied permanent losses of civic and professional rights (unless the whole debt was later repaid).

16 In England, the return to some formula for confirming a majority vote under bankruptcy was quite difficult; only a succession of failed reforms in 1825, 1849, 1861 and 1869 eventually delivered the 1883 Act. From then on, a judicial procedure working on a standard, "continental" majority basis worked in tandem with private compositions, which apparently remained the norm for the largest businesses. This latter, typically English, private law approach remains common today under the name of the "London Approach." See J. Armou and S. Deakin, "Norms in Private Bankruptcy: The 'London Approach' to the Resolution of Financial Distress," University of Cambridge ESRC Working Paper, No. 17 (2000). It is actually strongly defended both by the authorities and by the media, most clearly against the influence of the more heavy-handed US Chapter 11. For the former, see P. Brierley and G. Vlieghe, "Corporate Workouts, the London Approach and Financial Stability," *Financial Stability Review* (1999): 168–183; for the latter, see J. Willman, "Salvage System Faces its Toughest Test," *Financial Times* (20 July 2008).

17 Bankruptcy

> has something in it of Barbarity; ... It contrives all the ways possible to drive the Debtor to despair, and encourages no new Industry, for it makes him perfectly incapable of anything but starving. This Law, especially as it is now frequently executed, tend wholly to the Destruction of the Debtor, and yet very little to the Advantage of the Creditor.
>
> (D. Defoe, *An Essay Upon Projects* (Rockville 2008), 88)

18 R. Harris, Industrializing English Law: Entrepreneurship and Business Organization (Cambridge, UK 2000).

19 On the Act of Anne, see E. Kaddens, "The Last Bankrupt Hanged: Capital Punishment for Bankruptcy in 18th Century England," *Duke Law Journal* 59 (2010). On the history of debt discharge more generally, see D.G. Boshkoff, "Limited, Conditional and Suspended Discharge in Anglo-American Bankruptcy Proceedings," *University of Pennsylvania Law Review* 131 (1982): 69–125; C.J. Tabb, "The Historical Evolution of the Bankruptcy Discharge," *American Bankruptcy Law Journal* 65 (1991): 5–51. On eighteenth-century bankruptcy practices in England, see among others J. Hoppit, *Risk and Failure in English Business, 1700–1800* (Cambridge, UK 1987).

20 Sir W. Blackstone, *Commentaries on the Laws of England* (London 1811).

21 The comprehensive Bankruptcy Act of 1732 only rehearsed and added formal clarity to the existing regulations; this code then remained the touchstone of legislation until 1825.

22 The point is also underlined by Blackstone, *Commentaries on the Laws of England*, 472.

23 This latter rule was not completely remorseless: many commentators noted that debtors remained morally obliged to their creditors after they had benefited from a *concordat*. The true custom of merchants, they suggested, probably condemned majority votes; but they would immediately add that, quite reasonably, judges never endorsed such principle and indeed helped control collective-action problems.

24 Available analysis and documentation on these arrangements are sparse, however. These accords being private, the archives are apparently rare and fragmented. See Hoppit, *Risk and Failure*; T.M. Luckett, "Credit and Commercial Society in France, 1740–1789" (unpub. Ph.D. diss., Yale University, 1992); and, critically, B. Montagu, *A Summary of the Law of Composition with Creditors* (London 1823). In what is possibly the first treatise on private compositions, the author, a former bankruptcy commissioner, comments on tens of cases brought to the courts, mostly during the four preceding decades. Forsyth also mentions that these agreements were "common practice" and that they benefited from "the constant anxiety by the English Courts of law and equity to uphold and give effect to such arrangements." See Forsyth, *A Treatise of the Law relating to Compositions with Creditors* (London 1841). He then differentiates between *assignments* that transferred the debtor's property to one or more creditors, who would act as trustees and liquidate the estate, and *deeds of inspectorship*, that allowed the debtor to manage the firm though under the control of an agent of creditors.

25 Initially, the concept of a penal act of bankruptcy responded to the intent of Common Law to protect private property. Defining the bankrupt as a criminal was the only means actually to take the control of all his assets and share the proceeds.

26 "One of the most fascinating tales in the development of bankruptcy jurisprudence concerns the monumental transformation by which the unthinkable – voluntary bankruptcy – became commonplace." D. Baird, "The Initiation Problem in Bankruptcy," *11th International Review of Law and Economics* 223 (1991): 142. See also, J.C. McCoid, "The Origins of Voluntary Bankruptcy," *Bankruptcy Development Journal* 5 (1998): 361–389.

27 The *Code Michaud*, written in 1629 but never enacted, already introduced this difference.

28 Under the *Ordonnance* as under the *Code*, prosecution would immediately close the door to composition.

Bibliography

Abu-Lughod, J., *Before European Hegemony: The World System A.D. 1250–1350* (Oxford 1989).

Ajello, P., "I depositi, le fedi di credito e le polizze dei Banchi di Napoli," in: R. Filangieri (ed.), *Storia del Banco di Napoli: I Banchi di Napoli dalle origini alla costituzione del Banco delle due Sicilie, 1539–1808* (Naples 1940).

Ankum, J.A., *De Geschiedenis der "*Actio Pauliana*"* (Zwolle 1962).

Arru, A., de Rosa, M.R. and Muldrew, C., *Debiti e crediti*, special issue of *Quaderni Storici*, 47 (2011).

Avallone, P., *Stato e banchi pubblici a Napoli a metà del '700: Il Banco dei Poveri: una svolta* (Naples 1995).

Avallone, P., "Delitti e castighi nei banchi pubblici napoletani tra XVII e XVIII secolo," in: L. Cajani (ed.), *Criminalità, giustizia penale e ordine pubblico nell'Europa Moderna* (Milan 1997), 171–98;

Banchi pubblici, banchi privati e monti di pietà nell'Europa preindustriale: amministrazione, tecniche operative e ruoli economici. Atti del convegno, Genova 1–6 ottobre 1990 (Genoa 1991).

Barbour, V., *Capitalism in Amsterdam in the Seventeenth Century* (Ann Arbor, MI 1963).

Bauer, C., *Unternehmung und Unternehmungsformen im Spätmittelalter und in der beginnenden Neuzeit* (Jena 1934).

Beachy, R., "Bankruptcy and Social Death: The Influence of Credit-Based Commerce on Cultural and Political Values," *Zeitsprünge. Forschungen zur Frühen Neuzeit* 4 (2000): 329–43.

Becker, C. (ed.), *"Consuetudines almae Reipublicae Augustanae" von Matthaeus Laimann und Georg Tradel mit "Notwendigs Bedenckhen" von Georg Tradel: Eine Zusammenstellung Augsburger Stadtrechts mit einer Denkschrift zu seiner Reform vom Ende des sechzehnten Jahrhunderts* (Berlin 2008).

Becker, C., "Bancarottierer" *Konkurs, Treuhand, Sanierung: Zeitschrift für Insolvenzrecht* (2008).

Becker, C., *Insolvenzrecht* (Cologne 2010).

Beckmann, J. and Bergius, J., *Sammlung auserlesener teutschen Landesgesetze, welche das Policey- und Cameralwesen zum Gegenstande haben*, 14 vols. (Frankfurt am Main 1781–1793).

Bell, G.J., *Commentaries on the Law of Scotland*, 7th ed., edited by J. M'Laren (Edinburgh 1870).

Bouvier, J., "Vers le capitalisme bancaire: l'expansion du crédit après Law," in: F. Braudel and E. Labrousse (eds.), *Histoire économique et sociale de la France, 1660–1789*, Vol. II (Paris 1970).

Boyer-Xambeau, M.-T., Delaplace, G. and Gillard, L., *Private Money and Public Currencies in the Sixteenth Century Challenge* (Paris 1994).

Braudel, F., *Civilisation matérielle, économie et capitalisme, Xve–XVIIIe siècle*, 3 vols. (Paris 1979).

Braudel, F., *Civilization and Capitalism: 15th–18th Century*, 3 vols. (New York 1981/1984).

Brook, T. and Luong, H.V. (eds.), *Culture and Economy: The Shaping of Capitalism in Eastern Asia* (Ann Arbor, MI 1997).

Carande R., *Carlos V y sus banqueros* (Madrid 1949).

Carande R., *El crédito de Castilla en el precio de la politíca imperial* (Madrid 1949).

Carrière, C., *Négociants marseillais au XVIIIe siècle: contribution à l'étude des économies maritimes*, 2 vols. (Marseille 1973).

Cassis, Y., *Capitals of Capital: A History of International Financial Centres, 1780–2005* (Cambridge, UK 2006).

Chassagne, S., "Faillis en Anjou au XVIIIe siècle: Contribution à l'histoire économique d'une province," *Annales. Économies, sociétés, civilisations* 2 (1970): 477–97.

Chaunu, H. and Chaunu, P., *Séville et l'Atlantique*, 8 vols. (Paris 1955/1959).

Cipolla, C.M., *Money in Sixteenth-Century Florence* (Berkeley, CA 1989).

Coleman, P.J. *Debtors and Creditors in America: Insolvency, Imprisonment for Debt, and Bankruptcy, 1607–1900* (Madison, WI 1974).

Coquery, N., *Tenir boutique à Paris au XVIIIe siècle. Luxe et demi-luxe* (Paris 2011).

Dalrymple, J., Viscount Stair, *The Institutions of the Law of Scotland*, edited by D. Walker (Edinburgh 1981).

Day, J., *Money and Finance in the Age of Merchant Capitalism* (Oxford 1999).

De Simone, L., *La fede di credito* (Naples 1922).

De Stefano, M., *Banchi e vicende monetarie nel Regno di Napoli, 1600–1625* (Livorno 1940).

Demarco, D., *Storia del Banco di Napoli: Il Banco delle Due Sicilie, 1808–1863* (Naples 1958).

Demars-Sion, V., "Contribution à l'histoire de la faillite: étude sur la cession de biens à la fin de l'Ancien Régime," *Revue historique de droit français et étranger* 75 (1997): 33–91.

Dickson, P.G.M., *Finance and Government under Maria Theresia 1740–1780*, 2 vols. (Oxford 1987).

Dillen, J.G. van, *A History of the Principal Public Banks* (The Hague 1934).

Doucet, R., *L'état des finances en 1567* (Paris 1929).

Doucet, R., *La Banque Capponi à Lyons en 1556* (Paris 1939).

Duffy, I., *Bankruptcy and Insolvency in London during the Industrial Revolution* (New York 1985).

Ehrenberg, R., *Die Zeitalter der Fugger: Geldkapital und Creditverkehr im 16. Jahrhundert*, 2 vols. (Jena 1896).

Eigner, P. and Štefanová, D. (eds.), *Banken und Unternehmenskultur* (Vienna 2009).

Filangieri, R., *Storia del Banco di Napoli: I Banchi di Napoli dalle origini alla costituzione del Banco delle due Sicilie, 1539–1808* (Naples 1940).

Finn, M.C., *The Character of Credit: Personal Debt in English Culture, 1740–1914* (Cambridge, UK 2003).

Fontaine, L., "Antonio and Shylock: Credit and Trust in France, *c.*1680–*c.*1780," *Economic History Review* 1 (2001): 39–57.

Fornasari, M., *Famiglia e affari in età moderna: I Ghelli di Bologna* (Bologna 2002).

Forner i Delaygua, J.J., *La protección del crédito en Europa: La acción pauliana* (Barcelona 2000).

Frank, A.G., *ReORIENT: Global Economy in the Asian Age* (Berkeley, CA 1998).

Frank, A.G. and Gill, B.K. (eds.), *The World System: Five Hundred Years or Five Thousand?* (London 1993).

Gerhardt, W., *Die systematische Einordnung der Gläubigeranfechtung* (Göttingen 1969).

Gerschenkron, A., *Economic Backwardness in Historical Perspective: A Book of Essays* (Cambridge, MA 1966).

Goldthwaite, R., *Private Wealth in Renaissance Florence* (Princeton, NJ 1968).

Gorißen, S., "Der Preis des Vertrauens: Unsicherheit, Institutionen und Rationalität im vorindustriellen Fernhandel," in: Ute Frevert (ed.), *Vertrauen: Historische Annäherungen* (Göttingen 2003), 90–118.

Goudy, H., *Treatise on the Law of Bankruptcy*, 4th edn, edited by T.A. Fyfe (Edinburgh 1914).

Greif, A., *Institutions and the Path to the Modern Economy* (Cambridge, UK 2006).

Grenier, J.-Y., *L'Économie d'Ancien Régime: Un monde de l'échange et de l'incertitude* (Paris 1996).

Guerra, E.G. and De Luca, G. (eds.), *Il mercato del credito in età moderna: Reti e operatori finanziari nello spazio europeo* (Milan 2009).

Häberlein, M., *Brüder, Freunde und Betrüger: Soziale Beziehungen, Normen und Konflikte in der Augsburger Kaufmannschaft um die Mitte des 16. Jahrhunderts* (Berlin 1998).

Häberlein, M.,"Firmenbankrotte, Sozialbeziehungen und Konfliktlösungsmechanismen in süddeutschen Städten um 1600," *Österreichische Zeitschrift für Geschichtswissenschaften* 19 (2008): 10–35.

Hassenpflug-Elzholz, E., *Böhmen und die böhmischen Stände in der Zeit des beginnenden Absolutismus: Eine Strukturanalyse der böhmischen Adelsnation um die Mitte des 18. Jahrhundert* (Munich 1982).

Hellmann, F., *Das Konkursrecht der Reichsstadt Augsburg* (Breslau 1905).

Hilaire, J., *Introduction historique au droit commercial* (Paris 1986).

Hildebrandt, R., "Wirtschaftsentwicklung und Konzentration im 16. Jahrhundert: Konrad Rot und die Finanzierungsprobleme seines interkontinentalen Handels," *Scripta Mercaturae* 4 (1970): 25–50.

Hildebrandt, R., "Zum Verhältnis von Wirtschaftsrecht und Wirtschaftspraxis im 16. Jahrhundert: Die Fallitenordnungen des Augsburger Rates 1564–1580," in: A. Mächler, E. Grünert, H. Kraemer and K.-R. Seidel (eds.), *Historische Studien zu Politik, Verfassung und Gesellschaft: Festschrift für Richard Dietrich zum 65. Geburtstag* (Bern 1976), 153–60.

Hirschman, A.O., *The Passions and the Interests: Political Arguments for Capitalism before its Triumph* (Princeton, NJ 1977).

Hoffman P.T. and Norberg, K. (eds.), *Fiscal Crises, Liberty, and Representative Government, 1450–1789* (Stanford, CA 1994).

Hoffman, P.T., Postel-Vinay, G. and Rosenthal, J.-L., *Priceless Markets: The Political Economy of Credit in Paris, 1660–1870* (Chicago, IL 2000).

Hoppit, J., *Risk and Failure in English Business, 1700–1800* (Cambridge, UK 1987).

Jones, J.W., *The Foundations of English Bankruptcy. Statutes and Commissions in the Early Modern Period* (Philadelphia, PA 1979).

Justice commerciale et histoire économique, special issue of *Histoire & Mesure*, 23 (2008).

Kadens, E., "The Last Bankrupt Hanged: Balancing Incentives in the Development of Bankruptcy Law," *Duke Law Journal* 59 (2010): 1229–319.

Kellenbenz, H., "Le banqueroute de Melchior Manlich en 1574 et ses répercussions en France," in: *Villes, bonnes villes, cités et capitals: Études d'histoire urbaine (12e–18e siècle) offertes à Bernard Chevalier* (Tours 1989), 153–9.

Kerridge, E., *Trade and Banking in Early Modern England* (Manchester 1988).

Kessler, A.D., *A Revolution in Commerce: The Parisian Merchant Court and the Rise of Commercial Society in Eighteenth-Century France* (New Haven, CT 2007).

Köstlin, R., "Darstellung der Lehre vom strafbaren Bankerott überhaupt und besonders nach der neueren deutschen Gesetzgebung," *Archiv für preußisches Strafrecht* 5 (1857): 721–44.

Lamoreaux, N.R., *Insider Lending: Banks, Personal Connections and Economic Development in Industrial New England* (Cambridge, UK 1996).

Lapeyre, H., *Simon Ruiz et les Asientos de Philippe II* (Paris 1954).

Lapeyre, H., *Une famille de marchands: Les Ruiz* (Paris 1955).

Léon, P. (ed.), *Histoire économique et sociale du monde*, Vol. III (Paris 1978).

Liedl, E., *Gerichtsverfassung und Zivilprozess der freien Reichsstadt Augsburg* (Augsburg 1958).

Luckett, T., "Credit and Commercial Society in France, 1740–1789" (unpub. Ph.D. diss., Princeton University, 1992).

Lüthy, H., *La Banque Protestante en France*, 2 vols. (Paris 1959/1961).

McBryde, W.W., *Bankruptcy* (Edinburgh 1995).

McDouall, A., Lord Bankton, *Institute of the Laws of Scotland* (Edinburgh 1993).

Mackenzie, G., "Observations upon the 18th Act of the 23d Parliament of King James the Sixth against Dispositions made in Defraud of Creditors," in: *The Works of that Eminent and Learned Lawyer, Sir George Mackenzie of Rosehaugh*, Vol. II (Edinburgh 1722).

Mann, B.H., *Republic of Debtors: Bankruptcy in the Age of American Independence* (Cambridge, MA 2002).

Marsilio, C., *Dove il denaro fa denaro: Gli operatori finanziari genovesi nelle fiere di cambio del XVII secolo* (Novi Ligure 2008).

Martin, J.-C., "Le commerçant, la faillite et l'historien," *Annales. Économies, sociétés, civilisations* 6 (1980): 1251–68.

Mathias, P., "Risk, Credit and Kinship in Early Modern Enterprise," in: J.J. McCusker and K. Morgan (eds.), *The Early Modern Atlantic Economy* (Cambridge, UK 2000).

Meuvret, J., "Circulation monétaire et utilisation économique de la monnaie dans la France du XVIe et du XVIIe siècle," in: *Études d'histoire économique. Recueil d'articles. Cahier des Annales*, Vol. 32 (Paris 1971).

Muldrew, C., *The Economy of Obligation: The Culture of Credit and Social Relations in Early Modern England* (New York 1998).

Müller, J., "Der Zusammenbruch des Welserschen Handelshauses im Jahr 1614," *Vierteljahresschrift für Sozial- und Wirtschaftsgeschichte* 1 (1903): 196–234.

Müller, K.O., *Welthandelsbräuche, 1480–1540* (Stuttgart 1934).

North, D.C., *Institutions, Institutional change and Economic Performance* (Cambridge, UK 1990).

North, D.C., *Understanding the Process of Economic Change* (Princeton, NJ 2005).

Ogilvie, S., "The Use and Abuse of Trust: Social Capital and its Development by Early Modern Guilds," *Jahrbuch für Wirtschaftsgeschichte* (2005): 15–52.

Paulus, C., "Entwicklungslinien des Insolvenzrechts," *Konkurs, Treuhand, Sanierung: Zeitschrift für Insolvenzrecht* (2000).

Piergiovanni, V. (ed.), *The Courts and the Development of Commercial Law* (Berlin 1987).

Reynard, P.C., "The Language of Failure: Bankruptcy in Eighteenth-Century France," *Journal of European Economic History* 30 (2001): 355–90.

Rocco, M., *De' Banchi di Napoli e della loro ragione*, Vols. I–III (Naples 1785–1787).

Rosa, L. de, *Il Mezzogiorno spagnolo tra crescita e decadenza* (Milan 1987).

Roover, R. de, *Money, Banking and Credit in Medieval Bruges* (Cambridge, MA 1948).

Safley, T.M., "Bankruptcy: Family and Finance in Early Modern Augsburg," *Journal of European Economic History* 29 (2000).

Safley, T.M., "Business Failure and Civil Scandal in Early Modern Europe," *Business History Review* 83 (2009): 35–60.

Sandage, S.A., *Born Losers: A History of Failure in America* (Cambridge, MA 2005).

Santarelli, U., *Per la storia del fallimento nelle legislazioni italiane dell'età intermedia* (Padua 1964).

Sella, D., *Crisis and Continuity: The Economy of Spanish Lombardy in the Seventeenth Century* (Cambridge, MA 1979).

Sgard, J., "Do Legal Origins Matter? The Case of Bankruptcy Laws in Europe 1808–1914," *European Review of Economic History* 10 (2006): 389–419.

Skeel Jr., D.A., *Debt's Dominion: A History of Bankruptcy Law in America* (Princeton, NJ 2001).

Sombart, W., *Der moderne Kapitalismus*, 4th ed., 2 vols. (Leipzig 1916/1921).

Spann, M., *Der Haftungszugriff auf den Schuldner zwischen Personal- und Vermögensvollstreckung* (Münster 2004).

Spooner, F.C., *The International Economy and Monetary Movements in France, 1493–1725* (Cambridge, MA 1972).

Strieder, J., *Studien zur Geschichte kapitalistischer Organisationsformen* (Leipzig 1925).

Strieder, J., *Aus Antwerpener Notariatsarchiven* (Stuttgart 1930).

Silvestri, A., "Sui banchieri pubblici napoletani nella prima metà del '500: Notizie e documenti," *Bollettino dell'Archivio Storico del Banco di Napoli* 2 (1950).

Silvestri, A., "Sui banchieri pubblici napoletani dall'avvento di Filippo II al trono alla costituzione del monopolio. Notizie e documenti," *Bollettino dell'Archivio Storico del Banco di Napoli* 3 (1951).

Silvestri, A., "Sui banchieri pubblici nella città di Napoli dalla costituzione del monopolio alla fine dei banchi dei mercanti: Notizie e documenti," *Bollettino dell'Archivio Storico del Banco di Napoli* 4 (1952).

Silvestri, A., "Sull'attività bancaria durante il periodo aragonese," *Bollettino dell'Archivio Storico del Banco di Napoli* 6 (1953).

Tortora, E., *Il Banco di Napoli. Raccolta di documenti storici e statistici* (Naples 1883).

Uhlenbruck, W., "Zur Geschichte des Konkurses," *Deutsche Zeitschrift für Wirtschafts- und Insolvenzrecht* (2007).

Wallerstein, E., *The Modern World-System*, 3 vols. (New York 1974).

Weber, M., *Die protestantische Ethik und der "Geist" des Kapitalismus* (Tubingen 1904).

Weber, M., *Wirtschaft und Gesellschaft: Grundriss der verstehenden Soziologie* (Tubingen 1956).

Westermann, A., "Die Zahlungseinstellung der Handelsgesellschaft der Gebrüder Zangmeister zu Memmingen 1560," *Vierteljahresschrift für Sozial- und Wirtschaftsgeschichte* 6 (1908): 460–516.

Wong, R.B., *China Transformed: Historical Change and the Limits of European Experience* (Ithaca, NY 1997).
Zambrana Moral, P., *Derecho Concursal Historico. I: Trabajos de Investigacion* (Barcelona 2001).
Zambrana Moral, P., *Iniciacion Historica al Derecho Concursal: Planteamientos institucionales* (Malaga 2001).

Index